A READER IN FEMINIST KNOWLEDGE

The 'minority' feminist viewpoints have often been submerged in the interests of maintaining a mainstream, universal model of feminism. This anthology takes into account the various differences among women while looking at the important areas of feminist struggle. While sisterhood is indeed global, it certainly does not mean that all women are required to submerge their specific differences and assimilate to a universal model.

Consequently, the collection includes essays by leaders in the field of post-structuralist inquiry as well as by those immersed in the new spirituality, and the social consequences of recent biological research. Other essays reflect the political struggles which continue to be waged with different strategies by socialist and radical feminists, and the self-searching analyses undertaken by feminists uneasy about their inclusion within educational institutions and the radical new interpretations of sexuality within the cultural domain. Significantly, the collection begins with a powerful critique of white mainstream feminism emanating from Aboriginal women in Australia. While the critique is specific its implications concerning a pervasive racism within the feminist movement have global implications for all feminists.

A Reader in Feminist Knowledge and the companion volume *Feminist Knowledge: Critique and Construct* will be of great value to students on courses dealing with feminist theory, both Women's Studies courses and courses on current political and social movements. It will also appeal to anyone interested in recent developments in feminist theory.

A READER IN
FEMINIST KNOWLEDGE

edited by
Sneja Gunew

London and New York

First published 1991
by Routledge
11 New Fetter Lane, London EC4P 4EE

Simultaneously published in the USA and Canada
by Routledge
a division of Routledge, Chapman and Hall, Inc.
29 West 35th Street, New York, NY 10001

Printed in England by Clays Ltd, St Ives plc

British Library Cataloguing in Publication Data

A Reader in Feminist Knowledge.
1. Feminism
I. Gunew, Sneja
305.4′2

Library of Congress Cataloging in Publication Data

A Reader in Feminist Knowledge / edited by Sneja Gunew.
p. cm.
Includes bibliographical references.
ISBN 0 415 04698 X. – ISBN 0 415 04699 8 (pbk.)
1. Feminism.   I. Gunew, Sneja Marina
HQ1154.R4   1991
305.42 – dc20   89-10959

CONTENTS

v

CONTENTS

Part III Male theories of power

Part IV Feminism and subjectivity

Part V Philosophy

Part VI Psychoanalysis and feminism

Part VII Biology and feminism

Part VIII Religion

Part IX Radical feminism

ACKNOWLEDGEMENTS

Many of the chapters in this *Reader* have been published before. We are grateful for permission granted to use the following material:

In Part I

Jackie Huggins, 'Black women and women's liberation', *Hecate*, 13.1 (1987), pp. 77–82.

Diane Bell, 'Aboriginal women and feminist politics' (extract from 'The politics of separation'), *Dealing With Inequality*, ed. M. Strathern (Cambridge: Cambridge University Press, 1987).

Bell Hooks (Gloria Watkins), 'Sisterhood: political solidarity between women', *Feminist Review*, 23 (Summer 1986), pp. 125–38. This is an edited version of chapter 4 of B. Hooks, *Feminist Theory: From Margin to Centre* (Boston South End Press, 1984).

In Part II

Marian Lowe and Margaret Lowe Benston, 'The uneasy alliance of feminism and academia', *WSIF*, 7, 3 (1984), pp. 177–83.

Linda Gordon, 'What's new in women's history?' *Feminist Studies/ Critical Studies*, ed. T. de Lauretis (Indiana University Press, 1986), pp. 20–30.

Susan Sheridan, 'From margin to mainstream: situating women's studies', *Australian Feminist Studies*, 2 (1986), pp. 1–14.

In Part III

Nancy Jay, 'Gender and dichotomy', *Feminist Studies*, 7, 1 (Spring 1981), pp. 38–56, by permission of the publisher Feminist Studies, Inc., c/o Women's Studies Program, University of Maryland.

In Part IV

Moira Gatens, 'A critique of the sex/gender distinction', *Beyond Marxism? Interventions After Marx*, ed. J. Allen and P. Patton (NSW: Intervention Publications, 1983), pp. 143–60.

In Part V

Genevieve Lloyd, 'Reason as attainment', in *The Man of Reason: 'Male' and 'Female' in Western Philosophy* (London: Methuen & Co., 1984). Moira Gatens, 'Feminism, philosophy and riddles without answers', in *Feminist Challenges*, ed. C. Pateman and E. Gross [Grosz] (London: Allen & Unwin, 1986), pp. 13–29.

In Part VI

Luce Irigaray, 'This sex which is not one', Ch. 2 of *This Sex Which is Not One* (NY: Cornell University Press, 1985), pp. 23–33. Ellie Ragland-Sullivan, 'Jacques Lacan: feminism and the problem of gender identity', *Sub-stance*, 36 (1982), pp. 6–20 (edited). Hélène Cixous, 'The laugh of the Medusa', in *New French Feminism: An Anthology*, ed. E. Marks and I. de Courtivron (Amherst, Mass.: University of Massachusetts Press, 1980), pp. 245–64 (edited).

In Part VII

Susan Leigh Star, 'The politics of right and left: sex differences in hemispheric brain asymmetry', in R. Hubbard, M.S. Henifin, and B. Fried, *Women Look at Biology Looking at Women*, (Cambridge, Mass.: Schenkman Publishing Co., 1979), pp. 61–74, by permission of Schenkman Books, Inc. Ruth Bleier, 'Introduction' (extract), in *Science and Gender: A Critique of Biology and its Theories on Women*, (NY: Pergamon Press, 1984), pp. 7–14.

In Part VIII

Elisabeth Schüssler Fiorenza, 'Introduction', in *Bread Not Stone: The Challenge of Feminist Biblical Interpretation* (Boston, Mass.: Beacon Press, 1984), pp. ix–xxv. Rosemary Radford Ruether, 'Renewal or new creation? Feminist spirituality and historical religion', 1985–86 Dudleian Lecture, in the *Harvard Divinity Bulletin* (February–March 1986), pp. 1–7.

Carol P. Christ, 'Why women need the Goddess', *Womanspirit Rising: A Feminist Reader in Religion*, ed. C.P. Christ and J. Plaskow (NY: Harper & Row, 1979), pp. 273–387.

In Part IX

Jessica York *et al.*, 'We are the feminists that women have warned us about: introductory paper', *Feminist Practice: Notes From the Tenth Year* (London: The Theory Press, 1979), pp. 1–3.

Susan Hawthorne, 'In defence of separatism', extract from unpublished thesis (LaTrobe University, 1976).

Charlotte Bunch, 'Not for lesbians only', in *Building Feminist Theory: Essays from Quest*, ed. C. Bunch *et al.* (NY and London: Longman, 1981), pp. 67–73 (© Charlotte Bunch 1975). Also included in C. Bunch, *Passionate Politics: Feminist Theory in Action, Essays 1968–86* (NY: St Martin's Press, 1987).

Anne Koedt, 'The myth of the vaginal orgasm', *Radical Feminism*, ed. A. Koedt, E. Levine, A. Rapone (NY: Quadrangle, 1973), pp. 198–207.

Mary Daly, 'The spiritual dimension of women's liberation', *Radical Feminism*, ed. A. Koedt *et al.* (NY: Quadrangle, 1973), pp. 259–67.

Janice Raymond, 'The visionary task: two sights-seeing', *Women's Studies International Forum*, 8, 1 (1985), pp. 85–90

In Part X

Barbara Taylor, 'Lords of Creation: Marxism, feminism and "utopian" socialism', *Radical America*, 14, 4 (1980), pp. 41–6.

Mia Campioni and Elizabeth Gross [Grosz], 'Love's labours lost: Marxism and feminism', in *Beyond Marxism? Interventions after Marx*, ed. J. Allen and P. Patton (NSW: Intervention Publications, 1983), pp. 113–41.

Part I

FEMINIST KNOWLEDGE: CRITIQUE AND CONSTRUCT

INTRODUCTION

Sneja Gunew

The readings offered in this first section address in various ways the fact that feminist knowledge also has its orthodoxies and exclusions. Over the past three decades of second-wave feminism, particular kinds of feminist mainstream have come into being, emanating, in the main, from Britain, France, and America. The last decade has produced a number of critiques of this hegemonic feminism issuing from groups of women who, for a variety of reasons, have found themselves marginalized even in this movement which purports to deal with and attempt to change women's oppression everywhere. As Hazel Carby puts it,

> anonymity and the tendency to generalize into meaninglessness, the oppression of an amorphous category called 'Third World women', are symptomatic of the ways in which the specificity of our experiences and oppression are subsumed under inapplicable concepts and theories.[1]

In 1985 the British feminists Michèle Barrett and Mary McIntosh published an article dealing with the unacknowledged ethnocentrism within the white women's movement.[2] In a later issue, Caroline Ramazanoglu argued that it was not simply a matter of ethnocentrism, 'but of a crushing, institutionalized racism'.[3] Increasingly, there has grown an awareness within all areas of the women's movement that we too are not free of the tendency to universalize and thereby to construct an exclusionary norm. As women within the left-wing movement had to learn, an emancipatory politics does not in itself necessarily and inevitably serve their particular needs. The women's movement has tended to treat race and class as subservient in ways that the left-wing movement saw gender as being of secondary importance.

Within Australia, the specific needs of Aboriginal women have only recently surfaced and, in the first reading, Jackie Huggins takes up the point that in its current constitution, the Australian women's movement is irrelevant to Aboriginal women since white women are still unable to confront their own racism. That particular painful battle is finally on the feminist agenda in Australia as it is in Britain and America. Huggins

3

continues that white women have also not concentrated on the specific effects of sexism as regards black women. She also emphasizes the fact that class differences must be kept in mind since Aborigines in general are economically discriminated against within the workforce. One disturbing element she identifies is the increasing incidence of black male chauvinism, which has eroded Aboriginal women's traditional rights and powers within their own communities.

Diane Bell starts from the proposition that only certain privileged whites are in a position to delineate the niceties of whether class, or race, or gender are of primary significance. Bell carefully differentiates the position from which these categories are defined for white feminists and for Aboriginal women. Her central contention is that these terms are not necessarily as separate as they may appear and that for Aboriginal women racism too is gendered. She then focuses on the different experience of Aboriginal women's so-called separatism. It is necessary to view this in the larger context of Aboriginal society where the equal but different relationships between the sexes prevails. Whereas white feminists are concerned with infiltrating dominant male power structures, Aboriginal women have always maintained their separate spheres. She goes on to summarize points made by black women activists concerning the differences between black and white women's experiences. She cites Roberta Sykes' thesis that, in a way not recognized by white women, Australian culture was predicated on the rape of black women and that their struggle centres on the right to say no to sex at a time when white feminists were to some degree fighting for the right to attain a certain kind of sexual initiative. The black activist Pat O'Shane's emphasis has been on the primary need for Aboriginal women to co-operate with Aboriginal men to combat racism in general, similar to Huggins' point in the previous reading. Marcia Langton argues that black women, from their different experiences, 'mock and satirize' white women, but that their strategy is not yet coherent.

Bell herself makes the point that Aboriginal women's traditional strategy of retreat (*jilimi*) differs in several important respects from a variety of such moves by white women. These differences need to be understood so that Aboriginal women are not excluded from current important decisions being made between blacks and whites here in Australia. Because Aboriginal women's sexuality is not intertwined with their economic status, *jilimi* does not constitute a retreat from heterosexuality in ways that are associated with a radical feminist position. Women-only groups have always posed a threat in the past when men are denied sexual access to women, as in the medieval nunneries, and this has been compounded when the women also enjoyed economic independence, as did the *béguines*. Bell argues that, unlike white separatists, Aboriginal women do not operate with the notion of battlelines between

4

the sexes and that their emphasis is rather on dialogue: between men and women on the one hand, and with white women on the other. As well, the paper examines the responsibility white feminists have to engage with issues relating to Aboriginal women and to cross-cultural women in general.

In the third reading, Bell Hooks (Gloria Watkins) contends that rather than pretend that there is no conflict among women, we need to work through racism in order to move beyond it. She identifies the model for sisterhood created by white women as one based on shared victimization and that such a model did not encourage the visibility of class and race as analytical categories as well as excluding the concept of women's strength and strategies of resistance. It encouraged women not to confront their own sexism as displayed in violence against other women. She points out, furthermore, that the women's movement is not owned by white women to the extent that they can decide whether and when to invite other women to participate and on what terms. After the recognition that racism exists, the next step is to transform it by actively translating culture-specific codes of behaviour across all groups. Only this, in conjunction with the redistribution of wealth, will transform society.

NOTES

1 Hazel Carby, 'White women listen! Black feminism and the boundaries of sisterhood', in *The Empire Strikes Back* (Centre for Contemporary Cultural Studies, Hutchinson, London, 1982), p. 220.
2 Michèle Barrett and Mary McIntosh, 'Ethnocentrism and socialist-feminist theory', *Feminist Review*, 20 (Summer 1985), pp. 23–47.
3 Caroline Ramazanoglu, 'A response to Barrett and McIntosh', *Feminist Review*, 22 (Spring 1986), p. 84.

BLACK WOMEN AND WOMEN'S LIBERATION

Jackie Huggins

Black women have yet to see even their menfolk attain positions of power and influence in the mainstream culture. It is understandable then, that in terms of priorities, black women seek to raise the life chances of the whole group. They view disadvantages of race and class before disadvantages of sex.[1]

This paper focuses on the women's liberation movement and its proven irrelevance to Aboriginal women, the role of Aboriginal women and men with a strong theme of women's 'independence' prevailing, and the multitude of social problems faced by Aborigines. I argue that Aboriginal men and women both are fighting for the same things, regardless of gender differences. The overall scenario is that, in such a deprived and oppressed culture, it would seem ludicrous to suggest that either sex could be a victor.

Although the women's liberation movement was first activated in the 1960s from such movements as the anti-war and civil rights groups in America, the contemporary women's movement has a much longer history. It dates back to at least the nineteenth century with struggles over universal suffrage, the exploitation of women's labour, unionization of women, and the temperance movements. However, several black American critics insist that blacks are always left to fight their own battles: 'Women's Liberation won't be any different. White women won the right to vote but black people, including black women, didn't get it for another hundred years.'[2] There is also a commonly voiced suspicion that the women's liberation movement has 'attached' itself to the black movement in order to take advantage, for its own interests, of the momentum and attention that the blacks have recently achieved.

Historically, the women's liberation movement in Australia began some eighteen years ago and, in that time, it has developed a size and diversity which has made it a nebulous and rather elusive body, with feminists having had different priorities in their agendas for change. These divergences have led also to different tactics and strategies, and to competing ideologies and world views.[3]

As the movement grew, some feminists saw that class and race differences meant that women experienced different forms and degrees of oppression. However, if the white women who organized the contemporary movement towards feminism were at all aware of racial politics in Australian history, they would have known that overcoming barriers that separate women from one another would entail confronting the reality of racism; not just racism as a general evil in society, but the race hatred they might harbour in their own psyches. Despite the predominance of patriarchal rule in Australian society, Australia was colonized on a racially imperialistic base and not on a sexually imperialistic base. No degree of patriarchal bonding between white male colonizers and Aboriginal men overshadowed white racial imperialism.[4] In fact, white racial imperialism granted to all white women, however victimized by sexist oppression, the right to assume the role of oppressor in relationship to black women and black men.

White liberation leaders are also fond of pointing to the analogy between blacks and women as second-class citizens in a white, male chauvinist society. One of the clearest points of similarity between the situation of blacks and women is that they have both been brainwashed into the same 'low self-image'; they are not supposed to use their minds, they are incapable of making decisions. They are both second-class members of the society who should be kept in their place.

If white women in the women's movement needed to make use of a black experience to emphasize women's oppression, it would only seem logical that they focus on the black female experience – but they have not. Had white women desired to bond with black women on the basis of common oppression, they could have done so by demonstrating an awareness of the impact of sexism on the status of black women. Unfortunately, despite all the rhetoric about sisterhood and bonding, white women are not sincerely committed to bonding with black women to fight sexism. They are primarily interested in drawing attention to the oppression they consider they experience as white upper- or middle-class women.[5]

The further notion that all women as a sex have more in common than do members of the same class is false. Upper-class women are not simply bedmates of their wealthy husbands. As a rule, they have more compelling ties that bind them together. They are economic, social, and political bedmates united in defence of private property, profiteering, militarism, racism – and the exploitation of other women. It would be quite another matter to expect any large number of wealthy women to endorse or support a revolutionary struggle which threatened their capitalist interests and privileges. Will the wives of bankers, generals, corporation lawyers, and big industrialists be firmer allies of women fighting for liberation than working-class men, black and white, who are fighting for theirs?[6]

7

The ruling powers breed and benefit from all forms of discrimination and oppression. Therefore, for a middle-class white woman to compare her environmental situation with that of a black is totally naive. While white women are fighting to get out of the kitchen, black women are fighting to get into it.

For these reasons, many black women do not see the women's movement as relevant to their own situation. Black women, who have worked from necessity are apt to view women's liberation as a white middle-class battle irrelevant to their own, often bitter, struggle for survival. As Ida Lewis commented: 'The women's liberation movement is basically a family quarrel between white women and white men.'[7] Similarly, Aboriginal women are aware of the divisiveness of feminism in terms of their own black movement. Women's liberation has meant very little to both black American women and Aboriginal women who believe that the black woman has always been placed in a position of asserting herself.

The patriarchal nature of contemporary society means that Aboriginal women were subject to further specific oppression by both Aboriginal and white men. They have been typecast as capable only of roles and deserving only of treatment deemed unworthy or undesirable for that more highly valued, rarer 'commodity' – the white woman.[8] Male dominance was, and is, a major ingredient in the culture Europeans brought with them to Australia. The message came through to Aborigines, directly or indirectly, in words and deeds, in almost all their contacts with Europeans.

Black women have never been interested in being jockeyed into the position of fighting their own men. Women must support their every effort for equality and to emerge as a valuable force in this society: it is a time for uniting, not dividing. 'We should stand behind our men, not against them' is a popular militant battle-cry. There are, none the less, black women who question just how far behind that is. The black militants' idea of a submissive female, walking silently five paces to the rear, is a little more than many independent black women can stomach. Black men today are not necessarily innocent of the chauvinist attitudes charged against white men by white women's liberationists. Black male chauvinism is creeping into Aboriginal society, particularly with the advent of more visible and vocal Aboriginal and Islander women's groups. When once Aboriginal women were encouraged to enter the workforce, they are now being pulled down by their own black males. Pat O'Shane exemplifies this: 'It's not easy being a black woman at the top of a white bureaucracy. The hardest part has been dealing with chauvinist males (mostly black) who are threatened by a woman having this much power.'[9] Black men may perhaps be more inclined to be comfortable with men in power rather than women. Today, black men, as well as white men, are finding an assertive woman a threat.

8

In some ways Aboriginal women have suffered less trauma than their menfolk. It is often observed in culture-contact situations that the men of the culture that is disrupted by a more dominant culture have in a sense further to fall and, hence, suffer a worse shock and dislocation in terms of identity than the women. The men had controlled the society, had been the chief sacred and political figures. Now they found men of an alien culture controlling the parameters of their existence. Women were accustomed to taking direction in some areas, and could transfer autonomy less painfully. Their roles in the family did at least continue, even if carried out under drastically changed circumstances, which gave their lives greater continuity.[10]

Today, women's status has been changing, their prestige and opportunities increasing more rapidly than men's. Aboriginal women have continued important work-roles. But, of course, to add to the disadvantage of sex and class, black women carried the additional burden of racism. Women have been prominent as workers, office-bearers, and spokespersons in Aboriginal lobby groups and pressure groups arousing public awareness of Aboriginal needs. Women have also participated in the various state and Commonwealth consultative bodies,[11] along with many men.

Black liberation for men and women seems a more important goal to many black women than women's liberation. What is holding black men back is the same thing that holds back their black mates: the white power structure. In other words, the main oppressor is a class society.

For instance, the occupational distribution of Australian males shows that Aborigines are virtually absent from the white-collar world. Only 2 per cent of Aboriginal males occupy the top seven occupation groups, which are the most responsible, least onerous physically, and best rewarded materially, compared with 35 per cent of non-Aboriginal workers.[12] A large percentage of the Aboriginal workforce is locked into the least rewarded and least promising occupational spheres, and experienced in jobs with little or no transfer value to dynamic parts of the economy. Aborigines are not only highly concentrated in the poorest-paid jobs, in some areas they monopolize them.

Aborigines have also been easy to ignore till now because they have been geographical, political, and social outcasts. They are non-European, with few technologically useful skills; they are often unemployed; they suffer from malnutrition and sickness to such a degree that, by the age of forty, many are unemployable; they figure prominently in crime statistics and have a low reputation in the larger society.[13]

The position of black Australians compared with white Australians is daily eroding, in relative and absolute terms – relative because the life-chances for the white majority improve at a faster rate, and absolute because the rate of population growth is much higher among black

Australians: any change in the position of Aborigines, for better or worse, affects a continuously expanding population.[14] While the formal legal and political barriers to full citizenship have been removed, the barriers that remain are social; the legacy of generations of training in dependency, poverty, and isolation from the mainstream of the national life. In a highly urbanized nation, Aborigines are the least urban element, in a rich nation they are the poorest, in a well-educated nation they are the least educated. In the Australian capitalist economy they participate as an under-class, moving from unemployment into unskilled labouring jobs or into invalidity.[15]

Aborigines do not have the training to take advantage of opportunities in expanding industries, and there is every evidence that, as a consequence of their weak educational backgrounds, their occupational disadvantages will persist. At 45 and above, one-half to three-quarters of the Aboriginal population report no formal education and are presumptively illiterate. Even among ages 25–9, nearly one-quarter of Aborigines have not been to school, and at ages 15–19 the fraction is one-tenth. By comparison, in the non-Aboriginal population, even among those aged 50 or older, only 1 or 2 per cent have no formal schooling.[16] While white capitalist education leaves much to be desired, the basic skills it provides are necessary for employment or, sometimes, even for survival within the system.

Health, housing, and education make up a complex of interrelated factors that mutually reinforce one another. Poor health is often caused by poor housing, and poor health retards future growth. Moreover, whatever happens in the schools is likely to be wasted, unless a parallel effort is directed to improving the home environment. Educational performance is a function not only of innate intelligence and educational exposure, but also of the reinforcement that a child gets from the home. To make effective gains in health, housing, or education, inputs are needed in all three areas simultaneously.

Like health, decent housing is recognized as an elementary right. Aborigines are among the worst-housed people in the world. The poor housing conditions of Aboriginal Australians reflect their past low earning power, and their status in Australian society as economic drop-outs and cast-offs. The structures in which they live are made of the most fragile materials. They are the most segregated group, they have least access to community facilities such as schools, sewerage, rubbish removal, reticulated water, or adequate or clean water of any kind.

Jobs and income come last in the chain of causation that maintains Aborigines in a depressed status. In the absence of good health, jobs are uncertain. In the absence of education, unskilled and poorly paid work is the only realistic expectation. In the absence of a living wage, housing will be poor, overcrowded, and insanitary. Poorer health follows as a

10

consequence. And so the chain of causation continues.[17]

Unless Aborigines are to remain social and political outcasts, they must be able to participate on an equal footing in the central institutions of the society. To do that, they must be able to achieve educational levels that permit them to manipulate the symbol system and the legal-bureaucratic system. Aboriginal women particularly are aware of this factor, and are striving to instil into their young children the importance of education.

If enough effort is applied, the vicious circle of poor education, poor jobs, low income, and poverty could be broken at any one of several points, or several points simultaneously. For many Aboriginal people, the 1982 election was designated 'the election of hope', and was seen as producing major changes in economic, political, and social development programmes. However, in fact, what has occurred (nothing) has been a disaster for our people. The present Labor Party's backdown on land rights has opened and festered the old wounds of the deprivation and dispossession of our people. Neither has the Bicentennial convinced Aboriginal people of their welcomed participation (in a genuine way that will focus on the true history of this country and the sufferings Aboriginal people have endured), or that they will receive their rightful place in Australian society.

Without question, it is easier for a black woman to consider herself first a human being, second an Aborigine, and only third a member of the female sex. As Hilary Saunders eloquently sums up the feelings of many black women:

> We must not let this awareness as women go too far. We are a race of people who have suffered many injustices, we are fighting for self-determination. Women must play a large part in this yet we can only hope to achieve this as one people not a race of men, nor a race of women but of Black United People.[18]

NOTES

1 Patricia Grimshaw, 'Aboriginal women: a study of culture contact', Norma Grieve and Patricia Grimshaw, *Australian Women: Feminist Perspectives* (London: OUP, 1981), p. 94.
2 B. Day, *Sexual Lives Between Black and Whites* (London: Collins, 1974), p. 286.
3 Grieve and Grimshaw (1981), p. 229.
4 B. Hooks, *Ain't I A Woman* (London: Pluto, 1987), p. 122.
5 ibid., p. 142.
6 E. Reed, *Problems of Women's Liberation* (New York: Pathfinder, 1971), pp. 73–4.
7 Day (1974), p. 283.
8 E. Windschuttle (ed.), *Women, Class and History* (Melbourne: Fontana, 1980), p. 258.

FEMINIST KNOWLEDGE: CRITIQUE AND CONSTRUCT

9 S. Mitchell (ed.), *Tall Poppies* (Melbourne: Penguin, 1984), p. 159.
10 Grieve and Grimshaw (1981), p. 90.
11 ibid., p. 86.
12 L. Broom and F. Lancaster Jones, *A Blanket A Year* (Canberra: ANU Press, 1973), p. 33.
13 ibid., p. 3.
14 ibid., p. 11.
15 ibid., p. 12.
16 ibid., p. 20.
17 ibid., p. 89.
18 Grieve and Grimshaw (1981), p. 87.

ABORIGINAL WOMEN, SEPARATE SPACES, AND FEMINISM[1]

Diane Bell

Aboriginal women in central Australia clearly have a view of themselves as women. Witness the daily routine where the majority of waking hours is spent with other women in hunting parties away from the general camp, in social intercourse in an area taboo to men, in ritual activities known as 'women's business'. *Yawulyu* ceremonies in which women celebrate their rights in land and give form to their responsibility for the maintenance of harmonious relations of people to land, are performed on the 'women's only' ground located behind the *jilimi*, as the women's camp is known in Warlpiri.[2] It is here, away from the gaze of men and children, that precious sacred objects are stored and that women's knowledge is passed to younger generations.

Forming the permanent core of the *jilimi* are those widows who have chosen not to remarry and other women who, although married, are not domiciled with their husbands. Joining them in this camp are single girls who are reluctant or too young to go to their promised husbands; women who are seeking a safe environment while visiting without their spouses or who, following a dispute, have temporarily vacated the *swag* of their spouse; women who are ill or in need of emotional support; and those not yet through their final stages of mourning. Accompanying all these women are their dependent children and charges. During the day, married women from nearby camps come to the *jilimi* to socialize, but at night return to their family camps.

In times past, in the smaller family camps of hunter-gatherer bands, there would have been at most three or four women to form a *jilimi* but on the large government settlements of the 1960s and 1970s *jilimi* residents numbered twenty or more. In these unwieldy, strife-torn communities, the refuge function of the women's camp is marked: in the *jilimi* women find female support and a safe environment. Living with other women, rather than becoming a second or third wife, may be seen as one response women have made to enhanced male solidarity (see Bell, 1980). But, in the 1980s, the proud assertion of independence of *jilimi* life is illusory. Women, through the receipt of old age pensions, may have the capacity of economic self-sufficiency but they do not control the

13

means by which their living is produced. Social security cheques issue from an office little affected by their ritual standing, prowess as hunters, or kinship obligations.

In the past, separation allowed women and men to demonstrate independence without compromising the essential complementary nature of male/female activities in the maintenance of their society. Today, the separation of the sexes and women's independence are no longer mutually reinforcing values. The persistence of separate domains of action effectively denies women participation in the emerging political and economic spheres within which power and authority have come to reside. In exploring this erosion of women's power-base and the differential impact on gender relations for different groups in central Australia, I argued that the concept of women having the right to live in an area which is under their control and which is taboo to men is not new, but the reasons for and the values placed on the separation are (Bell and Ditton, 1980/4; Bell, 1983).

In charting the changing contours of gender and spatial relations, I have found it useful to focus on the dynamics of decision-making, particularly with reference to population-intensive settlement. Drawing on experiences of Aboriginal women living in Alice Springs and on government settlements (environments that present partial and very different faces of urbanization), I traced the shifting relations of power in decision-making and suggested we treat with caution the assumption that the *jilimi* and women's refuge are built on common ground. Both permit the maintenance of separate spaces, but each does so by reference to different systems of gender relations and with different ramifications for economic viability. I proposed that at stake, both for Aboriginal and non-Aboriginal women, was 'the right to retreat' and to make decisions concerning her life. For Aboriginal women these rights existed by virtue of the sex-segregated nature of the society, while for feminists they were asserted in strategies such as seeking state support for women's centres.

This is a subject over which I have worried for at least two decades and no doubt will continue to do so.[3] The state my musings had reached by 1985 is recorded in the *Politics of Separation*, in the final section of which I discussed aspects of Aboriginal women's political practice and that of feminists (Bell, 1987, pp. 123–9). Here, my intention was to build on the conceptual frame enunciated in that earlier work and to look to concrete examples of cross-cultural exchange, to particular moments where central Australian Aboriginal women have begun to clarify and explore not only the basis of their right to be separate but also their relationship to feminist politics.

The Pine Gap protest of 1983 brought together a number of interests in peace, land rights, and women's issues.[4] The cross-cutting affiliations forged by the women and men, Aborigines and non-Aborigines, who were involved in the action are clear evidence that we cannot simply ask: which has salience, 'race' or 'gender'? As an anthropologist I look to behaviour, the patterning, the shared meanings, and I learn of otherness through participant observation. This is fundamentally different from a literature survey which establishes that Aboriginal women privilege 'racism' or 'class' over 'sexism'.[5] Reflected in such endeavours is the platform of the left in the 1960s and while feminists identified with their protests, they also found it necessary to have a critique of sexism inherent in the practice of leftist politics. If Australia follows the trend of North America, we can expect to see closer attention to the points of intersection of gender, race, and class; to a mapping of the convergence and divergence of interests; to an exploration of the shifting power relations; to dialogues between radical feminists on the nature of racism within the women's movement (see Aickin Rothschild, 1979; Dill, 1983; Fisher, 1984). More recent autobiographical and oral historical work indicates that while racism is pervasively oppressive, for Aboriginal women, the experience is gendered and thus *may* be illuminated by feminist analyses.[6] Such deliberations may, however, be difficult to locate.

The fourth Women and Labour conference in Brisbane, July 1984, had racism as a major theme. The organizers of the conferences attempted to include Aboriginal women but the proceedings bear no record of feminists' deliberations on the topic. Two days before the Brisbane conference was due to begin, an Aboriginal women's committee raised objections to three papers written by white women about Aboriginal women. These papers had already been accepted by the organizing committee of the conference, printed, and bound in the compilation of papers to be distributed to participants. Two withdrew, but one author sought clarification from the committee on how she should proceed. After some discussion among the Aboriginal women, it was decided that the oldest present, a woman from central Australia, should speak for her 'sisters'. On her instruction the paper was removed from the printed volume and presented orally under conditions negotiated by the author and committee: men were excluded and an Aboriginal woman was delegated to be present.[7]

The purported reason for these actions was that the paper violated Aboriginal law regarding matters sacred. The author was shocked she had unwittingly transgressed. In her understanding she had merely repeated material that was published and thus available for public comment. Her intention had been to discuss material that had been inspirational for her writing of fiction. She did not seek to speak *for* or to appropriate the knowledge of another. In her view the episode was instructive. 'I was glad I wrote the paper. . . In the meeting I saw their attitudes to knowledge and the need to earn the right to use it' (personal communication 1988). At that personal level exchanges can be frank but the episode raised important questions: on what basis do Aboriginal women claim their experience is privileged? When is consultation licence for censorship? Who may operate in the 'market-place' of ideas? The offending material concerned myths from Arnhemland – not country for which the women present had specific responsibility – but it did allude to themes that are found within the corpus of sacred mythological knowledge in central Australia. By what authority then does one speak for another?[8]

In an interview following the conference, several of the angriest of the Aboriginal women made it plain that they were the experts and that they were tired of white academics growing rich on their knowledge. They contended they had been over-researched, under-consulted, and that it was inappropriate for white women to undertake research in Aboriginal society.[9] Thus the Brisbane conference became a forum through which these women spoke to a wider audience. It was an exercise in power, which set one minority group against another. Feminists, like Aboriginal women, are vulnerable in this respect and on such occasions media and male-stream academics alike gratefully note the 'squabbles of the girls'.

But the vulnerability of feminists to charges of 'unsisterly' or 'racist behaviour' from Aboriginal women is another matter. Holding that sisterhood is global, they make every effort to incorporate all women. At conferences and in volumes dealing with 'Australian women' feminist scholars have been anxious to include the voices and views of Aboriginal women but the success rate is poor. Reason for invitations not being accepted range from the irrelevance of questions addressed, the alien and intimidating forum, to the spokeswomen being over-committed. Invitations are always subject to charges of tokenism. As I have suggested, it is by reference to shared moments in particular actions that we find the most rigorous confrontations of sexism and racism. The concrete focus of organizing and executing a particular protest, establishing a women's advisory council, co-authoring a report, giving evidence on matters of customary law in a court of law provide ample opportunities for cross-cultural negotiations by Aboriginal and white women.

Despite the use of disruptive tactics in public fora, there are enduring points of contact between feminists and Aboriginal women, which range from personal and work relationships established in the field to more diffuse relationships through federal organizations.[10] The Aboriginal Women's Task Force, an initiative of the Federal government, established within the Office of The Status of Women in late 1982, provided links to femocrats. But the Task Force suffered the same lack of funding that has stifled other women's projects. Two Aboriginal women set out to consult throughout Australia and report in twelve months on an impossibly wide range of issues. Under the Hawke government, the Task

Force was restructured: it became a body of national representation. But, as women both Aboriginal and white have pointed out, it was government-funded and government-controlled. It answered questions that perplex governments and the recommendations call for increased funds, more liaison committees, in fact more research (Daylight and Johnstone, 1986).

About the same time, another organization, the Federation of Aboriginal Women, whose tactics were quite different, emerged. If women wanted action, they went directly to the organization involved: the need they argued was obvious – they did not need an inquiry to tell them. Further, they addressed a wide range of issues felt by the bureaucrats to be adequately covered by existing organizations. Not surprisingly the Department of Aboriginal Affairs was not prepared to recognize the need for such an organization.[11] The Federation argued organizations funded by the state were male-dominated and that their role was to bring women's opinions forward. Although they did not pursue their relationship to feminist politics as a conceptual issue, they clearly recognized that the experience of racism was gendered. The particular way in which Aboriginal women are treated, the violence, the discrimination, the exclusion they acknowledged was because they are both female and black.

How, then, may we contrast the ends Aboriginal women seek to achieve and those of white feminists? A common strategy of reformists in white Australian society has been to seek the right to a place within the dominant power structures. Thus women have looked to occupy positions which will allow an equality of action, the right to negotiate at the same table. This contrasts with the Aboriginal model of decision-making based on negotiated agreements underwritten by the differentiation of the sexes. In this process when clarifying issues and identifying priorities, the separation of men and women is important, but when it comes to achieving consensus, complementarity between the sexes is critical. However, we cannot leave a discussion of decision-making there for such now occurs at the interface of Aboriginal and white society. As yet no strategy which ensures that Aboriginal women will be both informed and heeded as well as safe has emerged. And, as I have suggested, their stress on separation has become a non-functional strategy. In the past the right to retreat did not need to be asserted and by retreating, women were not living a less meaningful or an impoverished life. The retreat afforded them space. Today it locks them out of arenas where decisions affecting their lives are made.

Yet Aboriginal women have not been prepared to endorse the ideology of these white feminists who seek equality of action in male-dominated areas. They have given different reasons for their reticence. In central Australia, Aboriginal women have sought to have their distinctively female contribution to their society recognized and that entails a role in

17

decision-making. Superficially, we appear to have a variation on the 'different but equal' theme. This has proved a dangerous platform for white feminists and, given that the constraints on Aboriginal woman's participation in decision-making derive from the nature of gender relations in the wider society, it is a dangerous position for her also (Hartmann, 1981, p. 29).

Black activist Roberta (Bobbi) Sykes (1975, pp. 313–21), writing in the early 1970s, stated that black women would not join white women's groups because there was no shared experience. For her, the common ground was that all black women had been raped, literally and metaphorically.[12] The racism of white women was apparent in their inability to respond to or even address such facts. Rape was a taboo subject. In Sykes' view white women sought the right to say yes to sexual advances without social condemnation, while black women sought the right to say 'no'. This is a generalization which most radical feminists would reject: they too sought the right to say no. Sykes' position was very much that of black America and it is significant that she says 'black' not 'Aboriginal'. The focus on sexuality is, in a sense, reactive. It was an issue with which white feminists struggled in the 1970s but in my experience of central Australia, the key issue was decision-making and political representation, not sexuality.

A theme not fully developed in Sykes but given weight by a barrister, Pat O'Shane (1976, pp. 31–4), is that of the special relationship of black women to black men in their joint struggle against racism. The argument runs that for Aboriginal women to seek liberation in terms of the feminist platform is divisive, a further cause for injury of their menfolk. The major fight O'Shane concludes is against racism, not sexism: 'We don't want to put men down, they have suffered enough.' She does, however, see a situation in which all women may work together.

> When the white women's movement takes head-on the struggle against racism, which is the greater barrier to our progress, then we've got a chance of achieving sisterhood and, through our combined struggles, liberation of all humankind. (1976, p. 34)

Eve Fesl (1984), on the other hand, declares that Aboriginal women have no need for women's liberation as they already have a sisterhood. She defines herself first as an environmentalist, second as Aboriginal, and last as a woman (ibid., p. 109).

Marcia Langton (1982, 1983, pp. 11–16), in her enunciation of the dynamics of what she calls 'the black gin syndrome', provides the most devastating account yet of Aboriginal women's perceptions of white women. She argues that Aboriginal women recognize the taboos of white women and violate them. They mock and satirize white women's response to men. But, as she rightly points out, their strategy is, in the end, incoherent. They are jailed for offensive behaviour (see NSW Anti-Discrimination Board, 1982, p. 31).

I think I have said enough to indicate that Aboriginal women respond to white feminists in a number of ways. After all, Aboriginal women are in very different situations in different parts of Australia. To this point I have spoken of feminist strategies as if they were endorsed by all white feminists. Of course, this is not so. In conclusion, let me briefly draw some comparisons with features of separatism in our society. Superficially, the radical separatists of the 1980s appear to be advocating a solution similar to that of Aboriginal women. They concentrate on the establishment of institutions which look remarkably like the *jilimi*.[13] Encapsulated in their catch-cry, 'women have no country' is the recognition that women need space that is theirs. Further, they share the dilemma of Aboriginal women in that if they are separate, how will their voices be heard? No doubt some would respond that men have never listened so not much is lost. There is little point in attempting to convince the enemy of your right to equality of opportunity. Political lesbianism, by isolating the heterosexual couple as the basic unit of the political structure of male supremacy, and refusing to engage in heterosexual activity, seeks to undermine the power of man as a class (Leeds Revolutionary Feminist Group 1981, pp. 5–10; Rich, 1980).

There is, however, a significant difference in the politics of separation as pursued by the Aboriginal and white separatists. For Aboriginal women a retreat to the *jilimi* is not a retreat from heterosexual activity. Many women in the *jilimi* maintain relationships with men: some marital, some more casual. Celibacy is not a feature of *jilimi* life. For the Aboriginal women with whom I worked, sexuality is not and never has been associated with the responsibility of wife in marriage, nor was it tied to their economic well-being. A retreat to the *jilimi* does not threaten her economic well-being. A husband enjoys no automatic control over a wife's sexuality any more than he has the right to distribute her produce. Her sexuality is hers to bestow, and further, she has real choices. A young wife may withdraw to the company of other women or return to her family. She is not bereft of social and economic support. She can expect sympathy from both male and female kin. An older woman may leave a husband and her retreat could occasion both shame and fear in the man. Aboriginal women may move in and out of sexual relations with men without undermining their relationship with other women and without suffering economic deprivation. The emphasis on denial of sexual access to women's bodies is not a defining feature of Aboriginal women's separation, though it may motivate individual instances of retreat.

One action in which Aboriginal and white women adopted a range of positions and formed some unholy alliances was the battle over the Alice

Springs Women's Centre. In 1977, several white women, concerned with the lack of access to abortion in the Northern Territory, formed a health group. A local refuge was suggested as a suitable venue. Women from the health group assumed control of the refuge, and in 1978 it became the Alice Springs Women's Centre. Its reputation had been as a racist institution – black women were not admitted, but then neither were many white women. Those few middle-class women who did use the refuge argued that they could not admit black women because they did not understand them. Under the health group, the refuge was run as a collective and several Aboriginal women who worked in the Aboriginal organizations of Alice Springs and who came into contact with these white women began to take an interest. Indeed, in its second year of operation the dominant group became the urban Aboriginal women who formed an *ad hoc* advisory group. There was much discussion concerning the needs and aspirations of the Aboriginal women. In its third year of operation, the dominant group became the women of the town camps and bush communities – women stranded when they were in town, ill, discharged from hospital with no way to get home. These women co-existed with the urban women who at no stage moved out.

There were cross-currents and heated discussions between these groups of women with very different needs and backgrounds, but seeking very similar solutions. They all needed a place that was set apart. They all needed a safe place to which they could retreat in time of stress. A *de facto* parallel structure began to develop within the Centre, but the potential for this arrangement was not realized because the refuge folded after a further six months.[14] The refuge had come under increasing criticism; white women accused black women of misusing government resources by dominating the refuge. The reverse had never been an issue. To certain bureaucrats and administrators the refuge was politically dangerous for it provided a basis from which Aboriginal women, already discontent with their lot, could engage in wider political protest. Criticism of the American installation at Pine Gap was another clear example.

It is interesting to note that one of the arguments for closing the Women's Centre in Alice Springs was that it encouraged 'deviant' relationships: that men were not allowed access to their wives and that the family was not promoted as the basic structuring unit of society. Here the threat was not celibacy but lesbianism; it was not the withdrawal of women from heterosexual activity but the existence of an alternative that affronted the sensibilities of certain influential *Women for Christ* in Alice Springs. For white women generally, the separation usually implies a negation of heterosexual activity, it is a retreat from what Cheryl Hannah has aptly termed 'the heterosexual battleline'. Here we have the nub of the conflict of models. Historically, any 'women-only' groups

20

must necessarily be deviant, because to withdraw is to pose a threat to the right of men to define women in terms of sexual access. If the all-women's community also achieves a measure of economic independence, the threat is compounded. This becomes clear if we compare two accounts of closely related yet very different women's communities: a nunnery and the *béguinage* of medieval France and Germany.

Of these two the threat posed by the nuns was considerably less than that of the politically and economically independent *béguines*. For many, a nunnery may appear to constitute an artificial or 'unnatural' community (Williams 1975, pp. 105–25), but the women do not violate the principle that all women are either daughters or wives, that is, women under the control of a male. At the head of the Church is the 'father', the nuns themselves are 'the brides of Christ', chaste wives whose sexuality poses no threat. While particular orders may have exercised a degree of autonomy in the handling of their affairs, ultimately they were subject to the dictates of a religious code which categorically denied them the right to assume the position as head of the Church.

Unlike nuns, the *béguines* were not initially subject to direction from male clergy. Against the background of the religious revival of the twelfth century, certain women who wished to develop a lifestyle separate from men, to uphold Christian values, to pursue independent careers in the cities where women were in a majority, formed communities that provided a supportive and powerful alternative to family life or the life of a nun (see Clark, 1975, pp. 72–80). The organization of the *béguinage* had much in common with the *jilimi*. There was a core of women who were living without men but they were joined by others in need of a safe environment. Meetings were secret and the women discussed matters of intellectual and spiritual import in a way not possible for those women subject to male control. Families sent their daughters to the *béguines* to be educated in reading, religion, and other matters before marriage (Clark, 1975, p. 78). However the strength and number of women choosing a life of chastity outside the Church eventually proved too much for the Church authorities who succeeded in dispersing the women and absorbing the remaining groups within the Church structure. The tactics and the reasons given were in essence very similar to those members of the Alice Springs Christian community who sought the dispersion and absorption of the Women's Centre in 1982.

The position to which the women of these separatist communities retreat and that from which they retreat are fundamentally different for white and Aboriginal women. Perhaps to use the word *retreat* pre-empts the issue. White women who withdraw permanently from the hetero-sexual battleline threaten not only men, but also many of those women who remain in heterosexual relationships. Those women who retreat occasionally tend to use the 'women's camps' of the separatists for brief

21

respite. Not surprisingly, the women who have chosen to live there permanently are sceptical of the visitors' motives: they see little point in returning. Further, the occasional visitors in need of recharging the batteries before re-engaging in combat on the battleline engender resentment (see Leeds Revolutionary Feminist Group, 1981; Rich, 1980).

The battleline is an artefact of white society and it is one that Aboriginal women recognize and treat with a wry scorn. Those Aboriginal women who see some common ground in feminism and their own struggles direct their energies at attempts to create both a basis on which a dialogue between men and women may fruitfully occur and a context within which Aboriginal women may talk to white women. By focusing on the nature of the changing gender and spatial relations in two specific situations and comparing strategies of white and Aboriginal women, I have sought to provide the basis for a better understanding of the dynamics of the politics of separation in both societies.

The nature of my research in central Australia and engagement as consultant by Aboriginal organizations and various state agencies has forced me to think through my position as a feminist working in another culture. It is, I have found, by reference to such situations that the hardest thinking is achieved but I share the concern, voiced by Burgmann a decade earlier, that there is little of substance written by feminist scholars.[15] Feminists confronting charges of racism in relation to Aboriginal women show signs that they are still locked in the guilt/shame cycle so well explored by Fisher (1984) for the United States. She argues that feminists who are concerned not just to understand the social order but who are also committed to changing it, need to confront the interplay of emotions and political action.

I am often asked for sources authored by Aboriginal women and I am struck by the lack of material. Several articulate Aboriginal women have addressed the question of the relevance of feminist theory and practice (Fesl, 1984; O'Shane, 1976) but when compared to the volume of writing by black women elsewhere (Moraga and Anzaldua, 1981), and in particular by women who identify as feminists, there is a real dearth. There are a number of possible explanations the most obvious of which is scale. Aborigines constitute 1.1 per cent of the Australian population. Of the 90,000 who are women about 80 per cent live in major urban centres, but of those who live in remote locations some 92 per cent live in communities of less than 400 persons.[16] Thus we find Aboriginal women living under very different circumstances across Australia. Not surprisingly, their needs are also very different. In terms of comparisons with North America, a more profitable analogue could be made with American Indian women than with black Americans. But even here we find a well-developed body of literature. A further consideration is that Aboriginal social and local organization establishes strict knowledge boundaries. Decisions are made on the basis of who has the right to know and that number is limited by ties of locality.[17] My position, in writing about Aboriginal women, is that I do have a legitimate voice; I have been allowed access to certain beliefs and practices; I have used that knowledge responsibly; there has been no covert research, no breaches of confidence; I have made publications available to those who contributed. This is all a form of paying one's dues. But as a social scientist, I see my responsibility as not speaking *for* Aboriginal women but rather to provide a basis on which cross-cultural understanding may build, to locate issues of gender and race within a wider perspective, to offer an analysis of social change.

NOTES

1 I gratefully acknowledge the permission of Cambridge University Press to draw on material in *The Politics of Separation* (Bell, 1987, pp. 206–36).

2 Warlpiri is a desert language with over 2,000 primary speakers (see Bell, 1983). Aranda speakers refer to the 'single women's camp' as *alukwerre* and it is interesting to note that when women of the Central Australian Aboriginal Congress in Alice Springs sought to establish a women's 'birthing centre' this was the name chosen.

3 At some future date my continuing concern with the subject of the 'politics of protest' will surface in a more detailed exploration of the many occasions on which the feminists have confronted Aboriginal issues.

4 On 11 November 1983 a number of Aboriginal women joined white feminist groups in a protest camp at Pine Gap, central Australia. Inspired by the Greenham Common peace camp, the women chose to focus attention on this American communication base just outside Alice Springs. For a discussion of the event, see *Chain Reaction*, No. 34 (1983), pp. 26–9 and No. 36 (1984), pp. 12–17. For a feminist analysis from a participant observer, see Lloyd (1988).

5 In a paper published in 1984 but written in 1975, Burgmann (1984, pp. 20–1), in agreement with Grimshaw and disagreement with Larbalestier, posits that race and class are the locus of women's disadvantage. Giving emphasis to personal perception, she notes the disenchantment of her Aboriginal friends with existing feminist theory and practice. Of course, Burgmann writes of urban women whose experience of racism and access to fora within which to discuss feminist issues is markedly different from that of women in more remote rural areas. Further, it is worth entertaining the proposition that Aboriginal women, like other women, find a comfortable niche if their analyses do not take on mainstream theory. It is very convenient for males – Aboriginal and white – who occupy positions of power, to be able to argue it is class and race that are the locus of oppression. They are thus shielded from confronting the sexism of their own practices. It is unreasonable to ask that Aboriginal women provide a critique of gender relations which feminists, long schooled in political theory, still have failed to do.

6 See, for example, Eatock (1987, p. 28), Watson (1987, p. 51), and Williams (1987, p. 72) whose first-hand accounts provide the basis for further analysis. The unwillingness of Sykes (1984) and Fesl (1984) to embrace wholeheartedly the women's movement does not render a feminist analysis of the place of

Aboriginal women within Australian society irrelevant.

7 Pages 219–25 were removed at midday of the first day. The paper had been presented earlier that morning. Some of the compilations in circulation retain the contentious section.

8 Secret material may be acknowledged only by those who have rights in the country and/or ceremony to which it refers. There are further restrictions based on age and gender. Sacred material refers to religious beliefs and practices, is considered powerful but is not necessarily secret. Improper behaviour with respect to sacred material is believed to be dangerous. Publication of restricted material has caused considerable distress in the past and, in one case, distribution of an already printed book was halted by an order of the Supreme Court, Northern Territory.

9 I provided a commentary for the ABC *Coming Out Show* on a tape-recording of this interview (recorded 27 September 1984). The author had declined to respond on air.

10 Dominy (1985, p. 14) provides an interesting comparative case in her exploration of the alliances between separatists' politics and Maori women seeking a distinctive identity. With reference to the 'conference', she argues that its modelling on the white/male/middle-class experience alienates both separatists and Maori women.

11 The then Minister for Aboriginal Affairs, Mr Clyde Holding, in response to a question from a member of the Federation at the Aborigines and International Law Conference, Canberra, 21–2 November 1983, stated that organizations already existed through which women could make their views known. The terms of reference of the Task Force contradict this and no doubt the Federation was an important force in keeping the broader issue of self-determination on the agenda.

12 Dominy (1985, p. 16) argues that every generation uses the past to define self and that these are formulated in the current social context. Authenticity, she argues, is always contextualized, always defined in the present. Her suggestion that the land/mother/nurture and rape/subjugation be seen as symbolic complex accords with Sykes' representations (ibid., p. 17).

13 Striking parallels are evident with the New Zealand experience. Dominy (1985, 1986) explores the cross-cutting affiliations between Maori and Pakeha women, the alliances which are forged within contexts of social protest, and the consequences for lesbian gender conceptions.

14 The history of the closure may be traced through the pages of the *Centralian Advocate* (7 February, 14 February, 23 February, 6 March, 20 March, 27 March, 2 April, 10 April, 17 April, 1 May, and 15 May 1980). The engineering of the collapse of the Women's Centre was one of the dirtiest pieces of Northern Territory sexual politics I can remember.

15 See Burgmann (1984). In the volumes edited by Rowland (see Sykes, 1984; Fesl, 1984) and Scutt (see Eatock, 1987; Watson, 1987; Williams, 1987) we hear from familiar voices – Bobbi Sykes, Pat O'Shane, and Eva Fesl. More recent Australian volumes on the general theme of feminism have not included the obligatory article on Aboriginal women. See, for example, Grieve and Burns (1986).

16 Statistics dealing with Aboriginal demography are notoriously variable. Here I am drawing on those in the Department of Aboriginal Affairs, *Community Profile Statistical Collection* (1981), tables 1–11.

17 Unlike Maori women for whom pre-contact forms of governmental structure permitted decision-making at a number of levels, in Australia until governments sought 'representative councils', there were no bodies at the national

level with authority, ascribed or achieved, who could speak for Aborigines (Weaver, 1985, pp. 113–50).

REFERENCES

Aickin Rothschild, Mary, 'White women volunteers in their freedom summers; their life and work in a movement for social change', *Feminist Studies*, Vol. 5, No. 3 (1979), pp. 466–95.

Australian Law Reform Commission, 'Aboriginal customary law reference', *Field Trip*, No.7, Central Australia (1982), pp. 47–8.

Bell, Diane, 'Desert politics: choices in the "marriage market"', in *Women and Colonization: Anthropological Perspectives*, ed. Mona Etienne and Eleanor Leacock (New York: Praeger, 1980), pp. 239–69.

Bell, Diane, *Daughters of the Dreaming* (Melbourne/Sydney: McPhee Gribble/ Allen and Unwin, 1983).

Bell, Diane, 'The politics of separation', in *Dealing with Inequality*, ed. Marilyn Strathern (London: CUP, 1987), pp. 112–29.

Bell, Diane and Pam Ditton, *Law: The old and the new* (Canberra: Aboriginal History, 1980/4).

Burgmann, Meredith, 'Black sisterhood: the situation of urban Aboriginal women and their relationship to the white women's movement', in *Australian Women and the Political System* (Melbourne: Longman Cheshire, 1984), pp. 21–47.

Clark, Gracia, 'The béguines: a medieval women's community', *Quest*, Vol. 1, No. 4 (1975), pp. 73–80.

Daylight, Phyllis and Mary Johnstone, *Women's Business: Report of the Aboriginal Women's Task Force* (Canberra: Department of Prime Minister and Cabinet, Office of Status of Women, AGPS, 1986).

Dill, Bonnie Thornton, 'Race, class and gender: prospects for an all-inclusive sisterhood', *Feminist Studies*, Vol. 9 (1983), pp. 131–50.

Dominy, Michele D., 'Lesbian–feminist gender conceptions: separatism in Christchurch, New Zealand', *Signs*, Vol. 11, No. 2 (1986), pp. 274–89.

Dominy, Michele, D., '"To forge a distinctive New Zealand identity from a Maori point of view": feminist expressions of Maoritanga', unpublished paper (1985).

Eatock, Pat, 'There's a snake in my caravan', in *Different Lives*, ed. Jocelynne A. Scutt (Harmondsworth: Penguin, 1987), pp. 23–31.

Fesl, Eve, 'Eve Fesl', in *Women who do and Women who don't join the Women's Movement*, ed. Robyn Rowland (Melbourne: Routledge and Kegan Paul, 1984), pp. 109–15.

Fisher, Bernice, 'Guilt and shame in the women's movement: the radical ideal of action and its meaning for feminist intellectuals', *Feminist Studies*, Vol. 10, No. 2 (1984), pp. 184–212.

Grieve, Norma and Ailsa Burns, *Australian Women: New feminist perspectives* (Melbourne: OUP, 1986).

Hartmann, Heidi, 'The unhappy marriage of Marxism and feminism: towards a more progressive union', in *Women and Revolution*, ed. Lydia Sargent (Boston, Mass.: South End Press, 1981).

Hawthorne, Susan, 'Traditional Aboriginal stories and Australian feminism – a white perspective in Fourth Women and Labour Conference Papers' (Brisbane, 1984), pp. 219–25.

Langton, Marcia, 'The black gin syndrome', unpublished paper (1982).

Langton, Marcia, 'Medicine Square: For the recognition of Aboriginal swearing and fighting as customary law' (BA (hons) thesis, Prehistory and Anthropology Department, ANU, 1983).

Leeds Revolutionary Feminist Group, 'Political lesbianism: the case against heterosexuality', in *Love Your Enemy?* (London: Only Woman Press, 1981).

Lloyd, Jane, 'Politics at Pine Gap: women, Aborigines and peace', (unpublished B Litt (hons) thesis, Australian Studies, Deakin University, 1988).

Moraga, Cherrie and Gloria Anzaldua, *This Bridge Called My Back: writings by radical women of color* (New York: Kitchen Table: Women of Color Press, 1981).

New South Wales Anti-Discrimination Board, *Study of Street Offence by Aborigines* (AGPS, 1982).

O'Shane, Pat, 'Is there any relevance in the women's movement for Aboriginal women?' *Refractory Girl*, 12 (1976), pp. 31–4.

Rich, Adrienne, 'Compulsory heterosexuality and lesbian existence', *Signs*, Vol. 5, No. 4 (1980), pp. 631–60.

Sykes, Bobbi, 'Black women in Australia: a history', in *The Other Half*, ed. Jan Mercer (Harmondsworth: Pelican, 1975).

Sykes, Bobbi, 'Bobbi Sykes', in Rowland (1984), pp. 63–9.

Watson, Lilla, 'Sister, black is the colour of my soul', in Scutt (1987), pp. 45–52.

Weaver, Sally, 'Political representivity and indigenous minorities in Canada and Australia', in *Indigenous Peoples and the Nation-State*, ed. Noel Dyck (Canada, 1985), pp. 113–50.

Williams, Drid, 'The brides of Christ', in *Perceiving Women*, ed. Shirley Ardener (London: Malaby Press, 1975).

Williams, Elizabeth, 'Aboriginal first, woman second', in Scutt (1987), pp. 67–73.

SISTERHOOD

Political Solidarity Between Women

Bell Hooks (Gloria Watkins)

INTRODUCTION: SUNDAY AFTERNOON, 12 JANUARY 1986

Weeping, the sound mingles with the music of Lole y Manuel, Paco de Lucia, and Camaron, all singers of flamenco, I confront the frustration of trying to begin writing; the worry that I shall not find words to say what needs to be said; the fear that I daily lose the capacity to speak in writing. I know I cannot listen to this music and write at the same time. The sound will overcome me, carry me into a world of passionate speech that is beyond words. It is a singing filled with tension, intensity – in its own way a music of struggle. In this new year I feel it is imperative that feminist activists recognize the primacy of struggle – the significance of struggle in political work on an individual and collective level. Radical commitment to political struggle carries with it the willingness to accept responsibility for using conflict constructively, as a way to enhance and enrich our understanding of one another, as a guide directing and shaping the parameters of our political solidarity.

Within the feminist movement racial conflict between white women and women of colour continues to be one area of struggle. Often these conflicts are so overwhelming that they cause us to despair that we can ever live and work together in social spaces that are not irrevocably tainted by politics of domination. Since energy wanes and hope diminishes it is absolutely necessary for feminist activists to renew our commitment to political struggle and strengthen our solidarity. This means that we must work with greater diligence to confront racism and the conflicts that it engenders with the conviction that sustained committed struggle will lead towards a liberatory feminist political agenda.

Feminist Theory: From Margin to Center is one expression of the current attempt on the part of concerned feminist activists to formulate a liberatory theory, one that is more inclusive, that challenges rather than perpetuates domination. To some extent racism has shaped responses to *Feminist Theory: From Margin to Center*. Unlike my first book *Ain't I A Woman: Black Women and Feminism*, which was accepted for publication at a time when white women had decreed that 'race' was an acceptable topic for feminist discussion, *From Margin to Center* appears

27

at a time when many white women act as though there is no need for women of colour to play a central role in the making of feminist political theory. Although they make references to the work of a few privileged voices (that is to say, voices they choose to listen to, for example, Audre Lorde, Barbara Smith) for the most part theoretical writing by less known or unknown women of colour is ignored, particularly if it does not articulate the prevailing ideology. In women's studies classes throughout the US theoretical feminist writing by women of colour is often ignored and attention given rather to works of fiction or confessional autobiographical writing. Since its publication, *Feminist Theory: From Margin to Center* has received only a few reviews (I know of only two). Despite a lack of full recognition, critique, or discussion of *From Margin to Center* by established voices within feminist circles, I receive positive feedback from readers. It is not my intent to complain, for on a personal level I am pleased with both the writing of the book and the fact that sales are steady. This does not blind me to the reality that racism along with an established star system (which ensures that the work of certain individuals will receive widespread attention while other work will be ignored) influences response to the book.

Coming from a politically conservative, southern black working-class background, I am sometimes awed by the circumstances that enable me to claim and assert a radical politic. I cannot believe that I have written two feminist books. Lately, pure chance has brought me to a life in the north, to New Haven, Connecticut, where I teach in Afro-American Studies and English at Yale University – my first full-time teaching job. For me, teaching is political work and the classroom a space for radical political action. It is subversive to make the university a site for education for critical consciousness, for politicization – and it is difficult. It is not a course of action that ensures acceptance or prolonged employment.

I am grounded in a radical politic that is based on the belief that politics of domination as manifest in imperialist, capitalist, racist, and sexist oppression must be challenged and changed so that a new social order can emerge. At times I declare myself a socialist. At times I am disillusioned and express doubt about socialism in the United States, particularly a socialist-feminist or socialist politic which seems to be rooted in an established framework of academic discourse that is not directed at mass-based political movement or social change. Much socialist-feminist writing has focused on a feminist critique of socialism rather than on the imagining of a liberatory radical theory of socialism that would more adequately address interlocking systems of domination like sexism, racism, class oppression, imperialism, and so on. This is the agenda that socialist-feminists and all feminists who are committed to revolutionary change must ultimately address.

SISTERHOOD: POLITICAL SOLIDARITY BETWEEN WOMEN

Women are the group most victimized by sexist oppression. As with other forms of group oppression, sexism is perpetuated by institutional and social structures; by the individuals who dominate, exploit, or oppress; and by the victims themselves who are socialized to behave in ways that make them act in complicity with the status quo. Male supremacist ideology encourages women to believe we are valueless and obtain value only by relating to or bonding with men. We are taught that our relationships with one another diminish rather than enrich our experience. We are taught that women are 'natural' enemies, that solidarity will never exist between us because we cannot, should not, and do not bond with one another. We have learned these lessons well. We must unlearn them if we are to build a sustained feminist movement. We must learn to live and work in solidarity. We must learn the true meaning and value of sisterhood.

Although the contemporary feminist movement should have provided a training ground for women to learn about political solidarity, sisterhood was not viewed as a revolutionary accomplishment women would work and struggle to obtain. The vision of sisterhood evoked by women's liberationists was based on the idea of common oppression. Needless to say, it was primarily bourgeois white women, both liberal and radical in perspective, who professed belief in the notion of common oppression. The idea of 'common oppression' was a false and corrupt platform disguising and mystifying the true nature of women's varied and complex social reality. Women are divided by sexist attitudes, racism, class privilege, and a host of other prejudices. Sustained woman bonding can occur only when these divisions are confronted and the necessary steps are taken to eliminate them. Divisions will not be eliminated by wishful thinking or romantic reverie about common oppression despite the value of highlighting experiences all women share.

In recent years sisterhood as slogan, motto, rallying-cry, no longer evokes the spirit of power in unity. Some feminists now seem to feel that unity between women is impossible given our differences. Abandoning the idea of sisterhood as an expression of political solidarity weakens and diminishes feminist movement. Solidarity strengthens resistance struggle. There can be no mass-based feminist movement to end sexist oppression without a united front – women must take the initiative and demonstrate the power of solidarity. Unless we can show that barriers separating women can be eliminated, that solidarity can exist, we cannot hope to change and transform society as a whole. The shift away from an emphasis on sisterhood has occurred because many women, angered by the insistence on 'common oppression', shared identity, sameness, criticized or dismissed feminist movement altogether. The emphasis on sisterhood was often seen as the emotional appeal masking the opportunism of manipulative, bourgeois, white women. It was seen as a cover-up hiding the fact that many women exploit and oppress other women. . . .

Women are enriched when we bond with one another but we cannot develop sustaining ties or political solidarity using the model of sisterhood created by bourgeois women's liberationists. According to their analysis, the basis for bonding was shared victimization, hence the emphasis on common oppression. This concept of bonding directly reflects male supremacist thinking. Sexist ideology teaches women that to be female is to be a victim. Rather than repudiate this equation (which mystifies female experience – in their daily lives most women are not continually passive, helpless, or powerless 'victims'), women's liberationists embraced it, making shared victimization the basis for woman bonding. This meant that women had to conceive of themselves as 'victims' in order to feel that feminist movement was relevant to their lives. Bonding as victims created a situation in which assertive, self-affirming women were often seen as having no place in feminist movement. It was this logic that led white women activists (along with black men) to suggest that black women were so 'strong' they did not need to be active in feminist movement. It was this logic that led many white women activists to abandon feminist movement when they no longer embraced the victim identity. Ironically, the women who were most eager to be seen as 'victims', who overwhelmingly stressed the role of victim, were more privileged and powerful than the vast majority of women in our society. An example of this tendency is some writing about violence against women. Women who are exploited and oppressed daily cannot afford to relinquish the belief that they exercise some measure of control, however relative, over their lives. They cannot afford to see themselves solely as 'victims' because their survival depends on continued exercise of whatever personal powers they possess. It would be psychologically demoralizing for these women to bond with other women on the basis of shared victimization. They bond with other women on the basis of shared strengths and resources. This is the woman bonding feminist movement should encourage. It is this type of bonding that is the essence of sisterhood.

Bonding as 'victims', white women's liberationists were not required to assume responsibility for confronting the complexity of their own experience. They were not challenging one another to examine their sexist attitudes towards women unlike themselves or exploring the impact of race and class privilege on their relationships to women outside their race/class groups. Identifying as 'victims', they could abdicate responsibility for their role in the maintenance and perpetuation of sexism, racism, and classism, which they did by insisting that only men were the enemy. They did not acknowledge and confront the enemy within. They were not prepared to forgo privilege and do the 'dirty work' (the struggle and confrontation necessary to build political awareness as well as the many tedious tasks to be accomplished in day-to-day organizing) that is necessary in the development of radical political consciousness, the first task being honest critique and evaluation of one's social status, values, political beliefs, etc. Sisterhood became yet another shield against reality, another support system. Their version of sisterhood was informed by racist and classist assumptions about white womanhood, that the white 'lady' (that is to say, bourgeois woman) should be protected from all that might upset or discomfort her and shielded from negative realities that might lead to confrontation. Their version of sisterhood dictated that sisters were 'unconditionally' to love one another; that they were to avoid conflict and minimize disagreement; that they were not to criticize one another, especially in public. For a time, these mandates created an illusion of unity suppressing the competition, hostility, perpetual disagreement, and abusive criticism (trashing) that was often the norm in feminist groups. Today, many splinter groups who share common identities (e.g. Wasp working class; white academic faculty women; anarchist feminists, etc.) use this same model of sisterhood, but participants in these groups endeavour to support, affirm, and protect one another while demonstrating hostility (usually through excessive trashing) towards women outside the chosen sphere. Bonding between a chosen circle of women who strengthen their ties by excluding and devaluing women outside their group closely resembles the type of personal bonding between women that has always occurred under patriarchy; the one difference being the interest in feminism.

To develop political solidarity between women, feminist activists cannot bond on the terms set by the dominant ideology of the culture. We must define our own terms. Rather than bond on the basis of shared victimization or in response to a false sense of a common enemy, we can bond on the basis of our political commitment to a feminist movement that aims to end sexist oppression. Given such a commitment, our energies would not be concentrated on the issue of equality with men or solely on the struggle to resist male domination. We would no longer accept a simplistic good girls/bad boys account of the structure of sexist oppression. Before we can resist male domination we must break our attachment to sexism; we must work to transform female consciousness. Working together to expose, examine, and eliminate sexist socialization within ourselves, women would strengthen and affirm one another and build a solid foundation for developing political solidarity.

Between women and men, sexism is most often expressed in the form of male domination, which leads to discrimination, exploitation, or oppression. Between women, male supremacist values are expressed through suspicious, defensive, competitive behaviour. It is sexism that leads women to feel threatened by one another without cause. While sexism teaches women to be sex objects for men, it is also manifest when women who have repudiated this role feel contemptuous and superior in relation to those women who have not. Sexism leads women to devalue parenting work while inflating the value of jobs and careers. Acceptance of sexist ideology is indicated when women teach children that there are only two possible behaviour patterns: the role of dominant or submissive being. Sexism teaches women woman-hating, and both consciously and unconsciously we act out this hatred in our daily contact with one another. . . .

All over the United States, women spend hours of their time daily verbally abusing other women, usually through malicious gossip (not to be confused with gossip as positive communication). Television soap operas and night-time dramas continually portray woman-to-woman relationships as characterized by aggression, contempt, and competitiveness. In feminist circles, sexism towards women is expressed by abusive trashing, total disregard, and lack of concern or interest in women who have not joined feminist movement. This is especially evident at university campuses where feminist studies is often seen as a discipline or programme having no relationship to feminist movement. In her commencement address at Barnard College in May 1979, a black woman writer, Toni Morrison, told her audience:

I want not to ask you but to tell you not to participate in the oppression of your sisters. Mothers who abuse their children are women, and another woman, not an agency, has to be willing to stay their hands. Mothers who set fire to school buses are women, and another woman, not an agency, has to tell them to stay their hands. Women who stop the promotion of other women in careers are women, and another woman must come to the victim's aid. Social and welfare workers who humiliate their clients may be women, and other women colleagues have to deflect their anger.

I am alarmed by the violence that women do to each other: professional violence, competitive violence, emotional violence. I am alarmed by the willingness of women to enslave other women. I am alarmed by a growing absence of decency on the killing floor of professional women's worlds.

To build a politicized, mass-based feminist movement, women must work harder to overcome the alienation from one another that exists when sexist socialization has not been unlearned, e.g. homophobia, judging by appearances, conflicts between women with diverse sexual practices. So far, feminist movement has not transformed woman-to-woman relationships, especially between women who are strangers to one another or from different backgrounds, even though it has been the occasion for bonding between individuals and groups of women. We must renew our efforts to help women unlearn sexism if we are to develop affirming personal relationships as well as political unity.

Racism is another barrier to solidarity between women. The ideology of sisterhood as expressed by contemporary feminist activists indicated no acknowledgement that racist discrimination, exploitation, and oppression of multi-ethnic women by white women had made it impossible for the two groups to feel they shared common interest or political concerns. Also, the existence of totally different cultural backgrounds can make communication difficult. This has been especially true of black and white female relationships. Historically, many black women experienced white women as the white supremacist group who most directly exercised power over them, often in a manner far more brutal and dehumanizing than that of racist white men. Today, despite predominant rule by white supremacist patriarchs, black women often work in situations where the immediate supervisor, boss, or authority figure is a white woman. Conscious of the privileges white men as well as white women gain as a consequence of racial domination, black women were quick to react to the feminist call for sisterhood by pointing to the contradiction – that we should join with women who exploit us to help liberate them. The call for sisterhood was heard by many black women as a plea for help and support for a movement not addressing us. . . . Many perceived that the women's liberation movement as outlined by bourgeois white women would serve their interests at the expense of poor and working-class women, many of whom are black. Certainly, this was not a basis for sisterhood and black women would have been politically naive had we joined such a movement. However, given the struggles of black women's participation historically and currently in political organizing, the emphasis could have been on the development and clarification of the nature of political solidarity.

White females discriminate against and exploit black women while simultaneously being envious and competitive in their interactions with them. Neither process of interaction creates conditions wherein trust and mutually reciprocal relationships can develop. After constructing feminist theory and praxis in such a way as to omit focus on racism, white women shifted the responsibility for calling attention to race onto others. They did not have to take the initiative in discussions of racism or race privilege but could listen and respond to non-white women discussing racism without changing in any way the structure of feminist movement, without losing their hegemonic hold. They could then show their concern with having more women of colour in feminist organizations by encouraging greater participation. They were not confronting racism. . . .

Racism is not an issue simply because white women activists are

33

individually racist. They represent a small percentage of women in this society. They could have all been anti-racist from the outset but eliminating racism would still need to be a central feminist issue. Racism is fundamentally a feminist issue because it is so interconnected with sexist oppression. In the West, the philosophical foundations of racist and sexist ideology are similar. Although ethnocentric white values have led feminist theorists to argue the priority of sexism over racism, they do so in the context of attempting to create an evolutionary notion of culture, which in no way corresponds to our lived experience. In the United States, maintaining white supremacy has always been as great if not a greater priority than maintaining strict sex-role divisions. It is no mere coincidence that interest in white women's rights is kindled whenever there is mass-based, anti-racist protest. Even the most politically naive person can comprehend that a white supremacist state, asked to respond to the needs of oppressed black people and/or the needs of white women (particularly those from the bourgeois classes), will find it in its interest to respond to whites. Radical movement to end racism (a struggle that many have died to advance) is far more threatening than a women's movement shaped to meet the class needs of upwardly-mobile white women.

It does not in any way diminish the value of, or the need for, a feminist movement to recognize the significance of anti-racist struggle. Feminist theory would have much to offer if it showed women ways in which racism and sexism are immutably connected rather than pitting one struggle against the other or blatantly dismissing racism. A central issue for feminist activists has been the struggle to obtain for women the right to control their bodies. The very concept of white supremacy relies on the perpetuation of a white race. It is in the interest of continued white racist domination of the planet for white patriarchy to maintain control over all women's bodies. Any white female activist who works daily to help women gain control over their bodies and is racist negates and undermines her own effort. When white women attack white supremacy they are simultaneously participating in the struggle to end sexist oppression. This is just one example of the intersecting, complementary nature of racist and sexist oppression. There are many others that need to be examined by feminist theorists.

Racism allows white women to construct feminist theory and praxis in such a way that it is far removed from anything resembling radical struggle. Racist socialization teaches bourgeois white women to think they are necessarily more capable of leading masses of women than other groups of women. Time and time again, they have shown that they do not want to be part of a feminist movement – they want to lead it. Even though bourgeois white women's liberationists probably know less about grass-roots organizing than many poor and working-class women, they were certain of their leadership ability, as well as confident that theirs should be the dominant role in shaping theory and praxis. Racism teaches an inflated sense of importance and value, especially when coupled with class privilege. Most poor and working-class women or even individual bourgeois non-white women would not have assumed that they could launch a feminist movement without first having the support and participation of diverse groups of women. Elizabeth Spelmann stresses this impact of racism in her essay, 'Theories of race and gender: the erasure of black women':

> this is a racist society, and part of what this means is that, generally, the self-esteem of white people is deeply influenced by their difference from and supposed superiority to black people. White people may not think of themselves as racists, because they do not own slaves or hate blacks, but that does not mean that much of what props up white people's sense of self-esteem is not based on the racism which unfairly distributes benefits and burdens to whites and blacks.

One reason white women active in feminist movement were unwilling to confront racism was their arrogant assumption that their call for sisterhood was a non-racist gesture. Many white women have said to me, 'we wanted black women and other non-white women to join the movement', totally unaware of their perception that they somehow 'own' the movement, that they are the 'hosts' inviting us as 'guests'.

Despite the current focus on eliminating racism in feminist movement, there has been little change in the direction of theory and praxis. While white feminist activists now include writings by women of colour on course outlines, or hire one woman of colour to teach a class about her ethnic group, or make sure one or more women of colour are represented in feminist organizations (even though this contribution of women of colour is needed and valuable), more often than not they are attempting to cover up the fact that they are totally unwilling to surrender their hegemonic dominance of theory and praxis, a dominance which they would not have established were this not a white supremacist, capitalist state. . . .

Another response to racism has been the establishment of unlearning racism workshops, which are often led by white women. These workshops are important, yet they tend to focus primarily on cathartic individual psychological acknowledgement of personal prejudice without stressing the need for corresponding change in political commitment and action. A woman who attends an unlearning racism workshop and learns to acknowledge that she is racist is no less a threat than one who does not. Acknowledgement of racism is significant when it leads to transformation. More research, writing, and practical implementation of findings must be done on ways to unlearn racist socialization. Many white women

35

who daily exercise race privilege lack awareness they they are doing so (which explains the emphasis on confession in unlearning racism workshops). They may not have conscious understanding of the ideology of white supremacy and the extent to which it shapes their behaviour and attitudes towards women unlike themselves. Often, white women bond on the basis of shared racial identity without conscious awareness of the significance of their actions. This unconscious maintenance and perpetuation of white supremacy is dangerous because none of us can struggle to change racist attitudes if we do not recognize that they exist. . . .

Women will know that white feminist activists have begun to confront racism in a serious and revolutionary manner when they are not simply acknowledging racism in feminist movement or calling attention to personal prejudice, but are actively struggling to resist racist oppression in our society. Women will know they have made a political commitment to eliminating racism when they help change the direction of feminist movement, when they work to unlearn racist socialization prior to assuming positions of leadership, or shaping theory, or making contact with women of colour so that they will not perpetuate and maintain racial oppression or, unconsciously or consciously, abuse and hurt non-white women. These are the truly radical gestures that create a foundation for the experience of political solidarity between white women and women of colour.

White women are not the only group that must confront racism if sisterhood is to emerge. Women of colour must confront our absorption of white supremacist beliefs, 'internalized racism', which may lead us to feel self-hate, to vent anger and rage at injustice at one another rather than at oppressive forces, to hurt and abuse one another, or to lead one ethnic group to make no effort to communicate with another. Often women of colour from varied ethnic groups have learned to resent and hate one another, or to be competitive with one another. Often Asian, Latina, or Native American Indian groups find they can bond with whites by hating blacks. Black people respond to this by perpetuating racist stereotypes and images of these ethnic groups. It becomes a vicious cycle. Divisions between women of colour will not be eliminated until we assume responsibility for uniting (not solely on the basis of resisting racism) to learn about our cultures, to share our knowledge and skills, and to gain strength from our diversity. We need to do more research and writing about the barriers that separate us and the ways we can overcome such separation. Often the men in our ethnic groups have greater contact with one another than we do. Women often assume so many job-related and domestic responsibilities that we lack the time or do not make the time to get to know women outside our group or community. Language differences often prevent us from communicating; we can change this by encouraging one another to learn to speak Spanish, English, Japanese, Chinese, etc.

One factor that makes interaction between multi-ethnic groups of women difficult and sometimes impossible is our failure to recognize that a behaviour pattern in one culture may be unacceptable in another, that it may have different signification cross-culturally. Through repeated teaching of a course titled 'Third World Women in the United States', I have learned the importance of learning what we called one another's cultural codes. An Asian-American student, of Japanese heritage, explained her reluctance to participate in feminist organizations by calling attention to the tendency among feminist activists to speak rapidly without pause, to be quick on the uptake, always ready with a response. She had been raised to pause and think before speaking, to consider the impact of one's words, a characteristic that she felt was particularly true of Asian-Americans. She expressed feelings of inadequacy on the various occasions she was present in feminist groups. In our class, we learned to allow pauses and appreciate them. By sharing this cultural code, we created an atmosphere in the classroom that allowed for different communication patterns. This particular class was peopled primarily by black women. Several white women students complained that the atmosphere in the class was 'too hostile'. They cited the noise level and direct confrontations that took place in the room prior to class starting as an example of this hostility. Our response was to explain that what they perceived as hostility and aggression, we considered playful teasing and affectionate expressions of our pleasure at being together. Our tendency to talk loudly we saw as a consequence of being in a room with many people speaking as well as cultural background: many of us were raised in families where individuals speak loudly. In their upbringing as white, middle-class females, the complaining students had been taught to identify loud and direct speech with anger. We explained that we did not identify loud or blunt speech in this way, and encouraged them to switch codes, to think of it as an affirming gesture. Once they switched codes, they not only began to have a more creative, joyful experience in the class, but they also learned that silence and quiet speech can in some cultures indicate hostility and aggression. By learning one another's cultural codes and respecting our differences, we felt a sense of community, of sisterhood. Respecting diversity does not mean uniformity or sameness.

A crucial concern in these multi-racial classroom settings was recognition and acknowledgement of our differences and the extent to which they determine how we will be perceived by others. We had continually to remind one another to appreciate difference since many of us were raised to fear it. . . .

Cutting across racial lines, class is a serious political division between women. It was often suggested in early feminist literature that class would not be so important if more poor and working-class women would join the movement. Such thinking was a denial of the existence of class privilege gained through exploitation as well as a denial of class struggle. To build sisterhood, women must criticize and repudiate class exploitation. The bourgeois woman who takes a less privileged 'sister' to lunch or dinner at a fancy restaurant may be acknowledging class but she is not repudiating class privilege – she is exercising it. Wearing second-hand clothing and living in low-cost housing in a poor neighbourhood while buying stocks and shares is not a gesture of solidarity with those who are deprived or under-privileged. As in the case of racism in feminist movement, the emphasis on class has been focused on individual status and change. Until women accept the need for redistribution of wealth and resources in the United States and work towards the achievement of that end, there will be no bonding between women that transcends class. . . .

Women from lower-class groups had no difficulty recognizing that the social equality women's liberationists talked about equated careerism and class mobility with liberation. They also knew who would be exploited in the service of this liberation. Daily confronting class exploitation, they cannot conveniently ignore class struggle. In the anthology *Women of Crisis*, Helen, a working-class white woman, who works as a maid in the home of a bourgeois white 'feminist', expresses her understanding of the contradiction between feminist rhetoric and practice:

> I think the missus is right: everyone should be equal. She keeps on saying that. But then she has me working away in her house, and I'm not equal with her – and she doesn't want to be equal with me; and I don't blame her, because if I was her I'd hold on to my money just like she does. Maybe that's what the men are doing – they're holding on to their money. And it's a big fight, like it always is about money. She should know. She doesn't go throwing big fat pay checks at her 'help'. She's fair; she keeps on reminding us – but she's not going to 'liberate' us, any more than the men are going to 'liberate' their wives or their secretaries or the other women working in their companies.

Women's liberationists not only equated psychological pain with material deprivation to de-emphasize class privilege; they often suggested it was the more severe problem. They managed to overlook the fact that many women suffer both psychologically and materially and for that reason alone changing their social status merited greater attention than careerism. Certainly, the bourgeois woman who is suffering psychically is more likely to find help than the woman who is suffering material deprivation as well as emotional pain. One of the basic differences in perspective between the bourgeois woman and the working-class or poor woman is that the latter knows that being discriminated against or exploited because one is female may be painful and dehumanizing, but it may not necessarily be as painful, dehumanizing, or threatening as being without food or shelter, as starvation, as being deathly ill but unable to obtain medical care. Had poor women set the agenda for feminist movement, they might have decided that class struggle would be a central feminist issue; that poor and privileged women would work to understand class structure and the way it pits women against one another.

Outspoken socialist-feminists, most of whom are white women, have emphasized class but have not been effective in changing attitudes towards class in feminist movement. Despite their support of socialism, their values, behaviours, and lifestyles continue to be shaped by privilege. They have not developed collective strategies to convince bourgeois women who have no radical political perspective that eliminating class oppression is crucial to efforts to end sexist oppression. They have not worked hard to organize with poor and working-class women who may not identify as socialists but do identify with the need for redistribution of wealth in the United States. They have not worked to raise the consciousness of women collectively. Much of their energy has been spent addressing the white male left, discussing the connections between Marxism and feminism, or explaining to other feminist activists that socialist-feminism is the best strategy for revolution. Emphasis on class struggle is often incorrectly deemed the sole domain of socialist-feminists. Although I call attention to directions and strategies they have not employed, I wish to emphasize that these issues should be addressed by all activists in feminist movement. When women face the reality of classism and make political commitments to eliminating it, we shall no longer experience the class conflicts that have been so apparent in feminist movement. Until we focus on class divisions between women, we shall be unable to build political solidarity.

Sexism, racism, and classism divide women from one another. Within feminist movement, divisions and disagreements about strategy and emphasis led to the formation of a number of groups with varied political positions. Splintering into different political factions and special-interest groups has erected unnecessary barriers to sisterhood that could easily be eliminated. Special-interest groups lead women to believe that only socialist-feminists should be concerned about class; that only lesbian-feminists should be concerned about the oppression of lesbians and gay men; than only black women or other women of colour should be concerned about racism. Every woman can stand in political opposition to sexist, racist, heterosexist, and classist oppression. While she may choose to focus her work on a given political issue or a particular cause, if she is firmly opposed to all forms of group oppression, this broad perspective will be manifest in all her work irrespective of its particularity. When feminist activists are anti-racist and against class exploitation, it will not matter if women of colour are present or poor women, etc. These issues will be deemed important and will be addressed, although the women most personally affected by particular exploitations will necessarily continue in the forefront of those struggles. Women must learn to accept responsibility for fighting oppressions that may not directly affect us as individuals. Feminist movement, like other radical movements in our society, suffers when individual concerns and priorities are the only reason for participation. When we show our concern for the collective, we strengthen our solidarity. . . .

Women need to come together in situations where there will be ideological disagreement and work to change that interaction so communication occurs. This means that when women come together, rather than pretend union, we would acknowledge that we are divided and must develop strategies to overcome fears, prejudices, resentments, competitiveness, etc. The fierce negative disagreements that have taken place in feminist circles have led many feminist activists to shun group or individual interaction where there is likely to be disagreement which leads to confrontation. Safety and support have been redefined to mean hanging out in groups where the participants are alike and share similar values. While no woman wants to enter a situation in which she will be physically annihilated, women can face one another in hostile confrontation and struggle and move beyond the hostility to understanding. Expression of hostility as an end in itself is a useless activity, but when it is the catalyst pushing us on to greater clarity and understanding, it serves a meaningful function. Women need to have the experience of working through hostility to arrive at understanding and solidarity if only to free ourselves from the sexist socialization that tells us to avoid confrontation because we will be victimized or destroyed. . . .

When women actively struggle in a truly supportive way to understand our differences, to change misguided, distorted perspectives, we lay the foundation for the experience of political solidarity. Solidarity is not the same as support. To experience solidarity, we must have a community of interests, shared beliefs, and goals around which to unite, to build sisterhood. Support can be occasional. It can be given and just as easily withdrawn. Solidarity requires sustained, ongoing commitment. In feminist movement, there is need for diversity, disagreement, and difference if we are to grow. As Grace Lee Boggs and James Boggs emphasize in *Revolution and Evolution in the Twentieth Century*:

> The same appreciation of the reality of contradiction underlies the concept of criticism and self-criticism. Criticism and self-criticism is the way in which individuals united by common goals can consciously utilize their differences and limitations, i.e., the negative, in order to accelerate their positive advance. The popular formulation for this process is 'changing a bad thing into a good thing . . .'

Women do not need to eradicate difference to feel solidarity. We do not need to share common oppression to fight equally to end oppression. We do not need anti-male sentiments to bond us together, so great is the wealth of experience, culture, and ideas we have to share with one another. We can be sisters united by shared interests and beliefs, united in our appreciation for diversity, united in our struggle to end sexist oppression, united in political solidarity.

REFERENCES

Boggs, Grace Lee and James, *Revolution and Evolution in the Twentieth Century* (New York: Monthly Review Press, 1975).
Hooks, Bell, *Ain't I a Woman: Black Women and Feminism* (London: Pluto Press, 1982).
Hooks, Bell, *Feminist Theory: From Margin to Center* (Boston: South End Press, 1984).

Part II

FEMINIST KNOWLEDGE AND WOMEN'S STUDIES

INTRODUCTION

Susan Sheridan

The purposes and ideas of women's studies are shaped by its location within educational institutions as well as by its relations to the women's movement. Current debates around women's studies in the academy include whether its principal role should be the critique of existing disciplines and traditions of thought or the construction of a new inter-disciplinary model of knowledge production; whether its energies should be directed towards transforming the general curriculum or establishing its own autonomous existence and concerns; whether women's studies is by definition in conflict with the present structures of the academy, especially its hierarchies of personnel, assessment procedures, and research/teaching priorities; how far its work can be relevant and useful to the women's movement; and, finally, what its relationship should be to women's studies projects in other fields of education, especially adult and community education, where the majority of women are to be found.

The first of the three readings in this section takes its impetus from the debate around 'mainstreaming', or integrating women's studies into the general curriculum, which surfaced in the United States during the early 1980s. Benston and Lowe regard the pressure towards 'mainstreaming' as part of a backlash against the existence of independent women's studies programmes, and argue for a redefinition of the priorities of women's studies in response. They locate this argument within a sharp account of the contradictory position occupied by women's studies, as an oppositional mode of knowledge within the academy. Pointing out that it was developed primarily as one of the major feminist strategies for 'educating for change' they also express a widely-shared scepticism about the possibilities of effecting significant social change through education alone. They argue that educational institutions are themselves implicated in the structures and ideologies of patriarchal capitalism and cannot be transformed without major changes in the society as a whole – that the university is, in effect, an agent of social control. In developing this Marxist analysis they present a somewhat monolithic account of institutional power/knowledge relations, one which appears not to allow much

45

possibility of interventions and challenges of the kind that women's studies most often claims to make. Yet when they move on to discuss political strategies, in the final section, their suggestions are both practical and far-sighted: they emphasize the need to push both feminist scholarship and links with the women's movement, and to lessen the present emphasis on teaching, largely because 'mainstreaming', which is principally a matter of teaching, requires the production of ideas that are easily acceptable to the mainstream itself.

The second reading concerns women's studies in transition from 'margin' to 'mainstream' in terms of the academy's structure: that is, women's studies as an independent interdisciplinary field of teaching and research rather than as a 'perspective' within each of the traditional disciplines. This kind of structural positioning of women's studies is perhaps more common in Australia than anywhere else, and it provides the occasion for an enquiry into the nature of interdisciplinary studies which is conducted in terms of both institutional and intellectual considerations. Having argued in this piece that its institutional location will inevitably shape the model of women's studies that is developed there, I concluded (too sanguinely, I now think) that these various models would have in common a commitment to interdisciplinarity and a high degree of self-consciousness about the positions from which we were constructing this new feminist knowledge (positions intellectual, political, cultural). Disciplinary training is proving to have a pronounced effect not just on the scholarship produced but on the nature and process of debates among feminist scholars. There is currently a major problem about the status of 'theory' within the disciplines and this has had its effect on the women's studies enterprise. At its most polemical, this takes the form of claims by some disciplines (notably philosophy and literary criticism) to being the major channels of feminist theory, and concomitant disclaimers by practitioners of traditionally empirical disciplines, like history and sociology. Other issues to do with disciplinary training and interdisciplinary aims take the form of practical anxieties about maintaining credibility within one's discipline, resisting denigration of the 'generalist', and the wider problem of losing ties with the political movement where questions were formulated outside of such frameworks.

Finally, Linda Gordon's essay exemplifies some of these issues in a particular discipline, that of history. It characterizes feminist history as pulled between two opposing imperatives – to fill in the empirical detail of women's hidden history, and to provide for the political movement the requisite 'humanistic narratives'. This may be read as a particular instance of the political vs academic determinations of women's studies, but Gordon's shorthand version of the feminist historian caught between 'fact' and 'myth' has led fellow historian Joan Scott to question its implication that historians' methods are themselves free of 'myth'

46

(*Women's Review of Books*, vol. 5, no. 1, 1987). Gordon's most urgent concern is the tendency for women's history to celebrate women's 'difference' without directly challenging the hegemonic definition of history as the story of men, particularly (but not always) those of the dominant class. She warns that 'women's history' is in danger of losing its critical, oppositional force, and adds that even the rhetoric of 'difference' applied to differences *among* women can, in a depoliticized climate, dwindle to a liberal-relativist celebration of variety, and deny the possibility of making generalizations at all. There is a timely reminder, too, that feminism is not the only social and political movement with claims to be reconstructing knowledge, questioning dominant definitions and frameworks. This suggests possible allies for women's studies within the academy, while still maintaining the importance of its autonomy as a field of enquiry.

THE UNEASY ALLIANCE OF FEMINISM AND ACADEMIA

Marian Lowe and Margaret Lowe Benston

SYNOPSIS

The authors argue that some integrationists are seriously underestimating the degree to which the university is embedded in the overall social structure, a role that has not developed accidentally, and that is not likely to change without concurrent major changes in other institutions. Although it is understandable why integrationist strategies have developed and why some projects may be useful, it is also important to think about how they may undermine the radical goals of feminist scholarship and our ties to the community.

The debate in women's studies about the proper balance between integration of feminist scholarship into the mainstream curriculum and autonomous women's studies programmes has been with us since the first programmes were developed. However, these questions have acquired a particular urgency now, as an increasing emphasis is placed on integration. At issue is not only the success women's studies is likely to have reaching its goals but, potentially, also the long-term survival of feminist programmes within universities and colleges.

Assessments of the proper balance between integration and autonomy should be done keeping in mind the origins and goals of women's studies (Boxer, 1982). Feminist scholarship and women's studies both came, of course, directly out of the women's movement. Feminist scholarship has taken on not simply the task of developing an understanding of the world that takes women into account. It also has as its explicit goal the search for the origins of women's oppression and the formulation of effective strategies for change. Women's studies was developed primarily as one of these strategies for change. It was seen as a way of disseminating feminist scholarship and of 'educating for change'. The basis of feminist scholarship and of women's studies is thus a commitment to social change, specifically addressed to ending the oppression of women.

The central questions and the major theoretical approaches of feminist scholarship were developed within the different branches of the women's movement. The major underpinning common to all is the conception of

48

human characteristics as having been divided along gender lines. Feminists, albeit in different ways, have as a major goal, the healing of this split and a redefinition of the meaning of 'human' in a way that does not depend on gender. Feminists thus see themselves as ultimately speaking for everyone. There has been a general recognition that changing women's role will require change in social institutions as well as in individual consciousness, although the degree to which institutions are questioned and the emphasis placed on individual or institutional change varies in the different branches of feminism.

FEMINISM AND WOMEN'S STUDIES

To the extent that choice has been possible in institutional settings, feminist principles have been the basis of the development of the structure of women's studies. More than any other social movement in contemporary society, feminism has shown a sensitivity to oppression in all of its forms. As a consequence of this, there is a strong egalitarian and anti-elitist element in feminism which has strongly affected women's studies. Feminism has also given women's studies a strong collectivist tendency because of the feminist conviction that individual development and strength depends on support from a community. Most important, perhaps, is the influence of that part of feminist theory which deals with the interaction between the individual and social context. This was expressed in early feminist writing as 'the personal is political', and was initially an exploration of the ways in which hierarchical, authoritarian, elitist, patriarchal, and exploitative elements in society are part of our own consciousness. Feminists, including those in women's studies, have been committed to overcoming such elements and to resisting 'honorary maleness' in our lives. As a consequence, autonomous women's studies programmes have been seen as places where a structure could be developed to support styles of work and relations to colleagues and students that differ significantly from overall university or college norms.

The understanding of the effect of social context on the individual has had a profound effect on feminist scholarship as well, and has led to feminist critiques of 'objective' scholarship and a recognition of the way personal bias can affect scholarly work. In fact, the quest for objectivity is seen as futile by feminist scholars, since biases are inherent in our view of the world. This recognition, that social context inevitably structures one's perception of reality and one's production of knowledge is probably the most revolutionary aspect of the new scholarship on women and is the main reason that feminists are convinced that acceptance of feminist scholarship by other disciplines implies a restructuring of knowledge within those disciplines.

The different branches of feminism have each made significant

49

contributions to feminist scholarship and to women's studies. In discussing these contributions, we shall use here the usual labels for different kinds of feminists. But it should be recognized not only that the labels are imprecise and represent abstractions of real positions but also that most feminists share all of these views to some extent and differ primarily in emphasis.

Liberal feminists ask for equal opportunity to compete within the existing system. This branch of feminism is much less committed to egalitarian aims and collective work styles than the others and makes the general assumption that women will act like men given the equal opportunity. Attempts at institutional change are directed towards those ideas and institutions that seem to keep women in disadvantaged positions, such as sex-role socialization, inequality of opportunity, unequal access to education, and female responsibility for childrearing and housework. The assumption is that women's oppression serves no real social function, so that the institutions seen as specifically oppressive to women can be changed without any fundamental change in other social institutions.

The liberal feminist idea that changes in individual consciousness are the critical factors in eliminating women's oppression has been a strong element in the development of women's studies and has provided a useful, if limited, focus on the very real legal and social barriers faced by women in our society. In women's studies, the elimination of sexism in the curriculum and 'balancing the curriculum' has been an important goal.

Radical feminists argue that the oppression of women is built into the very structure of our society. The division between the sexes, based on the patriarchal family, is seen as fundamental to social organization. Other hierarchical, oppressive social structures are developments that come out of patriarchy. Thus, all such structures must be rejected if women are to be liberated. This branch of feminism sees equality for women within the present system as impossible and calls for a radical restructuring of society, involving the elimination of patriarchy and along with it all other hierarchical structures.

The radical feminist analysis has led to a focus on women's lives and strengths and has been particularly concerned with an examination of power in personal and sexual relationships. The separatism that has resulted from the radical feminist viewpoint has led to the creation of a separate and exciting women's culture in contemporary society. In women's studies the analysis given by radical feminism has provided an important framework for much of feminist scholarship, while the existence of a separate women's culture has helped to create a sense of community.

The Marxist and socialist feminists also believe that women's oppression is so deeply rooted that only a basic restructuring of society can change it. This branch of feminism emphasizes the way in which the specific form of women's oppression changes from one society to another and links the position of women to economic and social institutions characteristic of a particular society. The contributions made by these feminists to feminist scholarship have been an emphasis on the interplay of social structures and the details of people's lives, an examination of the economic and social functions of women's roles in particular societies and thus an idea of what kinds of barriers exist to changing them, and finally, an idea of the relationship of women's oppression to that of other groups. A particular contribution to women's studies has been an analysis of the university as a social institution and its function as an agent of social control.

The different political points of view have led to a great deal of conflict within women's studies, but their interaction has also been responsible for the extreme richness of feminist scholarship and has contributed to the ability of feminists to think outside the prevailing belief systems.

Much of feminist scholarship to date has been done by feminist scholars based in traditional disciplines. Separate women's studies programmes to a large extent have provided a means for feminists based in different departments to communicate, to discuss their work with others who hold similar assumptions, to find support and a sense of community, and to find a space for attempting to put feminist principles into practice. The major activities of most women's studies programmes have been around teaching.

The focus on teaching developed for several reasons. Among these was a commitment to social change which implied that knowledge ought to be used. The choice of teaching as the vehicle for using feminist knowledge was then a natural result of the skills that many of the founding women's studies feminists already had. In addition, resources were made available to support teaching. From the beginning students have responded eagerly to women's studies offerings. In general, women's studies teaching has offered something useful to the teaching programmes of colleges and universities, and most institutions have taken advantage of it. Teaching in women's studies has cost universities little, and they have received a great deal in return in terms of student response.

WOMEN'S STUDIES AND ACADEMIA

In spite of the phenomenal growth since its appearance in the late 1960s women's studies has never fitted easily into academia. It has been a continuing question whether the goals and practices of women's studies were incompatible with the university system. This, of course, has to do with the political nature of women's studies and the supposedly objective nature of the university.

As feminist and other critical scholarship has shown, universities are not independent of the rest of society. There is an ideal of the unfettered search for knowledge and wisdom by scholars on behalf of the larger community. Objectivity – that is, neutral, unbiased work – is supposed to ensure the steady march towards more complete knowledge. But universities are political and economic institutions and, as such, they serve political and economic interests. The knowledge produced within them reflects this. Among other things, the universities are major agents of social control. Work done within the university in many ways serves the interests of those who benefit from our present social system. Specifically, university scholarship has been an important source of the ideology which has supported and, in part, created women's oppression.

Although the knowledge produced in the universities is not objective and value-free, those producing the work are convinced that it is. This blindness is possible because of the narrow meaning given to objectivity. Objective and unbiased have come to mean unemotional and uninvolved. By this criterion, any work that advocates political action or social change is non-objective and unsound. As a result, there is a systematic bias towards maintaining the status quo in the mainstream disciplines, making the universities important sources of social stability. Feminist and other scholars have repeatedly shown the lack of objectivity and the bias towards the status quo, in the behavioural and social sciences in particular, to the point where some are bored with the need to have the same discussion over and over (among others see Spender, 1982; Coyner, 1983; Hubbard and Lowe, 1979; and Miles and Finn, 1983). The feminist analysis of the interaction between knower and the object of knowledge has shown the effect of the world-view and the preconceptions that the knower brings to any scholarship. Given a scholarship that takes place in a competitive society, full of vested interests and decidedly imperfect, with sexism, racism, and poverty among its faults, it is not surprising that psychologists (as just one example) produce theories of 'male' vs 'female' brains or do research aimed at finding ways to get working people to accept boredom and lack of interest in their jobs. History, economics, literature, and the whole range of scholarly activities in the university look very different when done by people with different starting-points from the normal ones.

Work styles within universities are based on the ideal of the competitive meritocracy, with its accompanying hierarchy and elitism. These, coupled with the lack of women and minorities in most professions, act to reinforce the norms of the outside world. Scholars working within this framework are able to produce work that rationalizes and stabilizes social structures and protects various interests, including patriarchal ones, while still retaining the illusion that they are doing impeccably unbiased, objective work. Current academic research on theories that sex differences in behaviour and in social roles are rooted in biological differences between the sexes is an important example of this phenomenon. The myth of objectivity is an extremely strongly entrenched one. It has been very important in shaping the various disciplines and it is not clear how much impact the critiques have had or are likely to have. The illusion of objectivity where there is none is not a misperception that occurred by chance (Karier, 1975). It has been carefully fostered (whether consciously or no is another matter). The argument that the objective, scientific method somehow frees one from any question of whom that approach serves is one which has consistently appeared in the academic freedom literature of the twentieth century. In fact, the emphasis on objective scholarship acts to limit enquiry to topics which do not threaten the social order, since any scholarship which explicitly discusses the desirability of social change is seen as special pleading and non-objective.

A look at the history of the development of the various disciplines makes it clear that the professions and professional associations were set up so as to take control of knowledge, primarily through enforcing standards of objectivity. As part of this control, radical thought tied to social movements has been consistently and overtly excluded. The rhetoric of objectivity has been fostered to obscure very real political purposes of knowledge produced within the universities.

Given the degree to which a distorted objectivity has been established as a basic criterion for judging scholarship, the explicitly political orientation of feminist scholarship and of women's studies has inevitably made it suspect to anyone who is in the mainstream. Feminist scholarship is regarded by many non-feminists as lacking in rigour, as tainted by politics, or simply as special pleading. All of the other aspects of women's studies programmes which represent significant deviations from the norm have been seen as additional evidence for feminists' basic lack of soundness and untrustworthiness as scholars, since both control of knowledge and work styles are so closely tied to the biases inherent in work in the traditional disciplines. Thus, recognition of the validity of knowledge gained by non-professionals, non-hierarchical work styles, and treatment of students as active participants in the educational process are all viewed with deepest suspicion.

This has led to a basic dilemma for feminists. It has not been clear that women's studies could remain feminist and still remain in the university. As Mary Howell points out, feminists who attempt to work in professional areas face a fundamental conflict between the principles they hold and the imperatives of their jobs. For some, the choice has been clear:

Many feminists have thus decided not to become scholars, not to

53

become physicians, not to become professional in any area of work that is male-defined. There has been a thread of anti-intellectualism in the women's movement that is more apparent than real, for it reflects a deep mistrust of the *arenas* of intellectual activity.

(Howell, 1979)

This fear resulted, as just one example, in the resignation of the entire women's studies faculty at San Diego State in the mid-1970s. They felt that remaining was contrary to their principles.

Clearly, others *were* willing to try to work within the institution and try to use it for feminist ends. The separatists, however, have shared the mistrust Howell describes. Their commitment to separate women's studies programmes represents a recognition that 'feminist studies' represents ideas and practices that are incompatible with many (if not most) of the assumptions and procedures of universities and colleges.

THE DEBATE

Since the inception of women's studies, participants have debated tactics and to some extent goals. While a source of conflict, these debates have also been a source of vitality. How has it happened, then, that integration or 'mainstreaming' has come to dominate discussion in women's studies at the present time, particularly given this history of doubt about whether feminists belong in the university at all?

The availability of resources for mainstreaming has clearly played a major role. However meagre they may be, more resources appear to be available for integration than for other aspects of women's studies. But many women's studies faculty have also actively sought such resources. The concept of mainstreaming has been seen as both appropriate and as desirable by many of those in women's studies.

One reason for this may be an evangelical spirit. Having discovered all of the wonders opened up by feminist scholarship, there is a feeling on the part of many that it is simply too good and too powerful to keep to ourselves. As intellectuals we are rather awestruck at our discoveries and we want to share them with our unenlightened colleagues, particularly since we know that our movement is one for human liberation. In addition, we recognize the tenuousness of any discipline that is not accepted as legitimate by the rest of the academic community and many people feel a need for our colleagues to understand and accept our work in order to assure our survival.

The most compelling reason is probably that integrating material on women into the general curriculum appears to be the obvious thing to do. Since teaching has been one of the major tactics adopted by women's studies as a way of spreading the new scholarship on women, mainstreaming is a rather natural direction in which to move. It offers the possibility of reaching both colleagues and students, through activities that people are good at, and it offers the appearance of achievable results. The political origins of women's studies create pressure for action and for immediate results. Both the resources available and available skills make teaching the most obvious place for this action.

Integration, for a number of reasons then, is clearly a very attractive strategy and is consistent with the goals of women's studies. However, there are a number of problems. It is not clear that mainstreaming can fulfil all of its promises. In fact, it seems likely that it cannot. Furthermore, the tactic carries a fair amount of danger for women's studies as well.

Those who believe that women's scholarship can be made an integral part of the undergraduate curriculum and that, somehow, in the process the structure of the traditional disciplines will be radically changed are seriously underestimating the degree to which the university is embedded in the overall social structure and the importance of its social functions. The 'truth' of university scholarship is such that it presently serves vested interests. Since this role has not developed accidentally, it is not likely to change in any fundamental way without changes in other social institutions occurring at the same time. There is a certain amount of leeway because of the liberal ideal, but as long as we live in a society dominated by the male, white, corporate class the scholarship coming out of the disciplines will be their voice. Specifically, a sexist society will produce sexist scholarship. The integrationists in women's studies ask that a deviant voice be given a place in the mainstream. When this voice is heard, the argument goes, it will lead to an intellectual revolution based on new social values. If we believe in a liberal, open, objective university devoted to the disinterested pursuit of truth, this would make sense. But our own analysis tells us that this is not the case. We know that scholarship is never neutral and certainly is not now objective. The prevailing paradigms in the various disciplines arise out of social conditions and the social perceptions of those who practice the disciplines. In turn, the paradigms shape what can be perceived. There are strong pressures to retain these paradigms. Yes, if our ideas were to be listened to, they would lead to an intellectual revolution. The difficulty is that it will take a social revolution before most of our colleagues will be able to hear us. If we truly believe that the end of women's oppression can only come with radical social change, we cannot really expect to have our ideas accepted and taught in the mainstream. It is only if we accept the liberal ideas that sexism serves no real purpose, or that knowledge can be value-free, that we might expect our colleagues to change their point of view as soon as we present them with the insights of feminist scholarship.

This is not to imply that we should not try to talk to others. It is just that we need to be realistic about how far we can expect to get and about how much effort to expend. Our work is closer to the truth and also strikes directly at basic contradictions in the current production of knowledge. There will be some who can hear us. However, we are dealing in general with colleagues and students who are not advocates of radical social change. In order to be heard at all, it is clear what is most likely to happen. Material that is not too radical will be selected, in the hope that it will be palatable to those in the mainstream. Feminists have from the beginning felt pressures to compromise in order to get a hearing for our ideas, as the choice of the name women's studies rather than feminist studies makes clear. We have felt the need to look as objective and non-political as possible within our feminist standards. The same process is already happening with material selected as most suitable for integration into the general curriculum. A number of feminists have pointed to the diversity of feminist critiques of the disciplines and have asked how we are going to choose which to present. However, in practice this problem will probably disappear. There will be strong pressure to focus on the liberal side of feminist scholarship, and there is already evidence that even this material will be tolerated with difficulty, by students and faculty both, in courses outside women's studies (Froines, 1980; Wilson, 1981). As long as women's position is fundamentally unchanged in society (and it is now getting worse if anything), it is hard to see how faculty especially will respond in ways that are significantly different from the social norms.

At this point integration's main successes may come in slowing down the current inroads on the few gains which we have already made in women's social position. That, in fact, may be the main reason why our political programme as feminists must include some integration. There is now a large body of non-feminist scholarship on women which has been triggered in reaction to feminist demands for equality and the end of oppression. Non-feminists (to put it mildly) have taken up the question of the origins of women's oppression and they have produced a number of theories which, under the guise of objectivity, act to reinforce women's social roles. The 'biology is destiny' theories are the most widespread and probably the most dangerous. The most influential theories represent revivals of the biological determinism of the nineteenth century. There are evolutionary arguments, ideas about sex differences in the brain, and theories involving sex hormones, but they all claim that behavioural differences rooted in biological differences between the sexes have led to the differences we observe in social roles. They all carry the message that women's position arises from innate characteristics and that it would be very hard, and probably undesirable, to change. Such theories are extremely widespread at the present time. They are not only widely accepted within academia, but are receiving a great deal of attention in the media. It seems very likely that this kind of work will get at least equal time with feminist theories in the mainstream curriculum, since in many cases they are more compatible with the points of view of those working in the mainstream. We do have to do our best to counteract their influence, not simply by pointing out their flaws, but by offering their own alternatives.

POLITICAL STRATEGIES

If women's studies is to fulfil its commitment to the cause of women and ultimately to ending oppression for everyone, then we must continually assess our strategies in terms of goals, and we must explore a number of different paths. There are a number of areas besides integration in which we ought to be working.

First, if our aim is to educate for change through integration, then we need to do a great deal more to introduce feminist ideas into the secondary and primary schools and we also ought to be educating outside of the schools, in the community, as well. Even within the universities, mainstreaming may not be the best way to use feminist scholarship. Our personal experience has been that the existence of a separate women's studies programme is often itself a significant factor in the introduction of feminist material into the mainstream curriculum. This happens partly simply because the existence of the programme continually raises the issue and partly because students from our courses press for such material in their other courses.

Second, what we need at this point is more emphasis on scholarship, not less. We have undertaken a large task: 'to understand the world in order to change it', and we have just begun. If, as part of our political programme, we are in the university at all, it is because we recognize the resources of academia for producing knowledge. We need to take full advantage of our opportunities to generate the knowledge we need. The emphasis of the integration model is on teaching, and this will likely be at the expense of scholarly activity, given our time and resource constraints. Furthermore, as is discussed below, if we put too much of our effort into integration, we may damage our scholarship and our ability to provide an alternative vision of the future in irreparable ways.

Third, if our aim is to get closer to the truth and to develop a strategy for the future, then we have to have connections outside academia. If we work primarily within universities and colleges, then our scholarship will inevitably remain distorted and limited by the elitism and class bias of our environment. Only autonomous programmes have any possibility of having significant involvement in the community and still surviving.

Finally, if our aim is to have an impact on what is accepted as truth in our society generally, then an emphasis on integrating feminist scholarship into the classroom is not the proper way to go about it. The structure of knowledge is not defined there. It is defined by scholars in the major research centres, working through such institutions as journals, book publishing, and informal structures (the 'old-boy networks'). We need to learn much more about how to get past the 'gatekeepers' of knowledge in order to make our work legitimate and widely accepted. This will involve understanding more about not only the production but the distribution of knowledge. Circulation within the profession and teaching are, of course, the main methods that academic scholars use to distribute their results. But there are already a number of other ways in which knowledge produced within universities becomes part of the public sphere. These most often eventually involve presentation in one or another of the media, either directly by academics or indirectly by popularizers. The print media are particularly important and material appears in the whole range from low-circulation, intellectual magazines to the Sunday supplements of newspapers and the *Reader's Digest*. A relatively new phenomenon is the appearance of magazines such as *Psychology Today* whose purpose is the popularization of academic work. Using such channels is something we need to explore.

In the end, too much integration may impede rather than help our attempt to develop committed scholarship. The integration of material into other disciplines involves convincing others to redefine their assumptions, while at the same time trying to get our own questions on their agendas, instead of trying to formulate and answer our own questions. The focus on mainstreaming is likely to increase emphasis on producing, as well as teaching, ideas that will be acceptable to others. It will also continue to emphasize critiques of existing work in the traditional disciplines at a time when we should be moving beyond this.

Radical feminists and Marxist/socialist feminists have been the source of the most revolutionary aspects of the new scholarship on women. They are the ones who have raised questions that are outside the scope of the traditional disciplines and the ones who have developed the analyses based on 'the personal is political'. Their work has begun to give us alternative visions for the future. But it is just these aspects of feminist scholarship that are least understandable to non-feminists and which are least explainable in traditional frameworks. These are the parts of feminist scholarship that are likely to suffer from integration. They are also the parts that are most important to develop if we are to start looking to the future as well as the past and present, and so begin constructing our own model of change.

A focus on communicating with others who do not share our view of the world may make it significantly harder to keep up our intellectual revolution, since our own consciousness will be affected in the process as well. We as feminists share a world-view that is significantly at odds with the norm. As our analysis has made clear, society and social norms are extremely powerful in shaping the way people see the world. We internalize our most fundamental ideas without being aware that we have them, and it is extremely difficult to become aware of the assumptions behind our thinking and to hold views which deviate from the prevailing belief system. (The difficulties that many feminists have had in dealing with heterosexism in their own thinking is an example of our own problems with this.) It is well known that such deviant views require a large measure of support and legitimation if individuals are to continue to carry such views and to act on them. All of the pressures in the university run counter to feminist theory and practice. The way of viewing the world is simply different, and if we integrate ourselves too much into the mainstream, it may be hard to resist the pressures. In order to maintain our ability to raise new questions, to question the structure of knowledge, we must retain some status as outsiders. In order to maintain any measure of the co-operative and egalitarian work styles that support our scholarship, we must maintain an institutional base where we have some measure of control. The only counter to the pressures to think and act in accord with academic norms available to those of us in women's studies is support from other feminists, both within the university and in the larger feminist community. If we lose our primary identification with women's studies through turning our attention too much towards integration with others, we run the risk of losing this support and possibly our unique intellectual content with it.

Even in terms of survival, it is not clear that the need to appear legitimate in the eyes of others is best served by increased emphasis on integration and teaching. Our scholarship is the criterion used by others, much more than our teaching (although, of course, our unorthodox teaching methods have not helped our acceptance). They may not agree with everything we do, but even with the charge of special pleading, they may begin to grant us a grudging respect if we insist on retaining our own identity and the legitimacy of our own approach.

For all of these reasons, it appears that our goals will be best served by building programmes which are largely autonomous whenever that is possible. There is a major difficulty with this suggestion, of course, and that has to do with the question of choice. To what extent are we able to actually choose integration or autonomy at present and to what extent are we being guided by the way resources are being made available? Certainly the potential of the integration model for co-opting the radical potential of women's studies and feminist scholarship should make us cautious when we receive encouragement and resources from others to go in that direction. Our interests in the long run may be in rejecting available resources for integration and working as best we can with less in autonomous programmes.

POSTSCRIPT

Even with a separate women's studies department or programme the institutional pressures are severe and in many cases overwhelming. A separate women's studies programme is not a guarantee that feminist thinking can flourish, but an integrated programme is almost certainly a guarantee that it will not. Estelle Freedman has made a strong argument for the role played by the decline of separate women's organizations in the disappearance of American feminism in the 1920s (Freedman, 1979). The situation in many ways appears the same today. Strong external pressures exist in our society which are undermining feminist gains and there is an urgent need for feminist organizing and feminist organizations to combat these pressures. Autonomous women's studies programmes have an important role to play.

REFERENCES

Boxer, Marilyn, 'For and about women: the theory and practice of women's studies in the United States', *Signs*, 7 (3) (1982), pp. 661–95.

Coyner, Sandra, 'Women's studies as an academic discipline: why and how to do it', in Gloria Bowles and Renate Duelli Klein (eds), *Theories of Women's Studies* (London: Routledge & Kegan Paul, 1983).

Freedman, Estelle, 'Separation as strategy: female institution building and American feminism, 1870–1930', *Feminist Studies*, 5 (3) (1979), pp. 512–29.

Froines, Ann, 'Integrating women into the liberal arts curriculum: some results of a modest survey', *Women's Studies News*, 8 (4) (1980), pp. 11–12.

Howell, Mary, 'Can we be feminists and professionals?', *Women's Studies Int. Q.*, 2 (1) (1979), pp. 1–7.

Hubbard, Ruth and Marian Lowe, 'Pitfalls in research on sex and gender', *Genes and Gender II* (New York: Gordian Press, 1979).

Karier, Clarence, *The Shaping of the American Educational State* (New York: Macmillan, 1975).

Miles, Angela and Geraldine Finn, *Feminism in Canada: From Persuasion to Politics* (Montreal: Black Rose Press, 1983).

Spender, Dale, *Men's Studies Modified* (London: Pergamon, 1982).

Wilson, Joan Hoff, 'A grand illusion: continuing the debate', *Women's Studies Q.*, 9 (4) (1981), pp. 5–6.

FROM MARGIN TO MAINSTREAM
Situating women's studies
Susan Sheridan

Women's studies is often used as an umbrella term to cover a wide range of research and teaching on women and gender: it is used in this way in the now-established Women's Studies Section of ANZAAS, the Australian and New Zealand Association for the Advancement of Science.[1] In addition, women's studies in Australia has a history of over a decade of feminist study groups and projects[2] with no institutional location or support, like *Refractory Girl*, which first appeared in late 1972 and was originally subtitled 'a women's studies journal'. In the discussion that follows here, by women's studies I mean a distinctively interdisciplinary project in feminist research and teaching that is institutionally located in higher education but which has some degree of independence from particular disciplines and vocational courses.

In the past few years we have seen a number of women's studies initiatives of this kind which seem to be moving it from the margins to the mainstream of higher education. What distinguishes these women's studies initiatives from most earlier ones is the presence of one or more of the following factors:

1 tenurable appointments made specifically in women's studies;
2 accredited courses which constitute or contribute to recognized academic awards;
3 the disposition of a budget and some degree of administrative independence.

These factors could be said to give women's studies 'mainstream' status, certainly in contrast to the feminist study groups and projects mentioned above, but also in contrast to the 'multidisciplinary' mode of women's studies that operates in many tertiary institutions, where optional courses are offered by feminist teachers within the disciplines/ departments where they work. Multidisciplinary women's studies can establish itself as a strong presence in an institution that is committed to offering students a range of optional courses and where the staff involved have tenure. But often such discipline-based courses come and

61

go with the untenured women who initiated them, or they become isolated and marginalized within departments.

What are some of the implications of women's studies moving into the mainstream in the sense I have indicated? The strong tradition within the women's liberation movement that marginal or minority status is both the spur and the guarantee of the integrity of feminist activism must prompt us to ask whether the interventionist purposes of women's studies as it was originally conceived are compromised or even rendered irrelevant as it moves into the educational mainstream. Yet that tradition should also be examined lest it dwindle into the easy assumption that all diversification is necessarily a diffusion of political purpose and energy. In this paper I want first to give two local examples – one of a 'marginal' interdisciplinary women's studies course and its fate, and the other as an illustration of the anomalies and conflicts that can be involved in the formal recognition of women's studies. I want then to look at several theories about the nature and province of women's studies and its relationship to established institutions and disciplines, asking how they each understand the changes and challenges involved, and what strategies they suggest for women's studies projects in a variety of 'mainstream' circumstances.

There has been to date very little reflective comment on women's studies in Australia, and nothing with the scope of Marilyn Boxer's survey, published in *Signs* in 1982, of 'the literature about women's studies as a field in American higher education: its history, political issues, theories and structures',[3] and so my two illustrations of 'margin and mainstream' as an issue for women's studies in Australia cannot be placed in such a context, though it is much needed. The few critical analyses that have been written here have appeared in overseas journals,[4] and early discussions were published in pamphlets that are now hard to find, or else never reached print.[5] Although editorials in *Refractory Girl* and *Hecate* have from time to time discussed theoretical issues concerning the study of women and gender, neither journal has made women's studies as a field in education part of its brief. In 1976 *Refractory Girl* dropped the reference to women's studies from its subtitle in order to dissociate the journal from university courses which it described as 'conservative in methodology and reactionary in content'.[6]

The fierceness of this dismissal indicates how high were the expectations ten years ago of women's studies as a revolutionary force for change. The women's studies course which emerged at Flinders University in 1973 from this climate of ideas pursued the radical educational goals of student group self-management and self-assessment, believing that these were crucial for the development of women's confidence and solidarity.[7] The curriculum of its foundation course was not discipline-based but was rather a classic of the kind of integrative feminist work

62

that shapes itself around the women's liberation movement concerns with the nature of oppression and the conditions for liberation.[8] The course had marginal – indeed, precarious – status in the university, being dependent on one department's setting aside some of its part-time teaching funds and agreeing to appoint a philosophy tutor who would also be qualified to convene women's studies. But it was marginal in a more purposeful and deliberate way, too, in that the participants wanted the course to remain on the edge of the university in order better to involve women from outside the academic community.

After a decade of struggle this particular project has been abandoned, and a new women's studies major is about to be developed. The Flinders story, as told by Rita Helling,[9] ends on a note of warning about the lessons that can be drawn from it. At a time of restricted university financial resources in the early 1980s, women's studies got less support from other staff than it had in the past: 'It's not only a matter of scarce resources, but of priorities – of distribution of those resources,' she adds. It could also be pointed out that the radical education movement had by that time lost its impact among students, who had increasingly to take on part-time jobs in order to survive and who have consequently had less time and energy for campus activism, a crucial factor in the course as it was. Also, by about 1980 many of the purposes of the original course were being fulfilled elsewhere in Adelaide: when technical and further education courses became available they attracted many of the women from outside the university who wanted from women's studies an introduction to women's liberation ideas and support for their return to the paid workforce; and the College of Advanced Education women's studies diplomas drew in those who wanted an opportunity to get formal accreditation for studies in this field and to apply this new knowledge to their work in teaching or various kinds of social and community work.

The Flinders story also illustrates the containment of feminist challenges to 'the traditional, therefore patriarchal, academic mode': 'I cannot see any way out of this dilemma,' Rita Helling concludes, 'for courses merely reflect the institutional structures' of formal learning itself. While I believe this to be an unduly pessimistic generalization, for some institutional structures are more open to change than others and some women's studies courses are more favourably placed within them, there is no denying that, at least where the universities are concerned, it is even more difficult to effect radical changes in access, teaching, and assessment than it is to introduce some form of women's studies curriculum. My second example concerns just this distinction between women's studies curriculum content, on the one hand, and the radical education principles of teaching and learning that have been associated from the outset with the women's studies movement. It illustrates a clash

between certain principles of feminist pedagogy and traditional definitions of a properly academic subject of study and its appropriate mode
of assessment.

This illustration comes from my experience as a member of a working
party appointed by the Senior Secondary Assessment Board of South
Australia to draw up a submission for a Year 12 women's studies course.
In developing the syllabus and assessment sections of this submission we
kept in mind the following considerations:

1 that the course would not be publicly examinable but school-assessed.
Thus it could be flexible enough to provide scope for students aiming
for matriculation as well as those who would not pursue further
academic studies beyond Year 12;
2 that given this range of potential students, and the likelihood that
women's studies would be new to them, the course should place
particular emphasis on self-reflection and collective work:

Women's Studies recognises the need for women to define their own
nature and being, in reaction to the defining forces of social stereotyping. While an obvious first step is the analysis of social structures
which contribute stereotyped definitions, the educational process of
Women's Studies must begin from and continue to value the experiences and perceptions of the individual student.

Teaching strategies thus focus *first* on the personal, drawing
generalised knowledge from it. Students are then encouraged into
active participation in all activities, in order both to extend their
confidence and co-operation within a group, and to test the validity
of generalised theory against individual experiences.[10]

The appointed accreditation panel received this proposal unfavourably.
It advised that the course *should* be made publicly examinable in order
that *women's studies be taken seriously as an academic area*, equivalent
in status to subjects such as economics. Such a procedure would, we felt,
drastically undermine the pedagogical principles described above, and
one member of the working party resigned on the grounds that she could
not as a feminist teacher agree to women's studies being publicly
examinable. Those of us who agreed, albeit unwillingly, to rework the
syllabus in accordance with this directive from the accreditation panel so
that there might be at least some women's studies at Year 12, envisage
a split into two streams, the academic and the school-assessed – and it
seems that the latter will inevitably be perceived as inferior.

If this dual-stream women's studies course is accepted it will mean that
the academic stream will be 'taken seriously' by the universities as a
matriculation subject and by the Education Department as an area
requiring training and resources – at least, one hopes so. Against this,

the principles of a feminist pedagogy are compromised by the requirement of assessment by public examination which, if it gives any consideration at all to personal and political development, will undoubtedly reduce these to some collection of moral pieties. In the long term, the results of defining women's studies as an academic subject in this particular context will undoubtedly inhibit the development of local initiatives appropriate to specific schools, and may well serve to fossilize women's studies as an area of received knowledge 'about women' which bears no relation to the ongoing social and political movement for women's liberation from which it arose.

A second consideration here is that the disagreement between the working party and the accreditation panel about public assessment and its implications was a disagreement between two groups of feminist teachers, positioned within a hierarchical structure which they had no part in shaping. Positioned as judges, the accreditation panel refused the proposal that women's studies should be school-assessed only. Positioned as petitioners, the working party had no power position from which to negotiate. If women's studies is to continue to move – albeit unevenly – into the educational mainstream, how can we take advantage of this without becoming imprisoned in pre-existing institutional structures *and* without getting into situations where we are set against each other? The example I have given is perhaps extreme in that it is situated on the interface between secondary and tertiary education, in a territory that is, quite literally, no woman's land. But I believe it points to the kinds of conflict and anomaly that may beset women's studies in its present stage of development in higher education.

Concluding her discussion of the sharp disagreements over women's studies among United States feminists during the 1970s, Marilyn Boxer remarks that since then 'academic women's studies has become less directly a strategy for institutional change and more specifically an attack on sexist scholarship and teaching'.[11] It is a useful formulation of alternatives, although they need not be mutually exclusive in any absolute sense, because it highlights the dangers of using women's studies as a strategy, as a means to the end of structural changes in the institution, in circumstances where it stands alone in demanding such changes. In such circumstances women's studies can too easily be dubbed 'political' or 'not up to standard' and rejected, or simply let drop, from the institution altogether. On the other hand, Boxer's phrase, 'an attack on sexist scholarship and teaching' can connote a variety of strategies that are employed by women's studies courses, depending on their location, resources, and priorities.

The attack may be conducted largely in terms of the discourse of equality: a demand that women and gender be included in the curriculum and a campaign to end discrimination against women students and

65

teachers. There is much to be achieved by the application of equal opportunity principles and affirmative action policies to education in this country. Where such principles and policies are officially endorsed by the institution, they might be activated to challenge the traditional curriculum. This happened, for example, at a state university in Virginia, where the joint efforts of the Women's Studies Director and the Affirmative Action Director succeeded in having the university include in its 'mission statement' the following resolution:

The university is committed to the ideal of equality; therefore, it will provide a multicultural curriculum that adequately represents women, minorities and Third World as well as nonwestern peoples; and it will include on its faculty those who do research on topics that enrich such a curriculum.[12]

However, when comparable recommendations were included among affirmative action proposals at Macquarie University following a 1981 national conference on women in higher education, they met the strongest objections of all. Efforts to move in the direction of reforming course content to include the experiences of women and removing sexist language 'were seen to interfere with academic autonomy, with individual freedom', and proposals to this effect had to be dropped.[13]

Yet there are dangers accompanying the success of such moves where women's studies are concerned, as witnessed by the acrimonious debate over integration vs autonomy in the US recently:[14] it is feared that the integration of women's studies materials into the traditional curriculum will be achieved at the expense of the kind of independent women's studies courses that I am concerned with in this paper. Without the development of independent and interdisciplinary women's studies, there is another problem with the strategy of attacking sexist scholarship without changing institutional structures: when feminists are obliged to work exclusively within the disciplinary construction of knowledge there is a very real danger of becoming merely reactive, of inverting the categories of 'men's studies' to produce a 'women's studies' which is defined by its focus on women but incapable of coming up with new questions and new modes of enquiry.[15]

An alternative reading of the phrase, 'an attack on sexist scholarship and teaching' yields more radical implications. Feminist criticism of patriarchal scholarship is no longer directed at the exclusion or denigration of women per se, but at the implications for knowledge and for social change generally of analyses based upon this exclusion or denigration. Women's studies is at its strongest points an attack on androcentric knowledge and practices, and the production of new analyses of the position and activities of women which 'extend to whole social formations'.[16] As such, it has the potential to redraw the map of knowledges:

66

it is more than a corrective, more than a supplement to received truths. To realize this potential and still to take account of the present realities of its relationship to existing disciplines and institutions is the challenge facing women's studies in the educational mainstream.

How this is to be done is the question asked of each of the three approaches that I want now to discuss. Each proposes a position of some independence for women's studies within the university, and some form of interdisciplinary work as its major intellectual task. It is worth noting at the outset, however, that each proposal is to some extent shaped by its institutional context. The first, by a United States writer, refers to a situation that is common in universities and colleges in Australia as well, where the autonomy of women's studies rests solely in its courses and not in its staffing or its place in the institutional structure; thus she argues strongly for setting up women's studies 'as an academic discipline' as a solution to the problem of fragmented energies for both students and staff in a multidisciplinary series of courses. The second approach derives from the development of an interdisciplinary major in women's studies as a distinct field of study with its own staff within a traditional arts faculty at the Australian National University. The third comes from a women's studies major that contains both disciplinary and inter-disciplinary work, the latter constituting the core courses; here women's studies consists in an interdisciplinary course-team structure and thus an administrative unit, like others within the school, which is characteristic of the newer universities involved, Deakin and Murdoch.

In 'Women's studies as an academic discipline: why and how to do it',[17] Sandra Coyner proposes that feminist scholars should give up the attempt to transform the existing disciplines because what they require is an intellectual revolution of the kind described by Thomas Kuhn as a 'paradigm shift'[18] – and this is a long, slow process, no simple matter of 'accumulating or improving the quality of explanation'. Instead, women's studies should be set up as an academic discipline in its own right, parallel to the established ones, a separate department within a faculty:

> What I am suggesting, at this point in our history, is a new option, the specialist in 'pure' Women's Studies who can work with our existing staffs, and a new orientation, the disciplines contributing to Women's Studies, not just the other way around.

While such a change would have obvious strategic advantage, Sandra Coyner also spells out its intellectual implications – and these raise further questions. For instance, she sees the need to train graduates as women's studies specialists so that 'the same person might teach, for example, "Women in American History", "Psychology of Women", "The Family" and a Women's Studies survey or seminar'. Thus the area is seen as a multidisciplinary one, a collection of bodies of knowledge about women; and this, it seems to me, has all the disadvantages of multidisciplinarity (separate knowledges, unable to question their boundaries or their key concepts, such as 'the family') as well as the requirement that they be present but kept separate in one person's head rather than in a course developed by several specialist heads.

There is a counter-tendency, however, to this notion of multiple knowledges. Sandra Coyner suggests that women's studies work be organized around two central questions, namely:

1 What are key generalizing concepts that explain large amounts and disparate kinds of information about women?
2 How do these key women's studies concepts relate to each other?

But I am not convinced that the search for shared assumptions and the attempt to construct large-scale explanatory models would save women's studies from breaking into the many feminisms that make up the women's movement. Yet she claims that women's studies should keep its distance from the movement for exactly this reason, its lack of consensus. Her belief that women's studies as a discipline should, or does already, rise above all this dispute is illustrated in her easy reference to 'our' shared priorities, as if they were always everywhere fixed, when she claims that:

> We study different literature [from the established disciplines], we put family and reproductive relationships near the top of the list, not the bottom; we want to know about women's relationships with women, and a women's culture previously ignored; we see qualities of sensitivity and nurturance as achievements, not leftovers.

In this account of priorities there is an obvious tendency to put first the things that have previously been invisible, yet many of us would find unsatisfactory a list of key concepts that lacked, for instance, reference to women's wage labour under capitalism. Also, any list of key concepts is going to be shaped, willy nilly, by current concerns of the women's movement, as the reference to 'women's culture' above shows.

Finally, I am worried by Sandra Coyner's reference to getting from our colleagues 'an admission that we have another, separate body of knowledge of which we are the guardians'. The figure of knowledge as a kind of pre-capitalist accumulation of value, a treasure trove that requires guardians, immediately suggests piracy – and I must say I would rather be a pirate than a guardian. More pertinently, I think the opposing figure of knowledge as a toolbox is more congenial to the experimental purposes of women's studies: tools are exchangeable and reproducible, so they do not need guardians; they are used to produce new things, they are the means of producing other ends; none the less they do need to be fashioned for specific purposes, sometimes from existing models, sometimes invented anew. Feminist knowledge as a toolbox implies a conception of knowledge and learning that is quite different from the dominant one in western culture, but one which feminism shares with some other oppositional movements, such as Marxism; and a model of separate women's studies that could blind us to the possibilities of tool-swapping would be unnecessarily restrictive.

An alternative model of women's studies as a distinct entity both intellectually and institutionally within the university is proposed by Susan Magarey in an article entitled 'Towards transdisciplinary learning'.[19] She argues that women's studies involves a distinct approach to intellectual enquiry in that it must draw on and transcend a specific range of disciplines in order to investigate issues and questions that derive, not from these disciplines, but from the women's movement. It is 'transdisciplinary' in that it moves, not between disciplines, but beyond them; such an enterprise

endeavours to transcend a specific range of disciplines, and this must mean that it establishes criteria for assessing and selecting techniques and procedures according to their usefulness in illuminating a particular field of knowledge or in facilitating synthesis of information from a variety of intellectual traditions.

Like Sandra Coyner, but for different reasons, she rejects the attempt to transform existing disciplines. The transdisciplinary model would not set itself up as a parallel discipline but would function, rather, as a contrary example, critically borrowing from various disciplines and at the same time 'subverting [the institution's] patriarchal domination of learning, if not so much by an explicit challenge to its hierarchical material structure, then certainly by a clear and explicit challenge to its ordering and use of knowledge'.

As a 'field' of knowledge rather than a discipline, women's studies can remain eclectic and develop in ways appropriate to local and specific needs; it can keep drawing on the expertise of feminists working outside of academe, and thus keep in close touch with the wider women's movement. (Not sharing Sandra Coyner's distrust of this connection to a political movement, I would see it as 'the lifeblood of feminist scholarship, not its tragic flaw'.[20]) The ANU transdisciplinary model, with its emphasis on the activity of learning rather than the accumulation of knowledge-capital, mobilizes the notion of knowledge as a toolbox, discussed above. And this emphasis also keeps alive the issue of collaborative learning, which occupied such a central place in early discussion about the project of women's studies.

However this model still leaves the traditional disciplines unchallenged except, as I mentioned, by the *example* of a transdisciplinary alternative.

Yet the relation of women's studies to the discipline remains a problem to be addressed, if only because the great majority of us have been trained and still work within that structure of the division of knowledge. The work of re-vision exerts an undeniable attraction when we can experience ourselves as blessed/cursed with double vision: as able, from a feminist position, to see both the androcentric bases on which our knowledge was built *and* the ghostly presence of women to which that knowledge was blind. Such re-vision has a powerful influence on the research and teaching we do, for it is clear that feminist analyses do not fall in pure form from the skies but are forged out of debate with received knowledge, as well as out of political activism. A further reason for continuing to attend to the disciplines and specializations of knowledge is that they are always in process and not, however much they may appear to be for long periods, static and fossilized. There are often points of contact and indeed mutual influences between feminist and other innovative theoretical enterprises: in my own discipline-by-training, literary studies, there have recently emerged dynamic points of contact, for instance, between feminism and some forms of Marxism and post-structuralism. The process of feminist critique of received knowledges is not, it turns out, a linear one of supersession, but a dialectical one.

The final approach to women's studies which I want to consider here is one which attempts to incorporate a critique of the disciplines as well as the construction of new knowledge. This construction is inter-disciplinary in that it operates characteristically in the spaces between disciplines and traditions of thought like Marxism, psychoanalysis, and structuralism. This approach is developed in a women's studies course at Deakin University entitled 'Feminist Knowledge as Critique and Construct'. To quote from the course introduction, it poses the following questions:

> The rather cumbersome title of this course is designed to alert you to the paradox at the heart of Feminist Knowledge: where does the construct, which allows the critique to operate, come from? If women are trying to resist the many ways in which they have been defined, then where are they going to find new definitions – when all languages in which theories are couched (and all sign systems built on the linguistic model) are totally permeated by centuries of gender inequality? Languages of all kinds (visual, gestural, verbal, etc.) reflect women back to themselves as objects of patriarchy. How then can they possibly find a way around this structure?[21]

In its attempt to highlight, and to theorize, the positions from which one 'critiques' and 'constructs' knowledge, the course draws attention to the variety of structural positions from which we who call ourselves feminists speak – from our disciplines-by-training, our political commitments, and more generally by our cultural positioning in terms of class and race as well as gender. It is an attempt to recognize the diversity of feminisms without simply falling back into a vague liberal pluralism. '"Feminism" means knowing that there is a debate on.'[22]

A variety of models of women's studies will continue to emerge from different institutional structures. There is a range of ways in which it can situate itself as a relatively autonomous enterprise which challenges disciplinary divisions while keeping open lines of communication to existing traditions of thought. There will also be differing degrees of connection to the wider women's movement. But as women's studies moves into the educational mainstream in these various ways, we can well take on board Catharine Stimpson's early vision of the politics most appropriate to such a movement:

Women's Studies will embody . . . a politics of energy. The movement will consist of a cluster of self-generating forces. . . . Each will devise its own goal and methods. One group may negotiate with conservatives. Another may consolidate the experiments of other groups. Still another may serve as a cutting edge of action and theory. . . . The virtues of a politics of energy are the stimulus to women to be autonomous and self-defining; the creation of a number of models of local activity . . . and the winning of time until Women's Studies is both more internally coherent and more muscular.[23]

NOTES

1 An earlier version of this paper was presented at the ANZAAS Congress held in August, 1985 at Monash University. My thanks to Judith Allen, Sneja Gunew, and Susan Magarey, as well as to the participants in that discussion for responses that generated this revision.

2 The range of such projects in the US is indicated in C. Bunch and S. Pollack (eds), *Learning Our Way: Essays in Feminist Education* (New York: The Crossing Press, 1983).

3 M.J. Boxer, 'For and about women: the theory and practice of women's studies in the United States', in N.O. Keohane et al. (eds), *Feminist Theory: A Critique of Ideology* (Sussex: Harvester Press, 1982), pp. 237–72.

4 R. Rowland, 'Women's studies courses: pragmatic and political issues concerning their establishment and design', *Women's Studies International Forum*, 5 (1982), pp. 487–95. S. Magarey, 'Women's studies in Australia – towards transdisciplinary learning?' and R. Helling, 'The personal is political', *Journal of Educational Thought*, 17 (1983), pp. 162–71 and 172–81.

5 e.g. several undated pamphlets published around 1974: E. Haley, M. Burn, and C. Yates (eds), *A Guide to Flinders Women's Studies*; S. Higgins and M. Venner (eds), *Women and Sexist Education*; P. Ryan (ed.), *A Guide to Women's Studies in Australia* (Australian Union of Students).

6 Editorial, *Refractory Girl, A Journal of Radical Feminist Thought*, 10 (March 1976).

7 See note 4; also R. Helling, *The Politics of Women's Studies* (Adelaide: University Relations Unit, 1981).
8 The definition of interdisciplinary work offered in E.C. DuBois et al. (eds), *Feminist Scholarship. Kindling in the Groves of Academe* (Urbana and Chicago: University of Illinois Press, 1985), pp. 7–10.
9 Helling, 'The personal is political', op. cit., p. 180.
10 Draft submission on women's studies to S.S.A.B.S.A., 1985 (unpublished).
11 Boxer, op. cit., p. 252.
12 N.T. Bazin, 'Expanding the concept of affirmative action to include the curriculum', *Women's Studies Newsletter*, 8, 4 (1980), pp. 9–11.
13 Sabine Willis, 'Domino theory: affirmative action at Macquarie', *Refractory Girl*, 26 (June 1980), pp. 39–43.
14 e.g. G. Bowles and R. Duelli-Klein (eds), *Theories of Women's Studies* (London: Routledge & Kegan Paul, 1983); G. Bowles (ed.), 'Strategies for women's studies in the 80s', *Women's Studies International Forum*, special issue, 7 (1984).
15 Thanks to Sneja Gunew for this observation.
16 Magarey, 'Towards transdisciplinary learning?', op. cit., p. 167.
17 In Bowles and Duelli-Klein, op. cit., pp. 46–71.
18 See the critique of feminist appropriations of the Kuhnian paradigm shift by M. Strathern, 'Dislodging a world view, challenge and counter-challenge in the relationship between feminism and anthropology', *Australian Feminist Studies*, 1 (Summer 1985), pp. 1–26.
19 Magarey, 'Towards transdisciplinary learning?', op. cit.
20 DuBois et al., op. cit., p. 8.
21 Introduction, *Feminist Knowledge as Critique and Construct* (Victoria: Deakin University, 1985).
22 Strathern, op. cit., p. 21.
23 C. Stimpson, 'What matter mind? A theory about the practice of women's studies', *Women's Studies*, 1 (1973) pp. 293–314.

WHAT'S NEW IN WOMEN'S HISTORY

Linda Gordon

1

The feminist reconstitution of knowledge no longer seems to me so radical a break as it once did. In history, and probably in other fields as well, our critiques of old scholarship, and our attempts to construct a new scholarship, seem to me rather to follow in paths already opened. That does not, I think, belittle or weaken the feminist contribution. On the contrary, the emphasis on the uniqueness and novelty of what we are doing may reflect the bravado of inadequate confidence.

In attempting to reconstruct history, feminists do no more and no less than many groups battling for political power have done before. If history is the king of the political arts, its power to legitimate sovereignty is frequently under attack and must constantly be defended. From the classical world to Tudor England to the Reagan administration, ideologues write and rewrite histories of their imperialisms, successions, and legitimacy, with an eye to raising money for armies. Opponents counterattack, now scoring points as the rulers reveal their hypocrisy, now writhing in helplessness, unable to reach the masses with their counterarguments. The stakes may be higher today, but the ability of the dynasties to buy historians is greater too.

Naming the new women's history 'herstory' does us no favour. Implying that we are the first to fight this ideological battle deprives us of a history we already have. Indeed, I would venture to say that the rhetoric of the uniqueness of our intellectual project reflects a growing distance of scholars from the totalizing tendencies of a strong political feminist movement, and its desire to incorporate, even to subsume, other radical traditions. But most historiographic progress – perhaps most intellectual progress – proceeds by rearranging relationships within old stories, not by writing new stories. The old stories have been ours and I shall return to argue it shortly.

I hardly need to mention that the feminist retellings of the past are stimulated by feminist political challenges to present-day structures and relationships. I may, however, need to mention that there was a first wave of women's history in the late nineteenth and early twentieth centuries. If this first wave was forgotten, it was not because it was modest. Elizabeth Cady Stanton reinterpreted the Bible. Alice Clark began to rewrite the rise of capitalism. Their influence was negligible, but within the academy the evidence is not overwhelming that we have had much more influence in the last decade. I respond with a cold sweat when I remember how completely this first wave of history was suppressed. When I became a feminist and began, with a group of historians-turned-feminist, to find out something about women's situation in the past, I discovered these books, dusty, in the Widener library stacks, untouched for decades. It is not good for the ego to contemplate a similar fate for one's own work. Only the continued existence of a strong feminist movement will make our own work remembered long enough to contribute to other generations.

Because of the hiatus in the feminist political tradition, the new wave of women's historians had to regain some lost territory. For a second time we had first to render the invisible visible, the silent noisy, the motionless active. In doing so, we were answering a call from a massive and powerful women's liberation movement for useful myths and counter-myths. Yet – and here is an optimistic sign – we left that task more quickly than our nineteenth-century ancestors did, they having produced scores of volumes of sketches of great women, descriptions of their country childhood, and tributes to their mothers. As historians, we were soon dissatisfied with myth-making, perhaps because the movement that gave birth to us was less elite (as were, for many of us, our own social origins); we moved to less glorious and also more ambivalent analyses of the past. Very soon many women's historians, and no doubt other feminist scholars, experienced friction with (or, worse, distance from) the social movement that had given birth to their careers. It frequently happened to me that the women's movement offered questions and topics, but my answers did not confirm all the slogans I had helped write.

Existing in between a social movement and the academy, women's scholarship has a mistress and a master – and guess which one pays wages. Undermining to some extent the co-opting effect of the academy, the rudeness with which women are treated there recreates some of the material conditions that provoked our social movement. But in history, at least, both academic and political impulses have been channelled at times into two different purposes, two poles of philosophical assumption and self-consciousness. One pole of energy, assimilated to the empiricism that dominated most history writing in this period, directed us to rectify past errors. Women's historians sought to proclaim a truth heretofore denied, disguised, distorted, defamed, and thereby to expose the meretricious lies of earlier mandarins. This goal, of course, presupposed the possibility of a truth, achieved through historical objectivity, and where this goal was dominant, women's historians used and assimilated the work of the new social history. Another pole, rejecting the possibility of objectivity and accepting the humanistic and story-telling function of history, stimulated us to create new myths to serve our aspirations.

I would like to find a method in between. This in-between would not imply resolution, careful balance of fact and myth, or synthesis of fact and interpretation. My sense of a liminal method is rather a condition of being constantly pulled, usually off balance, sometimes teetering wildly, almost always tense. The tension cannot be released. Indeed, the very desire to find a way to relax the tension is a temptation that must be avoided. Neither goal can be surrendered. It is wrong to conclude, as some have, that because there may be no objective truth possible, there are not objective lies. There may be no objective canons of historiography, but there are degrees of accuracy; there are better and worse pieces of history. The challenge is precisely to maintain this tension between accuracy and mythic power.

For the historian, the tension is further maintained by the nature of our sources. Among the particular constraints on the activity of producing history which embodies both truth and myth, is the finite, capricious, mottled nature of the evidence. Historians can be trained to creativity and imagination in the search for evidence, in sensitivity about what can constitute evidence, but we cannot always enlarge the available evidence through hard work or great intelligence. Moreover, we are not at ethical liberty to pick and choose among the shards available; our equivalent of the Hippocratic oath enjoins us to present all, or a representative sample, of the evidence relevant to a given inquiry; to search hard for the same; to seek out bits of evidence that might defeat our argument. These are neither outmoded nor unrealizable standards; nor are they standards inappropriate for feminists. They embody quite usefully the tension that we should seek to maintain between verifiable, fact-based truth and myth.

In our feminist version of this old task of reconstituting history, in negotiating between demands for truth and demands for myth, we encounter several issues at once old and new, feminist versions of traditional epistemological questions in history and politics. I would like to comment on four of them.

DOMINATION AND RESISTANCE

In the history of women's history, the greatest of our contradictions has been that between domination and resistance. Sometimes we feel impelled to document oppression, diagram the structures of domination, specify the agents and authors of domination, mourn the damages. Sometimes we feel impelled to defend our honour and raise our spirits by documenting our struggles and identifying successes in mitigating the tyranny. Neither aspect corresponds uniquely to myth-making; rather, we need different myths in different situations. In the history of women's history, Simone de Beauvoir and Mary Beard have stood respectively for each tendency, each with its shortcomings. In defining us as the other, de Beauvoir invited us to confront our pain, our jealousy of men, our humiliation. Her bravery was extraordinary. Mary Beard, much less well known, the clubwoman, the reformer, the no-nonsense capable matron, has been a far less attractive figure, because she wrote and embodied women's capability, not their fragility.

At other times the duality appears identified with the structure *vs.* agency debate in Marxism. This debate unfortunately has often been reduced to a schema in which structural analysis implies determination, while analysis in terms of human agency implies indeterminacy or contingency. Here, too, the dichotomy is not so neat. Usually, it is the dominant groups that can have individual agency, while the subordinated appear locked in 'structures'. The feminist critique, like that of good labour history, demands the recognition of structure and agency on all sides of a power equation.

My impression is that despite the long history of this historiographical problem, historians today have difficulty writing interpretations of the past that encompass both domination and resistance. Structural analysis is presented as deterministic, while discussion of women's agency is misunderstood as victim-blaming. Power itself becomes a pejorative. I remember some early second-wave feminist rhetoric and poetry calling for an end to power, indeed equating female beauty and kindness with the rejection of power; and I still read too many histories of female experience as powerless, which is false and impossible. To be less powerful is not to be powerless, or even to lose all the time. Analysis becomes moralistic rather than historical. Women's oppression is assumed to make us all angels, without character flaws.

POLITICAL OR SOCIAL HISTORY: REDEFINING POWER

A more recent contradiction in the new women's history is sometimes formulated as an argument between political and social history. To review a bit of the history of our discipline: once the only history was political or diplomatic (as studying inter-dynastic struggle has been called). It *was* history, by definition – the epics and apologia for kings. The age of democracy produced the so-called social history, a most revealing misnomer, for social means *hoi polloi*, the commoners, we who have no individuality. At first social history was like imperialist, primitive anthropology: writers chronicled the quaint culinary, marital,

76

and folk customs of the peasantry. Recently there have been a revival of social history and a contest for its meaning and purpose, in which historians on both ends of the continuum between fact and myth participate.

In the last few decades, particularly through developments in demography, social historians tended to study aspects of life seemingly removed from political domination. They studied household structure, marital patterns, friendships, childbirth. Political historians charged that the result was a romanticization of oppression. Eugene Genovese criticized some black history in this way. In women's history, the poles were identified as political and *cultural* history. Ellen DuBois, for example, criticized some of Carroll Smith-Rosenberg's work for photographing the positive aspects of the culture of the oppressed with a focus too close to show the framework: the prison bars.

Social or cultural historians have had several responses. One is, of course, that political historians still look only at the queens among us. Moreover, since the power of the rulers is far easier to see than the power of the ruled, the political/social history distinction tended to coincide with the domination/resistance dichotomy. Political historians charged that social history meant denial of oppression, constriction, suffering; social historians charged that political history missed the sources of popular cultural autonomy. It could hardly be true that the concept of a women's culture *per se* denies the problem of oppression. On the contrary, the imposition of concepts such as oppression often masks the specificity of women's own understanding of their condition.

Transcending this unproductive polarization requires, I think, that we integrate into the debate a critique of the definition of the political. If political is to do with power, there are ways in which the masses are involved in political activity and political relationships in their daily lives. There is no reason why questions of power, even the measurement of power, should not be fit into descriptions of, for example, women's writing, mothering, housework, or leisure. But here, too, I find that feminists cannot take unique credit for challenging definitions of the political as having to do with state power. Non-feminist libertarian social theorists began the exposure of hidden forms of power, although male supremacy remained invisible to them; while many feminists have, as I just argued, denied power, which is just another way of mystifying and thus upholding it.

The responsibility to situate one's work in an adequate analysis of power relations is not merely a problem for historians. While all scholarly work, in these post-encyclopaedic days, requires some specialization and particularity, that does not mean that any scholarly topic, any unit of study, is legitimate. It is not legitimate to define a topic that by its very boundaries creates a distorted view of reality. I am reminded particularly of women's scholarship that begins with the caveat that only white, or only middle-class, women are here included, as if the statement justified the exclusion. Similarly, choosing topics or sources of information that allow us to see only domination or only areas of women's autonomy can be illegitimate. Our collective goal ought to be to advance a theoretical framework to our scholarship that transcends the victim/heroine, domination/resistance dualism and incorporates the varied experiences of women. We need, I think, work that insists on presenting the complexity of the sources of power and weakness in women's lives.

DIFFERENCE

In the 1980s, perhaps the dominant emphasis in women's studies scholarship has been on what is generally called 'difference'. I have severe reservations about this emphasis because I fear that 'difference' is becoming a substitute, an accommodating, affable, and even lazy substitute, for opposition.

A development of the single greatest theoretical contribution of second-wave feminism, the notion of gender, *difference* is a code word that has now taken on two meanings. The primary meaning is that women have, according to discipline, a different voice, a different muse, a different psychology, a different experience of love, work, family, and goal. To varying degrees, all the disciplines have been involved in demonstrating not only the existence of that difference in experience but also the difference that recognizing it makes in the whole picture.

'Difference' may be hegemonic today, but it is not without critics, and it has not always defined feminist work. Feminist scholarship has another edge, examining the imposition of difference – i.e. gender – as a squeezing of possibility, and protesting the exclusion and subordination of women in the name of our uniqueness. Different but equal may be the gender version of separate but equal. Indeed, the very notion of difference can function to obscure domination, to imply a neutral asymmetry. The difference motif is not characteristic of all disciplines: strong in literature, psychology, and philosophy, it by no means dominates in history, sociology, or anthropology. Moreover, the difference motif does not seem to me to have the same meanings in all disciplines or in all pieces of work. In some, the discovery of hidden voices dominates; in others, it becomes a language of distinction, of dualism; in still others, it is used to define the nature of the feminine. Indeed, the meanings of difference can range from the essential to the trivial. In much historical and social-science work, for example, we are identifying the varying forms of labour and relations that produce certain patterns of response, making the difference a derivative rather than a primary category.

Moreover, in other contexts, difference takes on another meaning, that of difference *among* women, a meaning nearly opposite in implication – but more on that later.

If one uses the notion of 'difference' as an organizing principle, one can periodize the entire history of feminism in terms of the domination, in alternation, of an androgynous and a female-uniqueness view of women's subordination and liberation. The eighteenth- and early nineteenth-century Enlightenment feminists, religious *and* secular, tended towards an androgynous vision of the fundamental humanity of men and women; that is, they emphasized the artificial imposition of femininity upon women as part of a system subordinating, constricting, and controlling them, with the result that 'women', as an historically created category, had had their capacities as well as their aspirations reduced. By contrast, the later nineteenth-century feminists tended towards a female moral superiority view. They applauded what was different in women, and while they were not always biologistic in their assumptions about how we became different, the process of differentiation was less interesting to them than the result: a world divided between a male principle of aggression and a female one of nurturance. Motherhood was for them the fundamental defining experience of womanhood.

In our second wave of feminism, a similar movement from androgyny to female uniqueness occurred. The early women's liberation movement, both radical and liberal, emphasized equal rights and equal access for women to previously male privilege. In the past decade, we have seen again a celebration of women's unique and superior qualities with, again, an emphasis on mothering as both source and ultimate expression of these qualities. But it is not as if an acute shift occurred from one perspective to another; rather, this duality persists continuously within feminism. Moreover, it can be described and evaluated according to one's point of view: one historian might see a conflict between libertarian opposition to gender and sentimental acceptance of a separate sphere for women; another might see it as male-stream abstract egalitarianism *vs.* the assertion of an alternate female value system. The implications of each perspective are also contextual. Denial of difference can mean inauthenticity, while assertion of difference can mean retreat from supporting women's transcendent aspirations. Put another way, love of difference can mean a retreat from anger at the limitation of possibility, while hatred of difference can mean self-hatred for women.

One of the worst things about the emphasis on difference is that it allows the development of new 'fields' and the adoption of new styles of critique that do not fundamentally challenge the structure of the disciplines. It does not force the reinterpretation of all existing interpretation on the basis of new evidence but instead creates, potentially, pockets of women's literature, women's psychology, women's morality, and so forth. That is not an argument against separate women's studies programmes; it is an argument about what should be the content of our women's studies.

Science, perhaps because it excludes women most determinedly, and perhaps also because it is the most violent and destructive of disciplines, has evoked the most radical critiques of its basic assumptions. I am sceptical about whether such critiques can be applied directly to history. Neither do I like the segregation of women's history, its establishment, so to speak, as the description of a parallel course on which women ran through time. One main reason women do not, did not, keep to a separate track is, of course, the institution of heterosexuality. Institutionalized heterosexuality simultaneously helps to create gender and thus difference, and set limits on that difference. Lesbians and straight women alike, we are members and participants in all sorts of heterosexual institutions – economic, educational, cultural, and commercial – which construct our identity, willy-nilly.

Women's history is not just different, it is critical; it is against men's history. One reason the discourse about difference matters so much is that through it, feminists debate the conceptions of domination and resistance. Both seem to me drained of their experience, of the ways in which they *matter* so much, when they are rephrased in terms of difference.

Another meaning of difference, which equally results from feminist debates about oppression and resistance, points to differences among women. It is directly related, and negatively so, to the first meaning of difference, for the emphasis on a *unique* female voice almost always becomes an assumption of a *homogeneous* female voice. Naturally, people get angry at arrogant uses of 'we'. The women's movement becomes several women's movements, both because new movements are stimulated by older ones and out of rage at the pretensions of some to speak for all – worse, at the replication of elitist patterns within our work and society. Thus, if the multiplicity and variety of feminist perspectives are a strength and a richness, they are also a reflection of inequality among women.

One response to this disunity has been a flowering of narratives of varieties of femaleness. Historians do that to some extent through the documentation of individual lives and collective conditions, visible particularly in the publication of many oral-history 'biographies' and autobiographies. These works are supplying sources that other historians may incorporate into larger studies. But too often these narratives do not criticize the generalizations we have made about femaleness, and instead confine themselves to the assertion, in a liberal relativist way, of variety. Indeed, by implication, they sometimes deny the legitimacy of generalization. Too often the response to Afro-American women's analyses, for example, is a tolerant acceptance of difference rather than an attempt to *integrate* that experience as part of our whole approach to the study of women.

METHODOLOGY

Everything I have said so far skirts the issue of whether there is a feminist methodology and epistemology. In history writing, one could look for feminist or different female methods of 1) defining what counts as evidence, 2) collecting evidence, 3) generalizing from specifics, and 4) drawing conclusions. Only in the first category do I see any unique contribution – I repeat, I am speaking only of methodology – in women's history. But the question of what counts as evidence is far more substantive than methodology, really. I consider as evidence material once thought of as outside history – gossip, menstruation, latrines; but historians once considered black people outside history too. Critics of science have raised the question of a gendered methodology most forcefully, but when applied to the social sciences or the humanities, a critique such as, say, Evelyn Keller's critique of male science is not clearly a uniquely female method. The incorporation of the subjectivity of the object of study is a theme that has been raised by sociologists, anthropologists, and historians for decades, men as well as women. It is a method that I recognize in my own work; I listen very hard to my subjects, and operate on the assumption that their own self-interpretation is likely as good as mine, or at least worth a respectful hearing. But that does not seem to me different from the methods employed by Herbert Gutman, say, in his reconstruction of slave families, or E.P. Thompson in his interpretations of working-class religion. Good historical listening embodies a critique of the concept of false consciousness. But this critique was raised by anti-Leninist socialists before we second-wave feminists argued it; and feminists have also been involved in branding disagreements as inauthentic.

I would like to clarify what I take to be the political import of what I am saying. In order to do that, my working definition of feminism, as a historian, needs to be specified. It is clear to me that an ahistorical, unchanging definition that posits a fixed content for feminism won't do, because it cuts us off from our tradition, or, rather, narrows that tradition to a part of itself. Feminism is a critique of male supremacy, formed and offered in the light of a will to change it, which in turn assumes a conviction that it is changeable. What counts as feminist is markedly different today from what was considered so 200 years ago. Moreover, as I have argued, there is today a great variety within feminism, and we should expect, each of us, to disagree with much that is feminist. If every feminist scholar knew something of the history of the feminist tradition, that might serve as a corrective to dogmatism, if nothing else.

If there are contradictions within feminism, it should be understood that there are traditions of female thought, women's culture, and female consciousness that are not feminist. Female and feminist consciousness stand in complex relation to each other: clearly they overlap, for the female is the basis of the feminist, yet the feminist arises also out of a desire to escape the female. That seems to me an inescapable tension.

I have wanted to raise here a troubling question. Throughout various parts of feminist scholarship today, historical and otherwise, there is an attempt to reach a false resolution of the tension I have just defined, a resolution that would obliterate the distinction between the female and the feminist. It seems to me important to claim both. The female is ourselves, our bodies, and our socially constructed experience. It is not the same as feminism, which is not a 'natural' excretion of that experience but a controversial political interpretation and struggle, by no means universal to women. I find a tendency to celebrate the female and to distinguish ourselves as sharply as possible from the male, in method as well as substance. This tendency is then mixed with, and sometimes supported by, the inadequate integration of women's experience as victims of oppression with our own voluntary, responsible activity against it. I cannot evade the question whether a scholarship focused on liberation must not also criticize, and even reject, part of what is constituted female. If it does not, then we may be sacrificing the understanding of gender, reverting to an operating assumption that some eternal female principle defines our destiny beyond our control.

Part III

MALE THEORIES OF POWER

INTRODUCTION

Elizabeth Grosz

Nancy Jay's paper, 'Gender and dichotomy' is one of the first feminist texts directly to address the question of the phallocentrism of the structure of binary oppositions. These have, within the history of western thought, functioned in the humanities and social sciences as self-evident, pre-eminently rational, *a priori* principles for categorizing and describing a rich multiplicity of phenomena. Jay's paper provides a clear introduction to the logic underlying this binary structure. This logic, contrary to common presumptions within western thought, is not simply a neutral way of dividing a continuum into two equal but opposite terms or poles. As Jay argues, the relation between these terms is a hierarchical, non-reversible and non-reciprocal relation, one that privileges one term from a pair of binary opposites, thereby making its opposite logically dependent on it. Two apparently equal, substantive, self-subsisting terms are reduced, through a binary logic, into one term and its other, or opposite.

Jay is, of course, not the first to note the insidious form of binary polarizations, but she is among the first to analyse the ways in which this structure functions to produce and reinforce the hierarchized relations between the sexes in patriarchal cultures. Taking as her critical object the structures of opposition pervasive in anthropology, especially in Durkheim's writings, she challenges the ways in which the sacred and the profane, nature and culture, and ultimately, male/masculine and female/feminine are theorized within the anthropological mainstream. She reveals that underlying these apparently methodological or neutral divisions are pervasive, if largely unrecognized, power relations.

Although she does not refer directly to Lacan and Althusser, her analysis may be of considerable use in assessing the theoretical and political assumptions made by each. Althusser's conceptions of the relations between nature and culture, economic base and ideological superstructure, science and ideology, 'men's' 'real' relations and their 'imaginary', reflected representations of their real relations, are all clearly amenable to Jay's criticisms of Durkheim. In each of these binary pairs, the primary term – culture, base, science, real relations – is privileged and its opposite or other – nature, superstructure, ideology, lived relations – is defined only by the absence, lack or deprivation of the positive term. The subordinated terms here are amorphous, universal categories that lack a clear-cut definition or substance in so far as they are defined as categories only negatively. Nature is what is left behind by culture, the superstructure is everything in the social besides the economy, ideology consists not only in falsehoods, untruths, and 'propaganda', but also in cultural products, artefacts, social relations, psychological characteristics, and so on; what makes ideology ideological is the fact that it is not scientific and not economic. In each case, the category has no internal coherence; its rationale is provided only by its other.

It seems more difficult to ascribe clear-cut binary structures to Lacan's work. His writings are more ambiguous than Althusser's, and he seems to have a preference to ternary, rather than binary forms of classification. For example, where Althusser opposes nature to culture, here following Lévi-Strauss (as indeed does Lacan, at least in certain texts), Lacan instead conceives of a relation between need (which is as close to nature as he comes), and demand and desire (which, taken together, comprise Lacan's approximation of culture). In no sense do these terms refer to an objective, distinct nature, considered in its purity, nor of a culture conceived as the transcendence of nature. Need, demand, and desire are psychical impulses: need is the biological antecedent and precondition of demand and desire; demand is the verbalization of need (and is thus dependent on it) and desire is the unspeakable and unconscious residue unarticulated in demand's 'translation' of need.

Where Althusser distinguishes science from ideology, Lacan opposes truth and knowledge (which are usually closely allied). Where Althusser divides a scientific knowledge from the ideology of lived relations, Lacan sees an intersubjective relation between an analyst who is supposed to know (but does not) and an analysand who knows (but does not want to). Yet in spite of his aversion to simple binary polarization, Lacan nevertheless remains embroiled in binary oppositions whenever he theorizes about the two sexes. Masculine and feminine remain, as in Freud's work, defined by the relations between active and passive, subject and object, and phallic and castrated. In this sense, Jay's critique remains highly pertinent to feminist readings of Lacan. As she herself notes, it is often difficult to distinguish relations of opposition (or contradiction) from relations of difference (or contrariety) and this seems particularly relevant to Lacan's elusive and complex work.

As I see it, Jay's text provides an introduction to the Derridean notion of deconstruction, without, however, the strongly 'French', 'foreign' (for the Anglo-Saxon reader) style of Derrida and many of his English-speaking commentators. The terrain Jay covers is also that of Derrida. His deconstructive readings of various philosophical texts interrogate the ways in which terms (such as presence, speech, identity) gain their privileged positions only at the expense of other, negative, oppositional terms (absence, writing, difference). Like Derrida, Jay aims not only to reveal these oppositional pairs and to analyse them, but also to question, criticize, and undo them.

It is not adequate simply to refuse the oppositional structure, pretending it does not exist; it pervades all our conceptual systems and criteria for their assessment. It is the heritage of our intellectual history, the terms by which we are able to think or articulate our various conceptual systems. Nor, however, can this structure simply be accepted without question. It must be continually challenged and displaced, pushed to its limits. Jay's paper not only shows how such an interrogation may be possible within the disciplines of anthropology, sociology, and elsewhere, but how the oppositional form is ultimately allied with the ways in which the two sexes are conceived. The binary form of relations between the sexes, in which man defines the woman in terms of oppositions to himself – she is what he is *not* – underlies and provides something of a political explanation for the tenacity of an oppositional logic in western philosophy.

In other words, Jay's paper shows that the binary structure is implicitly *sexualized*, pervaded with sexual-political values, and related to the patriarchal differentiation of the sexes. She shows how relations of *difference* – where the two terms are autonomous and capable of self-definition – are constricted into a binarized form – where one defines the other as its negative. Arguably, this binarized form exhibits the most insidious and powerful forms of patriarchal (mis)representation. In this sense, her analysis, while different from Foucault's understanding of power, seems compatible with and complementary to it. Foucault himself seems to avoid the familiar binarized methods and terminology of many of his predecessors, or else self-consciously to problematize them. This is most clear in his earlier writings, particularly in *Madness and Civilisation*, where, in taking the oppositions between madness and reason, and speech and silence, he undertakes an archaeology of the silencing of madness, that is, an archaeology of the investment of reason in the silencing of madness or unreason.

However, in his later works, Foucault seems less concerned about conceptual or textual devices of power than in the ways texts *do things*, perform functions, or act, on bodies. This does not mean Jay's analysis is incommensurable with or irrelevant to his conception of power as a network of acts, forces, and effects. For a position more interested than Foucault in understanding the interrelations between the *internal* discursive mechanisms (such as Jay and Derrida outline) and powers that act on bodies and behaviours, clearly a deconstructive challenge to binary polarizations, given its link to the social and psychological subordination of women would be necessary. Jay's work seems especially relevant to Foucault's analysis of the powers operating within discourse to control, refine, and supervise the production and circulation of discourse, techniques that ensure the predictability and on-going cohesion of discourses. Binary polarization remains one of the major theoretical methods by which certain kinds of power relations – especially those governing relations of oppression – are represented and rationalized.

Jay's paper provides as clear, concise, and convincing an analysis of the ways in which the binary structure pervades our conceptual categories as I have seen. Above all, she makes explicit the ways in which it has functioned to define the sexes according to patriarchal norms by providing a naturalistic or self-evident justification for women's (conceptual, social, sexual) subordination. In this sense, her paper provides a powerful critical tool in feminist displacements and re-writings of patriarchal knowledges.

GENDER AND DICHOTOMY

Nancy Jay

The social conditions and consequences of the radical use of logical dichotomy are generally neglected by logicians and sociologists alike. Logicians, no doubt, can safely ignore them, but social theorists do so at their own risk. This paper examines some ways in which logical dichotomy and radical gender distinctions are associated, some consequences of conceiving of gender distinctions as formally dichotomous, and some reasons why it is in the interest of certain social groups to understand gender distinctions in that way. The point of departure will be an examination of Emile Durkheim's *The Elementary Forms of the Religious Life*. This book serves as a model of how one may begin to understand relations between intellectual concepts and social distinctions. It also serves as a cautionary tale, for Durkheim's uncritical use of dichotomy can be shown to create certain problems, among them that he wrote a brilliant sociology of knowledge, which if followed closely, leads directly to the conclusion that women are unable to think.

One of Durkheim's major interests in primitive religions was as material for a theory of knowledge. He wanted to find the origin of those essential ideas which 'philosophers since Aristotle have called the categories of the understanding: ideas of time, space, class, number, cause, substance . . . etc.' These concepts 'are like the solid frame which encloses all thought: this does not seem to be able to liberate itself from them without destroying itself, for it seems that we cannot think of objects that are not in time and space, which have no number, etc.'[1]

Empiricist thinkers, Durkheim claimed, who must derive everything in consciousness from the individual's sense impressions, are unable to account for the origin of these categories; and idealist thinkers account for them only by claiming they are given, *a priori*, in the nature of the mind. Durkheim proposed to find a source that has empirical reality for the categories in society itself, through religion. The categories, he said, 'are born in religion and of religion: they are a product of religious thought.'[2]

Durkheim chose to study Australian religion because it was well described, and at the time was universally believed to be a truly primitive

89

or 'elementary' religion. He claimed that Australian men, in performing rituals, represent their own society to themselves, thus making aspects of their society available to consciousness as concepts. This representation and conceptualization in turn reinforces and actually creates and recreates the social structure as represented in ritual. It is in these 'collective representations' that the categories originated. For example, the category of class grew out of totemic rituals symbolizing the clan and phratry divisions of society. Ritual is the medium that, by symbolizing these social divisions, transforms them into concepts, and in so doing reciprocally creates them. 'It is the phratries which have served as classes and the clans as species. It is because men were organized that they were able to organize things.'[3]

It is only through ritual representation that the categories first arise in consciousness. Furthermore, ritual is essential not merely to give birth to the categories, but also to maintain them, so that society can continue to conceptualize itself and the world. This is an essential function that religion performs, and a reason for its continued existence. A secular society is only possible when science and philosophy are sufficiently developed so as to take over the cognitive work originally accomplished only in ritual action.

This sociology of knowledge, this recognition of religion as not only a way of knowing, but as originally *the* way of conceptual knowing, is tied to a truly dichotomous understanding of religion. Durkheim both defines and identifies religion by reference to the radical separation of, the total opposition between, the sacred and the profane. 'This division of the world into two domains, the one containing all that is sacred, the other all that is profane, is the distinctive characteristic of religious thought.'[4]

Durkheim found a social origin for this split between sacred and profane, but it is a strangely vague and subjective one, unlike those 'with empirical reality' that he found for the categories. We are somehow aware of purely moral forces in society:

> But the sentiments which they inspire in us differ in nature from those we have for simple visible objects. . . . Consequently, we get the impression that we are in relations with two distinct sorts of reality and that a sharply drawn line of demarcation separates them from each other: on the one hand is the world of profane things, on the other that of sacred things.[5]

We can certainly make that distinction in reflection, but it is difficult to find there the same kind of dichotomy that Durkheim did. Even Durkheim found it hard to identify the character of the sacred more precisely. He tried to specify the features that distinguished it from the profane, and having ruled out a number of possibilities, concluded:

'There is nothing left with which to characterize the sacred in relation to the profane except their heterogeneity', the opposition itself which is made between them.

However, this heterogeneity is sufficient to characterize this classification of things and to distinguish it from all others, because it is very particular: *it is absolute.* In all the history of human thought there exists no other example of two categories of things so profoundly differentiated or so radically opposed to one another. The traditional opposition of good and bad is nothing beside this: For the good and the bad are only two opposed species of the same class, namely morals, just as sickness and health are two different aspects of the same order of facts, life, while the sacred and the profane have always and everywhere been conceived by the human mind as two distinct classes, as two worlds between which there is nothing in common.[6]

The sacred possesses no objective features that necessarily distinguish it from the profane; on the contrary, mere proximity with the profane destroys the distinction. The dichotomy is only maintained by constant effort (like the urgency in parts of the Old Testament about keeping 'the difference between' the clean and the unclean). But Durkheim does not ask why this should be so. He offers no functional analysis for the sacred/profane dichotomy; he never asks what it is for. Unlike other aspects of religion that he did take as fully problematic, it does not serve as one of the sources of the categories of understanding.

Following Durkheim, the radical separation of the sacred and profane leads directly and necessarily to a radical separation of women and men in religious life. Because women are profane in relation to men, they are, according to Durkheim, excluded from all rituals, even from knowledge about them.[7] In fact, women are not supposed to know *any* of the process by which conceptual thought is formed. Over and over he refers to their exclusion.[8] For Durkheim, the exclusion of women even provides an identifying sign to distinguish truly religious practices from those that are mere magic. Religion performs its essential function – of establishing conceptual thought – for men only. If it serves women, Durkheim never shows how.

We can understand why Durkheim himself was not troubled by the anomaly of the thinking woman from convictions he expressed in his earlier work, *The Division of Labor in Society*: 'The two great functions of psychic life are . . . dissociated . . . one of the sexes [female] takes care of the affective functions and the other of intellectual functions.'[9] But this explanation is troublesome, for according to Durkheim, the dissociation grows with the progress of civilization.

The woman of past days was not at all the weak creature that she has become with the progress of morality. . . . Dr Lebon has been able to establish directly and with mathematical precision this original resemblance of the two sexes in regard to the pre-eminent organ of physical and psychic life, the brain. By comparing a large number of crania chosen from different races and different societies, he has come to the following conclusion: 'The volume of the crania of man and woman, even when we compare subjects of equal age, of equal height and equal weight, show considerable differences in favor of the man, and this inequality grows proportionally with civilization, so that from the point of view of the mass of the brain, and correspondingly of intelligence, woman tends more and more to be differentiated from the male sex. The difference which exists, for example, between the average cranium of Parisian men and women is almost doubled that observed between male and female of ancient Egypt.'[10]

But this only explains why women no longer think, not why they were originally able to do so.

If the capacity for conceptual thought is not inherent in human beings, but is acquired only through participation in a process that specifically excludes women, how does it come about that women can think? There is no way whatsoever, based strictly on Durkheim's analysis, to answer this question. The question only arises when someone says, but they *can* think. Similarly, the tendency of certain forms of religion to split the world into good, right, male, light, spirit, and so forth, and evil, left, female, dark, flesh, and so forth becomes problematic only when it is observed that women are not more evil, mortal, dark, or left-handed than men. But Durkheim took sexist, dualist religion utterly for granted (and, as we shall see, even created his own brand of dualist religion in his sacred/profane dichotomy). Had he wanted to question it, his own method would have allowed him to do so easily, and in the same process to provide a functional explanation for his sacred/profane dichotomy, and also to account for women's ability to think.

Suppose he had set out to account for the origin, not of the categories of understanding, but of something quite similar: the basic laws of formal logical thought.[11] These too were first classically formulated by Aristotle, and (as Durkheim said about the categories) they comprise 'a certain number of essential ideas which dominate all our intellectual life'.[12] Also similar to the categories: 'They are inescapable because any attempt to disregard them reduces our thoughts and words to confusion and gibberish.'[13]

The most basic of these logical rules are three. They are the Principle of Identity (if anything is A, it is A); the Principle of Contradiction (nothing can be both A and Not-A); and the Principle of the Excluded

Middle (anything, and everything, must be *either* A *or* Not-A). As Durkheim claims for the categories, the origin of these principles cannot be explained by either the empiricist or the idealist. They are not representative of the empirical world: they are principles of order. In the empirical world almost everything is in a process of transition: growing, decaying, ice turning to water, and vice versa. Because these logical laws cannot apply directly to anything in transition, they cannot have their origin in the individual's sense impressions. Similarly, the idealist can account for them only as given, *a priori*, in the nature of the mind. But if we follow Durkheim, and try to account for their origin in society, as represented in religion, we find that he has done almost all the work for us.

In his sacred/profane dichotomy, we find a clear religious representation of these laws. The dichotomy creates, he says,

> a bipartite division of the whole universe, known and knowable, into two classes which radically exclude each other. Sacred things are those which the interdictions protect and isolate [A]; profane things, those to which these interdictions are applied and which must remain at a distance from the first [Not-A].[14]

Durkheim believed that the distinction between the sacred and profane is unique: 'In all the history of human thought there exists no other example of things so profoundly differentiated or so radically opposed to one another.' But this kind of dichotomous distinction is not unique at all; on the contrary, it is the same principle by which logicians have wished to understand every proposition (known and knowable) to be *either* true *or* not true, one or the other but not both, separated by the excluded middle. In Durkheim's contrast of this discontinuous distinction with that between good and bad, or sickness and health, he is turning to the empirical world, where things are indeed found to be on a continuum and do not fall into rigid either/or distinctions.[15]

Between the sacred and the profane, says Durkheim:

> There is a break in continuity. . . . Since we picture a sort of logical chasm between the two, the mind irresistibly refuses the two corresponding things to be confounded, or even to be put in contact with each other; for such a promiscuity, or even too direct a contiguity would contradict too violently the dissociation of these ideas in the mind.[16]

All that is true of A, Not-A, and the excluded middle, as it is of the sacred and the profane. Durkheim does not use the phrase 'excluded middle', instead he speaks of the need 'to create a sort of vacuum between them'.[17]

Now there is, in every society, a dichotomous distinction: that between

93

male and female. Although this dichotomy need not be phrased in terms of A and Not-A, it is particularly susceptible to such phrasing. In societies through the world, *everyone*, 'known and knowable', is either male or female, one or the other, but not both. Furthermore, there is no third possibility (*tertium non datur*); neither we nor the Australians sort people into female, male, and 'other'. Although biologically sex is a continuum, it is not one socially. A modern transsexual does not move a certain distance along the continuum socially; she or he makes a complete leap from one category into the other.[18]

Still following Durkheim, we can say that because society was dichotomously organized, people were able to organize the world dichotomously. This formulation also solves the problem of the woman who can think: in being female and profane, that which must be excluded, and therefore Not-A, women have just as immediate social experience of A/Not-A dichotomy as do men in being male and sacred, that which must be kept pure, A. Thus women have fully adequate access to knowledge of the rules of identity, contradiction, and the excluded middle, or, in Durkheim's sense, to the social grounds of the capacity for formal logical thought. This formulation is especially Durkheimian because A/Not-A gender distinction is necessarily a *social* distinction. It cannot arise from biological sex difference. But Durkheim himself could not have made this analysis because he took rigid dichotomous gender distinction for granted, a biological given, and never looked at it sociologically.

Religious dualism certainly exemplifies the process that Durkheim described: formal representation of social distinctions acting reciprocally to recreate those very distinctions. But if this process were sufficient explanation, because all societies make dichotomous gender distinctions, they would all end up making them with comparable rigidity, all religions would be dualist, and all thinkers would rely equally on formal logic. In fact, great variety exists in all these institutions. So here we must part company from Durkheim. Because we no longer hope to find the origin of social institutions by looking back down a linear evolutionary line to the Australians, we are spared many a confusing chicken-or-egg problem. We can simply assert that our social institutions shape our thought, which in turn shapes our society. In these very general terms I want to examine some relations between ways of thinking and ways of making gender distinctions.

Although gender distinctions are regularly dichotomous, they do not always carry out the full implications of formal A/Not-A phrasing. When they *are* so phrased, men and women are conceived of in ways that cannot be a consequence only of conceptualization and reinforcement of empirical distinctions between them. Concepts of femaleness and maleness come into being that have nothing whatever to do with human sexual differences, but follow from the nature of contradictory dichotomy itself. First I shall examine what these concepts are, and then shall suggest why it is in the interest of some social groups to distort human sexual differences in that way.

To begin with, all dichotomous distinctions are not necessarily phrased as A/Not-A. Consider some differences between the phrasings A/B and A/Not-A. A and B are mere contraries, not logical contradictories, and continuity between them may be recognized without shattering the distinction. (Durkheim's good/bad and sickness/health distinctions are A/B distinctions.) Continuity between terms is a logical impossibility for distinctions phrased as contradictories, as A/Not-A. Thus men and women may be conceived as men and not-men, or women and not-women, between which there is logically not continuity, or as two forms (A,B) of the class 'human' which may be supposed to have a good deal in common. Further, in A/B distinctions both terms have positive reality. In A/Not-A dichotomies only one term has positive reality; Not-A is only the privation or absence of A. A/B distinctions are necessarily limited; in themselves they do not encompass C, D, and so forth. But there is nothing about them that necessarily prevents also considering C (a third possibility), and then the distinction becomes A/B/C. In other words, mere contrary distinctions are not eternally tied to dichotomous structure, and as dichotomies they are limited in scope. The structure of A/Not-A is such that a third term is impossible: everything and anything must be either A or Not-A. Such distinctions are all-encompassing. They not only cover every possible case of the category (gender, propositions, and so forth) to which they are applied, but they can, and logically do, order 'the entire universe, known and knowable'.

This all-encompassing capacity is a consequence of a quality of Not-A called 'the infinitation of the negative'. As John Dewey has written, 'If, say, "virtue" be assigned to A as its meaning, then Not-A includes not only vice, but triangles, horseraces, symphonies, and the precession of the equinoxes.'[19] The infinitation of the negative, and the consequent lack of internal boundaries in Not-A, is the logical structure behind the 'contagion' of pollution. For example, the notion in the Levitical law that a man who touches a menstruating woman, or anything directly in contact with her, becomes unclean himself. Only the excluded middle, the essential empty space between A and Not-A (the 'difference' that must be kept between the clean and the unclean), holds the chaos of Not-A at bay. Whatever is contiguous with Not-A is necessarily Not-A itself.

The infinitation of the negative can also be used very differently. It is why theologians sometimes like to 'define' God negatively (the *via negativa*): God is not this, and not that. This keeps Him infinite as no other method of definition can do. But this is not what is ordinarily meant by 'definition'. Except that it is not A, Not-A is wholly undefined and undefinable.

Where gender dichotomy is a form of A/Not-A dichotomy, can we decide who is Not-A and consequently 'tends towards infinitation'? At first glance, societies with dualist religion may seem to put maleness in the infinite, Not-A, position: immortality, spirit, and transcendence are male in such religions. For the Greeks, said Jane Harrison, becoming a man was ceasing to be a woman. Anthropologists are generally agreed that one function of male initiation rites is to separate boys from women and children, to make them not-women. It is claimed that, because in infancy males were physically and experientially part of women, they need an experience of radical separation. Thus societies with strong sex segregation, where young children of both sexes spend their time almost exclusively in the company of women and other children, are the most likely to provide radical separation experiences for boys. It is probably true that, in all societies, men go through a more marked separation experience than do women in the development of gender identity. Girls can go on being women: boys must become something different.[20]

If we try to interpret men as not-women, tending towards infinitation, all finitude appears compressed into a female, A, side of the dichotomy. But it is nowhere near that simple: dualist religion will not fit this formulation. In dualist religion, the *female* side is regularly phrased as Not-A, and therefore tends towards infinitation: impurity, irrationality, disorder, chaos, change, chance (the goddess Fortuna), error, and evil. That which is defined, separated out, isolated from all else, is A and pure. Not-A is necessarily impure, a random catch-all, to which nothing is external except A and the principle of order that separates it from Not-A. Those very Greeks, who seemed to Jane Harrison to see men as not-women, offer the clearest expression of the reverse.

The Pythagorean table of opposites, cited with approval by Aristotle, puts the 'limited' (A) on the male, good, light, right side, and the 'unlimited' on the female, evil, dark, left side. You might expect that this formulation would lead to a reversal of the nature of an infinite God, approached by the *via negativa*, who perhaps would turn out to be female. Not at all, divinity and immortality are still safely male. For example, Plato's *Phaedo* opposes what is 'divine and immortal and intelligible, and uniform and indissoluble and ever constant and true to itself', on a positive, A, side to what is 'human and mortal and manifold and not intelligible and dissoluble and never constant nor true to itself', on a negative, Not-A side.[21] Eternal, perfect form is opposed to its own negation, privation, or absence. Immortality and divinity are limited, A, because the transitory ways of the flesh, birth and death, growth and decay, are all alike imperfections (the womb–tomb equation). All change falls necessarily into Not-A.

Aristotle thought all dichotomous terms had this structure: the one a positive, the other a mere negative.[22] All contraries then become contradictories. If the sexes are distinguished in this way, there can be only one perfect form, which, not surprisingly, is the male. Opposed to it can be only not-male, not form. Consequently, the female 'form' is not really a form at all, but only a deformation of the male. Deformities, privations of form, are unlimited, as is formlessness itself.

This formal logic is behind Aristotle's famous notion of woman as 'misbegotten male', an idea endorsed by patristic and scholastic theologians. A woman, having no positive sexual reality of her own, is only a failure to become a man. Aristotelian embryology claimed that, because all form, like the soul, is in the semen, and only formless matter is contributed by the mother, it is the true nature of all pregnancies to result in boy babies only. If girl babies are born, it is because of some failure in the gestation process, probably the south wind blowing too much, thought Aristotle, or perhaps something else went wrong. (The possibilities of error tend towards infinitation.)

You do not have to move very far from this position to *appear* to be no longer expressing gender distinctions as dichotomous, as for example, in Tennyson's line, 'Woman is the lesser man'. The notion of woman as 'the lesser man' is fairly common. You find it in Freud, for example, with the notion of women as castrated men, 'sexually inferior'. Hidden behind this notion is still the idea of femaleness as only a privation of maleness, of women as deformed or diminished men, lacking positive sexuality of their own.

The suggestion of continuity in the 'lesser man' notion is deceptive for A/Not-A gender distinction is only concealed, not abandoned in such notions. In some societies women may be given diminutive, 'lessened', and therefore feminized, men's names (Henrietta, Jaqueline). The absence of the reverse reveals the hidden dichotomy. Men are almost never given aggrandized or masculinized women's names. (You can imagine some: Annelegrand, Susanissimo; but you will not find them being used.) If women were truly similar to men, but only lesser, men would acceptably be greater women.

Hidden, taken for granted, A/Not-A distinctions are dangerous, and because of their peculiar affinity with gender distinctions, it seems important for feminist theory to be systematic in recognizing them. Sometimes such distinctions are obvious, as in clean/unclean, but more often they are concealed and go unrecognized. Durkheim failed completely to see the A/Not-A structure of his own sacred/profane dichotomy, and among criticisms of it, I know of only one that recognizes that structure. The anthropologist W.E.H. Stanner, in describing the confusion in the category 'profane', wrote: 'Things so disparate cannot form a class unless a class can be marked by a property, its absence, and its contrary.'[23] What he recognized was the infinitation of the negative and the consequent lack of internal order in Not-A.

Feminist theory can similarly be alert to structural clues revealing unstated A/Not-A gender distinctions. One such clue is the presence of only one positive term, the other being characterized only by privation of that positive, as in the 'lesser man' notion. Evidence of the infinitation of the negative is another clue. The A/B/C distinction 'men/women/children' is harmless, but it is well to be suspicious of the dichotomy 'men/women and children', with its hint of infinitation of the negative, for it may reflect the notion that women and children have in common that they are not-men. In this case, the logically inevitable absence of internal boundaries within Not-A lends powerful support to the notion of women as immature, as infantile in relation to men. This widespread distortion is evident in such disparate cases as ancient Roman law and early psychoanalytic theory. An example is Marie Bonaparte's acceptance of the idea that 'a woman is a man whose development has been arrested, a sort of adolescent to whose organism is subjoined, in a kind of symbiosis, the apparatus of maternity, which is responsible for the check in development'.[24]

Other clues to hidden A/Not-A distinctions are the threat of chaos (or pollution) if the excluded middle is not maintained, the insistence on rigid either/or distinctions without alternatives (third possibilities). The social dichotomies on which orthodox Puritans understood their social order to rest were not overtly phrased as A/Not-A. At first glance they look like mere contrary distinctions, but they could be understood (and were understood by many New England thinkers) as inseparably part of a single dichotomous system of formal logic that encompassed the entire universe, known and knowable.[25] When that dangerous woman, Anne Hutchinson, was banished from Massachusetts in 1638, she was accused of having violated social dichotomies: 'You have stept out of your place, *you have rather bine a Husband than a Wife and a preacher than a Hearer; and a Magistrate than a Subject.*'[26] The hidden A/Not-A structure of these dichotomies is indicated by the frightful sexual and social chaos threatened by her actions and beliefs:

> The filthie Sinne of the Comunitie of Woemen and all promiscuous and filthie cominge togeather of men and Woemen without Distinction or relation of Marriage, will necessarily follow. And though I have not herd, nayther do I thinke, you have bine unfaythfull to your Husband in his Marriage Covenant, *yet that will follow upon it* . . . and soe more dayngerous Evells and filthie Unclenes and other sines will followe than you doe now Imagine or conceave.[27]

It is not only feminist theorists who need to be wary of A/Not-A distinctions. As a fundamental principle of formal logic, the A/Not-A dichotomy is wonderfully simple and supremely all-encompassing. But it is necessarily distorting when it is applied directly to the empirical world, for there are no negatives there. Everything that exists (including women) exists positively. Dewey has warned of the dangers of giving A/Not-A distinctions direct existential reference:

> The notion that propositions are or can be, in and of themselves, such that the principle of the excluded middle directly applies is probably the source of more fallacious reasoning in philosophical discourse and in moral and social inquiry than any other one sort of fallacy.[28]

This is well illustrated by Durkheim's direct application of his sacred/profane dichotomy to religion. For him, all religion was actually founded on that contradictory dichotomy and anything that did not exhibit that characteristic was not religion. But his dichotomy has not been found by most good ethnographers studying 'primitive' religion. Evans-Pritchard, Nadel, Lienhardt, Goody, Turner, *all* fail to find it.[29] This is not surprising. These ethnographers were not concerned with purely formal logical structures found only in the mind, but attended to what real people were doing in the world. From this perspective there is a continual interpenetration of religious and mundane affairs, which are never wholly separable from one another. What Stanner, a fine ethnographer of Australian religion, has written of Durkheim's sacred/profane is also true of A/Not-A gender dichotomy: 'The dichotomy itself is unusable except at the cost of undue interference with the facts of observation. . . . To use the dichotomy is to disregard what is the case.'[30]

Another illustration of the distorting effects of direct application of A/Not-A can be found in Greek science. In opposing eternal, perfect form to its own privation or absence, some Greek thinkers created a realm of fixed and eternal essences. These perfect and permanent forms were not merely ways of knowing, but were ultimate ontological reality itself: Being. The realm of Being necessarily excluded, by its very nature, all that was changing, contingent, and therefore ontologically imperfect: Non-being (which logically did not have real existence). Science was a process of purification, of separating eternal from transitory, form from matter, essence from accident, order from disorder. But then, because the transitory natural world, as Non-being, had been stripped of all possibilities for order, science could consist only in the definition and classification of the perfect unchanging forms which (from our point of view) it constituted itself. Only Being was a proper subject for science; the material world, and with it all changing individuals of any kind, was ruled out as Non-being.

It is worth noting that the 'eternal' realm of Being has vanished with Greek civilization, while the transitory natural world is still with us. This is because direct applications of A/Not-A to the world are unsupported by any natural order, but are social creations, and as such require continual work to maintain them. Especially in the case of the direct social applications of A/Not-A distinctions, like gender distinctions, this work is done with deadly seriousness. Ethnographers, even comparatively recent ones such as Lloyd Warner,[31] claim that if an Australian woman happened to see the rituals of sacred objects that were to be known by men only, she was immediately killed, thus removing the anomaly and keeping the dichotomy intact. Joan of Arc, a woman in armour, muddying up the excluded middle, met a similar fate. Measures taken nowadays are a good deal less extreme, but they still exist, and are still a source of suffering.

One cannot but be struck by the enormous amount of social effort expended, of sustained, co-operative work performed, and of oppression and violence done in the creation and maintenance of such social dichotomies. Is all that effort necessary simply for the creation and maintenance of logical categories? Surely we can tell the sheep from the goats, the quick from the dead, the males from the females, and A from Not-A, without resorting to traditional forms of oppression, both physical and spiritual. A disinterested respect for formal logic is inadequate as a motive for murder. Then what is radical social dichotomy 'really' for?

There are, of course, many ways to answer this question. I want to suggest one answer based on the resistance of formal logic to the understanding and acceptance of change. Within such thinking, because change, natural and social, falls into Not-A it is experienced as disorder, as unintelligible. (Thus modern science and formal logic have long parted company, although formal logic was fully adequate for Greek science, a science specifically uninterested in problems of change.) In this brief exploration of some relations between formal logic and resistance to change, I shall look in turn at social theory, religion, and political ideology. These will be only glimpses, necessarily superficial, but they may suggest another way of thinking about a phenomenon long recognized by feminist theory: the persistent relation between conservatism and rigid gender dichotomy.

Consider first some differences between Durkheim's sociology of religion and that of Max Weber. A central concern of Weber's sociology is the role of religion as a factor in social change. In marked contrast, Durkheim's sociology of religion is not in any way useful for understanding either religious or social change, although it has proved valuable for studying religion as a source of social stability. Both men relied heavily on dichotomous distinctions, but they differed in the kinds of dichotomy they made and in how they used them. As we have seen, Durkheim's theory depended on the use of A/Not-A, not merely as a way of thinking, but also as having direct existential reference, as accurately

100

describing real religion. Weber's dichotomies were mere contrary A/B distinctions: otherworldly/innerworldly, asceticism/mysticism, and so forth. In further contrast to Durkheim, Weber did not give these distinctions direct existential reference. They were only ways of thinking about religion, 'ideal types' not real ones, 'theoretically pure', not actually pure, used only to clarify aspects of religious phenomena, not completely or directly to describe them. Weber frequently reminded his readers of this withholding of direct existential reference; for example, of 'priest' versus 'prophet': 'Yet even this distinction, which is clear enough conceptually, is fluid in actuality.'[32]

This difference is also evident in their respective attitudes to the problem of definition. (An exhaustive definition is a creation of a dichotomy, an isolation of A as distinct from everything else, which is Not-A.) Both men began the first paragraphs of their major monographs in the sociology of religion with the question of a definition of religion. Durkheim said it was impossible to begin without one and produced one based on his sacred/profane dichotomy. Weber said it was impossible to produce one at the beginning of such a work and went ahead and wrote *all* of his enormous work in the sociology of religion without ever making one.[33] The two men also differed radically in the kinds of gender distinctions they made. Although Weber cannot be called a feminist sociologist, his work is most definitely not characterized by the monolithic, unexamined, rigid, and distorting sexism that mars Durkheim's work.

In his *Logic: The Theory of Inquiry*, Dewey has shown how the attempt to retain the structure of Aristotelian logic in a world recognized to be a changing one resulted in a purely formal logic without reference to the existential world. Thinkers who still try to apply such logic directly to the world fall into traps as did Durkheim, for if you congeal the world in order to clarify it, you lose more than you gain. Because, says Dewey, we cannot simply disregard the principles of identity, contradiction, and the excluded middle, needing them as we do to order our thought, he proposes a 'functional use', very like Weber's ideal types, which

denies that affirmative and negative propositions have a one-to-one correspondence with objects as they are, but it gives them the operative and instrumental force of means of transforming an unsettled and doubtful situation into a resolved determinate one.[34]

But suppose it is not merely in our thought, but directly in the social world that we wish to transform 'an unsettled and doubtful situation into a resolved determinate one'. Suppose we want not social theory, but social order. The direct social application of A/Not-A distinctions is an effective means of achieving just that.

Louis Dumont, in *Homo Hierarchicus: an essay on the caste system*, claims that members of that most conservative of all social organizations, the Indian caste system, conceptualize it as the social elaboration of 'a single true principle, namely the opposition of the pure and the impure'.[35] This particular social order is legitimated by religion, a religion grounded in an A/Not-A distinction. (Although all religion is by no means characterized by Durkheim's sacred/profane dichotomy, many religions do insist on A/Not-A distinctions of various kinds.) We can look within our own Judaeo-Christian tradition for illustrations both of the insistence on A/Not-A dichotomy (associated with resisting change) and of abandoning dichotomy (associated with striving for change). For example, contrast the prophets (second and third) Isaiah and Ezekiel (who, as Weber observed, was more priest than prophet).

Ezekiel, whose mission was to restore a *former* order, lost in the Babylonian exile, always insisted: keep things separate, don't mix the clean and the unclean.[36] And he was also profoundly sexist, regularly identifying sin with femaleness, horrified of 'menstruous women', and utterly condemning of women who had minds of their own. 'And you, son of man, set your face against the daughters of your people who prophesy out of their own minds,' said the Lord to Ezekiel.[37]

Isaiah's mission was to tell of a *new* kingdom. 'Remember not the former things, nor consider the things of old. Behold, I am doing a new thing,' said the Lord to Isaiah.[38] In this new kingdom, dichotomous distinctions will vanish; the wolf and the lamb, who ordinarily keep discreetly separate, shall dwell together, and, Isaiah proclaimed, 'every valley shall be exalted, and every mountain and hill shall be made low'.[39] When 'the glory of the Lord shall be revealed, *all flesh* shall see it *together*.'[40] Neither the Lord nor Isaiah was fussy about gender dichotomy: 'As one whom his mother comforts, so will I comfort you,' said the Lord to Isaiah, or even more startlingly: 'You shall suck the breast of kings.'[41] There is also a remarkable passage in which the Lord unites in Himself the two halves of the dualist split, losing any clear gender identity, but solving the problem of theodicy:

I form the light and create the darkness: I make peace and create evil: I the Lord do all these things. . . . Shall the clay say to him that fashioneth it, what makest thou? Woe unto him that saith unto a father, What begettest thou? or to the woman, What hast thou brought forth?[42]

(Notice that both darkness and evil have positive reality; they are not mere privations of light or good.)

The Pauline Epistles represent both these positions: stressing dichotomous social distinctions and order, and denying dichotomy and striving for change. Paul's letters have long provided both arch-conservatives and religious revolutionaries with appropriate texts. Paul himself was an advocate of radical religious change who also needed at times to insist on order in the young church.

The Corinthians were the most wildly disordered of the early congregations. Paul scolded them for orgies and incest as well as for unfettered prophecy and speaking in tongues. It was to these enthusiasts that Paul made his most extreme and dichotomous gender distinctions.[43] For example, in 1 Cor. 11: 3, the distinction between woman and man is the same as that between man and Christ, between Christ and God. (Although this is not overtly phrased as A/Not-A, its tendency to be all-encompassing makes it suspicious.)

The Galatians, on the other hand, seem to have been conservatives, in danger of deserting the new gospel and returning to established religion, order, and the Law. To them Paul wrote a perfect expression of contradictory dichotomy abandoned for the sake of change: 'For neither circumcision counts for anything, nor uncircumcision, but a new creation.'[44] To them he also wrote, 'There is neither Jew nor Greek, there is neither slave nor free, there is neither male nor female; for you are all one in Christ Jesus.'[45]

It is clear that the degree of direct application of formal dichotomy to the social world varies within complex societies, and even from social situation to social situation. One can ask in *whose* interest it is to preserve social dichotomies, *who* experiences change as disorder. Within the Indian caste system, it is those at the top of the hierarchy who are most endangered by pollution from contact with the impure, and who have the greatest interest in maintaining the social order unchanged. It is not only women, but all inferior persons, who are kept in their place by this social application of the pure/impure dichotomy. Weber has observed: 'The religion of disprivileged classes is characterized by a tendency to allot equality to women.'[46]

The association of abandoning rigid gender dichotomy with striving for change is most obvious in revolutionary movements. This is true of the English[47] and French revolutions as well as the Chinese, which is perhaps the most dramatic example, both in degree of social change and of reduction of rigid gender dichotomy.[48] It is worth noting that traditional Chinese society, far more profoundly than the English and French aristocracies and monarchies, embodied in its very structure the principle of A/Not-A, with women in the Not-A position. This is the structure of exogamous patrilineal descent groups, in which 'A' men must always marry 'Not-A' women. Like the eternal, unchanging quality of A/Not-A, such structures are characterized, as Meyer Fortes has said, by 'presumed perpetuity in time'.[49]

Turning to our own society, the association between conservative political thought and the insistence on rigid gender distinctions is clear.

The feminist movement in this country grew out of an attempt to bring about social change, to abolish another social dichotomy, the movement to end slavery. And it was revitalized in the 1960s along with massive resistance to racial barriers and the emergence of other kinds of movements for social change and 'alternative lifestyles'. Now, in a new conservatism (as it were, an Ezekiel-like attempt to restore a lost social order), the Republican Party, for the first time in forty years, has failed to endorse the Equal Rights Amendment.

Attention to relations between conservatism and dichotomous thinking seems particularly important for feminist theory because of the great susceptibility of gender distinction to A/Not-A phrasing. The exclusively binary structure of gender distinctions may explain this susceptibility, but not why women, rather than men, are so consistently put in the Not-A position. Those who seek an 'origin' for this widespread tendency need to look elsewhere than to Durkheim for help. They may, perhaps, do better looking at individual development, where, in the process that Margaret S. Mahler[50] has called 'separation-individuation', an I/Not-I experience of the self or ego as distinct from all the rest of the world (known and knowable) comes into being. Because infancy begins in undifferentiated union with the mother, separation from *her* is fundamental in this process. Thus all those who, for whatever reason, tend towards formally dichotomous thinking, have at the roots of their development an experience of femaleness in a Not-A position. The degree of rigidity, of impermeable ego boundaries, of intolerance for continuity, developed in this process is, of course, influenced by many factors, including social structural ones. (Notice, by the way, the great degree of continuity that Isaiah accepts both with women *and* with infancy. This is in sharp contrast to Ezekiel.)

No doubt there are other, and perhaps better, ways to understand why women are so regularly Not-A. It is far easier to understand why almost any ideology based on A/Not-A dichotomy is effective in resisting change. Those whose understanding of society is ruled by such ideology find it very hard to conceive of the possibility of alternative forms of social order (third possibilities). Within such thinking, the only alternative to the *one* order is disorder.

NOTES

My thanks to Rosalind Ladd for help with philosophical concepts and to Nancy Chodorow, Robert Jay, Sherry Ortner, Rayna Rapp, Michelle Rosaldo, and Kurt Wolff for criticism and encouragement.

1 Emile Durkheim, *The Elementary Forms of the Religious Life*, trans. Joseph Ward Swain (London: George Allen and Unwin, 1915), p. 9.
2 ibid., p. 9.

3 ibid., p. 145.
4 ibid., p. 37.
5 ibid., p. 212.
6 ibid., p. 38-9.
7 Actually, Australian women do take part peripherally in some men's rituals, and they also have their own rituals from which men are excluded. See Phyllis M. Kaberry, *Aboriginal Women, Sacred and Profane* (New York: Philadelphia: Blackstone, 1939). The male ethnographers who were Durkheim's source did not describe women's rituals, and Durkheim himself gave little significance to women's marginal role in men's rituals. But I am not trying here to test the accuracy of Durkheim's description of Australian religion, rather to follow out some consequences of his theory.
8 For example, Durkheim, *Elementary Forms*, pp. 120, 126, 137-9, 303-5, 319.
9 Emile Durkheim, *The Division of Labor in Society*, trans. George Simpson (New York: The Free Press, 1964), p. 60.
10 ibid., pp. 57-8.
11 Durkheim does devote much of his conclusion to claiming to show the origin of logic and 'logical thought' in society through religion, but he limits himself to examining logical thought as 'conceptual thought' and does not touch on problems of identity, contradiction, and the excluded middle.
12 Durkheim, *Elementary Forms*, p. 9.
13 Morris R. Cohen and Ernest Nagel, *An Introduction to Logic and Scientific Method* (New York: Harcourt, Brace and Co., 1934), p. 187.
14 Durkheim, *Elementary Forms*, pp. 40-1.
15 A/Not-A dichotomy will not work for propositions in the world either, for the truth of these can change as with the proposition 'I am hungry', which is sometimes true and sometimes not true.
16 Durkheim, *Elementary Forms*, p. 40.
17 ibid., p. 318.
18 Cf. M. Kay Martin and Barbara Voorhies, *Female of the Species* (New York: Columbia University Press, 1975), ch. 4. For how this leap is managed, see Harold Garfinkel, *Studies in Ethnomethodology* (Englewood Cliffs, N.J.: Prentice Hall, 1967), pp. 116-85.
19 John Dewey, *Logic: The Theory of Inquiry* (New York: Holt, 1938), p. 192.
20 Nancy Chodorow, *The Reproduction of Mothering: Psychoanalysis and the Sociology of Gender* (Berkeley, Calif.: University of California Press, 1978).
21 Quoted in G.E.R. Lloyd, *Polarity and Analogy: Two Types of Argumentation in Early Greek Thought* (Cambridge: Cambridge University Press, 1966), p. 23.
22 ibid., p. 65.
23 W.E.H. Stanner, 'Reflections on Durkheim and Aboriginal religion', in *Social Organization: Essays Presented To Raymond Firth*, ed. Maurice Freedman (Chicago: Aldine, 1967), p. 232.
24 Marie Bonaparte, 'Passivity, masochism and femininity', in *Psychoanalysis and Female Sexuality*, ed. Hendrik M. Ruitenbeek (New Haven, Conn.: College and University Press, 1966), p. 136. Bonaparte is here citing the ideas of 'the great biologist Maranon', but she claims he 'was in the right'. ibid., p. 132.
25 Perry Miller, *The New England Mind: The Seventeenth Century* (Boston, Mass.: Beacon Press, 1961), pp. 111-53.
26 David O. Hall (ed.), *The Antinomian Controversy, 1636-1638: A Documentary*

History (Middletown, Conn.: Wesleyan University Press, 1968), p. 383. Italics in original.

27 ibid., p. 372.

28 Dewey, *Logic*, p. 346.

29 For good discussions, see Jack Goody, 'Religion and ritual: the definitional problem', *British Journal of Sociology*, 12 (1961): 142–64; Steven Lukes, *Emile Durkheim, His Life and Work: A Historical and Critical Study* (New York: Harper and Row, 1972), pp. 24–8; and Stanner, 'Reflections'.

30 Stanner, 'Reflections', pp. 229–30.

31 Lloyd Warner, *A Black Civilization: A Study of an Australian Tribe*, rev. edn (New York: Harper and Row, 1937).

32 Max Weber, *The Sociology of Religion*, trans. Ephraim Fischoff (Boston: Beacon Press, 1963), p. 29.

33 I am indebted to Karen Fields for this observation about Max Weber.

34 Dewey, *Logic*, p. 198.

35 Louis Dumont, *Homo Hierarchicus; an essay on the caste system*, trans. Mark Sainsbury (Chicago: University of Chicago Press, 1970), p. 43.

36 For example, Ezek. 22: 26; 44: 23.

37 Ezek. 13: 17.

38 Isa. 43: 18–19.

39 Isa. 40: 4.

40 Isa. 40: 5 (emphasis added).

41 Isa. 66: 13; 60: 16.

42 Isa. 45: 7–10.

43 1 Corinthians also contains a passage (14: 34–6) used for centuries of legitimate untold repression: 'the women should keep silence in the churches. For they are not permitted to speak, but should be subordinate as even the law says. . . .' This passage is almost certainly a later interpolation. In both vocabulary and theology it is unlike anything else by Paul. See William O. Walker, Jr, 'First Corinthians 11: 2–16 and Paul's views regarding women', *Journal of Biblical Literature*, 94 (March 1975), pp. 94–110. It is not surprising, however, that it was interpolated into 1 Corinthians; it would never fit in Galatians.

44 Gal. 6: 15.

45 Gal. 3: 28.

46 Weber, *Sociology of Religion*, p. 104.

47 Keith V. Thomas, 'Women and the civil war sects', *Past and Present*, 13 (April 1958): pp. 42–62.

48 Judith Stacey, 'When patriarchy kowtows: the significance of the Chinese family revolution for feminist theory', *Feminist Studies* 2, no. 2–3 (1975), pp. 64–112.

49 Meyer Fortes, 'The structure of unilineal descent groups', *American Anthropologist*, 55 (1953), pp. 17–41.

50 Margaret S. Mahler, in collaboration with Manuel Furer, *On Human Symbiosis and the Vicissitudes of Individuation, vol. 1: Infantile Psychosis* (New York: International Universities Press, 1968).

Part IV

FEMINISM AND SUBJECTIVITY

INTRODUCTION
Philipa Rothfield

There are so many different ways of understanding what it is that we are. Some regard humanity as having an immutable essence, or attribute to every living creature a soul.[1] Others posit that the nature of humans changes, tying such changes to the ways in which the subject is inscribed in discourses, or is produced through ideology, or is a reflection of the spirit of a particular age (*Zeitgeist*).[2] Some of these accounts exhibit a teleological bent, others are more inclined to privilege material determinations or the machinations of history. It may not be possible, nor even desirable, to produce a singular account of human subjectivity.[3] A more productive approach might be to argue that there are multiple determinants of the self, some self-produced, some socially determined, and that there are multiple *discourses* on the self, evidencing different interests and perspectives on subjectivity. Depending on which account one might choose, different factors have been posited as determining difference amongst subjects (people). In particular, sexuality, sexual difference, religion, race, and ethnicity have operated as categories to identify difference. These differences have been exploited at times so as to facilitate forms of domination. The identification and significance of difference is one thing, but it is the *interpretation* and *evaluation* of difference which enables differential social actions. Sometimes, the very identification of a group is intertwined with its social treatment (see Foucault's work on madness and incarceration), and sometimes the identification of a group also encourages its emancipation (see Marx's work on the self-identification of the working class as a potentially revolutionary act).

There are two senses to identification which I would like to highlight. One sense would regard identification as a reference to an objective, given reality, such as religious preference. Another looks at the process of identification as intrinsic to the very production of difference. Of course, the productive sense may very well utilise objective elements as its means of identification, such as skin colour or sexual identity. However, the act of identification is seen to be embedded in a discursive process which characterizes the very nature of that which is selected. This latter emphasis on the productive nature of identification and difference relates to the work of Foucault who looks at discourse, the constitution of knowledge and its relationship to power. The artist, Mary Kelly, also discusses 'the construction of femininity as a representation of difference within a specific discourse'.[4] She attempts to *re-present* sexual difference or subvert it through a variety of means and media. In her work, *Interim*,[5] she interrogates femininity, fashion, and ageing through pictures of fashion clothes and highlighted snippets of conversation between women in cafés. In this piece, one can see her decision not to include figures of women (in the clothes) because of the tendency to see such bodies in conventional ways – ways she is attempting to de-centre.

An implication of the productive kind of approach to subjectivity is that it is not a fixed process. It therefore has appeal for some perspectives which are looking to change the 'givens' of subjectivity. Feminism is one such discourse.

Feminists have drawn attention to the question of *sexual difference* and its relation to subjectivity. The identification of sexual difference is prevalent in all societies – although its manner of representation, and the social practices which surround it, vary. For feminists, the elements of sexual differences are vital to understand if we are to apprehend and change the workings of patriarchy. Such understandings have proved to be multifarious. If post-modernist theory is to engage fruitfully with feminism, I think one of its benefits will be to provide support for a heterogeneity of feminist discourses and the usage of a wide spectrum of materials.

In the early days of the women's liberation movement, feminists argued for a distinction between sex and gender: sex is assigned at birth, whereas one's gender is socially produced. Together, they form the sexually differentiated person. This was a fundamental position regarding male and female subjectivity. It characterized sex-role behaviour as that which is socially produced as appropriate activity for men and women. Often, the notion of socialization is invoked to stand for the process by which social expectations and roles are internalized.[6] At the time, the sex/gender distinction was considered an important rebuttal to those who wanted to say men and women are essentially different, and that male-dominance has a biological and (hence) immutable basis. The opposition between innate and learned behaviour was a prominent controversy. The distinction was also used to counter sociobiology, a contemporary of the movement, which attempted to understand human behaviour in terms of animal and biological research, and to give humanistic studies the stamp of scientificity.[7] The sex/gender distinction was extremely important to the aims of the WLM in the 1970s. If gender rather than sex is the aspect of our subjectivities which constitutes masculinity and femininity, and it is socio-culturally produced, then it can be changed. Easier said than done. Writers such as Millett argued for an end to sex-role differences, the domain of gender difference. In her paper, Moira Gatens critically looks at what it is that the sex/gender distinction says about our subjectivity.

The sex/gender distinction no longer takes precedence in feminist writings on subjectivity and sexual difference. There are now several paths of approach. One group has taken up psychoanalytic theory. Initially, feminists of the early 1970s found little of interest in Freudian psychoanalysis with its emphasis on the penis and its assertion of female penis-envy. Kate Millett delivered an historic critique of Freud's bias towards the male. Juliet Mitchell's response to this, *Psychoanalysis and Feminism*, was a watershed defence of the utility of Freudian theory for feminism. One of the central problems in Freud's work is the apparent ahistoricity of his complexes, the Oedipal and more importantly, the Castration. The latter two are the most central factors in the determination of sexual difference for Freud. If history or society (patriarchy) has nothing to do with those elements which determine sexual difference and the meaning of masculinity and femininity, then perhaps sexual difference and the centrality of male sexuality – the phallus – is immutable. Mitchell argued instead that it is important to heed an account of subjectivity that relates to male dominance at the social level. Whilst perhaps not a simple reflection of patriarchy, it may be that the Freudian story allows us to understand how subjectivity, sexuality and sexual difference is constituted within patriarchy. The point was a decisive and influential one for the following reason – it represents an interest in the determinations of patriarchy on its male and female subjects, and a preparedness to look at writing which centres upon the male, or, masculinity, or, that which it represent, phallocentricity.[8] Prior to Mitchell, any feminist theory which showed women as somehow subject to the determinations of patriarchy would have been considered dubious to say the least. As it is, many feminists regard psychoanalysis with suspicion.

The question and role of history in feminist theory is addressed in various places. Feminists with a socialist (materialist) orientation have been careful to include the role of history in their modes of explanation. This means that the dynamics of sexual difference require an historical dimension to their characterization. This is the very issue which Teresa Brennan identifies and analyses within the context of contemporary feminist readings of psychoanalysis. She argues that there is an impasse at present between the terrains of feminism and psychoanalysis, which is creating a tension for the politics of feminism and the issue of change. She is thus addressing the feminist suspicion of psychoanalytic theory as regards political change. Brennan looks at the psychoanalytic theory of Lacan and the issue of the historical in one of his registers, the

111

Imaginary. She characterizes some of the dilemmas facing any feminist appropriation of Lacan, and the way in which the politics of feminism in this context cluster around the question of the historical. If the avowed phallocentricity of Lacanian theory is not tied to any particular historical reality, what hope for change?

Amidst the waxing fortunes of semiotics, structuralism, and post-structuralism came the theoretical elaborations of anti-humanism and a de-centred subjectivity. Anti-humanism depends in part upon the identification of the humanistic enterprise which is evident in post-Enlightenment philosophy, from Kant, through to empiricism and liberalism. The emphasis in anti-humanism is away from the self-creating individual of humanism – the knowing subject – and towards positing outside forces as the determining factors. Thus, Althusser's anti-humanist Marxism asserts the process of ideology as that which produces the subject. The ideological level is in turn said to be ultimately determined by the material level – all external social forces.[9] Foucault's approach is rather to look at relations of power, sexuality, and knowledge in the production of sexual difference through our continual participation in discursive institutions and the socio-cultural process. Alongside French anti-humanism, there are those who have taken pains to trace the origins of humanism in the historical productions of modernity.[10] Janet Wolff raises the issue of the gendered nature of the subject of modernity.[11]

Finally, one of the more recent topics for feminism and subjectivity is that of the body. Through the work of Luce Irigaray in particular, there is a good deal of interest in the body and sexual difference. Moira Gatens' paper discusses the body from a variety of perspectives. She introduces the body through her critique of the sex/gender distinction, which presupposes that the body is some *tabula rasa* upon which the productions of gender are inscribed. Gatens develops an alternative perspective to this in which the body is always to be situated socially and historically. She further examines the body in relation to questions of biology, masculinity/femininity, and the Imaginary.

The two papers in this section represent a diversity of feminist engagements with subjectivity. Each is concerned to highlight critically the relevance of certain themes. Brennan examines the relations between psychoanalysis, politics and feminism, and Gatens, the sex/gender distinction and the body. And each is a critical contribution to our understanding of such matters.

NOTES

1 Religious systems in particular espouse an essential spiritual nature or suggest timeless truths.

2 Foucault's work and other post-structuralist, cultural analyses look at the relations between subjectivity and discourse. Semiotic film analysis, Michel Pecheux, and the work of the Birmingham Centre for Cultural Studies all exhibit an interest in these connections. Althusser's structuralist Marxism is the strongest statement regarding the production of the subject through ideology, whereby our total subjectivity is a product of the workings of ideology. The connection between self and *Zeitgeist* derives from Hegel.

3 Mary Kelly expresses this view in an interview, 'No essential femininity, a conversation between Mary Kelly and Paul Smith', *Parachute*, Vol. 26 (Spring, 1982).

4 Kelly (1982), p. 32.

5 For its reproduction, see *Mary Kelly Interim* (Fruitmarket Gallery, Kettle's Yard, and Riverside Studios, 1986).

6 For a powerful critique of socialization theory, see *Changing the Subject. Psychology, Social Regulation and Subjectivity*, Henriques, Hollway *et al.* (London: Methuen, 1984), esp. Chapter 1.

7 The conclusions of sociobiology tended towards the reactionary.

8 It is thus in the slipstream of such a shift that we find Laura Mulvey's film criticism which sees all film viewing as subject to the structuring dominance of the male gaze.

9 See Althusser, 'Ideology and ideological state apparatuses', in *Lenin and Philosophy* (Monthly Review Press, 1971).

10 See Charles Taylor's introduction to *Hegel* (Cambridge University Press, 1975), and John Rundell, *Origins of Modernity. The Origins of Modern Social Theory from Kant to Hegel to Marx* (Cambridge: Polity Press, 1987).

11 In a paper entitled, 'The invisible flâneuse', Wolff looks at the literature of, or on, modernity, for example, by Baudelaire, Simmel, and Benjamin, and points out the social invisibility of women in these texts. She identifies Baudelaire's *Flâneur* (city stroller) – a person engaging in the *public* side of city life. This is at the very time in which the creation of separate spheres was pursued in the developing economies of capitalism. The attribution of women to the private sphere appears to have rendered them invisible for these texts of modernity and their concern with the public, urban, nature of existence. She projects a demand for a feminist sociology of modernity. See Janet Wolff, 'The invisible flâneuse', in *Culture, Theory, Society*, Volume 2, No. 3, Winter, 1985.

AN IMPASSE IN PSYCHOANALYSIS AND FEMINISM

Teresa Brennan

For over a decade, debates on psychoanalysis and feminism have foundered on a political issue. The issue is change: what is the relation between psychoanalytic theory and the socio-historical concerns of feminist strategies?[1] With reservations, Mitchell (1974) approached psychoanalysis as a tool for the socio-historical analysis of women's oppression; she saw it as a potential adjunct to a materialist theory of ideology. Using Freud and Lacan (who dominates the debate) Mitchell said that potentially, possibly, psychoanalysis theorised a socio-historical product. In this, it theorised something mutable.

The notion that psychoanalysis extends socialization or ideology theories was problematic from the outset. Those who opposed the feminist appropriation of psychoanalysis did so as they thought the theory was ahistorical. Later, those who endorsed that appropriation made a related point. Jane Gallop (1982) criticized Mitchell precisely because she tried to stay 'within the bounds of feminism'. Gallop argued that Mitchell made Lacan's theory of desire contingent; and that in doing so she misread Lacan. Gallop attributed the misreading to Mitchell's desire to uncover a feminist 'prescription for action' (1982: 11). The implicit meaning of this is that a contingent reading is a socio-historical one; and socio-historical theories underlie prescriptions for action. There are two ways of taking Gallop's criticism. One is that if 'desire' (and whatever it implies) is non-contingent, politics are based on illusion. Perhaps feeling along these lines contributes to the increasing popularity of textual strategies. Alternatively, Gallop's criticism of Mitchell could mean that 'prescriptions for action' have to be limited, or informed about what is and is not mutable.[2]

As far as the reading of Lacan goes, Mitchell had already changed. At the point when Gallop published her criticism, Mitchell together with Jacqueline Rose (1982) marked out a different position from that proposed in *Psychoanalysis and Feminism*. Mitchell and Rose argue that psychoanalysis is not a socialization theory, nor an extension of the theory of ideology. For them, psychoanalysis is not (primarily) a theory of how socially created sexual relations are internalized. It is about the

114

construction, rather than the internalization, of sexual difference. Most of what they write suggests that this construction is trans-historical, but this is not spelt out in terms. In fact one of the problems with their position is that it is defined in the negative. For instance they criticize Nancy Chodorow (1978) for 'sociologizing' psychoanalysis.[3] Chodorow argues that the psychical evidence of psychoanalytic theories could be explained by a socio-historical fact: women are responsible for the early nurturing of children. In saying that Chodorow 'sociologizes' psychoanalysis, Mitchell and Rose seem to say that (Lacan's) psychoanalytic account cannot be reduced to socio-historical facts, be they mothering or something else.

At the same time, Rose and Mitchell are acutely aware of the socio-historical rationale of feminist political action, and are evidently committed to it. For this reason I am taking their position as pivotal in this article; and will concentrate on the difficulties it represents. It is in no sense an apolitical position (Rose is critical of 'the dissipation of politics into a writing strategy').[4] Much French feminist, psychoanalytic writing is represented as apolitical. Toril Moi (1985) levels this charge against Irigaray, Cixous, and (with qualifications) Kristeva, writers she otherwise finds valuable. Written in a less politically conscious feminist context, psychoanalytically inclined French theories on women and the feminine concentrate more on controversies over femininity. Psychoanalytic theories of femininity, and the notion that women are psychically disadvantaged by the lack of a penis, have been central to the Anglo-American feminist critiques of Freud for some time. They have been just as important for recent French work on Freud and Lacan, particularly Irigaray's. In general, such work on femininity and its relation to the penis is not cast in relation to the feminist issue of change, ideology and history that I focus on here. While I will try to indicate in passing where the controversies over femininity intersect with the socio-historical question, that question occupies most of this article. But as 'femininity' and 'ideology' are obviously related, Mitchell and Rose again represent a good point of departure. When writing on Lacan and femininity, they represent (some of) the difficulties the French texts represent, while they write in a more socially oriented context.

When psychoanalysis is presented in a socialization account, or an extension of the theory of ideology, the cause(s) of women's oppression can be pinpointed in certain social relations which can be acted on. But if one agrees (as I do) that psychical sexuality cannot be reduced to 'sociology' then the political implications of psychoanalysis are not straightforward. The fact that the implications are unstated signals an impasse for psychoanalysis and feminism.

The nature of this impasse should be clarified. I mean that the relation between the psychoanalytic theory of psychical sexuality and the socio-historical concerns of feminism should be clarified. This is the condition of rethinking the political issues. As things stand the political implications of psychoanalysis for feminism are still being sidestepped. For instance the most recent contribution to the psychoanalytic, feminist discussions (Sayers 1986) assumes that the psychology of women's oppression has 'social and historical determinants'. In her timely, critical survey of key contributions to the debates on psychoanalysis and feminism, Janet Sayers is aware of the complexity of the psychoanalytic account of sexuality's formation. She dismisses Chodorow's and like accounts which explain gender difference in terms of internalized social relations. Yet her own account begins from and concludes with the notion that psychical reality is *determined* by material reality (Sayers 1986: ix and 179). As the burden of the idea that psychoanalysis cannot be 'sociologized' is that there is more to psychical sexuality than socio-historical determinants, this once more avoids the issue.

Why is the issue avoided? As I said, part of the problem is that Mitchell and Rose, who have carried the discussion so far in other respects, nevertheless define their own position negatively. Moreover it is not always clear where Mitchell's later use of Lacan differs from her initial, more socio-historical approach. The next section of this paper attempts to clarify these issues by returning to Mitchell's *Psychoanalysis and Feminism* and the origins of feminist interest in psychoanalysis. It shows how the case for psychoanalysis was allied to the critique of essentialism. In the first instance the feminist critique of essentialism was a critique of ahistoricism. After this I turn to the arguments in Mitchell and Rose (1982). These arguments remain anti-essentialist but the critique of essentialism has a different basis (Section II). In abbreviated comments on Lacan I try to indicate what the difference involves (Section III). Once the difference is drawn out, the basis of the socialization critique, and the nature of the impasse, are plainer. I then suggest that psychical sexuality has certain structural trans-historical determinants, but that it is also, necessarily, a socio-historical product. In filling this out I take Rose (1982) as a point of departure (Section IV). This last section indicates how the relation between psychical sexuality and socio-historical issues can be reformulated without abandoning social history one the one hand, or on the other, glossing over how the psyche is formed (in part) outside it.

Finally, a difficulty in writing this paper was that the issues it addresses have been pursued by fairly separate groups of feminist theorists. Work on the socio-historical dimensions of women's oppression has diverged from that on Lacanian psychoanalysis. The difficulty concerned how much of Lacan (and psychoanalytic theory) to take for granted. My brief exposition of Lacan presupposes some familiarity with him, but I concentrate on the socio-historical issues.

116

I

Althusser's Marxism (on which Mitchell relied) saw ideology as more than beliefs determined by economic social relations. Yet ideology remained grounded in the mode of production in the admittedly tardy last instance. For Marxist-feminism, the idea that psychoanalysis could supplement the theory of ideology meant this: psychoanalysis addressed sexuality, and Marxism needed a theory which did precisely that. Perhaps psychoanalysis could theorise the lived experience of sexual oppression, provided that psychoanalytic findings fitted the socio-historical conditions of oppression. Very generally, it was thought that psychoanalysis may elucidate the beliefs or material practices which devolved from those conditions, in the same way that the theory of ideology explained social beliefs and practices devolving from the mode of production. Of course, before the analytic findings could be said or seen to fit them, the conditions themselves needed to be established. And rightly, these conditions are still debated.

While Althusser's Marxism presupposes that the mode(s) of production anchor ideology, the notion of a relation between specific conditions of oppression on the one hand, and practices and beliefs perpetuating them on the other, is consistent with a more widespread feminist proposition. This is the notion that the conditions of women's oppression are socio-historically grounded; and that consciousness reflects their socio-historical content. While Marxist-feminism has traditionally (but not exclusively) looked to the economic, other feminisms have sought other conditions: a popular candidate is kinship structures, mothering is a second. The assumption that guides the search is that provided that the conditions of oppression are or can be made historically specific, they can be acted on politically. This is the basic reason for rejecting essentialist theories.

The now well-established critique of essentialist theories is based on the idea that because they assume or postulate an innate factor, they are basically akin to biological theories which ground women's inferiority in something natural. What is natural is not social or historical. Therefore, it cannot be changed.[5] Mitchell's early emphasis on ideology was consistent with a materialist feminism opposed to any form of ahistorical essentialism. In arguing against the received feminist wisdom about Freud, Mitchell said he 'precisely did *not* believe things were biological, instinctual and changeless; he thought they were cultural' (1974: 324). Freud's psychoanalysis was valuable because it was not essentialist.

This non-essentialist psychoanalysis attracted women who experienced their femininity as intractable, but did not believe it immutable. The interest in psychoanalysis was prompted by more than an abstract desire to extend the theory of ideology. Henriques *et al.* wrote that feminism turned to psychoanalysis to theorize issues brought up by its emphasis on consciousness-change: on contradictions between what is deemed politically correct and what is desired and the consequent question of *how women change their construction as feminine.*

(1984: 7; emphasis added)

By 1974, when psychoanalysis became an issue for English-speaking feminism, it was clear that collusive feelings do not change by polemical fiat. Many women experienced conflict between feminist reason and sexist desire. Mitchell's major initiative appealed to those whose reason insisted that if desire persisted in spite of its rational dismissal, it must be anchored in irrationality. If consciousness rejected a debilitating romanticism in theory, yet it survived, it must be anchored in something . . . unconscious. Freud's is the theory of the irrational unconscious. Whatever its patriarchal dross, it was 'fatal for feminism' to refuse it.

One could (and did) criticize *Psychoanalysis and Feminism* by contrasting its author's rendering of Freud with Freud's unequivocal biological statements. This criticism is standard. Michèle Barrett takes this approach (1980). So to some extent does Elizabeth Wilson (1981). Critics are preoccupied by Freud's biologism, because it seems essentialist, beyond the reach of social history, thus beyond change. To date, Mitchell has not engaged with her critics' concern with change. What she had done is to insist that Freud is about the psychical, not the biological. Both ways, the arguments here walk past each other. In retrospect, I suggest that the reality is that Mitchell was starting something new. Yet she to some degree, and certainly her critics, were trapped by the existing terms of debate. Her reasoning overall is that the logic of Freud's discoveries runs counter to the biological explanation he sometimes has recourse to;[6] and that Lacan's theory fills the explanatory gap Freud filled with biology. Effectively Mitchell says that it does not really matter if Freud is sometimes biological. What matters is that he shows how deep run the non-biological currents in human sexual identity. We shall see that the trap set by the existing terms of debate is that these 'non-biological currents' are not synonymous with 'socio-historical determinants'.

Mitchell also stressed that Freud's account of sexual difference is not complete (1974: 286). What Freud said psychoanalysis lacks is what some women want: namely a theory of femininity. *Psychoanalysis and Feminism* did not attempt to build on the theory of femininity as such. It did offer a general theory of patriarchy. Mitchell's concluding chapters argue through Freud and Lévi-Strauss that patriarchy is anchored in the exchange of women and the extended incest taboo. A taboo proscribing incest among an extended kin network is irrelevant to the logic of capitalist market exchange. Because it makes this extended network

118

irrelevant, capitalism, by its own contradictions, gives us hope. It seems to follow that if patriarchy goes, femininity will change. I will leave out further details of Mitchell's theory of patriarchy, kinship and any disagreement with them. It is enough for here that Mitchell seeks to isolate the social conditions producing patriarchy, in order to struggle against them. She makes those conditions historically specific. Thus the structure of her argument places Mitchell amongst the feminist writers who argue for a particular condition which has to change before patriarchy can be overthrown.

In short, in one respect, the structure of her argument is consistent with a firmly established association between the historically mutable and the politically actionable. Now since *Psychoanalysis and Feminism*, Marxism and Althusser's theory have been thrown into question (if not thrown out) in critical discussions on sexuality, and some on feminist politics. The notion of acting on the supposedly linear sweep of class-directed history has been somewhat displaced by that of intervening in specific sites of intersecting practices. The meaning of the term 'ideology' has also changed. But the contrast between socially structured ideas which can change, and natural givens which can't, persists.[7]

One reason for covering well covered territory in the preceding paragraphs was to show how in the initial stages of the psychoanalytic discussions, psychical factors were contrasted with non-biological ones. That contrast correlates with the political principle that what is socially done can be socially undone. I think this contrast contributed to the ideal that psychical reality was the product of social history, even though Mitchell stressed (again and again) that psychoanalysis was about the unconscious and its laws. But what did that mean? In retrospect, Mitchell was saying, or beginning to say, that the psychical really was about something other than biological or social determinants. Yet if psychoanalysis was also about ideology, it had to be about how ideas come from socio-historical relations. Significantly, in *Psychoanalysis and Feminism* Mitchell placed a caveat on this notion. It had yet to be seen how closely 'the analysis of ideology is tied . . . to a logic of sexual struggle'. She also queried how adequately psychoanalysis analyses 'ideology and sexuality, and if it does so, what is the political practice that follows from this theory?' (1974: xxii–iii).

II

In 1984 Mitchell wrote of her early work that she was 'still hoping it would prove possible to use psychoanalysis as an incipient science of the ideology of patriarchy – of how we come to live ourselves as feminine or masculine within patriarchal societies' (1984: 221). The implication of this is that the hope was misplaced. In which case we need to know why.

Rose and Mitchell in *Feminine Sexuality*, albeit indirectly, contribute to the answer.

The purpose of their book was to present some of Lacan's writings on femininity. In this, its reference point to the early feminist interest in psychoanalysis is to the problem of femininity. It would be very interesting to discuss how far Lacan's understanding of 'woman' illuminates Freud's unanswered questions on femininity, but I do not do that here. For while *Feminine Sexuality* is not about social relations as such, some of the material in Rose and Mitchell's introductions bears on why the relation between the psyche and the social is hard to formulate. Given my particular concerns in this paper, I am concentrating on this peripheral aspect of the book, rather than its contribution to theorizing femininity.

However, to help situate its socio-historical bearing, I will refer briefly to debates within psychoanalytic feminisms over the 'place' of femininity. For a related reason, although I have presupposed broad familiarity with Lacan's theory, I want to draw attention to the difference between his symbolic and imaginary orders. A major debate *within* psychoanalytic feminisms (as distinct from the socio-historical debates that intersect them) centres over where femininity is 'located'. Irigaray, Cixous and Kristeva think femininity is closer to, part of the imaginary. Rose and Mitchell comment that this pushes femininity outside the symbolic, and that the feminine side of sexual difference, as much as the masculine, has to be situated within it. To do otherwise is to make femininity into something innate (essential). At first glance, there seems no reason why femininity should become essential by virtue of its placement in the imaginary. In practice, when it is located there it is (as far as I am aware) always allied to the biology of the female body; and Adams has argued that the alliance is inescapable.[8]

For Lacan, the imaginary is the place that both precedes and co-exists with the symbolic in psychical development. One difference between the symbolic and imaginary is that the latter is the arena of fantasy allied with misperception, delusions of complete unity with another, and *imagined* relations of other kinds. The imaginary is not reducible to its deluded aspects. It is also what it sounds like: it is the world of sensory images. But I am concerned with its fantasmatic aspects here. The symbolic acts as 'a break' on the imaginary. In its most familiar, Oedipal form, the symbolic (as the 'symbolic father'/phallus) breaks up the infant's imaginary fantasies of union with the mother. In Lacan's theory the symbolic father not only breaks up the imaginary mother/child dyad. When it does so, it founds the symbolic order capable of breaking through fantasy. In this more general form, it is the ability to symbolize; to communicate through language. It is the logical capacity and ability to reason which breaks up the closed circle of imaginary thinking. In everyday experience, the symbolic is evident in the logic that puts, for example, imaginary fears into perspective. In the analytic, therapeutic situation, its presence is felt through a different chain of reasoning, found in free association.

There will be more on the symbolic and its relation to 'non-essentialist' sexual difference shortly. To begin again on the socio-historical issues: as I indicated, the short answer on why psychoanalysis cannot be a direct adjunct to a materialist theory of ideology is this. While it is non-essentialist in a highly specific sense, Lacan's account of the symbolic constitution of sexual difference cannot be made historically contingent. His theory of sexual difference overlaps with but it is not identical to the feminist critique of essentialism: it is a non-essentialist theory, but it is not a socio-historical theory. Before saying why in detail I want to point out that this ambiguity leads to confusion in a first reading of *Feminine Sexuality*. In passing, both Mitchell and Rose use language which because of its previous associations, suggests that the advantage of psychoanalysis is that it is a theory about sexuality as a socio-historical product. As their intention is to not to show this, but rather to show why Lacan's theory cannot be made contingent or 'sociologized', it is worth clearing up any confusion that language occasions.

More specifically: in *Feminine Sexuality* Lacan's reading of Freud is upheld as the one that eliminates Freud's biologistic residues in favour of a social account. Other analysts are criticized because they locate the origins of femininity in female biology, and thus fall back on the body.

> If . . . the actual body is seen as a motive for the constitution of the subject in its male or female sexuality, then an *historical or symbolic* dimension to this constitution is precluded. Freud's intention was to establish that very dimension as the *sine qua non* of the construction of the human subject. It is on this dimension that Lacan bases his entire account of sexual difference.
>
> (Mitchell 1982: 17; first emphases added)

Given that biological psychoanalysis specifically and essentialism generally were found wanting because they made sexual identity immutable, one can be forgiven for concluding that Lacan is preferable because he does not. However, Lacan's relation to history is complex. There is a socio-historical dimension in the imaginary, but the symbolic constitution of sexual difference is not historical in the sense that feminism, especially Marxist-feminism, uses that term. Elsewhere in *Feminine Sexuality* it is evident that the symbolic is only 'historical' by analogy. Freud called on Lamarck; on the acquired inheritance of a mythical prehistoric event to explain how it was that the subject acquired its Oedipal history so rapidly and often in the absence of the real father (Mitchell and Rose (eds) 1982: 14 and 36). Lacan said the same things were explained as effects of language. Language of course is social. But as Lacan links his explanation of sexual difference on the *structure* of language, that explanation cannot be historically specific *of itself*. In fact the reason I use the term 'socio-historical' throughout this chapter is to distinguish the socially mutable from the 'social', given that language is both social, yet structurally, trans-historical. In Lacan's theory, 'social' does not mean mutable, and sometimes 'historical' doesn't either.

As mentioned, Lacan's theory seems to have an affinity with feminism, because it is a 'non-natural' theory of sexual difference. Consider Rose:

> It is the strength of the concept of the symbolic that it systematically repudiates any account of sexuality which assumes the pre-given nature of sexual difference – the polemic within psychoanalysis and the challenge to any such 'nature' by feminism appear at their closest here.
>
> (Rose 1982: 45)

Immediately Rose points out that there is a problem with this 'closeness'. She writes that Lacan's early understanding of the symbolic 'is open to the same objections as Lévi-Strauss's account (on whom Lacan relied) in that it presupposes the subordination which it is intended to explain' (1982: 45). While it is clearly Rose's intention to show that there is more to this 'closeness' than is apparent, it needs to be stressed that it is very problematic indeed. Otherwise, the critique of sociologizing (below) makes no sense. For feminism, a non-natural explanation was significant because it was allied with the idea that sexual identity had historically specific mutable determinants. Lacan's non-natural account of sexual difference (in the symbolic) does not allow for change down the line of history. It does allow for it on the lateral level of the present. As both Mitchell and Rose establish, Lacan insists on the fact that the categories 'masculine' and 'feminine' are not fixed by biology. This shifts the concept of bisexuality – not an undifferentiated sexual nature prior to symbolic difference (Freud's earlier sense), but the availability to all subjects of both positions in relation to that difference itself (Rose 1982: 49, n. 14).

In sum, in terms of its historical connotations, the value accorded non-essentialism has changed. Non-essentialism now has a quasi-structural reference point. Yet the original non-essentialist ideal still has a defensive use. Mitchell shows how Freud's concept of femininity was lost in the first psychoanalytic debate on sexuality; Rose how Lacan's related concept is currently under siege. In both cases an idea of femininity which is non-biological is challenged by an essential femininity. For instance Freud's 'culturalist' opponent Karen Horney is very palatable. She none the less locates femininity outside social relations. Her discussion of those relations is superb. Yet as Mitchell establishes, it is limited by the femininity it presupposes. In this respect, it is similar to the more recent theories placing femininity in the imaginary, implicating the female body in the process. I mentioned that Irigaray (for instance 1985) is often accused of doing this. The rejection of such accounts (and a preference for the Freud/Lacan non-essentialist account in this context) is fully consistent with the political critique of essentialism.

But the point for here is that the non-essentialist theory of sexual difference is also a theory of why that difference is *not* imprinted by socio-historical relations. Significantly, the shift in meaning within the critique of essentialism has been overlooked. For instance Sayers endorses Mitchell's critique of essentialism, re-stating the claim that Horney and Irigaray are similar in this regard (1986: 40–9). Something more needs to be said about why Lacan's account of sexual difference cannot be made historically contingent.

III

As I have indicated, Lacan's theory is non-essentialist because, like Freud's, it argues that femininity is constructed. Femininity is a secondary formation, not a biological given. This fairly familiar formulation does not of itself show why Lacan's non-essentialism is structured, not socio-historically induced. So to draw this out, I will focus on the structural aspects of his account, although it makes the presentation one-sided. However I think it indicates why 'psychoanalysis' cannot make a 'currently popular sociological distinction' between an innate sex and a socially defined masculinity or femininity (Mitchell 1982: 2).

Psychoanalysis cannot make this distinction because the person acquires the means to function as human when becoming a sexed subject: the two events are one and the same. In Lacan's theory the small biological being becomes 'human' when it speaks, *and* is thus *placed* by language. The 'placement' process happens both with and by an analogy with the Oedipus complex and its resolution. It is possible to speak and not to be placed. This is what occurs in psychoses. To be 'placed' by language is to take up a certain position in relation to the phallus. The girl struggles to 'be' it; the boy to 'have' it. This 'putting in place' in relation to the phallus not only inaugurates the felt difference between the sexes. It also divides the mind into the conscious and the unconscious, for it inaugurates repression. The phallus signifies all these divisions, and is identified with the father who breaks up the mother/child dyad. Freud formulated the father's intervention in terms of the fear of castration. In Lacan's terms, the acceptance of the father's law involves a 'symbolic castration'. I am now going to look at a less familiar aspect of what symbolic castration and repression involve. They involve the process of being inserted into a chain of meaning. It is the basis on which the subject is able to think its own thoughts from the standpoint of 'I'. When it represses some ideas its *selects* others. But it can only do this through the fundamental division established by the phallus. Where the subject does not accept this division, it lacks the basis for differentiating and thus the basis for logic. In this respect, phallus is to non-phallus as 'a' is to 'not-a'. (My term non-phallus is inaccurate, but it is useful initially. In the next few paragraphs, it should be clear that the phallus *is* the non-phallus.) It is the *sight* of the mother's non-phallus that fixes the meaning, and brings the anatomical difference between the sexes and castration into play.[9]

Rose points out that this visual 'crude opposition' covers over a much more complex psychical life. And so it does. But as well as covering over and cutting off ('castrating') or repressing a rich kaleidoscope of perception, and instituting sexual difference in the process, it also seals off the subject from psychoses.[10] To be the object of auditory or visual images with no self-imposed 'meaning' attached to them is to be psychotic; and this may occur when the subject does not take up a place on the basis of the 'crude opposition'. The reason is that it cannot connect itself as a body that thinks with the oppositions inherent in the language it has to think in. That is to say, unless it finds an analogy between its body and language it cannot insert itself into a chain of meaning. The analogy is between having and not having a penis, or the visual anatomical difference between the sexes, and the means to differentiate as such: 'this' and 'not this'. This is one sense in which the phallus is the symbol of lack: it is the symbol of the 'not'. As the symbol of lack, it extracts the child from a free-floating world of signifiers: it enables it to differentiate itself and to differentiate through language at the same time. It puts it in a position where it is able to assign meanings from its own standpoint; to operate within the symbolic, to make sense.

On this level it is evident why the masculine and feminine positions are available to both sexes. The assignation of meaning is not the prerogative of the male sex. When a man thinks that having the penis guarantees certainty, or the right to lay down meaning, he is basing his conviction on illusion. In one sense, he is confusing the phallus with penis. At the level of desire however the confusion is liable to be perpetuated. That is, in Lacan's account of sexual difference, the feminine is simply *not* masculine. It has no content, no essence. But

> it is in order to be the phallus, that is to say, the signifier of the desire of the Other, that the woman will reject an essential part of her femininity, notably all its attributes through masquerade. It is for what she is not that she expects to be desired as well as loved. But she finds the signifier of her own desire in the body of the one to whom she addresses her demand for love. Certainly we should not forget that the

organ actually invested with this signifying function takes on the value of a fetish.

(Lacan 1958: 84)

Before saying a few words about this, I will sum up on this exposition so far: in fact there is more at stake here than a theory of sexual difference, and the division between the conscious and the unconscious. There is a theory of intelligibility. In this theory, sexual difference is tied to the ability to make sense of the world. In existing commentaries on Lacan, the necessary emphasis is on how the subject's construction and identity alike rest on a fragile basis. It is necessary because subjectivity and sexual identity have been taken for granted. Yet in showing how this constructed sexual subject comes into being, Lacan also shows what this fragile construction secures (making sense). Partly to avoid simply repeating what Mitchell, Rose, Gallop (and others) set out, I have stressed this other aspect of the theory. Partly too, I have tried to take the shortest route to illustrating the specifically structuralist nature of Lacan's non-essentialism.

Yet, as many have said, sexual difference rests on shifting ground. Lacan's stress on the shifting uncertain nature of sexual identity may have been overworked, but it is central both to his theory and to the feminist appropriation of it. Indeed it is on this peg that the feminist appropriation of Lacan's psychoanalysis hangs its hat. Masculinity and femininity are not fixed positions. Both the subject's identity and the subject's 'meaning' are precarious. The different 'positioning' of the subject revealed through unconscious primary process, reveals the precariousness of the notion of an 'I': 'the "I" of a dream can be someone else . . .' (Mitchell 1982: 5). The unconscious, constant sliding of signifiers reveals that the meaning the subject confers 'from its own standpoint' is not the only meaning.

The unconscious . . . is concerned more with the signifier than with the signified and the phrase 'feu mon pere' (my late father') may mean, as far as the unconscious is concerned, that my father was the fire of God ('le feu de Dieu'), or even that I am ordering him to be shot (Fire!).

(Lacan 1955/6: 210)

The subject's ability to confer meaning: and its distinct identity, which is sexual by definition rests on a repression which is always threatened by what is repressed. In other words the repression of the Oedipus founds identity, but its foundations are unconsciously, constantly challenged. Desire is inextricably bound in speech and language, for desire (lack) is continually created by speech. By speaking one is committing the act which maintains one's place as separate. While this confers distinctness, and the ability to express meaning, its price is an alienation. For speech can only express demand. It cannot express all that underlies the demand. One reason for this is that the subject wants not be separate. The difference between what underlies the demand, and the demand itself, is desire. (See Gallop (1982: 11). Given that she puts such a readable case for desire's non-contingency, I have abbreviated my note on it here.) What underlies the demand is usually termed 'need'. Desire, the better-known aspect of Lacan's theory, is why the phallus is not just the symbol of 'not-a'. As the sign of the desire formed out of demand, the phallus also signifies specifically sexual difference: the subject's desire to be what it is not once it takes up (necessarily) sexed identity. For consciously, it can only have one.

In other words, the phallus is the reference point for sexual identity. Masculinity, by an illusory equation to which I return, makes itself this reference point. Femininity is constructed in relation to it. It is constructed in relation to a sign that signifies a lot more (or less) than the penis, although the phallus also signifies that. Freud construed femininity as woman's reaction to her castration (lack of a penis). While he thought that femininity was an ambisexual psychical state, he identified it in the last resort with the biological woman, insofar as he construed it in terms of what she has not. Lacan puts the emphasis on symbolic castration. This brings me to a major tension and debate within and around Lacanian theory (on this, see particularly Heath 1978). As I understand it, symbolic castration is a condition of subjectivity. At the same time, women 'have difficulty' effecting it. Parveen Adams (1978), dissecting the analyst Montrelay's contribution to the debate, sees the difficulty in terms of how women represent lack: men represent it with the visually significant penis; women do not have this option. There is a world of difference between a 'difficulty' and a complete inability to effect a given state. Exploring this difference, and the debates on femininity, would take me beyond my scope. Enough to stress here that because the visually significant penis 'figures' in representing lack, 'a crude visual opposition' remains significant in fixing the subject in place. Literally, this is illusion. Yet because of it, we continue to think difference in terms of being or having the phallus. So on the one hand, anatomy still figures. On the other, Lacan's 'structuralism' is non-essentialist; his femininity is not a biological given. Despite women's 'difficulties' effecting symbolic castration, both sexes can and do take up masculine and feminine positions irrespective of biology. But the critical point here is that this non-essentialism remains historically irreducible. Without the 'sexual difference' established through the symbolic law

there is only either its denial (psychosis) or the fortunes and misfortunes ('normality' and neurosis) of its terms.

(Mitchell 1982: 23)

126

This stress on the ramifications of the structure of sexual difference means the psyche's intersection with the social has to be considered differently. For from the foregoing description, it is evident that Lacan's theory cannot be a direct adjunct to a materialist account of ideology. Its level of explanation is in another register. It does not look to the relations between social being and social consciousness but to how consciousness is and always must be divided by language. Lacan is explicit on this: 'language is so irreducible to a superstructure that materialism itself is seen to be alarmed by this heresy . . .' (1955: 125). Lacan's theory even looks to how the capacity for having (coherent) ideas is instituted. For related reasons, Mitchell and Rose argue against the sociologizing of psychoanalysis. Psychoanalysis cannot be a theory of how a socially constructed gender is internalized, as Chodorow and others suggest (Rose 1982: 37n). It cannot be this because it is a theory of how sexual difference and desire are created. These are conditions for taking social ideas about sexuality on board. For want of a better term, the space in which these conditions are formed (and which they form) is called 'the psychical'. It is not a straightforward socio-historical product.

IV

The problem so far is that if the structures of sexual difference are non-contingent, it looks as if the parameters of psychical sexuality are immutable. These parameters leave room to move (neither sex is confined to the feminine place – femininity is constantly resisted). But by Lacan's account, they set limits on how far the repressed can return, without damage to the coherent experience of subjectivity. *One* of these parameters *seems* to be the penis as a 'sham' referent for the phallus. Because this is *the* problem, it serves as the matrix for three diverging strands in feminist, psychoanalytic investigation. One does not doubt that psychical structures and the symbolic register exist at a level independent from socio-historical ideology. It accepts Lacan's account, but sees it as a problem to be reckoned with (Mitchell, Rose, Adams *et al.*). The second seeks to challenge or explore the limits of the symbolic, meaning 'the paternal metaphor', or how far the phallus is identified with the father and penis. It is here we can locate the work of Irigaray (who does not accept that this independent psychical level is inherently patriarchal), Kristeva (who thinks it is but wants it perpetually challenged), Gallop, and those women writers whose literary strategies are sometimes read as trivial, rather than a political intervention in an area whose independence is denied.[11] For it is denied wherever it is insisted that any trans-historical account is by definition inimical to feminism. This is the response of the third strand within feminist psychoanalytic theory. It seeks to read out that in Freud and other psychoanalytic theories which cannot be reduced to socio-historical relations. As indicated, Chodorow tries to do this. Similarly, Sayers rejects Lacan because she believes that 'the signifiers of femininity are determined by their signifieds, by the material reality of women's day-to-day lives' (1986: 85). It is because she believes this that she finds the Lacanian feminists wanting. Of course as I tried to show ('feu mon pere') the Lacanian idea is precisely that signifiers are not determined by their signifieds. To some extent, it is because signifiers have a life of their own that the 'psychical' exists on an independent level.

Let us for the time being assume the worst. Psychical structures are both non-contingent, and they define femininity as nothing more than the negative of masculinity. How can these structures be thought about in a socio-historical context? Where feminism concentrates exclusively on this context, the perpetuation of oppression becomes a one-way traffic, where the social gets into the psyche, and leaves an ideological deposit. From this standpoint psychical life simply reflects social relations. On the other hand, psychical sexuality is not, and should not be treated as if it was self-contained. In one paper, Rose (1983) seems to want to keep psychoanalysis out of 'broad social explanation'.[12] Psychical structures do not exist in isolation; there is far more to the psyche and psychical sexuality.

The force of desire, the force of fantasy, and of other factors that make up psychical sexuality has to vary (if it did not, there would be no psychopathology) and it varies because of (individual or) social historical contingencies. One can say (with Gallop) that desire as such is not contingent on the failure or fulfilment of prescriptive demands, and still say (with Lacan) that there is a 'dialectic of demand and desire' (1958: 84). Psychical structures intersect with socio-historical relations.

Yet how, exactly, is the intersection to be approached? Without falling into a psychoanalytic tendency to explain everything in psychoanalytic terms? Lacan and some Lacanians do this. At times they make social, sexual relations the direct consequence of a psychical structural difference. While Lacan's theory accounts for how sexual difference as such is formed it does not *appear* to explain why sexual identity changes; and does not explain variations in the social, sexual division of labour. Nevertheless it may account for certain *social* effects. I think that if one accepts certain psychoanalytic premises, one must also accept that 'the psychical' will have some ideational impact aside from the ideas engendered by social history. This impact may have a positive side, but the immediate concern is with the psychical structure of sexual difference. The impact of that is hard to formulate, but as it bears on questions of change, its nature has to be considered. I will try to establish that there is a difference between recognizing the impact, and deducing social relations from psychical structures. Both issues are brought into focus through examining a particular instance where Lacan finds the structures in the relations.

In Rose's outstanding presentation of Lacan's texts in *Feminine Sexuality*, she writes that 'Lacan sees courtly love as the elevation of the woman into the place where her absence or inaccessibility stands in for male lack' (1982: 48). What this says is that an ideology, courtly love, can result from a psychical state. This particular psychical state is inter-twined with Lacan's theory of the trans-historical symbolic. Yet 'courtly love' is an historically specific phenomenon. Lacan says that this elevating procedure covers over 'male lack'. Before looking at the ideological aspect, I'll first say more about this lack. Lacan draws atten-tion to the affinity between 'courtly love' and the idealization of women in other instances. The phenomenon recalls Freud's observation of certain men: where they love, they cannot desire, and where they desire, they cannot love (1912). Freud also located idealization (and its inevitable concomitant, denigration) in a universal imperative. For Freud the split-ting of the sexual and the affectionate currents rested on an unsatisfac-tory resolution of the Oedipus complex, often resulting in impotence. It rested on an inability to come to terms with the universal desire for the mother. For Lacan the 'male lack' is also universal. It is the correlate of the impossible object of desire, namely unity, or non-separation: it is impossible because lack and separation are conditions of subjectivity.[13]

It is a fantasy about 'woman' which holds out the promise of oneness. 'For the man, whose lady was entirely, in the most servile sense of the term, his female subject, courtly love is the only way of coming off elegantly from the absence of sexual relation' (Lacan 1972/3: 141).

However, Rose suggests that 'courtly love' is not the only instance where the fantasy of woman has social effects. At the end of her introduction to Lacan's texts she writes that he

> gives an account of how the status of the phallus in human sexuality enjoins on the woman a definition in which she is simultaneously symptom and myth. As long as we continue to feel the effects of that definition we cannot afford to ignore this description of the fundamen-tal imposture which sustains it.

> (1982: 57)

If we feel the effects of this definition, we feel them through the social. They may be psychically experienced, but to be experienced by women, they have to be conveyed across the space of a social relation. What kind of effects? I'll adopt the women's movement term 'pedestal treatment' as a possible example. The immediate issue is that insofar as such effects involve social discourse they could be explained as ideological effects. Lacan's account of the psychical fantasy of woman stems from something more (or less): 'male lack'. This lack is not the result of historically specific social relations. It is universal. Despite this, the suggestion is that its effects are felt in the social. Two things must be noted. First this account could simply be wrong. Courtly love or pedestal treatment (to continue with the same example – and it is only an example) can be explained in socio-historical terms. Second, these explanations *are not mutually exclusive*. Ideologies deriving from socially specific relations could reinforce the psychically derived fantasies. After all, why did 'courtly love' as such only happen once? Now it would be easy to say that the socio-historical explanation is sufficient. It is certainly necessary. However as the psychical fantasy of woman has its axis in the symbolic, it is intimately tied to the symbolic structure of sexual difference. As this structure is trans-historical, it should follow that some variation on this 'psychical fantasy of woman' theme will recur throughout history. I return to the issue of trans-historical fantasies below. Here I want to take up another aspect of Rose's comment. For in fact it points to an issue which has to be generally true of fantasy in psychical and social life. It points to how fantasies which are psychically derived are projected into social relations; and thus have their own idea-tional impact. It also suggests that whatever that impact is, it has to be limited or informed by history. The issues here, especially the workings of projection, are made plainer through considering another objection to 'sociologizing' psychoanalysis.

The objection is to any notion of a one-to-one correspondence between social relations and psychical experience. It is not premissed on the idea that there is no connection between social or life events and contents of the unconscious. It is rather that those events are always mediated through fantasy. Moreover those fantasies themselves need not have any direct connection with external reality. This premise is basic to Klein's object relations theory (see note 3 at the end of this chapter) to Lacanian theory, and all psychoanalytic thinking that distinguishes fantasies from real events. Take Sarah Kofman's comments on the complaint, common among Freud's women patients, that their mothers did not give them enough milk.

These reproaches are heard too frequently, however, to correspond to any reality; instead, they are much more often the sign of the insatiable hunger of the child . . . The mother or wet nurse is thus not 'really' at fault; the limitlessness of desire lies at the origin of a feeling of infinite frustration, and this feeling is the source of an endless hostility. To accuse the mother is to substitute a finite and external cause, one more easily overcome, for an infinite and internal cause: it is thus to attempt, fantasmatically, to overcome a frustration that is necessary for structural reasons.

(1985: 165)

This example shows that fantasy has a distorted, refracted relation to reality. It takes an ingredient from reality (the mother or wet nurse) but accusations of deprivation do not stem from her behaviour but from the child's desire. As the word desire is used fairly freely in recent writing, I should mention in passing that desire as 'lack' can be concretized not only in sexuality, but in the lacking emotions; like envy, greed, general frustration.

To date, examples similar to Kofman's have been used to show that psychical content cannot be deduced from social relations; and thus, that psychoanalysis cannot be sociologized. In fact more is at stake. The 'fantasy of woman' discussed by Rose is not an isolated case. Two things are at issue. The first (once more) is the mechanism of projection. The second is a basic proposition of Lacanian theory: namely, that while real objects are blamed for frustration (and other feelings of lack) these feelings exemplify the limitlessness of desire; and are thus structurally induced. Taking these issues in order:

One of the purposes (if not *the* purpose) of analysis is to uncover the imaginary basis of much that is brought into it. While fantasies may have a psychical origin, their effects are not restricted to the subject's own psyche. They influence behaviour towards others, the assessment of others' intentions, and so on. Fantasies in general are read into or projected into the social. Buying into psychoanalysis entails recognizing the existence of projection. Psychoanalysis is a theory of the derivation of certain fantasies and (inescapably) a theory of how fantasies go *out*, over there. Into the social, onto people and things who are thereby credited or confused with, or constructed by imaginary attributes.

For the full implications of projection to be apparent, more needs to be said about the structural derivation of fantasies. To fantasize is to represent, and the condition of representation is absence. That representation, when it is visual, prefigures the difference between demand and need established in language. When (for instance) the breast is *represented* in its absence, its absence is acknowledged. Thus fantasy is intertwined with desire (absence, lack) from the outset;[14] it is intertwined with a structural inevitability. Yet while desire is a non-contingent event, fantasies involve more than a structural inevitability. They draw both on the lacking emotions, and on external material reality. Take for example a classic Kleinian fantasy: the infant believes it has destroyed the breast by envious sadistic attacks and the breast is now in fragments. The fragments have no reference to external reality: the breast does. The fantasy as such is not grounded wholly in visual perception, but is in part. It derives both from a *psychical* reality: a child's unconscious fantasy about the consequences of its thoughts and emotions. It is also grounded in a material reality: the breast.

In brief, we can say that fantasies in general draw ingredients from external reality, as well as from psychical structure. The importance of the social/psychical juxtaposition in fantasy comes more into focus when the foregoing comments are summed up. I have noted that fantasies are projected out, not (only) contained within the individual psyche; and that fantasy is inseparably bound up in desire: where there is desire and sexual difference, there is fantasy. From this perspective, the impasse in psychoanalysis and feminism is that the constitution of certain psychical givens of itself propels ideas into the social. That is to say: one spur to these ideas does not derive from specific socio-historical relations. Schematically speaking, such spurs sit alongside, in some way intermesh with, the socially specific ideas that are also drawn on in fantasy. But as I have tried to establish, it is an intermesh that must exist on a social level. The logic of psychoanalysis takes it right into broad social explanation. The questions are: (1) how much of the content of these ideas is socio-historical? (2) how much force do they have in relation to ideas derived from socio-historical relations?

At one level, fantasy and projection may be devices for the refraction of socio-historically derived ideas. For instance in the Kofman example, the subject blamed either a mother or a wet nurse. In the current social reality, a mother will usually carry the blame. It is for this reason that Dorothy Dinnerstein argues for equal parenting, so that the blame gets spread around. Effectively, she argues for a relocation of the referents for the blame; an argument which is much subtler than Chodorow's, and allows for hate, although it ultimately forgets that 'blame' itself has a psychical rather than a social origin. Still, at the level of the social referent, a materialist theory of ideology and psychoanalysis may still be complementary. At another level, some of the psychically derived content of certain fantasies seems set by trans-historical factors. If those trans-historical factors do not of themselves feed the subordination of women, they are not an immediate concern. What of those that do?

Let us at this point pick up again at the 'psychical fantasy of woman'. By Lacan's account this is certainly trans-historical; it is a product of the symbolic and the structure of sexual difference itself. If it is universal, the tendency to simultaneously idealize and denigrate women should be universal too. Its psychically derived content could explain certain recurrent images of women: the virgin/mother (Freud's affectionate current), the whore (his sensual current), and (if it is recurrent) Lacan's elevated lady. Yet even these recurrent images must be limited by what social relations and a particular culture permit.

Working out the limitations (and the extent to which trans-historical factors operate) could only be done in concrete comparative study. For that reason the issue of essentialism remains unresolved in this chapter. Certainly Lacanian psychoanalysis is a non-essentialist theory in terms of the letter of the law: it eschews innate factors in the subject's formation.

Its relation to the spirit of the feminist critique of essentialism is dubious, precisely because of the trans-historical possibilities it raises. But like it or not, if trans-historical psychical factors exist, then knowledge about them matters. As I said, in part, what prompted the turn to psychoanalysis was the search for more knowledge about how the conditions of patriarchy are internalized. If 'transhistorical psychical factors' are not about the internalization, but rather contribute to the formation of patriarchy, that too needs to be known. Not because they make that formation inevitable, but because they are more likely to do so if we are ignorant of how they work. The degree of their power may stand in an inverse relation to the degree of our knowledge about them.

If the foregoing paragraphs sound overly sanguine about any question of trans-historical factors, it is because of what the socio-historical limitations on them imply. They imply a potential opposition between socio-historical relations and the psychical derivation of fantasies. This opposition is evident at a readily observable level. The rejection of the fantasy of pedestalled women in feminist theory and practice of itself shows that there are limits to the effectiveness of a fantasy. My appeal to observable facts here does not solve the problems raised so far. It does suggest how their ramifications might be explored. For in psychoanalytic theory, the idea that social relations can either oppose or reinforce psychical products is fundamental. This idea is intrinsic to the distinction between psychical reality on the one hand, and material reality on the other.

Psychical reality, grounded in 'unconscious desire and its associated fantasies' (Laplanche and Pontalis 1973: 36) has the force of actual reality for the subject. This last point has been well-established in the psychoanalytic and relevant feminist literature. The classic instance of it is the discovery that founded psychoanalysis: namely, that the fantasy of paternal seduction is real in its unconscious effects. Yet while this major point has been made, its corollary has been neglected. That corollary is the fact that fantasy can be reinforced or opposed. This occurs in two ways. Psychical reality is contradicted when an analyst refuses the projections of an analysand; or, to say the same thing differently, when an analyst is not co-opted to the imaginary relations of the subject. If the analyst did collude, adjusting speech and response to the inviting projections of the analysand, nothing would get analysed. The analyst's response would confirm that a projected fantasy was an external reality.

Psychical reality is also contradicted or reinforced by external material reality. In both neuroses and psychoses, the force of psychical reality varies in relation to material reality. The subject's beliefs about external reality may be completely at odds with it; psychical reality need not 'match up' with external reality. In another sense the distinction between psychical and material reality is a distinction between what can and cannot be done. If it is or can be done, it is not psychical reality, as distinct from material reality. It is not 'unreal'. In this respect, the limits on psychical reality are set by what social relations permit. The implication here is that even if certain trans-historical psychical factors persist, their impact will change. A further implication is that certain social relations can reinforce (as well as oppose) trans-historical psychical factors.[15] The opposition to those psychical factors is a psychically active process. Again (and this of course remains to be explored) this raises the question of how far active aims can be separated from the formation of masculinity and sexual difference as such. If the psychical fantasy of woman is not tied to concrete relations which disempower women, which literally 'passify' them, will it become no more than a pale myth with less noxious historical referents? I am beginning to suspect that there is an illicit equation between the split images of women generated by the symbolic, and the objectification of women (in and outside the psyche) at other levels; an objectification which could be shown to vary in its historical intensity. In the long-run, the value of psychoanalysis to feminist practice may lie not in the trans-historical factors it gestures to, but in its contribution to understanding the conditions of their relative strength. That too remains to be explored.

The condition of its exploration is this notion: psychical reality is not an automatic extension of social relations, or repository for social ideologies. In other words, to some *as yet to be determined extent*, psychical factors exist as a 'third force' in social relations. The terms of the original feminist encounter with psychoanalysis were set by two other factors, biological and social ones. I have tried to show that the psychical cannot be reduced to the social. Yet the idea that it has any over-riding power in the social is drastically qualified. The fact that trans-historical psychical factors can be opposed means they are not all powerful. They cannot exist in isolation: they can only exist in social relations and ideologies which contribute to their content at a formative level, and either oppose or reinforce them at a social level. Any fantasy has to have a 'match' in socio-historical relations for it to have any socio-historical impact. In short, psychoanalysis may not (only) be about how ideas go in. It may be about stopping some 'ideas' getting out.

Department of Political Science, University of Melbourne, 1986

NOTES

1 Wilson (1981: 71) points out that feminism inherited the Marxist view of theory as a guide to strategy. Partly, her criticisms of feminist interest in psychoanalysis are based on the neglect of strategic political issues.

2 Julia Kristeva seems to be avoiding politics because of the illusions she thinks are at base of them. For a discussion of this see Ann Rosalind Jones (1984). For a critique of the political implications of Kristeva's (earlier) theory as such see Allon White. At the same time, the more Anglo-centric critiques of the French

difference theorists reflect more than a variation in political cultural context. They also reflect the theoretical unevenness of the debate. When editing this paper I was reading Alice Jardine's outstanding overview of the feminine in contemporary French theory (1985), which brings home just how uneven the shared theoretical assumptions at base of critiques can become. This paper is written from the shared (English) assumption that the socio-historical dimension has to be addressed; an assumption which is not just ignored in France. It is also challenged. Still, for the significance of the challenge to be brought out, I think it has to be spelt out in terms: it needs to be tied back to a socio-historical point of departure, before the departure point can be queried.

3 Chodorow's *The Reproduction of Mothering* has had considerable influence. Because critiques of how Chodorow sociologizes psychoanalysis are inbuilt to the position advocated by Mitchell *et al.*, I do not repeat both an exposition and critique of Chodorow here. I am concentrating on the difficulties raised if one accepts the notion that psychoanalysis should not be sociologized. However it is worth noting that her account of psychoanalytic object-relations theories defines those theories in a very problematic way. For instance, she defines Melanie Klein as an instinct-theorist, although Klein is regarded in Europe as one of the founders (see Laplanche and Pontalis 1973: 278) if not 'the parent of object-relations theory' (Grosskurth 1986: 372). Chodorow's selective use of the object-relations label is consistent with an American (psychoanalytic) context: her emphasis on the actual social relation, and her denial of a specifically psychical reality. Klein's object-relations theory stresses the significance of psychical reality. Curiously, Sayers comes close to Chodorow in describing Klein as 'instinct-based', and using this as a reason to criticize Dinnerstein.

4 Other feminist theorists, notably Parveen Adams share this position. Adams has contributed a lot to is articulation in various publications (see 1978 especially).

5 Denise Riley (1978) points to problems in a biological/social dualism. Elsewhere, I suggest that the idea of the 'biological' as a fixed category is itself ideological; through arguing (1) that a rigid distinction between the 'biological' and the 'social' is produced by (and reinforces) the epistemological distinction between subject and object and (2) that the subject/object distinction is itself a product of how psychical sexuality is structured by the divisions of active/passive and conscious/unconscious. Aside from that the existence of 'emotions' makes any rigid distinction between the biological and social problematic ('Our politics begin with our feelings?' unpublished paper, 1979). For a similar argument, see M. Gatens (1983) who develops it while also showing that the sex/gender distinction should be criticized. Henriques *et al.* (1984: 21–2) query the biological/social distinction as well, by arguing against the dualism it assumes and providing empirical illustrations of where it breaks down. As my immediate concern is with changes in the feminist use of 'essentialism', the biological/social distinction as such is not at issue here. However that distinction has to be called into question in relation to Freud's concept of the 'drives', which has to be tackled before the concept of psychical sexuality can be filled out.

6 The fact that this argument is not always explicit in *Psychoanalysis and Feminism* (but see p. 401) and that (therefore) Mitchell sometimes writes as if Freud didn't say what he clearly did, means that the overall bearing of her work can be undermined by comments that her reading of Freud is charitable.

7 However the issue of the construction of natural givens is very much on the

agenda. One of the main aims of Henriques *et al.* in *Changing the Subject* is to suggest how human attributes which are taken for granted as givens are in fact constructed.

8 The issue here is Freud's insistence that there is only one libido, and it is masculine. The non-essentialist bearing of this one-only-masculine-libido idea is that it is constructed. 'When the anatomical distinction between the sexes is thought to already designate masculinity and femininity, the thesis of two libidos may result. The argument from two libidos is essentially essentialist. The argument from a single (male) libido is not essentialist because it is not a natural effect of a biological condition.' (Adams 1978: 65–6).

9 To say non-penis at this point would lose sight of the fact that what the subject discerns as a lack in the other is not the lack of a penis (for all subjects lack; this is what desire is about) but that it uses the lack of a penis to represent both lack in the more general sense, and as a symbol of the division in language which it needs to think. Thus the phallus, as the symbol of lack, has ambiguous status. It marks all these divisions (the differentiation needed for logic; the fact that the one is not the other, the child is not the mother) but *we* represent division in a one-sided way (with the penis).

10 There is considerable empirical psychiatric evidence for this Lacanian proposition. Confusion over sexual identity or sexuality is evident in many case studies of the psychoses. One of the best examples is Juliet Hopkins' analysis of a six-year-old psychotic girl (1978). 'Sylvia' was firmly convinced she was a boy. The case is particularly interesting because the little girl is also a fetishist. Lacan and Cranoff place fetishism on the border between the imaginary two-sided relationship, and the symbolic three-sided relationship. Somewhat incidentally, there is a convergence in the non-Lacanian, French analytic literature towards the idea that without repression, there is either perversion or psychoses. See particularly J. Chasseguet-Smirgel (1984).

11 These (somewhat misnamed) literary strategies take on their meaning in the context of trying to 'think difference differently'. They are not engaging with a socio-historical feminism, but with the notion that the (penile) phallus is the privileged signifier. I am sympathetic to these explorations. But I suggest they are putting the cart before the horse, and that one should continue to search socially for the circumstances which reify femininity, in and outside the psyche: without these, I doubt that the asymmetric psychical equation would come to much.

12 Rose's (1983) article was written in the context of a debate on the relevance of psychoanalysis to feminism; and attempts to shift the terms of that debate by arguing that psychoanalysis is not a socialization theory, but a theory of how feminine socialization is resisted. It should be possible to re-situate this idea in the context of my suggestion concerning activity turned against the social order. But Rose's own position seems to be that while psychoanalysis as a theory of (individual?) resistance and feminist practice in the social are both crucial, they should be kept separate. At the same time, by this means Rose avoids the trap of identifying feminism with the celebration of uncertainty; a tendency which can grow out of a one-sided reading (the other side of the exposition in this article) of Lacan. In fact she explicitly queries how psychoanalysis, which shows identity to be 'uncertain and shifting' bears on feminism's 'necessary' striving for a certain identity.

13 I am abstracting from Rose's discussion of Lacan's theory of knowledge.

She also draws a crucial distinction between 'unity' as a feature of the symbolic (something from Lacan's later work) and 'unity' as an established part of the imaginary.

14 For a full discussion of the concept of fantasy in psychoanalysis see Laplanche and Pontalis (1968). Mitchell (1984) uses this article in suggesting that the setting for fantasy might be external reality; a suggestion I pursue in the text of this chapter.

15 In the context of the notion that social relations could either reinforce or oppose certain psychical factors in fantasy, the issue raised by Parveen Adams of the apparent historicity of hysteria is very relevant. (Paper to Southampton Sexual Difference Conference, July 1985). Hysteria is a psychical affair, but one which appears to dominate in particular places at historically particular times.

REFERENCES

P. Adams, 'Representation and sexuality, m/f no. 1, 1978.

M. Barrett, Women's Oppression Today (London: Verso and NLB, 1986).

J. Chasseguet-Smirgel, Creativity and Perversion (London: Free Association Books, 1984).

N. Chodorow, The Reproduction of Mothering (Berkeley: University of California Press, 1978).

D. Dinnerstein, The Rocking of the Cradle and the Ruling of the World (London: Souvenir Books, 1978).

W.R.D. Fairbairn, Psychoanalytic Studies of the Personality (London: Tavistock Publications, 1953).

S. Freud, 'Three essays on the theory of sexuality' in The Standard Edition of the Complete Psychological Works of Sigmund Freud (ed.) James Strachey, 24 vols (London: The Hogarth Press and the Institute of Psychoanalysis vol. 7, 1905).

S. Freud, 'On the universal tendency to debasement in the sphere of love', vol. 11 (1912).

S. Freud, 'Female Sexuality', vol. 21 (1931).

J. Gallop, The Daughter's Seduction: Feminism and Psychoanalysis (New York: Cornell University Press, 1982).

M. Gatens, 'A critique of the sex/gender distinction', in J. Allen and P. Patton (eds), Beyond Marxism? Interventions After Marx (Sydney Intervention Publications, 1983).

P. Grosskurth, Melanie Klein: Her World and Her Work (London: Hodder and Stoughton, 1986).

S. Heath, 'Difference', Screen 19, 3 (Fall, 1978), pp. 51–112.

J. Henriques, W. Hollway, C. Urwin, C. Vern and V. Walkerdine, Changing the Subject (London: Methuen, 1984).

L. Irigaray, Speculum of the Other Woman (New York: Cornell University Press, 1985).

A. Jardine, Gynesis: Configurations of Women and Modernity (New York: Cornell University Press, 1985).

A. R. Jones, 'Julia Kristeva on femininity: the limits of a semiotic politics', Feminist Review 18 (1984).

J. Lacan, 'Aggressivity in psychoanalysis', in Jacques Lacan, Ecrits: A Selection (tr.) A. Sheridan (1948; London: Tavistock Publications, 1977).

J. Lacan, 'The function and field of speech and language in psychoanalysis' (1953, in Ecrits 1977).

J. Lacan, 'The Freudian thing' (1955; in *Ecrits* 1977).

J. Lacan, 'On a question preliminary to any possible treatment of psychosis' (1955/6; in *Ecrits* 1977).

J. Lacan, 'The meaning of the phallus', in *Feminine Sexuality: Jacques Lacan and the Ecole Freudienne*, (eds) J. Mitchell and J. Rose, (tr.) J. Rose (1958; London: Macmillan, 1982).

J. Lacan, 'God and the *Jouissance* of the woman' (1972/3, in *Feminine Sexuality* 1982).

J. Lacan and W. Granoff, 'Fetishism', in M. Balint and S. Lorand (eds), *Perversions Psychodynamics and Therapy* (London: Ortolan Press, 1956).

J. Laplanche and J-B. Pontalis, *The Language of Psychoanalysis,* (tr.) D. Nicholson-Smith (London: The Hogarth Press and the Institute of Psychoanalysis, 1983).

J. Mitchell, *Psychoanalysis and Feminism* (London: Penguin Books, 1974).

J. Mitchell, 'Introduction I' in *Feminine Sexuality* (1982).

J. Mitchell and J. Rose (eds), *Feminine Sexuality: Jacques Lacan and the Ecole Freudienne* (London: Macmillan, 1982).

J. Mitchell, *Women: The Longest Revolution* (London: Virago, 1984).

T. Moi, *Sexual/Textual Politics: Feminist Literary Theory* (London: Methuen, 1985).

D. Riley, 'Developmental psychology, biology and Marxism' in *Ideology and Consciousness,* no. 4 (1978).

J. Rose, 'Introduction II' in *Feminine Sexuality* (1982).

J. Rose, 'Femininity and its Discontents', *Feminist Review* 14 (1983).

J. Sayers, *Sexual Contradictions: Psychology, Psychoanalysis and Feminism* (London: Tavistock Publications, 1986).

E. Wilson, 'Psychoanalysis: psychic law and order?', *Feminist Review* 8 (1981).

A. White, 'L'eclatement du sujet: the work of Julia Kristeva'. Stencilled Occasional Paper, Centre for Contemporary Cultural Studies (Birmingham, n.d.).

A CRITIQUE OF THE
SEX/GENDER DISTINCTION

Moira Gatens

In recent years it has become increasingly prevalent, in texts and papers concerned with sexual politics, to encounter the sex/gender distinction. This distinction is used in both confused and confusing ways and it is the purpose of this paper to clarify first, what the theoretical basis of this distinction is, second, to ascertain whether or not it is a valid or coherent distinction, and finally, to consider the political effects of the use of this distinction by various political groups. This tripartite task will involve overlapping considerations of feminism's relation to socialist and homosexual politics. The tale of the uncomfortable alliance between feminist and socialist politics[1] and feminist and homosexual politics[2] has recently surfaced in a way that is potentially productive for all parties. A critical appraisal of past and continuing alliances is the least one expects from radical theorists who value dialectical and historical analysis. It is in this spirit that the question of the viability of analyses located at the intersection of 'sex' and 'class' can be addressed. The difficulty of reconciling sex and class, or feminism and Marxism, despite the intervention of a third party, psychoanalysis,[3] has been well demonstrated.[4]

In this context, the introduction of 'spot-lighting' of gender, as an analytical tool which purportedly yields high explanatory returns (as opposed to the barren category of 'sex') offers occasion for comment. Over the past five years or so, feminist theory, of an Anglo-American orientation, has taken up the notion of 'gender' with considerable interest and mixed intent.

Influential journals and texts such as *m/f*, *Ideology and Consciousness*, *Feminist Studies*, *The Reproduction of Mothering*, *The Mermaid and the Minotaur* and *Women's Oppression Today*, share if nothing else, this enthusiasm for the notion of 'gender' as a central explanatory and organizing category of their accounts of the social and familial and/or discursive construction of subjectivity.[5] In general, the favouring of the category 'gender' over the category 'sex' is defended in terms of the 'dangers of biological reductionism'. Theorists who favour analyses based on gender argue that it is indispensable to see 'sex as a biological category and gender as a social one'.[6] Additionally, it would appear that the role of prior or current political commitment to any one of a variety of 'left' politics plays a decisive role in this preference for 'gender'.[7] Given that the category 'gender' commands considerable theoretical centrality in contemporary feminist and socialist-feminist theorizing as compared with its peripheral employment in the early seventies,[8] it is appropriate, at this time, to critically reassess its credentials.

It is in the area of political analysis and practice that the recent proliferation of the sex/gender distinction becomes most worrying. The distinction has been used by groups as diverse as: Marxists; (usually male) homosexual groups; and feminists of equality.

The effect of the use of the sex/gender distinction by the three groups outlined above, though clearly they display discernibly distinct political and theoretical motivations, has been to encourage or engender a neutralization of sexual difference and sexual politics. This neutralizing process is not novel, it can be traced to nineteenth-century liberal environmentalism where 're-education' is the catchcry of radical social transformation. Much of contemporary radical politics is, perhaps unwittingly, enmeshed in this liberal tradition. A feminism based on difference rather than on *a priori* equality is representative of a decisive break with this tradition.

What I wish to take to task in implicit and explicit investigations of gender theory is the unreasoned, unargued assumption that both the body and the psyche are a post-natally passive *tabula rasa*. That is, for theorists of gender, the mind, of either sex, is a neutral, passive entity, a blank state, on which is inscribed various social 'lessons'. The body, on their account, is the passive mediator of these inscriptions. The result of their analyses is the simplistic solution to female oppression: a programme of re-education, the unlearning of patriarchy's arbitrary and oppressive codes, and the relearning of politically correct and equitable behaviours and traits, leading to the whole person: the androgyn. It is precisely this alleged *neutrality* of the body; the postulated *arbitrary* connection between femininity and the female body; masculinity and the male body; and the apparent simplicity of the ahistorical and theoretically naive solution, viz. resocialization, that this paper proposes to challenge.

Before proceeding to present a critique of the proponents of the sex/gender distinction I should clarify what I take to be the central issue at stake. It would appear that one of the most burning issues in the contemporary women's movement is that of sexual equality *vs* sexual difference. It is arguable that this debate brings to a crisis both feminism's association with socialism and feminism's association with (male) homosexual groups. Both associations are often predicated upon an assumed 'essential' or possible equality, in the sense of 'sameness' between the sexes. It is against the backdrop of this question that this paper is situated. I would maintain that the proponents of sexual equality consistently mischaracterize and distort the position of those feminists who favour a politics of sexual difference. The fault may well lie with those feminists who have not made clear what such a 'politics of difference' amounts to. This paper is an attempt to amend this situation and, in addition, to quell, once and for all, the tired (and tiring, if not tiresome) charges of essentialism and biologism so often levelled at theories of sexual difference.[9] Critics of feminists of difference tend to divide the entire theoretical field of social enquiry into an exclusive disjunction: social theory is *either* environmentalist *or* it is essentialist.[10] Therefore, and it follows quite logically from this premise, if feminist theories of difference are not environmentalist then they must be essentialist. The task remains, then, to reopen the field of social theory from its forced containment in this disjunction and demonstrate the practical and theoretical viability of the politics of difference. The latter task shall be effected indirectly, by way of a critique of the proponents of 'degendering'.

THE DEGENDERING PROPOSAL

The problem of the relationship between sex and gender is, of course, not a new one. Freud grappled with the problem of finding a suitable definition of masculinity and femininity and their relation to men and women in the 'Three Essays' published in 1905.[11] However, the authoritative source for the recent prominence of writings centring on gender is not Freud but Robert J. Stoller, a contemporary psychoanalyst. Stoller published a book titled *Sex and Gender*,[12] in 1968, a text wherein he reports the findings and theses arising out of his research and involvement with the Gender Identity Research Clinic at UCLA.

Stoller studies first various *biological* anomalies (for example, neuters and hermaphrodites) in order to ascertain the relationship between sex and gender, and second he considers the biologically normal but *psychologically* disturbed individual (for example, the transsexual). He claims, at the completion of his research, to be able to account for the aetiology of both the transvestite and the transsexual – although his account is self-avowedly more complete in the case of *male* transvestites and transsexuals than in the (much rarer) cases of female transvestites and transsexuals.[13] He claims to be able to account for these psychological anomalies largely in terms of the distinction which he develops and systematizes between sex and gender.

The explanation is as follows. The biological sex of a person has a tendency to augment, though not determine, the appropriate gender identity for that sex (i.e. masculinity in the case of the male sex; femininity in the case of the female sex). However, a person's gender

141

identity is primarily a result of post-natal psychological influences. These psychological influences on gender identity, he claims, can completely override the biological fact of a person's sex and result in, for example, the situation of the transsexual.[14]

Stoller takes the genesis of transsexualism to be wholly social, that is, not biologically or physically determined. He posits, as the cause of male transsexualism, the mother's attitude to the child from birth. He reports that in all normal infants there is an initial period of symbiosis with the mother but that this symbiosis must be broken, particularly in the case of the boy, if normal masculinity or femininity as a separate (and in the case of the boy, different) and independent identity is to develop.

Stoller posits, in the case of the male transsexual, an unwillingness on the part of the mother to allow the child to separate from her and develop as an individual.[15] It must be stressed that it is not only a matter of how long the child is held close to the mother's body but also in what manner.[16] If the mother sees the child as a part of or extension to her own body, then the child will respond by not developing an identity separate from the mother's (or developing it at a critically late stage) and so, in the case of a male child, will feel himself to be a woman trapped in a male body.

The details of Stoller's work are not terribly important for the purposes of this paper. What is important is that his work was generally heralded as a breakthrough in the area of sexuality and socialization. As such it was quickly taken up by feminist theorists as offering theoretical justification for the right to equality for all independently of sex. His work has been used by Greer, Millett, Oakley, and more recently by Chodorow, Dinnerstein, and Barrett, to name a few.[17]

Millett, writing in 1971, and acknowledging Stoller as support or 'proof' of her view, offers the speciously reasoned conclusion that since 'Psychosexually (e.g. in terms of masculine and feminine, and in contradistinction to male and female) there is no differentiation between the sexes at birth. Psychosexual personality is *therefore* postnatal and learned.'[18] Millett's contention that 'patriarchal ascriptions of temperament and role' to the sexes are arbitrary[19] leads to the inevitable and naive feminist tactic of the re-socialization of society. She writes

> since patriarchy's biological foundations appear to be so very insecure, one has some cause to admire the strength of "socialisation" which can continue a universal condition *"on faith alone"*, as it were, or through an acquired value system *exclusively*. What does seem decisive in assuring the maintenance of the temperamental differences between the sexes is the conditioning of early childhood.[20]

Greer and Oakley pursue the same line of reasoning, with idiosyncratic differences.

The initial appeal of the implications of Stoller's research, in the late 1960s and early 1970s, is consistent with the social context of liberal humanism. Education or re-education, at that time, seemed a particularly viable programme for radical social change. Ten years later, however, both the context and the sentiment have altered considerably. Previous demands and strategies of the women's movement have 'back-fired' or proved to be co-optable.[21] It is in this context that we need to examine, very carefully, both the 'politics of equality' and sentiments originating with the liberal humanists of the eighteenth and nineteenth centuries.[22] The unproblematic assumptions of Stoller's research by contemporary writers, such as Chodorow and Barrett, warrants careful scrutiny.

In order for a programme of 'degendering' to be successful or even theoretically tenable, one would have to allow the validity of at least two unargued assumptions central to the thesis put forward by Stoller and assumed by the 'degendering feminists'. These are: i) that the body is neutral and passive with regard to the formation of consciousness, consciousness is primary and determinant – implicitly a rationalist view; and ii) the important effects of the historical and cultural specificity of one's 'lived experience' is able to be altered, definitively, by consciously changing the material practices of the culture in question. If the validity of these assumptions is allowed then one could claim that cultural and historical significances or meanings receive their expression in or are made manifest by an (initially or essentially) neutral consciousness which, in turn, acts upon an (initially) neutral body. One could claim, in addition, that masculine and feminine behaviours are arbitrary forms of behaviour, socially inscribed on an indifferent consciousness that is joined to an indifferent body. However, the above-mentioned assumptions warrant no such validity. To clarify the problem in other words, socialization theory, which posits the social acquisition of a particular gender by a particular sex is, implicitly, a rationalist account, an ahistorical account, and an account which posits a spurious neutrality of both the body and consciousness. In order to substantiate this position vis-à-vis the resocialization feminists who uncritically adopt Stoller's account, these two assumptions, outlined above, will be treated in detail. Although they are obviously interrelated, they will be treated separately for the sake of clarity and manageability.

SEX/GENDER AND THE RATIONALIST CONCEPTION OF THE SUBJECT

It is in the area of the heredity *vs* environment debate that the extreme difficulty of avoiding conceptualizing the person as a split body/ consciousness is most apparent. The sex/gender distinction is situated in such a debate and, it will be argued, is deeply entrenched in the problems of confused terminology and conceptualizing that characterize that debate. The sex/gender distinction is understood, by socialization theorists, as a body/consciousness distinction. This is not to suggest that this understanding does not have an immediate, commonsense validity but rather that such an understanding commits its user to a series of assumptions that, historically, have proved untenable.[23] Theorists who uncritically use the mind/body distinction consistently characterize the subject as either predominantly (or wholly) determined by biological forces, i.e. heredity or predominantly (or wholly) determined by the influence of social or familial relations, i.e. environment. Both these positions, the latter being the one that would best characterize re-socialization feminists, posit a naive causal relation between either the body and the mind or the environment and the mind which commits both viewpoints, as two sides of the same coin, to an *a priori*, neutral, and passive conception of the subject. If we conceive of the body as neutral and passive and of consciousness as socially determined, then we are at least halfway to a behavioural conception of subjectivity. It is unclear if the behaviourist conception of conditioning, which is based on various experimental hypotheses in animal ethology, has any valid application in the sphere of human behaviour. The stimulus–response model of conditioned behaviour assumes a passive and non-signifying subject who can be trained to respond appropriately and who can be relied upon to *consistently* respond appropriately. Psychoanalysis read as a *descriptive* theory of the constitution of subjectivity in (western, industrialized) patriarchal society, seriously undermines the behaviourist conception of 'conditioning' and the assumed passivity of the subject.

The problem of the interrelation and interaction of the body and the mind is by no means an archaic theoretical preoccupation. It is out of this problem that psychoanalysis arose. The Freud of 1889, that is, Freud the neurophysiologist, was perplexed by the phenomenon of hysteria, a disorder he once described as representing a 'mysterious leap from the mind to the body'.[24] Since Freud's early work on hysterics with Charcot and Breuer both physiological and psychoanalytic understandings of the so-called mind–body problem have altered drastically.[25] A cogent and theoretically useful account posits that there is one unitary reality underlying two (or more) distinct levels of theoretical abstraction and that the 'mysterious leap' is actually a leap from one kind of discourse, say the psychological, to another, the physiological.[26] It remains to integrate this insight into everyday and theoretical conceptions of the person – a task not always achieved even by those who offer acknowledgement of the necessity of such integration.

Freud stressed, from his earliest papers, that even perception cannot be regarded as passive but rather is an active process.[27] He argues further that consciousness cannot be equated with the perceptual system and

144

that, in fact, most of what is perceived never even enters consciousness but remains pre-conscious or unconscious.[28] This implies an activity, and not necessarily a conscious activity, on the part of the subject that cannot be accounted for by the behaviourist. Perception can be reduced to neither the body nor consciousness but must be seen as an activity of the subject.[29]

Concerning the neutrality of the body, let me be explicit, there is no neutral body, there are at least two kinds of bodies; the male body and the female body.[30] If we locate social practices and behaviours as embedded in the subject, as we have with perception, rather than 'in consciousness' or 'in the body' then this has important repercussions for the subject as always a *sexed* subject. If one accepts the notion of the sexually specific subject, that is, the male or female subject, then one must dismiss the notion that patriarchy can be characterized as a system of social organization that valorizes the masculine *gender* over the feminine gender. Gender is not the issue; sexual difference is. The very same behaviours (whether they be masculine or feminine) have quite different personal and social significances when acted out by the male subject on the one hand, and the female subject on the other. Identical social 'training', attitudes, or, if you will, conditioning, acquire different significances when applied to male or female subjects.

This is largely a result of the activity of the subject and its drive to master social relations and meanings.[31] Each gesture, attitude, perception, that enters human consciousness, does so charged with significances that relate to all that has gone before. That the male body and the female body have quite different social value and significance cannot help but have a marked effect on male and female consciousness.[32]

The orthodox account of the gender/sex distinction claims that the social determination of personal identity operates at the level of ideas, the level of 'the mind'. What this account fails to note is the obvious divergence between feminine behaviour, experience, lived out by a female subject and feminine behaviour, experience, lived out by a male subject (and vice versa with masculine behaviour). This claim does not imply an commitment, on my part, to a fixity or essence of the social significance of bodily functions, events, or experience. Signification, and its constitutive role in the construction of subjectivity is curiously absent from the writings of the proponents of degendering. This is likely to be an effect of their implicit commitment to a behaviourist conception of the person and the resultant stress on passive conditioning and socialization rather than the active process of signification.[33]

While explicitly wishing to distance this paper from ahistorical and *a priori* accounts of the social significance of the sexed body and its behaviour, I would suggest that some bodily experiences and events, though lacking any *fixed* significance are likely, in all social structures,

145

to be privileged sites of significance. Various anthropological, ethological, and historical evidence would seem to support this claim. For example, menstruation is likely to be one of these privileged sites. The fact that menstruation occurs only in (normal) female bodies is of considerable import for this paper. Given that in this society there is a network of relations obtaining between femininity and femaleness, that is, between the female *body* and femininity, then there must be a qualitative difference between the kind of femininity 'lived' by men.[34] To take again the example of menstruation, in our culture it is associated with shame and modesty – both characteristically feminine attributes. An interesting speculation is whether this shame could be connected to the more general shame involved in the failure to control one's bodily fluids, excretions, wastes, given the high store put on this control in our culture. Freud's neglect of the effect of the menses on the pubertal girl's psyche is significant. That the flow of blood would have profound psychical significance for her is clear and that this significance would centre around ideas of castration, sexual attack, and socially reinforced shame is highly probable. The female's first act of coitus would probably also bear on this.

The point is that the body can and does intervene, to confirm or to deny, various social significances in a way that lends an air of inevitability to patriarchal social relations. A thorough analysis of the construction of the specificity to female experience, which takes account of the female *body*, is essential to dispelling this 'air'. To slide from 'male' and 'female' experience to 'masculine' and 'feminine' experience further confuses the issue. The 'feminine male' may have experiences that are socially ascribed as 'feminine' but – and this is the relevance of the body and its specific social value and meaning – in a way that must be *qualitatively* different from female experience of the feminine. He is parasitically dependent on the female body, more particularly the maternal body, by a process of identification.[35] This point shall be elaborated further.

It has been the purpose of this section to argue that the view that consciousness is wholly socially constituted and inscribed by means of a passively conditioned socialization which in turn acts upon a neutral and passive body is untenable. I have argued that the conception of a passive subject (supported by various behaviourist-oriented assertions), central to the programme of degendering is demonstrably inadequate to account for human behaviour and, in particular, the activity of signification.[36]

CONTEXTUAL SPECIFICITY

A most common claim made against feminists of sexual difference is that their theories are essentialist and *a priori*, in short, ahistorical. This claim operates like the infamous blade that cuts both ways. The irony of the accusation is that feminists who propose degendering propose it outside of history and without considering the extreme resilience of expressions of sexual difference and the network of language and other systems of signification that both constitute and perpetuate this difference. Again, Chodorow provides us with the stereotype of this claim. She states 'To see men and women as qualitatively different kinds of people, rather than seeing gender as processual, reflexive, and constructed, is to reify and deny relations of gender, to see gender differences as permanent rather than as created and situated.'[37] Note the slide from sex to gender in this passage – from biological terminology (men, women) to psychological terminology (feminine, masculine). What is quite remarkable in her article is that she does not write about the body at all, except in a footnote where she does little more than acknowledge this (convenient) 'oversight'. She writes there:

> We cannot know what children would make of their bodies in a non-gender or non-sexually organised world, what kind of sexual structuration or gender identities would develop. But it is not obvious that there would be *major* significance to biological sex differences to gender difference, or to different sexualities.[38]

This kind of speculative phantasy is merely veiled rhetoric – the point is that we are historically and culturally situated in a society that is divided and organized in terms of sex – an historical fact. The charges of essentialism and ahistoricism can be made both ways. The recognition of the historicity of the significance of sex and gender can be shown to be of prime importance to theories of sexual difference. It is this historicity, this specificity that the analysis is based upon. Theorists of sexual difference do not take as their object of study the physical body, the anatomical body, the neutral, dead body, but the body as lived, the animate body – the *situated* body.

It is striking that the body figures in socialization theory only as the biological anatomical or physiological body. There is little analysis of the body as lived: of the body's morphology or of the imaginary body. If one wants to understand sex and gender or, put another way, a person's biology and the social and personal significance of that biology as lived, then one needs an analysis of the imaginary body. It is here that the importance of the feminist rereadings of Freud's work in terms of a theoretical description of how it is that male and female biologies are lived as masculine and feminine subjectivities in patriarchal culture is located.

As I indicated at the beginning of the preceding section, it was largely due to Freud's early work with hysterics that the discipline of psychoanalysis arose. What Freud posited as crucial in order to understand the hysteric's symptom was an understanding of the emotional and libidinal investment obtaining between the subject and her (or his) body.[39] This insight opened the way for future advances in the still prevalent mechanism of dualist conceptions of the subject. Contemporary French psychoanalytic research, in particular the work of Laplanche[40] and Lacan, can be seen as such advances. In Lacan's formulation of the 'mirror phase' he claims to have shown 'an essential libidinal relationship with the body-image'.[41]

In both papers where Lacan treats, specifically, the genesis of the ego, he stresses the importance of the mirror phase in relation to both hysteria and the imaginary body. He writes:

To call these (hysterical) symptoms functional is but to confess our ignorance, for they follow the pattern of a certain imaginary anatomy which has typical forms of its own. In other words, the astonishing somatic compliance which is the outward sign of the imaginary anatomy is only shown within certain definite limits. I would emphasise that *the imaginary anatomy referred to here varies with the ideas (clear or confused) about bodily functions which are prevalent in a given culture.*[42]

The existence and operations of the imaginary body are most clearly demonstrated by the aetiologically related phenomena of 'phantom limb' and hysteria.[43] What these phenomena illustrate is a libidinal or narcissistic relation of the subject with its body. This relation defies mechanistic or purely empirical explanation along either rationalist or behaviourist lines. The dispute concerning the experience of the unity of the body tends to centre around what this experience is predicated upon, and whether it is an experience given immediately in perception or developed in a milieu of social meaning and value. There is abundant evidence to favour the latter description. Schilder maintains that both 'phantom limb' and hysteria can be understood only if we take into account the fact that all healthy people are, or have, in addition to a material body, a body-phantom or an imaginary body. This psychical image of the body is necessary in order for us to have motility in the world – without it we would not be intentional subjects. The imaginary body is developed, learnt, connected to the body-image of others, and is not static.[44]

Hysterical symptoms have a demonstrably clear relation to the (culturally specific) imaginary body. Hysterical paralysis, for example, conforms to the culturally and linguistically delineated imaginary body. Hysterical paralysis of the arm does not correspond to the anatomical or physiological organization of the body but rather to the anatomically naive conception of the body, where the arm ends at the place where the shirt-sleeve meets the shoulder seam. Or again, there is an intimate relation of equivalence between the mouth and the vagina[45] that is, in the case of Dora,[46] used to express her unconscious desire via the symptom of *Tussis nervosa*. Knowledge of the particular form of the culturally constructed imaginary body is essential in order to understand the social (rather than individual) character of hysteria. The surprising homogeneity in the expression of the hysterical symptom, such as *anorexia nervosa*, within a given culture, signals the social character of the imaginary body. The imaginary body is socially and historically specific in that it is constructed by: a shared language; the shared psychical significance and privileging of various zones of the body (e.g. the mouth, the anus, the genitals); and common institutional practices and discourses (e.g. medical, juridical, and educational) on and through the body.

It is by way of an analysis of the imaginary body that it can be shown to be the site of the historical and cultural specificity of masculinity and femininity. It is to the imaginary body that we must look to find the key or the code to enable the decipherment of the social and personal significance of male and female biologies as lived in culture, that is, masculinity and femininity.

In this connection it is also clear that there is a contingent, though not arbitrary, relation between the male body and masculinity and the female body and femininity. To claim this is neither biologism or essentialism but rather to acknowledge the extremely complex and ubiquitous network of signification and its historical, psychological, and cultural manifestations. To deny this network and the specific historical form of femininity and masculinity and their relation to female and male subjects and to favour instead a conception of the subject as essentially neutral or neutered and further, to base one's political practices on this conception, can only lead to the reproduction, at another site, of these relations.

When Freud describes femininity and masculinity as end results of a developmental chain, he is quite explicit. The respective tasks of women and men in our culture are, for women, to 'take over' the place of the object, passive, castrated, the feminine, and, for the man, to 'combine' the values of subject, active, phallic, masculine.[47] Among the traits that epitomize femininity for Freud (and our culture) are: passivity, masochism, narcissism, envy, shame. What I suggest is that these feminine behaviours are not merely the result of patriarchal socialization and conditioning, the strength of which Millett was so admiring, or a discursively constituted category lacking a referent, but additionally are modes of defensive behaviour that utilize the culturally shared phantasies about biology – that is, they are manifestations of and reactions to the (conscious and unconscious) ideas we share about our biology.

Freud saw the biology of women and men to be unproblematic – the ovum is passive, the sperm active – the problem for him was the

149

psychology of masculinity and femininity which 'mirrors' this biology: the man actively penetrates the passive vagina. However, and this is the role of cultural and historical specificity, it is not given *a priori* that the penis is active, the vagina passive. This concept has to do with the imaginary anatomy, where the vagina is conceived of as a 'hole', a 'lack' and the penis as a 'phallus'. One could just as well, given a different relational mode between men and women, conceive of the penis as being enveloped or 'embraced' by the active vagina. In this context an interesting addendum is provided by recent biological research which maintains that the ovum is not as passive as it appears – it rejects some sperm and only allows entry, or envelops, a sperm(s) of its 'choice'.

Masculinity and femininity as forms of sex-appropriate behaviours are manifestations of an historically based, culturally shared phantasy about male and female biologies, and as such sex and gender are not arbitrarily connected. The connection between the female body and femininity is not arbitrary in the same way that the symptom is not arbitrarily related to its aetiology. Hence, to treat gender, the 'symptom', as the problem is to misrecognize its genesis. Again, we can here note parallels between behaviourist psychology and 'degendering'. The therapeutic techniques of behaviourism – systematic desensitization, behaviour modification, and so on – treat the symptom only.

In the above analysis of the two assumptions taken to be crucial to the theory of degendering, it has been argued that masculine and feminine forms of behaviour are not arbitrary inscriptions on an indifferent consciousness which is joined to an indifferent body. To speak of 'acquiring' a particular gender is to be mistaken about the significance of gender and its intimate relation to biology-as-lived in a social and historical context. The account of 'difference' that has been affected only indirectly, is an ongoing project and as such is both tentative and incomplete. However, even at this stage we can oppose the naive simplicity of degendering and its questionable theoretical basis.

TRANSSEXUALISM RECONSIDERED

It has been argued throughout this paper that the relation between masculine behaviour acted out by a male subject and masculine behaviour acted out by a female subject (or feminine behaviour acted out by a female subject and feminine behaviour acted out by a male subject) cannot be symmetrical. In other words, it has been argued that masculinity and femininity do not differ with regard to the sexes in terms of quantity only, but *qualitatively*. If this thesis is correct then to suggest the degendering of society as political strategy is hopelessly utopian, ahistorical, and functions theoretically and practically as a diversionary tactic. Additionally, it has been argued that the programme of degendering is based on a misunderstanding of patriarchal social relations.

This all but concluding section is titled 'transsexualism reconsidered' because it is the case of the transsexual that most clearly demonstrates the dissymmetry between masculinity/femininity and male/female. An understanding of the determination of male and female transsexualism is not to be found in the sex/gender distinction or in an analysis of the acquisition of gender identity. It was mentioned early in this paper that Stoller's account of transsexualism is more complete in the case of male transsexuals than female transsexuals. Contrary to Stoller's hopes,[48] it is clear that the same account will not cover both cases. It has been suggested that the male transsexual can be understood only if we first understand the genesis of the primitive ego and the notion of the imaginary body. The male transsexual, due to his primary relations to his mother, is in the situation of being constituted in such a way that his (primitive) ego conflicts with his imaginary (and biological) body, leading to his subjectivity being conceived by him as 'female-in-a-male-body'. Briefly this would involve the non-resolution of the misrecognition of the body of the other for one's own, that is, the male transsexual's primitive (bodily) ego is predicated upon a female body (i.e. the maternal body)[49] and he does not develop, until comparatively late, a separate identity from his mother. His transsexualism, in fact, is evidence that this separation is never adequately achieved. The desire of the mother[50] is active in this non-resolution or critically *late* resolution.

The case of the female transsexual cannot be symmetrical. The relation of the female infant to the mother's body is not and can not be problematic *in the same way*.[51] This may partially explain the relative rarity of female transsexualism. (Though the extremely common phenomenon of the 'tom-boy' is transsexualism, of a sort.) Female transsexualism is much more likely to be a reaction against oppression, that is, against the socially required forfeit of activity that was once enjoyed and socially tolerated. This possibly is overlaid by the desire of the mother to make a husband-substitute of the girl and/or the mother's own resentment of the female role in patriarchy. The transsexual knows, most clearly, that the issue is not one of gender but one of sex. It is not masculinity *per se* that is valorized in our culture but the *masculine male*.

On another level, this dissymmetry between the sexes is reflected in feminist musings concerning whether women are excluded (or all but excluded) from certain professions *because they are prestigious* or whether those professions are prestigious *because women are excluded*. The implication being that it is not what is done or how it is done but who does it that determines its value. The problem is not the socialization of women to femininity and men to masculinity but the place of these behaviours in the network of social meaning and the valorizing of one (the male) over the other (the female) and the resultant mischaracterization of relations of difference as relations of superiority and inferiority.

There is another aspect to the theory of gender that is also important to consider, and that is the political use to which the sex/gender distinction is put.

THE EFFECT OF THE SEX/GENDER DISTINCTION IN POLITICAL ANALYSIS AND ACTION

The commitment to economism or humanism in many Marxist accounts of the social and political status of women each, in their different ways, effects the neutralization of sexual difference. Economism by its privileging of the relations of production over psychical and social forms of subjectivity that are prior to or inadequately captured by the capitalist mode of production. Humanism by its adherence to an *a priori* and universal conception of human nature that, also, takes no account of sexual difference. A coherent account of the construction of male and female subjectivity under patriarchy and capitalism is indispensable for effective political strategy. However, to shift the site of analysis from 'male' to 'masculine', from 'female' to 'feminine', claiming by the shift priority to gender in the construction of men and women, rather than avoiding the problems of 'individualism' merely presents us with another set of problems. For example, masculinity and femininity and their constitutive role in sexual difference are often, on this account, reduced to the status of a *deus ex machina*.[52]

M. Barrett in *Women's Oppression Today* uses the category of gender to argue that socialism and feminism are compatible and 'that the ideology of masculinity and femininity has a crucial role in the division of labour as it has developed historically'.[53] Barrett's extensive and central use of the category gender is problematic in that she does not state, support, or defend its theoretical status, but rather assumes that there is general agreement concerning its, apparently transparent, explanatory merits. She writes: 'The processes by which gender, and particularly femininity, is socially constructed in capitalist society have been extensively explored. This topic falls within the well-researched area of 'socialization studies' in sociology and has also been a major focus of feminist accounts.'[54] It has been argued, at some length, in this paper that both the explanatory value and theoretical adequacy of 'socialization studies' are extremely tenuous. The question arises then, 'why would a theorist, familiar with the implications of psychoanalytic theory for socialization theory,[55] adopt the use of gender, knowing it is based on questionable theoretical grounds?' A likely explanation is that prior political investments and allegiances lead some feminists to neglect casting their otherwise critical eye in the appropriate direction.

Recent issues of the local journal *Gay Information* reveal a similar commitment to the centrality of the category gender in sexual politics. What Carrigan and others[56] argue is that the diversity of sexual preference and practice is such that a biological distinction, male/female, is inadequate to account for forms of sexuality. There is no quarrel here. However, to introduce gendered forms of sexuality takes us out of one hiatus into another. This move adopts, in keeping with socialization theory, only a quantitative distinction between masculinity and femininity and their relation to the construction of male and female subjectivities. Again, the body is neutral and *a priori*, consciousness a passive *tabula rasa*.

It is in the above context that I maintain that the programme of degendering put forward initially by feminists such as Millett and Oakley and taken over by Chodorow, is based on a misunderstanding (originating with Stoller's mistaken thesis of the genesis of transsexualism) of masculinity and femininity as conditioned forms of behaviour. Rather, I would suggest that 'masculinity' and 'femininity' correspond at the level of the imaginary body to 'male' and 'female' at the level of biology. It bears repetition that this statement does not imply a fixed essence to 'masculine' and 'feminine' but rather an historical specificity.

What has brought equality feminists and difference feminists into the present sharp confrontation is, partly, the so-called 'crisis' in Marxism and the withdrawal of the labour of many feminists from Marxist-oriented research. Also, at another level, the influence of French feminism[57] has been instrumental in the formulation and defence of a politics of difference, which is often placed in opposition to the politics of Marxist-feminism.

One could also argue that the gradual demise of the call for sexual equality and the rise of the insistence on sexual difference can be accounted for in purely pragmatic terms, that is, trial and error – we asked for equality and it didn't work, let's insist on difference. Practically, this has been the case in a number of areas. For example, the demand for equal legal status is now thought by some to be counter-productive. The feminist campaign for the acquittal of the cases of Roberts and Krope were argued on the grounds that the law of provocation did not take account of the, in general, disproportionate strength of men and women.[58] Likewise, many feminists have pointed out the abuse by men of the recently introduced anti-discrimination legislation.

However, there are also, and more importantly for the purposes of this paper, several theoretical determinations of the tactical shift from equality to difference. The most important of these I take to be the growing belief in the inefficacy of key theoretical concepts in various analyses and understandings of oppression (whether racial, class, or sex), in particular the notion of ideology – a notion that has its base in a rationalist conception of the subject. It is from the assumption of this analysis that predictable and planned social change or revolution can be posited, initially, in terms of the radicalization of consciousness.

The early feminist contribution to this social change is typified by the challenge to the notion that the sexual division of labour is natural, claiming rather that it is ideological – the implication being that alongside the struggle against capitalism should be the struggle against patriarchy, that the struggle for male emancipation was not, necessarily, compatible with or inclusive of the struggle for female emancipation.[59] The stumbling block to the proposed 'equal society' was (either or both) women's reproductive capacity and the responsibility of childrearing. These feminist claims represented the first 'crack' in the edifice of the homogeneity of radical and/or socialist politics. However, this 'crack' was quickly sealed, often by feminists themselves, by recourse to the claimed necessity of the neutralizing of sexual difference. For example, Firestone's 'cybernetic communism',[60] proposed the literal neutering of bodies by means of the complete technologization, and hence socialization, of the reproductive capacity. So, in effect, the edge of sexual difference and the denial of sexual neutrality was quickly, but not effectively, blunted by the call to neutralize the difference.

What is overlooked in this megalomaniacal phantasy, leaving aside the desirability or otherwise of its details, is that the implied neutrality is not a neutrality at all but a 'masculinization' or 'normalization' (in a society where men are seen as the norm, the standard) of women – a making of 'woman' into 'man'.[61] This move has many echoes in discourse and politics, as many feminists have tirelessly pointed out.[62] An assumption implicit in the aim of neutralizing the body and to thereby allot primacy to the ideological is the total passivity of the body. What this analysis yields, at best, is the predominantly Anglo-American crass empirical equation between patriarchal sex-role socialization and patriarchal consciousness.

It is the revival, or continuation, of the above problematic that the proponents of the sex/gender distinction seek. In addition to the neutralization of sexual difference, the sex/gender distinction lends itself to those groups or individuals whose analyses reveal a desire to ignore sexual difference and prioritize 'class', 'discourse', 'power', or some other 'hobby-horse'. Their accounts attempt to co-opt or trivialize feminist struggles and feminist theory at its peak, reducing sexual politics to gender difference and positing as primary the relations obtaining between genders and power, gender and discourse, or gender and class – as if women's *bodies* and the repression and control of women's bodies were not a crucial stake in these struggles.

NOTES

1 Weinbaum, B., *The Curious Courtship of Socialism and Feminism* (Boston, Mass.: South End Press, 1978).

2 For example, local experiences in Camp Inc. and CAMP.

3 See, for example, J. Mitchell's attempt at the tripartite amalgamation in *Psychoanalysis and Feminism* (Harmondsworth, Penguin, 1974).

4 Gallop, J., *Feminism and Psychoanalysis* (London: Macmillan, 1982).

5 *m/f*, esp. vols 2, 5/6, and 7. *1 + C, Feminist Studies*. Chodorow, N., *The Reproduction of Mothering* (Berkeley, Calif.: UCP, 1978); Dinnerstein, D., *The Mermaid and the Minotaur* (NY: 1977); Barrett, M., *Women's Oppression Today* (Verso, 1980).

6 ibid., p. 13.

7 See ibid., ch. 1; any editorial of *m/f*; and Chodorow, op. cit., ch. 2, esp. pp. 34–5.

8 For example, Greer, G., *The Female Eunuch* (London: Paladin, 1971), pp. 25–30; and Millett, K., *Sexual Politics* (London: Abacus, 1971).

9 The question of difference is almost invariably understood by its critics as being essentialist. For example, see Plaza, M., '"Phallomorphic power" and the psychology of "woman"', in *Ideology and Consciousness*, no. 4 (1978) and *m/f*, no. 2 (1978), p. 2: 'When feminists explain the present position of women in terms of a point of origin of sexual difference, then they deny specific practices and politics any effectivity since they are thereby expressions of a fixed unchanging essence. Sexual difference is then not instituted within specific practices but functions outside it.'

10 For example, Chodorow, N., 'Gender relations and difference in psychoanalytic perspective', in Jardine, A. and Eisenstein, H. (eds), *The Future of Difference* (Boston: G.K. Hall & Co., 1980), p. 3.

11 Strachey, J. (ed.), *The Complete Psychological Works of Sigmund Freud*, Standard Edition (hereafter S.E.) vol. VII, pp. 219–20: 'It is possible to distinguish at least three uses. 'Masculine' and 'feminine' are used sometimes in the sense of activity and passivity, sometimes in a biological, and sometimes again, in a sociological sense. The first of these three meanings is the essential one and the most serviceable in psychoanalysis . . .' See also 'An outline of psychoanalysis', S.E. vol. XXIII, p. 188.

12 Stoller, R.J., *Sex and Gender* (London: Hogarth Press, 1968).

13 See pp. 140–2, 'Transsexualism reconsidered', for alternative suggestions concerning female transsexualism and Stoller himself in *The Transsexual Experiment* (London: Hogarth Press, 1975).

14 Stoller writes: 'A transsexual is a person who feels himself consciously and unconsciously to belong to the opposite sex while not denying his sexual anatomy', *Sex and Gender*, p. 187.

15 See case of Lance, ibid., pp. 118–25, esp. p. 125.

16 ibid., see p. 307f.

17 Greer, G., *The Female Eunuch* (London: Paladin, 1971); Millett, K., *Sexual Politics* (London: Abacus, 1971); Oakley, A., *Sex, Gender and Society* (London: Temple Smith, 1972); Chodorow, op. cit.; Dinnerstein, op. cit.

18 Millett, op. cit., p. 30 (my emphasis).

19 ibid., p. 32.

20 ibid., p. 31 (my emphasis).

21 For example, the number of men who have built their academic reputations on feminism and 'teach' feminism.

22 For example, Wollstonecraft, M., *Vindication of the Rights of Women*; and Mill, J.S., *On the Subjection of Women*.

23 First, Cartesian dualism and later reductionist attempts to overcome it – idealism and empiricism. All three positions yield demonstrably inadequate conceptions of the subject.

24 'Notes upon a case of obsessional neurosis', S.E., vol. X, p. 157.

25 For example, see Deutsch, F., (ed.), *On the Mysterious Leap from the Mind to the Body* (NY: IUP, 1973); Schilder, P., *The Image and Appearance of the Human Body* (NY: IUP, 1979), and Lacan, J., *Ecrits* (London: Tavistock, 1977), pp. 1–7.

26 See Deutsch, op. cit., part I.

27 See 'Project for a scientific psychology', S.E., vol. I, Letter 52 to Fliess, vol. II.

28 See 'The interpretation of dreams', S.E., vol. VI, pp. 537–42.

29 M. Merleau-Ponty has an interesting account of perception as an activity of the body-subject in *The Phenomenology of Perception* (London: Routledge & Kegan Paul, 1970), esp. pp. 203–7.

30 To insist on two bodies is strategically important given that we live in a patriarchal society that organizes itself around pure sexual difference, that is male or female, and will not tolerate sexual ambiguity, for example, hermaphrodites, but forces a definite either/or sex on each person. (See Foucault, M., *Herculine Barbin* (NY: Pantheon, 1980)). However, even the *biological* determination of sex is not so straightforwardly clear and we must acknowledge sex as a continuum and bodies as multiple.

31 A clear account of this drive for mastery can be found in 'Beyond the pleasure principle', S.E., vol. XVIII, where Freud describes the *fort/da* game, a game of mastering the conceptions of presence and absence necessary to the acquisition of both subjectivity and language.

32 It is interesting to remark, in this context, that Marxism does not object to the notion of class consciousness, that develops through the subject's 'awareness' of where its interests lie, but cannot tolerate the notion of a sex(ed) consciousness.

33 See Merleau-Ponty, M., 'The child's relations with others', in *The Primacy of Perception* (Northwestern University Press, 1964), for an account of signification, introjection, and projection closely paralleling Lacan's, especially in terms of the centrality of the body-image in both accounts.

34 Both Freud and Stoller describe masculinity and femininity and their relation to maleness and femaleness in *quantitative* terms only. See Freud, S., S.E., vol. VIII, pp. 219–20fn; and Stoller, *Sex and Gender*, op. cit., p. 9. *Qualitative* distinctions are not considered.

35 See Lacan, J., 'Mirror phase', in *Ecrits*, op. cit.; and 'Some reflections on the ego', in *International Journal of Psychoanalysis*, vol. 34, 1953.

36 See introduction to *The Child, his Illness and Others*, M. Mannoni (Harmondsworth: Penguin, 1970); 'The function and field of speech and language in psychoanalysis' and 'The agency of the letter in the unconscious or reason since Freud', in *Ecrits*, op. cit.

37 Chodorow (1980) op. cit., p. 16.

38 ibid., p. 18 (my emphasis).

39 See Freud, S., 'On narcissism: an introduction', S.E., vol. XIV.

40 Laplanche, J., *Life and Death in Psychoanalysis* (London: Johns Hopkins UP, 1976), esp. ch. 4.

41 'Some reflections on the ego', op. cit., p. 14.

42 ibid., p. 13 (my emphasis).

43 See Merleau-Ponty, M., *The Phenomenology of Perception*, op. cit., esp. pp. 76–88; and Schilder, P., *The Image and Appearance of the Human Body*, op. cit., p. 63f and p. 119f.
44 ibid., p. 66f.
45 This unconscious equation is the inverse of Freud's breast = faeces = penis = baby, that is, mouth = anus = vagina. This phantasy is revealed in the pornographic films of Linda Lovelace where she has a clitoris at the back of her throat.
46 'Fragment of an analysis of a case of hysteria' ('Dora'), S.E., vol. VII.
47 See 'Infantile genital organisation', S.E., vol. XIX, p. 145.
48 Although Stoller himself begins to doubt this view in 1975, in *The Transsexual Experiment*, op. cit. (see esp. pp. 223–46).
49 He is not, of course, peculiar in this respect. However, the point is that the *duration* of this misrecognition is much greater in his case, largely due to the *quality* of the mothering he receives and the desire of his mother.
50 'The desire of the mother' should not, necessarily, be understood as her conscious desire. It is important to note Freud's claim here that 'It is a very remarkable thing that the unconscious of one human being can react upon that of another, without passing through the conscious', S.E., vol. XIV, 'The Unconscious', p. 194. See also Lacan, J., *Ecrits*, op. cit., pp. 288–9.
51 The 'sense of self' developed in the first two years of the child's life is, in the case of both male and female children predicated upon identification with the mother. For girls this identification is not problematic as it is a sex-appropriate identification. However, for boys this identification must be overlaid with male identifications at a later stage if they are to develop an appropriate male identity.
52 For example, see *m/f*, 7 (1982), editorial discussion with M. Barrett and R. Coward, p. 87f.
53 op. cit., p. 79.
54 ibid., p. 62. She cites in this context L. Comer and E. Belotti.
55 As Barrett clearly is, see for example, p. 53f.
56 See 'Of Marx and men', T. Carrigan in *Gay Information*, No. 11 (1982); and C. Johnston, 'Radical homosexual politics', Nos 2–3 (1980).
57 See *The Future of Difference*, op. cit., part II.
58 See Bacon, W. and Landsdown, R., 'Women who kill husbands, the battered wife on trial', in O'Donnell, C. and Craney, J. (eds), *Family Violence in Australia* (Melbourne: Longmans-Cheshire, 1982).
59 For example, Mitchell, J., *Women's Estate* (Harmondsworth: Penguin, 1971).
60 See Firestone, S., *The Dialectic of Sex* (London: Paladin, 1972), esp. ch. 10.
61 In this context see Flax, J., 'Mother–daughter relationships; psychodynamics, politics and philosophy', in *The Future of Difference*, op. cit., for an account of the phantasy of no women in the state of nature, esp. p. 29f.
62 See, for instance, Moller-Okin, S., *Women in Western Political Thought* (Princeton, NJ: 1979); Miller and Swift, *Words and Women* (NY: Anchor Doubleday, 1977), ch. 10; and Spender, D., *Man-Made Language* (London: Routledge & Kegan Paul, 1980).

Part V
PHILOSOPHY

INTRODUCTION

Elizabeth Grosz

The two papers comprising this section are a chapter from Genevieve Lloyd's book, *The Man of Reason*, entitled 'Reason as Attainment' and Moira Gatens' paper, 'Feminism and philosophy or riddles without answers'. They present two related but different approaches feminists have made in developing criticisms of the apparent sexual neutrality of the so-called 'queen of knowledges', philosophy. Because philosophy sees itself, and is seen by others, as providing both an explanation for and a critique of the presumptions and forms of argument used in other knowledges, and because many disciplines rely on philosophical positions to justify themselves (whether they recognize this or not), feminist interventions into philosophy may be of major strategic significance in the assessment and transformation of both philosophy and other academic disciplines. Moreover, well-placed criticisms of the discipline may exert a ripple effect on related or dependent knowledges: if basic questions regarding methods, criteria, and underlying assumptions are questions within philosophy, then both the sciences and the humanities may also be implicated.

Genevieve Lloyd's chapter comes from her detailed and sustained analysis of the ways in which reason has come to be conceived as an inherently and (usually) implicitly male enterprise throughout the history of philosophy. While her book ranges from the period of Greek philosophy to the modern period, culminating in the work of Sartre and de Beauvoir in the twentieth century, her third chapter, reprinted here, concentrates on the ways in which the threshold of modern philosophy, usually marked by the advent of Descartes' work, sets up a series of methods, goals, and presumptions which will negatively or positively characterize all of contemporary philosophy as well. In this chapter, she pairs the rationalism associated with Cartesian philosophy, with the empiricism attributed to Hume. Rationalism and empiricism are today seen as two competing and opposed positions; the former presumes the priority of mind over matter and privileges reason over perception and observation; the latter, by contrast, positions sensation, observation, perception, and matter in a position of priority over pure reason or conceptual processes in the attainment of knowledge. Although in this sense, rationalism and empiricism can be seen as opposites, each preferring opposed sides of the binaries mind/matter, subject/object, and reason/perception, in another sense, they can be seen merely as two sides of a single coin, as participants in a struggle over one and the same intellectual territory.

Lloyd focuses largely on the most privileged concept within the history of philosophy and of Descartes' treatment of it – the notion of reason. For Descartes, reason is not to be understood as a variable mode of apprehending objects (objects are, after all, highly variable and a reason based on the specificity of objects would have to be as variable as those objects); rather, it is a specific and singular form of the operations of the knowing subject's mind. It is an ordered and rigorous set of intellectual procedures, 'certain and simple rules', that are designed to ensure that truth can be guaranteed. Descartes concentrates on providing a set of methodological foundations or guarantees that will yield truth independent of the objects investigated. In this sense, his method is abstract and general: its goal is to be applicable to any object of investigation, whether this be the purely abstract notions provided by mathematics and geometry, the empirical and conjectural contents of the physical sciences, or the day-to-day knowledge of subjects provided by perception. His method would, Descartes hoped, provide a single, cohesive unity to the disparate forms of knowledge, showing them all to be the products of a unified and self-knowing mind.

His aspiration to provide a single unified method for all forms of knowledge is, Lloyd argues, based on a rigid separation, indeed dichotomization of mind and body. Where the body, and those pragmatic knowledges based on the body's capacities are disparate and varied, where, for example, the method needed to produce a good carpenter is quite different from that needed to produce a good ballet dancer, the mind is singular and unified. The arts, based on the body's various skills and capacities, are thus to be dramatically distinguished from the sciences and humanities, in which the mind and reason are pre-eminent. The mind was considered to be a natural or innate source of truth, if only its proper functioning, independent of the accepted and taught dogmas of tradition, could be ensured. This meant sweeping aside the false and constricting overlay of opinion and prejudice in favour of allowing the uncluttered and unobstructed mind the disciplined use of its own facilities and techniques.

Descartes thus formulated what he considered to be a few simple and direct procedures to remove the various obstacles to the mind's proper functioning: his method involved the breakdown of complex mental processes into their simplest components – clear and distinct ideas – and then a method of synthesizing the ideas thus analysed using an orderly and logical form of recombining, a kind of conceptual process of building or reconstruction. By using this method, the mind could be guaranteed access to the truth into whatever matters it enquired. The clarity and distinctness of ideas, their 'purity', comes, not from perception or from the information provided by the senses or the body – for the senses can be mistaken, and perception often provides confused rather than distinct ideas – but from the rational and controlled use of the mind. The body is thus regarded as a kind of impingement on, a sullying of, the ideas that are the raw materials of knowledge. It is not the senses, he argues, that perceive wax, because wax is so empirically changeable and dependent on various conditions; it is the mind that perceives its underlying identity. Descartes, Lloyd argues, aligns the distinction between the mind and the body with the opposition between reason and non-reason. It is only in so far as the mind is capable of clearing itself of the extraneous interferences of the body that it is capable of transcending the accidents and errors of perception.

Lloyd argues that Descartes' separation of the mind from the body had an ambiguous relation to women's access to the production of philosophy. On the one hand, by taking reason out of the hands of educators and a scholastic pedagogical tradition from which women had been excluded, and by making reason quite independent of the specificities of bodies, there was no *a priori* reason why women should be excluded from philosophical activities. If bodies have no direct relation to and influence on minds, then women's minds are as philosophically inclined as men's. He thus presumes an egalitarianism, or at least an egalitarian potential, to the operations of mind. Yet, on the other hand, Descartes none the less leaves the division of labour so prevalent in patriarchal societies still intact. While women are not actively excluded from the operations of reason, neither can they be included as women. It is only in so far as women have neutral, sexually indifferent minds that they have access to reason. Moreover, in spite of his own objectives in securing for the individual a private or conceptual access to reason, independent of its subjective particularity, Descartes nevertheless affirms women as the guardians of the sphere of everyday life, in which reason, emotions, mind, and body, are interrelated:

Women's task is to preserve the sphere of the intermingling of mind and body, to which the Man of Reason will repair for solace, warmth and relaxation. If he is to exercise the most exalted form of Reason, he must leave soft emotions and sensuousness behind; women will keep them intact for him. (Lloyd, p. 50)

In recognizing the implicit masculinity in the concept of reason as it is received by the philosophical community, Lloyd does not advocate the abandonment of reason by feminists. To affirm that philosophy has

up to now functioned to oppress and subordinate women does not necessarily mean the abandonment of philosophical principles, the refusal of
logic, truth, or validity. The critique of reason posed by many feminists
can, Lloyd argues, be seen as part of an ongoing tradition of auto-
critique, a critique sustained by philosophers themselves in their relations
to past or prevailing philosophical positions and systems. In short, while
reason is a male-dominated concept up to now, there is no reason to
suppose that philosophical notions of reason cannot themselves be
reformed so that transformations compatible with feminist principles can
themselves become part of the philosophical enterprise. Philosophy is
itself open-ended enough to be radically transformed. Lloyd retains the
belief that feminists need not abandon reason in devising critiques of it.
Indeed, through the interventions of feminists, philosophy could itself
become a genuinely human rather than an exclusively male endeavour.

Lloyd's position entails questioning the ways in which the discipline of
philosophy conceives of itself, its underlying and unrecognized masculinity which parades as universality. In investigating its masculinity,
women's access to the discipline can no longer be regarded as a matter
of individual struggle and achievement, but must be seen as a series of
political struggles against philosophical systems for the rights of self-
definition and a philosophical perspective. These are also the issues
concerning Gatens in her paper.

Gatens sets out to examine the ways in which women have been positioned in the discipline of philosophy. She focuses not so much on
women's passive placement by the discipline as on the ways in which
feminists have, in recognition of philosophy's misogyny, attempted to
reconstruct a philosophy able to include, speak to, and about women.
However, certain strategies developed by feminists have themselves fallen
into some of the misogynist traps lying within philosophy: in particular,
the strategy of extending philosophy so that where it had previously
excluded women, it was now capable of including them. Recourse to
universalisms or humanisms, in which women's activities are added to
those of men to provide a 'complete picture' of human activity involves
the strategy of neutralization (or neuterization), including women only in
so far as they are the same as men, on men's criteria. Gatens, for example, sees de Beauvoir as *more than* a faithful adherent, an acolyte; her
claim is that de Beauvoir has actively transformed existentialism from an
individualized account incapable of dealing with concepts like oppression
to a dynamic (if problematic) account of the oppression of women. De
Beauvoir has not only rewritten existentialism, but more relevantly in this
context, she has not recognized the substantial overhaul of Sartre's position she has undertaken: she herself has seen her work as an addendum
to his. In other words, she has rendered her own work invisible.

The third strategy Gatens outlines which implies the recuperation of critical feminist challenges to mainstream philosophical texts is a project of reformulating misogynistic philosophy from within. In adhering too closely to the criteria governing philosophical assessment and credibility (clear, logical argument, statements in principle translatable into logical form, etc.) feminist philosophers risk submitting their feminism to the primacy of philosophy instead of reordering philosophy according to principles.

Gatens examines the ways in which feminists have struggled against philosophy's resolute containment of women, making clear that the task is not as straightforward as it seems. If philosophy or, for that matter, other academic disciplines, are not to be abandoned altogether, then feminists must negotiate a series of manoeuvres that will not only cast feminist principles in philosophical terms, but will submit philosophy itself to feminist scrutiny and transformation. This would involve questioning many of the most basic assumptions of the discipline, its arbitrary division from other forms of knowledge, its goals, means, and criteria of assessment. Gatens advocates an open-ended philosophy, one capable of admitting its absences, accepting its limits and its partiality. Only such a broad and open field would enable women's differences, their specific interests to find philosophical expression, to be discussed, contested, transformed – a recognized and valued part of philosophical history rather than its unspoken underside.

Between them, Lloyd's and Gatens' papers articulate the field in which the current interactions between feminist theory and philosophy are played out: should feminism abandon philosophy altogether? Should feminism function to augment and supplement philosophy's absences and inconsistencies? Should feminism embark on the exploration of different philosophies? How? By what means? In short, they explore the various layers posed by the question: (how) is a feminist philosophy possible?

REASON AS ATTAINMENT

Genevieve Lloyd

INTRODUCTION

In *The Philosophy of Right*, Hegel contrasted the 'happy ideas, taste and elegance' characteristic of female consciousness with male attainments which demand a 'universal faculty'. 'Women are educated – who knows how? – as it were by breathing in ideas, by living rather than by acquiring knowledge. The status of manhood, on the other hand, is attained only by the stress of thought and much technical exertion.'[1] These kinds of connection between maleness and achievement are not confined to Hegel. In western thought, maleness has been seen as itself an achievement, attained by breaking away from the more 'natural' condition of women. Attitudes to Reason and its bearing on the rest of life have played a major part in this; a development that occurred in the seventeenth century has been particularly crucial.

In the illustrations, in the last chapter*, of Reason's superiority over other aspects of human nature, it was seen as a distinctive human trait, with ramifications in all areas of life – the practical, no less than the contemplative – even if, as with Augustine, this was regarded as an inferior diversion of Reason. In the seventeenth century, Reason came to be seen not just as a distinguishing feature of human nature, but as an achievement – a skill to be learned, a distinctively methodical way of thinking, sharply differentiated from other kinds of thought – and its relationships with other aspects of human nature were also transformed. The most thoroughgoing and influential version of Reason as methodical thought was the famous method of Descartes. Something happened here which proved crucial for the development of stereotypes of maleness and femaleness, and it happened in some ways despite Descartes' explicit intentions.

DESCARTES' METHOD

In its Greek origins, the basic meaning of 'method' was a road or path to be followed; and the metaphor of a path whose goal is understanding recurs throughout the entire philosophical tradition which grew from

Greek thought. The method which proceeds without analysis, says Socrates in Plato's *Phaedrus*, is 'like the groping of a blind man'.[2] The follower of true method is preserved from such blind wanderings by understanding the reason for which things are done in a certain order. Descartes used the same metaphors. In expounding his 'rules for the direction of the mind', he attacked those truth-seekers who 'conduct their minds along unexplored routes, having no reason to hope for success, but merely being willing to risk the experiment of finding whether the truth they seek lies there'. It is, he says, as if a man seeking treasure were to 'continuously roam the streets, seeking to find something that a passer-by might have chanced to drop'.[3] But, although the description of the goal remained much the same, Descartes completely transformed the relationship between Reason and method which had been central in the intellectual tradition since the time of Socrates.

The original Socratic ideal of method, illustrated by the definition of love, is expounded in the concluding sections of the *Phaedrus*. Right method, says Socrates, involves processes of generalization, the 'survey of scattered particulars, leading to their comprehension in one idea'; and processes of division into species, 'according to the natural formation, where the joint is, not breaking any part as a bad carver might'. These processes are aids to speaking and thinking; they belong in the art of rhetoric. But they are also supposed to be guides to truth, helping those who practise them to discern a 'one and many' in Nature. Most of the ingredients for later developments in the idea of method can be found in these brief *Phaedrus* passages: the idea of an orderly procedure; of an analysis to be conducted in relation to an end to be achieved; the connections between method and teaching; the importance of understanding the nature of the soul, in which persuasion is supposed to be induced. The ability to impart the Socratic art of rhetoric involves grasping its nature and relating its parts to the end which is supposed to be achieved in the soul. However, Socrates' general description of the art of rhetoric passed into the tradition as a general rubric which could be extended to any art: the teacher must have an understanding of what the art deals with and be able to analyse and evaluate its parts in relation to the achievement of its end.

Aristotle developed the idea of a systematic treatment of the art of arguing and debating into a concern with a rational way – a reasoned procedure – for arriving at sound conclusions. But the relation of reason to the 'way' or 'method' was similar to the original Socratic version. Reason – whether applied to the art of persuasion, to other arts, or more narrowly to the investigations which are supposed to yield truth – was incorporated into method. Method was a reasoned way of pursuing an activity; and it was the grasp of this internal reason which was supposed to enable the activity to be taught.

In Descartes' system, in contrast, method became not so much a reasoned way of proceeding – a path to be followed rationally – as a way of reason*ing*: a precisely ordered mode of abstract thinking. And the right order of thought was to be determined not by the variable subject-matter and ends of the activities at issue, but by the natural operations of the mind itself. Descartes' actual definitions of method are on the surface not very different from earlier ideas of method. By a method, he says in his *Rules for the Direction of the Mind*, he means

certain and simple rules such that, if a man observe them accurately, he shall never assume what is false as true, and will never spend his mental efforts to no purpose, but will always gradually increase his knowledge and so arrive at a true understanding of all that does not surpass his powers.[4]

To see what is really distinctive and important about Descartes' method we must see it in the context of the metaphysical doctrine for which he is most notorious – the radical separateness of mind and body – and also in the context of his immediate predecessors in the development of ideas of method.

Descartes' method, he insisted, is unitary and yields truth regardless of subject-matter. He criticized his Aristotelian scholastic predecessors for holding that the certainty of mathematics was unattainable in other sciences and that the method of each science should vary with differences in the material it investigated. A single and identical method, he thought, could be applied to all the various sciences, for the sciences taken together were nothing else but the very unity of human reason itself. This vision of the unity of the sciences as reflecting that of Reason arose directly from Descartes' radical separation of mind and body. Where body is involved, the formation of one habit inhibits that of others. The hand that adapts itself to agricultural operations is thereby less likely to be adept at harp playing. But the sciences consist entirely in the cognitive exercise of the mind. The traditional conception of a multiplicity of methods for different subject-areas thus rests on a faulty assimilation of mind to body. The sciences do not share in the inevitable multiplicity of the bodily arts. Knowing one truth does not have the restricting effect that is the consequence of mastering a bodily art; in fact it aids us in finding out other truths. So the sciences, taken all together, are identical with human wisdom, which always remains one and the same, however applied to different subjects.[5]

All this is strongly opposed to what Descartes saw as the arbitrariness of the prevailing scholastic curriculum divisions. This concern was not new. Descartes' humanist predecessors had also been dissatisfied with the arbitrary methods of presentation of the traditional disciplines which, they thought, created needless difficulties for students. In the sixteenth century, Peter Ramus had devised 'one simple method' to bring order to the subjects taught in universities. Ramus' method proceeded from universal and general principles down to the more specific and singular, an order which he supposed to reflect the different degrees of clarity among the parts of a discipline. The clearer was to precede the more obscure, following the order and progression from universal to singular. Aristotle had distinguished what is prior in Nature and what is prior to us. Ramus' idea was a right order and progression of thought, which would reflect the priority in Nature of the universal over the particular. But there was no real justification for his conviction that what was prior in being should also be clearer to students.[6]

For Descartes, the idea of a right order of thought was grounded in an understanding of the nature of the mind. The correspondence between the basic structures of human thought and the order of the world, he argued, is divinely guaranteed. To find and to follow the mind's most basic operations was for him not just a prerequisite for ease in learning. His organization of subject-matter in accordance with what is more apparent to an attentive mind was not just a pedagogical device. Clarity and distinctness were the marks of truth. His method was directed to uncovering those basic ideas whose truth was assured by the fact that a veracious God created both the mind and the material world. Method was not confined to pedagogy; it was linked with criteria of truth.

As a development in the politics of learning, the significance of this approach to method cannot be overestimated. Earlier Renaissance reforms of educational procedures often found themselves in conflict with those who saw following the 'natural' processes of the mind as less important than following approved methods of strict demonstration and proof, however difficult these may have been to impart to students. Descartes' method undercut this conflict. Its aim went beyond the transmission of an already established art or the successful pursuit of a course of study; it aimed at valid knowledge. It should not be seen, he insisted, as a means of persuasion, belonging in the art of rhetoric; it belonged, rather, with the discovery of new truth. But such discovery was assured precisely through following the natural processes of thought. At the same time, Descartes' grounding of this unified method in the unity of Reason itself, accessible through introspection, enabled him to separate method entirely from the realm of public pedagogy and disputation.

The implications for Reason of thus severing the links between method and public procedures of discourse, debate, and successful argument were far-reaching. The right ordering of ideas was no longer associated with the best arrangement of the school curricula, but with private abstract thought, which can be pursued quite independently of public educational structures and procedures. Persuasion was internalized as what is clear and apparent to an attentive mind – the mark of truth itself. Reasoning in accordance with this new method does not demand conformity with the subtle forms of argument accepted as valid in the public disputations of the schools. The emphasis is entirely on unaided Reason. Descartes presented the method as simply a systematization of the innate faculty of Reason or 'good sense' – the power of 'forming good judgement and of distinguishing the true from the false'. And this natural light of Reason is supposedly equal in all.[7]

Descartes saw his method as opening the way to a new egalitarianism in knowledge. In a letter written shortly after the publication of the *Discourse on Method*, he commented that his thoughts on method seemed to him appropriate to put in a book where he wished that 'even women' might understand something.[8] From our perspective, this tone may sound patronizing, but the remark is to be understood against the background of associations between earlier Renaissance versions of method and pedagogical procedures. By and large, it was only boys who were given systematic formal education outside the home. The exclusion of women from method was a direct consequence of their exclusion from the schools in which it was pursued. Descartes' egalitarian intentions come out also in his insistence on writing the *Discourse on Method* in the vernacular, rather than in Latin, the learned language of the schools. The work, he stressed, should appeal to those who avail themselves only of their natural reason in its purity.[9] The point was political as well as practical. The use of Latin was in many ways the distinguishing mark of the learned. Women, being educated mostly at home rather than in the schools, had no direct access to the learned, Latin-speaking world. The teaching of Latin to boys thus marked the boundaries between the private world of the family, in which the vernacular was used, and the external world of learning, to which males had access.[10] The accessibility of the new method even to women was thus a powerful symbol of the transformation which it marked in the relationship between method and autonomous, individual reasoning.

In place of the subtleties of scholastic disputation, which can only, he thought, obscure the mind's natural clarity, Descartes offered a few supposedly simple procedures, the rationale of which was to remove all obstacles to the natural operations of the mind. The general rubric of the method was to break down the more complex operations of the mind into their simplest forms and then recombine them in an orderly series. The complex and obscure is reduced to simple, self-evident 'intuitions', which the mind scrutinizes with 'steadfast, mental gaze', then combines in orderly chains of deductions.[11] Anyone who follows this method can feel assured that 'no avenue to the truth is closed to him from which everyone else is not also excluded, and that his ignorance is due neither to a deficiency in his capacity nor to his method of procedure'.[12]

Descartes' method, with its new emphasis on the privacy of the mind's natural operations, promised to make knowledge accessible to all, even to women. Such was his intent. The lasting influence of his method, however, was something quite different, though no less a product of his radical separation of mind and body. In the context of associations already existing between gender and Reason, his version of the mind–body relationship produced stark polarizations of previously existing contrasts. This came about not through any intellectual move made within his system, but as a by-product of his transformation of the relations between Reason and its opposites. Descartes strongly repudiated his medieval predecessors' idea of a divided soul, which had Reason – identified with the authentic character of a human being – struggling with lesser parts of the soul. For him, the soul was not to be divided into higher (intellectual) and lower (sensitive) parts; it was an indivisible unity, identified with pure intellect. He replaced the medieval philosophers' divisions between higher and lower parts of the soul with the dichotomy between mind and body. In this limited respect, Descartes' system echoed the thought of the early Plato. In place of the older divisions within the soul he introduced a division between the soul – now identified again with the mind – and body; the non-rational was no longer part of the soul, but pertained entirely to the body.

> There is within us but one soul, and this soul has not in itself any diversity of parts; the same part that is subject to sense impressions is rational, and all the soul's appetites are acts of will. The error which has been committed in making it play the parts of various personages, usually in opposition one to another, only proceeds from the fact that we have not properly distinguished its functions from those of the body, to which alone we must attribute everything which can be observed in us that is opposed to our reason.[13]

The drama of dominance between human traits persisted in Descartes' philosophy, but it was played out as a struggle between the soul itself – equated with pure intellect – and body. He saw the encroachments of non-intellectual passion, sense, or imagination as coming not from lower parts or aspects of the soul, but from altogether outside the soul – as intrusions from body. Descartes' method is founded on this alignment between the bodily and the non-rational. It involves forming the habit of distinguishing intellectual from corporeal matters. And this search for the purely intellectual – the clear and distinct – made possible polarizations of previously existing contrasts, which had previously been drawn within the boundaries of the soul. Those aspects of human nature which Reason must dominate had not previously been so sharply delineated from the intellectual. The distinction between Reason and its opposites could now coincide with Descartes' very sharp distinction – than which, as he says, none can be sharper – between mind and body.

Descartes' alignment between the Reason–non-Reason and mind–body distinctions brought with it the notion of a distinctive kind of rational thought as a highly restricted activity. Augustine had presented the mind's dealings with practical matters as a diversion of a unitary Reason from its superior function of contemplation. This diversion was at risk of entanglement with sense, but it was not thereby different in kind from the Reason employed in contemplative thought. Descartes separated thought of the kind that yields certainty much more sharply from the practical concerns of life. It was for him a highly rarefied exercise of intellect, a complete transcending of the sensuous – a highly arduous activity which cannot be expected to occupy more than a very small part of a normal life. In the *Discourse on Method*, he stressed the contrasts between the demands of enquiry into truth and the attitudes appropriate to the practical activities of life. The foundations of the enquiry into truth demand that the mind rigorously enact the metaphysical truth of its separateness from body. This securing of the foundations of knowledge is a separate activity from the much more relaxed pursuits of everyday life, where mind must accept its intermingling with body. Descartes' separation of mind and body yielded a vision of a unitary pure thought, ranging like the common light of the sun over a variety of objects. Its unitariness, however, served also to separate it from the rest of life.

Pure thought of this rarefied kind secures the foundations of science. However, most of scientific activity itself involves exercise of the imagination rather than of pure intellect; scientific investigation, although it demands sustained effort and training, occupies an intermediate position between pure intellect and the confusion of sense. The rest of life is rightly given over to the sway of the senses, to that muddled zone of confused perception where mind and body intermingle. In his correspondence with Princess Elizabeth, Descartes again stressed that arduous clear and distinct thought, of the kind that secures the foundation of science, can and should occupy only a small part of a well-spent life. If we can take seriously his autobiographical remarks to her – as he insists she should – it is something to which he himself devoted only a few hours a year.[14] It is through pure intellect, transcending the intrusion of body, that we grasp the separateness of mind and body on which true science is founded. The greater part of the life of a Cartesian self is lived in the zone of confused, sensuous awareness. However, it is sustained there by the metaphysical truth, which pure thought can grasp, of the absolute separateness of mind and body; and by the possibility of a complete science grounded in this truth. Underlying the confusion of the senses, there is a crystalline realm of order, where sharply articulated structures of thought perfectly match the structure of intelligible reality. These clear, matching structures of mind and matter underlie the confused realm of the sensuous produced by the intermingling of both. Individual minds can rest assured that there is an underlying right order of thought, which provides a secure underpinning for lives lived predominantly in the realm of the sensuous; the confusions of sense and imagination hold no ultimate threat.

Arduous as the grasp of the metaphysical basis of Descartes' method may be, the method itself was supposed to be accessible to all. And within the terms of the system there is, in all this, no differentiation between male and female minds. Both must be seen as equally intellectual substances, endowed with good sense or Reason. The difference in intellectual achievement between men and women, no less than that between different men, must arise not from some being more rational than others, but 'solely from the fact that our thoughts pass through diverse channels and the same objects are not considered by all'.[15] But removing method from the restraints of public pedagogy did not, in practice, make knowledge any more accessible to women. Descartes' method may be essentially private and accessible to all. But for him, no less than Bacon, the new science was, none the less, a collective endeavour. It is by 'joining together the lives and labours of many', he says in the concluding section of the *Discourse on Method*, that science will progress.[16] It is through a corporate exercise, however non-corporeal may be its ultimate metaphysical foundation, that the new science will advance, rendering humanity the promised goal of becoming 'masters and possessors of nature'.[17] Descartes thought his account of the mind opened the way to a newly egalitarian pursuit of knowledge. But the channels through which those basically equal resources of Reason had to flow remained more convoluted, even for noble women, than for men. Elizabeth poignantly expressed the situation in one of her letters to Descartes:

the life I am constrained to lead does not allow me enough free time to acquire a habit of meditation in accordance with your rules. Sometimes the interests of my household, which I must not neglect, sometimes conversations and civilities I cannot eschew, so thoroughly deject this weak mind with annoyances or boredom that it remains, for a long time afterward, useless for anything else.[18]

The realities of the lives of women, despite their supposed equality in Reason, precluded them, too, from any significant involvement in the collective endeavours of science, the developing forms of which quickly outstripped the private procedures of Descartes' method.

It is not just impinging social realities, however, which militate against sexual equality in this new version of Reason's relations with science. There are aspects of Descartes' thought which – however unintentionally – provided a basis for a sexual division of mental labour whose influence is still very much with us. Descartes' emphasis on the equality of Reason had less influence than his formative contribution to the ideal of a distinctive kind of Reason – a highly abstract mode of thought, separable, in principle, from the emotional complexities and practical demands of ordinary life. This was not the only kind of thought which Descartes recognized as rational. In the Sixth Meditation he acknowledged that the inferior senses, once they have been set aside from the search for truth – where they can only mislead and distort – are reliable guides to our well-being. To trust them is not irrational. He does not maintain that we are rational only when exercising arduous pure thought, engaged in intellectual contemplation, and assembling chains of deductions. Indeed, he thinks it is not rational to spend an excessive amount of time in such purely intellectual activity.[19] None the less, through his philosophy, Reason took on special associations with the realm of pure thought, which provides the foundations of science, and with the deductive ratiocination which was of the essence of his method. And the sharpness of his separation of the ultimate requirements of truth-seeking from the practical affairs of everyday life reinforced already existing distinctions between male and female roles, opening the way to the idea of distinctive male and female consciousness.

We owe to Descartes an influential and pervasive theory of mind, which provides support for a powerful version of the sexual division of mental labour. Women have been assigned responsibility for that realm of the sensuous which the Cartesian Man of Reason must transcend, if he is to have true knowledge of things. He must move on to the exercise of disciplined imagination, in most of scientific activity; and to the rigours of pure intellect, if he would grasp the ultimate foundations of science. Woman's task is to preserve the sphere of the intermingling of mind and body, to which the Man of Reason will repair for solace, warmth, and relaxation. If he is to exercise the most exalted form of Reason, he must leave soft emotions and sensuousness behind; woman will keep them intact for him. The way was thus opened for women to be associated with not just a lesser presence of Reason, but a different kind of intellectual character, construed as complementary to 'male' Reason. This crucial development springs from the accentuation of women's exclusion from Reason, now conceived – in its highest form – as an attainment.

HUME ON REASON AND THE PASSIONS

Descartes' method transformed Reason into a uniform, undifferentiated skill, abstracted from any determinate subject-matter. This loss of differentiation gave rise to another crucial change. Reason lost the strong motivational force it had in earlier thought. In the lack of inner direction to specific ends, Descartes' Reason became an inert instrument, needing direction by an extraneous will. For him, the understanding lacked even the power to affirm or deny, and its polarization from the non-rational bodily passions deprived it also of the capacity to struggle directly with non-rational forces. Plato's Reason, in contrast, was presented as straining of its own resources towards truth; and in the 'divided-soul' model, Reason deliberated about ends, decided between them, and struggled with the passions to determine which end would prevail. Aristotle, too, despite his repudiation of the divided soul, presented Reason as controlling or subduing by its own force the emotional part of human nature.

For Descartes, Reason's origins ensured it a connection with truth and with human well-being, though one that depended on an extraneous divine benevolence. But if his supporting theological views are repudiated, the impotence of this methodical abstract thought becomes apparent. Spinoza, reacting against the passivity of Descartes' version of Reason, rejected the distinction between will and understanding, making Reason an active, emotional force, able – like the earlier Greek versions of Reason – to engage with passions in its own right. But it was Descartes' version of Reason that prevailed; and its inherent inertness and impotence appeared most starkly in Hume's version of Reason. For Hume, Reason has of itself no power to control passion or to deliberate about ends. Its motivating force lies always outside itself, in the driving force of passion. Under the aegis of different passions, it is directed to different ends. Reason has of itself no power to deliberate about ends or to choose between them; and it entirely lacks the affective force necessary to struggle with the passions. It 'is and ought to be nothing but the slave of the passions, pretending to no other office but to serve and obey them.'[20]

What are the implications of this reversal for the male–female distinction? We might expect it to loosen the alignment between maleness and Reason, but what actually happens is a subtle reinforcement of the older pattern. To see how this is so we must look more closely at Hume's restructuring of the Reason–passion distinction, and at its repercussions in Kant's treatment of the role of Reason in morality.

Hume turned on its head the seventeenth-century rationalists' picture of the role of Reason in knowledge and, more generally, in human life. For him, all our beliefs about the world, all our knowledge of matters of fact, resolve into expectations of stability, predictability, and constancy arising from customary associations in the mind. Reason plays no part in all this; belief is a function of our sensitive rather than of our cognitive nature. Reason can conjoin ideas in chains of necessary deduction; but these cannot yield understanding of the real natures of things. Reason yields knowledge in strictly limited areas of thought, such as logic and mathematics, where all that is involved is a grasp of entirely formal relations between ideas; knowledge of 'matters of fact', however, is the province not of Reason, but of imagination. The understanding

175

which delivers the world to us is reduced to 'the general and more established properties of the imagination', in contrast to the 'trivial suggestions of the fancy'.[21] Its reliability rests entirely on the force of our 'strong propensities', under the force of custom, to consider things in a certain way. For Descartes, conformity to Reason determined what is or is not to be regarded as 'natural'; for Hume, it was the other way round: Reason must rest on and conform to our natural propensities. 'Where reason is lively, and mixes itself with some propensity, it ought to be assented to. Where it does not, it never can have any title to operate upon us.'[22] These strong inclinations are the test of what is trustworthy in human thought, and provide the motivating force for a Reason which is of itself entirely inert.

A new and, at first sight, disconcerting picture emerges of the role of Reason in morality. Reason can still discover connections between things, but it has no role in how those connections affect us. Of itself it can never 'produce any action or give rise to volition'. Nor can it prevent volition, or 'dispute the preference' with any passion or emotion.[23] The supposed pre-eminence of Reason above passion rests on a misunderstanding; the principle which opposes our passion is called Reason only in an improper sense. Hume's argument for this conclusion is not altogether persuasive. Passions, he points out, are not susceptible of agreement or disagreement with relations of ideas or matters of fact, and are therefore incapable of being true or false – a prerequisite for being in conflict with Reason. But what is important here is not Hume's justification of the point, but its import for his understanding of morals.

Where a passion is neither founded on false suppositions, nor chuses meaning insufficient for the ends, the understanding can neither justify nor condemn it. 'Tis not contrary to reason to prefer the destruction of the whole world to the scratching of my finger. 'Tis not contrary to reason for me to chuse my total ruin, to prevent the least uneasiness of an Indian or person wholly unknown to me. 'Tis as little contrary to reason to prefer even my own acknowledg'd lesser good to my greater, and have a more ardent affection for the former than the latter.[24]

Hume's point is not that any of these stances should be regarded as acceptable to people of good sense, but rather that their being or not being so is in no way a matter of Reason. Moral distinctions are not the 'offspring of reason', which is wholly inactive.[25] They derive from a moral sense grounded in feelings or sentiment. Hume acknowledged that the idea that moral distinctions derive from passions, in relation to which Reason is utterly impotent, would meet with resistance. But he diagnosed this resistance as resulting from conflating with Reason what are in fact 'calm passions' – actions of the mind which resemble Reason in that they operate with the same calmness and tranquillity, producing little emotion in the mind. Such calm passions as benevolence, the love of life, kindness to children, or 'the general appetite to good, and aversion to evil' influence the mind no less than the more violent passions of resentment, fear, or apprehension. What we call 'strength of mind' implies the prevalence of the calm passions above the violent; and this, Hume suggests, is what is 'vulgarly' called reason. It refers to affections of the same kind as the passions, but 'such as operate more calmly, and cause no disorder in the temper'. But their comparative tranquillity causes us to regard them as conclusions only of our intellectual faculties. Generally speaking, it is the violent passions that have the more powerful influence on the will. But it is often found that the calm ones, 'when corroborated by reflection, and seconded by resolution', are 'able to controul them in their most furious movements'. This 'struggle of passion and reason', as it is called, Hume concludes, 'diversifies human life', making men different 'not only from each other, but also from themselves in different times'.[26]

On the basis of this general distinction between calm and violent passions, Hume reconstructs the distinction between Reason and passion in terms of two forms of acquisitiveness or self-interest; he argues that the curbing of one by the other is the basis of civil society.[27] The more primitive forms of the passion of acquisitiveness produce inevitable conflicts in large societies; for acquisitiveness combines destructively with partiality of affection – the tendency to give priority to our own interests and those of our immediate relatives. The 'first and most natural sentiment of morals' is associated with this immediate preference for ourselves and friends above strangers. But it combines with the passion of acquisitiveness to produce inevitable social conflict. The resources available to satisfy the passion of acquisitiveness are limited; and the avid desire to acquire goods and possessions for ourselves and our nearest friends is 'insatiable, perpetual, universal and directly destructive of society'. So the 'partial and contradictory motions of the passions of different individuals' must be restrained, if society is to survive.

However, this passion – like all passions, according to Hume – can be controlled only by a stronger one; and the only passion strong enough to regulate and restrain it is acquisitiveness itself. It alone has sufficient force and proper direction to counterbalance the love of gain and render men fit members of society by making them abstain from the possessions of others. If it is to play this restraining role, it must first undergo a change of direction. But this readily happens, Hume thinks, on the slightest reflection,

since 'tis evident, that the passion is much better satisfy'd by its restraint, than by its liberty, and that in preserving society, we make

177

much greater advances in acquiring possessions, than in the solitary and forlorn condition, which must follow upon violence and an universal licence.[28]

The preservation of society thus rests on the control of acquisitiveness by a more reflective and far-sighted version of itself: 'whether the passion of self-interest be esteemed vicious or virtuous, 'tis all of a case; since itself alone restrains it: So that if it be virtuous, men become social by their virtue; if vicious, their vice has the same effect.'

In this reconstruction of the old theme of the subordination of passion to Reason, control is exercised not strictly by Reason, but by a calm, reflective form of passion – an enlightened self-interest. But the resulting operations of justice in society can be ascribed to Reason in an improper sense, in that they involve considering objects 'at a distance'. From this more detached perspective, preference can be given to 'whatever is in itself preferable' – a principle that is 'often contradictory to those propensities that display themselves upon the approach of the object'.[29]

Reason, as reflective passion, remains for Hume a weak and vulnerable force in comparison with more immediate forms of acquisitiveness. In the normal course of events, it does not prevail over the more intense attractions of objects close by. To have efficacy it must be embodied in externally imposed authority. The social remedy for destructive self-interest depends on making the long-term observance of justice the immediate interest of particular persons who take responsibility for the execution of justice. When the reflective form of acquisitiveness is embodied in institutions of justice, 'men acquire a security against each others' weakness and passion, as well as against their own, and under the shelter of their governors, begin to taste at ease the sweets of society and mutual assistance'.[30]

This, then, is Hume's version of the relationship between Reason and passion: immediate self-interest subjected to the control of a higher and more reflective version of itself. Reason in its 'improper' sense – whether it be 'calm' as against 'violent' passions, 'reflective' as against 'immediate' and 'partial' self-interest, or 'remote' perspective embodied in magistrates as against the pursuit of short-term interests – controls passion. And this relation of dominance or control is articulated in terms of a distinction between 'public' and 'private' interests. The public passion of acquisitiveness is given the role of curbing private interest in acquiring goods and possessions for the sake of the individual and his family.

Hume does not pursue the implications of his reconstruction of the Reason–passion distinction for male–female relations. But the individual whose private interests must be controlled by considerations of justice is perforce, of course, the male head of a household. Women are associated with 'private' passion, because it is on their behalf that male household heads pursue private acquisitiveness. In its social context, Hume's version of Reason, like Descartes', which made it possible, takes on associations with maleness, even if these are not specifically required by their philosophical theory.

NOTES

1 Hegel, G.W.F. (1821) *The Philosophy of Right*, trans. T.M. Knox (Oxford: Oxford University Press, 1952), add. 107, para. 166, pp. 263–4.

2 Plato, *Phaedrus*, 270e. Quotations are from the translation by B. Jowett, in *The Dialogues of Plato*, vol. I (New York: Random House, 1937).

3 Descartes, R. (1701) *Rules for the Direction of the Mind*, rule IV, trans. E.S. Haldane and G.R.T. Ross, *The Philosophical Works of Descartes*, vol. I (Cambridge: Cambridge University Press, 1972), p. 9.

4 ibid.

5 ibid., rule I, in Haldane and Ross, op. cit., vol. I, pp. 1–2.

6 For an informative treatment of the contrasts between humanist pedagogical reforms and seventeenth-century versions of method, see Ong, W.J., *Ramus: Method and the Decay of Dialogue, From the Art of Discourse to the Art of Reason* (Cambridge, Mass.: Harvard University Press, 1958).

7 Descartes, R. (1637) *Discourse on Method*, pt I, in Haldane and Ross, op. cit., vol. I, p. 81.

8 Letter to Vatier, 22 February 1638; in Alquié, F., *Oeuvres Philosophiques de Descartes*, vol. II (Paris: Editions Garnier Frères, 1967), p. 27.

9 Descartes, R. (1637) op. cit., pt VI, in Haldane and Ross, op. cit., vol. I, p. 130.

10 For an interesting discussion of this aspect of the use of Latin, see Ong, W.J., 'Latin language study as a Renaissance puberty rite', in *Rhetoric, Romance and Technology: Studies in the Interaction of Expression and Culture* (Ithaca, NY: Cornell University Press, 1971).

11 Descartes, R. (1701) op. cit., rule XII, in Haldane and Ross, op. cit., vol. I, p. 46.

12 ibid., rule VIII, in Haldane and Ross, op. cit., vol. I, p. 28.

13 Descartes, R. (1649) *The Passions of the Soul*, pt I, art. XLVII, in Haldane and Ross, op. cit., vol. I, p. 353.

14 Letter to Princess Elizabeth, 28 June 1643, in Kenny, A. (ed.), *Descartes: Philosophical Letters* (Oxford: Oxford University Press, 1970), pp. 140–3.

15 Descartes, R. (1637) op. cit., pt I, in Haldane and Ross, op. cit., vol. I, p. 81–2.

16 ibid., pt VI, in Haldane and Ross, op. cit., vol. I, p. 120.

17 ibid., p. 119.

18 Princess Elizabeth to Descartes, 10/20 June 1643, trans. J. Blom, in *Descartes: His Moral Philosophy and Psychology* (Hassocks: Harvester Press, 1978), p. 111.

19 Letter to Princess Elizabeth, 28 June 1643, in Kenny, op. cit., pp. 140–3.

20 Hume, D. (1734–6) *Treatise of Human Nature*, ed. L.A. Selby-Bigge (Oxford: Oxford University Press, 1960), vol. II, pt III, sec III, p. 415.

21 ibid., vol. I, pt IV, sec. VII, p. 267.

22 ibid., p. 270.

23 ibid., vol. I, pt III, sec. III, pp. 414–15.

24 ibid., p. 416.
25 ibid., vol. III, pt I, sec. I, p. 458.
26 ibid., vol. II, pt III, sec. VIII, p. 438.
27 ibid., vol. III, pt II, sec. II, pp. 484–501.
28 ibid., p. 492.
29 ibid., vol. III, pt II, sec. VII, p. 536.
30 ibid., p. 538.
 * Readers are referred to the book-length study of which this is an extract: G. Lloyd, *The Man of Reason* (London: Methuen & Co., 1984).

FEMINISM, PHILOSOPHY, AND RIDDLES WITHOUT ANSWERS

Moira Gatens

'Would you tell me, please, which way I ought to go from here?'
'That depends a good deal on where you want to get to,' said the Cat.
'I don't much care where –' said Alice.
'Then it doesn't matter much which way you go,' said the Cat.
'– so long as I get *somewhere*,' Alice added as an explanation.
'Oh, you're sure to do that,' said the Cat, 'if only you walk long enough.'
Alice felt that this could not be denied, so she tried another question.
'What sort of people live about here?'
'In *that* direction,' the Cat said, waving its right paw around, 'lives a hatter: and in *that* direction,' waving the other paw, 'lives a March Hare. Visit either you like: they're both mad.'
'But I don't want to go among mad people,' Alice remarked.
'Oh, you can't help that,' said the Cat: 'we're all mad here, I'm mad. You're mad.'
'How do you know I'm mad?' said Alice.
'You must be,' said the Cat, 'or you wouldn't have come here.'
(Carroll, 1972, pp. 88–9)

This quotation is intended to act, thematically, as an allegorical description of the kind of argument presented in this paper concerning the relationship between feminism and theory, or more specifically, feminists working in philosophy. Some readers may recall that Alice opts for the path on the left, and thus, for the March Hare. However, regardless of her choice, she wanders into the Mad Hatter's Tea Party – she meets both the Hatter and the Hare, each in the company of the other. That the company Alice consciously seeks has little to do with the company she finds herself in is relevant to the present concern in the following way. It will be central to my argument throughout this chapter, concerning the relations between feminism and philosophy, that feminists working within the discipline of philosophy cannot *choose* to pursue and create a theory of women's subjectivity, of women's social and political existence, and so on, independently or in spite of the western philosophical tradition. Like the Mad Hatter, the assumptions and frameworks of traditional philosophy will crop up in the most unlikely places and in a most alarming manner. Traditional philosophy cannot, in my view, simply be ignored, particularly by those who find themselves in the Wonderland of philosophy. But perhaps I am jumping ahead here and offering solutions to the riddle before it has been posed. The riddle is 'What is the relation, if any, between feminism and philosophy?'

An overview of past and present relations between feminist theory and philosophical discourse suggests three dominant ways in which this relation could be characterized. I would like to examine, in detail, all three. Before doing so, however, a note of caution should be struck. These three approaches or attitudes to philosophy, by feminists, are not easily separated or discrete, nor necessarily in complete opposition to each other.

BELLEROPHONTIC LETTERS

The first way in which the relationship between feminist theory and philosophy has been characterized may be seen as a form of radical feminism or theoretical separatism. These feminists present two kinds of arguments. The first is that there is no relation between feminism and philosophy, or more generally between feminism and *theory*. Feminism, on this view, is pure praxis, the very activity of theorizing being somehow identified with masculinity or maleness. Perhaps the view of Solanas would be appropriate to quote here. She writes:

The male's inability to relate to anybody or anything makes his life pointless and meaningless (the ultimate male insight is that life is absurd), so he invented philosophy. . . . Most men, utterly cowardly, project their inherent weaknesses onto women, label them female weaknesses and believe themselves to have female strengths; most philosophers, not quite so cowardly, face the fact that male lacks exist in men, but still can't face the fact that they exist in men only. So they label the male condition the Human Condition, pose their nothingness problem, which horrifies them, as a philosophical dilemma, thereby giving stature to their animalism, grandiloquently label their nothingness their 'Identity Problem' and proceed to prattle on pompously about the 'Crisis of the Individual', the 'Essence of Being', 'Existence preceding Essence', 'Existential Modes of Being' etc., etc. (Solanas, 1969, p. 265)

These problems are described by Solanas as specifically *male* problems. The female, on her account, exhibits no such perverse relation to her being, which she grasps intuitively and without lack. Philosophy, or theory, on this view is a male enterprise, arising out of an inherent inadequacy of the male sex.

The second argument of feminists, still within this first approach, is that there is a relation between feminism and philosophy but that it is historically, and *necessarily*, an oppressive one. This group argues that philosophy is, necessarily, a masculine enterprise that owes its existence to the repression or exclusion of femininity and as such it is of no use to feminists or their projects. In fact, philosophy may be seen, on this view, as a dangerous and ensnaring trap (Daly, 1978, introduction). Political action, if it is to be effective, needs to dissociate itself from traditional theory. What is needed is not a new theory but, as d'Eaubonne argues, a mutation. She writes:

> It is essential today that the spirit of the revolution to be accomplished go beyond what has been called until now the 'revolutionary spirit', just as the latter went beyond reformism. Ultimately, it is no longer a revolution that we need, but a *mutation*. (d'Eaubonne, 1980, p. 66; emphasis added)

The history of philosophy is, on this view, obsolete, dead, or dying; we must 'start from scratch', and as for history, she cries: 'Spit on Hegel!' In terms of the first approach then, the reply to the riddle of relation between feminism and philosophy is that the relation is disjunctive. One chooses feminism *over* philosophy. This approach to philosophy has several problems. It is dependent for its rationale on an unspoken and unexamined proposition that philosophy, as a discipline or an activity, coincides with its past. It assumes that philosophy is and will be what it was. This reification of philosophy misses the point that philosophy is, among other things, a human activity that is *ongoing*. Some philosophers may have proposed that their systems were closed, complete, and able to transcend history, but this is no reason for us to assent to their propositions. Since the objects of philosophical enquiry (that is, the human being, its cultural, political, and linguistic environment), are not static entities, the project of philosophy is, necessarily, open-ended. The conceptions of philosophy as a system of truths that could, in principle, be complete, true for all time, relies on the correlative claim that nature or ontology and truth or epistemology are static. In that feminists in the first approach accept the picture that philosophy likes to present of itself it allows this dominant characterization free rein. Moreover, the first approach, if presented as a practical and viable alternative for feminism, rather than as a limited strategy, may have a lesson to learn from the story of Bellerophon.

Bellerophon, a brave warrior from Greek mythology, travels to a new land, unaware that he carries on his person, in the form of a letter, the orders for his own execution. Whether or not feminist consciousness is 'inscribed' in an analogous fashion is a matter of great debate. The response of any particular person to this question would be influenced by that person's commitment, or lack of commitment, to the psycho-analytic view of the unconscious, to various structuralist and post-structuralist claims concerning the social construction of consciousness, and so on. My own view is that one's *conscious* intentions have less to do with one's practical and theoretical behaviour than some feminists would have us think. It is the recalcitrant attitude of human beings to social change, regardless of their conscious intentions, that led many feminists, especially in the mid- and late 1970s, to study the unconscious and its relation to the production and reproduction of patriarchal and class ideologies. That this analysis has been abandoned by some and continues, for those who are still working within its parameters, to prove difficult, does not mean that it is, therefore, inessential. Perhaps the study needs to be tackled from another direction, a question I will consider in the third part of this chapter. For now I shall do no more than indicate that the first approach towards the question of the relation between feminism and philosophy, if presented as a long-term pro-gramme, is utopian and runs the serious risk of reproducing, elsewhere, the very relations which it seeks to leave behind.

THE PROJECT OF EXTENSION

Whereas the first approach, in its most extreme form, sees both the method or framework of philosophy and its concrete content as anti-thetical to feminist aims, the second approach is characterized by seeing the *content* only as oppressive to women. In other words, feminists in the second category, a category that may be typified by, though not limited to, the stance of liberal feminists, agree that historically, philosophy has had an oppressive relation to women (of misogyny, of omission) but that this relation is not a *necessary* one. They argue or assume that philosophy as a discipline and as a method of enquiry is entirely neutral with regard to sex. Researchers adopting this approach view the history of philosophy as male-dominated, but argue that women are presently in a situation of being able to correct this bias. Here, then, the relation between feminist theory and philosophy is envisaged as a complementary one, where feminist theory adds to, or completes, traditional or existing philosophy, by filling in the 'gaps' in political, moral, and social theory. By *adding* an analysis of the specific social, political, and economic experience of women, this approach seeks to transform philosophy from a male-dominated enterprise into a *human* enterprise.

In its more radical form this approach may do more than merely add the lived experience of women; it may also purport to offer the means by which that experience may be altered. Philosophy may be seen, in other words, as more than a merely *descriptive* tool – it may also be seen as a transformative activity which is capable not only of analysing social relations but also of providing a means whereby one may intervene and change those relations. The answer of these feminists to our riddle is to opt for the conjunction, at least initially. I say *initially* because implicit in much of their work is the notion of the 'inbuilt obsolescence' of feminism. Eventually, they suppose, it will be unnecessary to retain a specifically feminist perspective. Once the goal of equality is reached, feminism would be redundant.

What this approach usually entails is the adoption of a particular philosophical theory (for example liberalism, existentialism, Marxism), as a method of analysis which then takes 'woman' as its object, as its (philosophical) problem. Certainly, I think that this is what Wollstone-craft attempts, *vis-à-vis* egalitarianism, in *A Vindication of the Rights of Women*; what de Beauvoir attempts, *vis-à-vis* existentialism, in *The Second Sex*; and what Mitchell attempts, *vis-à-vis* both psychoanalysis and Marxism, in *Psychoanalysis and Feminism*. It is for this reason that I do not wish to reduce this second approach to liberal feminism alone. It is work done under the rubric of this second approach that epitomizes the dominant relation between feminism and philosophy since Wollstone-craft and is, for that reason, worth examining in detail.

Consider de Beauvoir's own contention concerning the use of existentialism in understanding the situation of women:

[I]t is regardless of sex that the existent seeks self justification through transcendence – the very submission of women is proof of that statement. What they demand today is to be recognized as existents by the same right as men and not to subordinate existence to life, the human being to its animality.

An existentialist perspective has enabled us, then, to understand how the biological and economic condition of the primitive horde must have led to male supremacy. The female, to a greater extent than the male, is the prey of the species . . . in maternity woman remained closely bound to her body, like an animal. (de Beauvoir, 1975, p. 97; emphasis added)

For the moment it is enough to note de Beauvoir's commitment to Sartre's view of the (female) body and its relation, for Sartre, to immanence. I will be picking up this point later in the section where I will consider the effect of the necessary precommitments of feminists who use existing philosophical systems to explore the existence and experience of women.

Wollstonecraft's views on the education of women reveal a similar pre-commitment, this time to egalitarianism. She writes:

[T]he most perfect education, in my opinion, is such an exercise of the understanding as is best calculated to strengthen the body and form the heart. Or, in other words, to enable the individual to attain such habits of virtue as will render it independent. In fact, it is a farce to call any being virtuous whose virtues do not result from the exercise of its own reason. This was Rousseau's opinion respecting men; I *extend* it to women. (Wollstonecraft, 1975, p. 103; emphasis added)

So, we see that the theory, the philosophical framework employed by these feminists, is considered unproblematic. The problem, the problem of how these philosophical paradigms relate to women, is seen as a problem of *content*. The framework remains intact while the content is *extended*, sometimes altered, to include women, to account theoretically for the position of women, and, possibly, to offer the means whereby that position may be transformed. Philosophy is thus employed as the *method* which takes women or feminism as its object of enquiry. It seems to me that there are several problems involved in this second approach that are connected to the nature of the critique these feminists offer. The explicit critique of Rousseau, offered by Wollstonecraft, for example, is *internal* to his philosophy. The philosophy of Rousseau *per se* is not a problem for Wollstonecraft; rather, it is its exclusive application to males that is, for her, the problem. The difficulties I see in this approach will be treated in turn.

The neutral framework, sexist content, claim

What I want to examine here is the claim that philosophy as a discipline, that the work of any particular philosopher, taken as a method of enquiry, is neutral and that it is the content only, that is, what a philosophical framework is 'filled' with that is sexist or inadequate in relation to women. To be clearer, I want to investigate the claim that, for example, existentialism, as a philosophy, is sex-neutral, to investigate the claim that the sexism of *Being and Nothingness* is limited to its use of misogynistic metaphors and sex-blind examples. I have no quarrel with the contention that philosophy, from Plato to the present, *is* riddled with statements that are anti-women or anti-feminist – this has been demonstrated, by feminists, *ad nauseam*. Rather, I am interested in taking to task the claim that it is to this extent *only* that philosophy has denigrated women or generally been inappropriate in terms of offering an adequate analysis of women. If it were the case that the misogyny or inadequacy (in relation to women) of philosophy were merely a problem of content (that is, of the philosopher's personal attitudes or values infecting his otherwise neutral system) then the project of extension and inclusion would be viable. I am no longer convinced, however, that Sartre's metaphors, for example, are incidental or accidental to his overall thesis. It is not only a matter of the specific content, the concrete examples, offered by him being inadequate as an account of *human* being. I would argue that his philosophy is inadequate in general outline too. In other words, the project of *extending* philosophies, which may have excluded or been oppressive to women in the past, in order that they may include women, non-oppressively, in the future, is viable only on condition that the general form or framework of any particular philosophy is sex-neutral. It is to this claim that I would like to turn, again by way of existentialism.

Consider Sartre's account of the existence of others, exemplified by 'the Look'. This entire section of *Being and Nothingness* is written in terms of an individual man encountering an individual man and in terms which assume the mutual apprehension of the intersubjective reciprocity of subjecthood. He writes: 'my apprehension of the Other in the world as probably being a man refers to my permanent possibility of being-seen-by-him; that is, to the permanent possibility that a subject who sees me may be substituted for the object seen by me' (Sartre, 1977, p. 257). Would this thesis, robbed of its apparent neutrality, convey the same meaning? Take a concrete situation, experienced by most, if not all, women at some time in their lives. The example is supplied by M. Tax.

A young woman is walking down a city street. She is excruciatingly aware of her appearance and of the reaction to it (imagined or real) of every person she meets. She walks through a group of construction workers who are eating lunch in a line along the pavement. Her stomach tightens with terror and revulsion; her face becomes contorted into a grimace of self-control and fake unawareness; her walk and carriage become stiff and dehumanized. No matter what they say to her, it will be unbearable. She knows that they will not physically assault her or hurt her. They will only do so metaphorically. What they will do is *impinge* on her. They will demand that her thoughts be focused on them. They will use her body with their eyes. They will evaluate her market price. They will comment on her defects, or compare them to those of other passers-by. They will make her a participant in their fantasies without asking if she is willing. They will make her feel ridiculous, or grotesquely sexual, or hideously ugly. Above all, they will make her feel like a *thing*. (Tax, 1973, p. 28)

The question we must ask is, 'Does this situation reveal to the men in it (in line with Sartre's thesis) that this woman's existence involves for them the possibility of their objectification?', that is, that the woman, as seeing subject, may be substituted for the woman, the seen object? I think not. What has happened to the purported reciprocity of 'the

Look'? What, on reflection, does this situation suggest about Sartre's philosophy? It suggests that it is a philosophy about men, about free and equal subjectivities that encounter each other in a situation of struggle for mastery. It is a description that is inappropriate for some men in some situations, and, I would argue, for all women in some situations. The point is qualitatively different from the predominant feminist criticism of the sexism of philosophers throughout the history of western thought. It is not a point directed at content, at what is said or what is *not* said about women, but rather, about what *can* and *cannot* be said about women within the terms of particular philosophical theories.

What are the limitations to what de Beauvoir can say, having adopted the existentialist method, about women, their situation, their character? What precommitments are entered into by feminists when they apply this or that philosophical view to the position of women? What factors are preselected and hence predetermined to rise to prominence? What will be excluded? Some questions are foreclosed by the method, whether it be existentialism, psychoanalysis, Marxism, or liberalism. For feminists employing existentialism, the problem of women's relation (or *lack* of it) to transcendence, is seen as crucial; for feminists employing psycho-analysis, the problem of the social construction of women as (symbolically) *lacking*, is seen as crucial; for feminists employing Marxism, the problem of women's relation (or *lack* of it) to productive labour is seen as crucial; and so on. The point I'm making is that the history of philosophy is the history of man defining man as having a particular relation to some essential faculty or power. This faculty or power may be rationality, transcendence, productive labour, etc.; what is important is that man's relation to this power or his capacity to embody it is deemed crucial to his subjectivity. The relation of many feminists to this history is revealed in the attempt to extend this analysis of man to include woman. This involves assuming the neutrality of the essential power or faculty under consideration with regard to sex and social position and positing it instead as crucial to the *human* subject. The tendency of these feminists to extend this analysis to women is encouraged by the implicit assumption, common in philosophy, that the analysis is universally applicable.

Where does this situate feminists who work within this mode? On my view it does *not*, necessarily, imply that they are wasting their time or that their contributions to feminist theory are minimal. On the contrary, I would argue that many feminists who believe themselves to be engaged in this kind of research are, in fact, doing something quite different. However, they are doing it in such a way that they make their work, and their contributions to philosophy *invisible*. This leads me to the second point of criticism of this second way of conceptualizing the relation between feminism and philosophy.

Women, philosophy, and invisibility

Michele Le Doeuff (1977, p. 10) has remarked that one area in which women have free access to philosophy, today, is in the area of commentary on the 'Great Classics'. She observes, in this context, 'Who better than a woman to show fidelity, respect and remembrance? A woman can be trusted to perpetuate the words of the Great Discourse: she will add none of her own.' Le Doeuff's point is, I think, misplaced, the point being not so much that woman, as philosophical commentator, will *add* no words of her own but that she will *claim* none as her own. She will endeavour, as far as possible, to make herself, her thought, and the reconstructive work necessary to interpretation, invisible. It is in terms of the exercise of this capacity – to order without appearing to interfere; to extract and clarify what was, apparently, there all along; to extrapolate and expand; to draw out consequences and point out repercussions of the thought of the Master, *as if* these thoughts and associations lie latent in the test, expectantly awaiting the discerning eye – that women who are philosophers often render themselves invisible. It is to this invisibility of the work of women in philosophy, including women who are feminists, that I would now like to turn. In the context of the employment, by feminists, of existing philosophies to explain and/or alter the position of women, the following question arises: Is it accurate to describe the work of these feminists as merely the *extension* of the content of existing philosophies, or is it the case that they are, in fact, offering alternative frameworks that bear only a superficial or historical relation to existing philosophies? In other words, is the existentialism of de Beauvoir the same as the existentialism of Sartre? Is Mitchell's account of psychoanalysis consistent with Freud's? and so on. In what way do these women make themselves and their contribution to the theory they employ invisible?

De Beauvoir states clearly in *The Second Sex* that women is the other, not only to man but also to herself. Her explanation of the oppression of women is partly in terms of the problem of female subjectivity, that is, that woman is perceived *and* perceives herself as *object*. This account is, already, clearly at odds with Sartre's account in *Being and Nothingness*. For Sartre, at least the Sartre of *Being and Nothingness*, the other is always a subject. His analysis of interpersonal and social relations, in 1943, has little to offer in terms of a theory of *structural* oppression. His analysis revolves around *individual* power relations and individual consciousnesses. Coupled with Sartre's conception of 'bad faith', this analysis can offer little more than an understanding of women's oppression as a form of bad faith. It is de Beauvoir, in 1949, who offers this theory of oppression, and – this is my point – in a way that obscures her contribution to the viability of existentialism as a *social* theory. The Sartre of 1952 has already picked this up. In a rare though half-hearted display of acknowledgement of the role that de Beauvoir had played in forming his philosophy, he writes: 'Genet is first an object – and an object to others . . . Simone de Beauvoir has pointed out that . . . woman is an object to the other and to herself before being a subject' (Sartre, 1964, p. 37). I do not believe Sartre could have offered his 'biography' of Genet, nor the view we find there on freedom, were it not for de Beauvoir's contributions to existentialism. Space does not permit me to offer similar examples of Mitchell's relation to psychoanalysis, or of other feminists' relation to Marxism. The examples I have chosen are those that I imagine to be the most accessible and familiar. My point is not to seek out past plagiarisms or even to demand that the work of women in the past be acknowledged – though both projects are worthy of investigation. My present concern is to make visible and analyse the mechanisms by which women's work in philosophy has been rendered negligible in order that those of us who are feminists, and who work within philosophy *as* feminists, do not duplicate this history.

The point I have made in this section concerning the process of rendering women's work invisible relates back to the first point concerning framework and content. The framework of any particular philosophy, I have argued, is not sex-neutral. Feminists who have attempted to extend or alter the content of these philosophies have done more than add and 'tidy up'. They have also, often, modified the *framework* of the philosophy they employ, though in a way that is not always readily visible. I have tried to indicate previously that this problem of the invisibility of the contributions of feminist philosophers to philosophy is compounded by the alleged neutrality of the framework with regard to sex or gender, on the one hand, and its patently inadequate applicability to *both* sexes, on the other. The inadequacy of any particular philosophy that is being put to this feminist purpose reflects then, because of these factors, back onto 'woman'. That is, women's existence is not seen as problematizing existentialism or psychoanalysis or Marxism but rather woman herself is seen as the problem. Somehow she is characterized as defying theorization. How many times have we heard: from Marxists – 'the woman question'; from psychoanalysts – 'woman, the dark continent'; 'woman the enigma'; and more recently from other quarters, 'Does woman exist?'. The supposed neutrality of both the framework and the particular faculty or power that is deemed essentially human in the terms of that framework contribute to a situation where the inadequacy of philosophical theory does not throw 'philosophy' into question but '*woman*'. This leads me on to the third and final point of criticism relevant to this second kind of relation between feminism and philosophy, that is, the question of legitimation.

Philosophy and legitimation

Part of the initial training of any philosopher involves grasping and being able to reproduce an appropriate philosophical style. Of course, this style varies historically and according to the particular tradition one finds oneself within. However, a PhD thesis in geometric form or in the genre of dialogue, though both are historically prevalent in philosophy, would not, I suspect, be favourably received, at present, in any tradition. What is deemed appropriate philosophic style by university authorities, by journal editors, and by publishing houses appears to have a consistency that is closely connected to a normative standard, decided, in part, by tradition, but also, no doubt, masking discursive power relations. What are some of the major factors that determine whether a piece of research is philosophical? Clearly it is not merely the subject-matter but also the mode of presentation of that subject-matter. *Nausea* is literature, *Being and Nothingness* is philosophy. *The Idiot* is not philosophical text although it deals with issues common to the philosophy of ethics. By what processes are some texts considered legitimate, philosophically, and others not? At the present time we could say that for work to be considered philosophical it should be clear and logically ordered and argued rather than ambiguous, descriptive, or merely persuasive. For work to be counted as philosophical it should be rational and objective, rather than emotive or subjective. The view presented should be evident, in principle, to all rather than relying on private knowledge or exclusive lived experience. Philosophy aims at the universal, the abstract, stressing rationality, the creation of a clear mind, whereby the universal may be apprehended. It is not concerned with the particular, with the contingent. Personal opinion is to be overcome or to be transformed, if possible, into public and authorized knowledge.

These criteria concerning the public legitimation of philosophy do not always sit comfortably with feminist research. One of the effects of this process by which work is considered legitimate is that any research that displays overt political or personal commitment or involvement is considered, for that reason, to be illegitimate, to be not-philosophy. This places most, if not all, feminist research in a difficult position apropos its philosophical credentials. One way for feminists who are also philosophers to retain both their feminism and their commitment to philosophy is to use *existing* philosophical theories in their study of women. The benefits attached to this option are obvious. First, feminists who work within this approach are able, by this means, to retain both their commitment to philosophy and their commitment to feminism by including feminist concerns in a way that does not disrupt the preset boundaries and assumptions of philosophy. Second, the accounts and findings of these feminist philosophers are more likely to be judged as legitimate by virtue of their close association with past or existing philosophies which, after all, do purport to be concerned with *human* existence. Hence, it is with this final point, the point concerning the process by which philosophy separates itself from other modes of enquiry, and legitimates this separation, that all three points that I have raised in this section converge. The questions of framework *vs* content, women's invisibility in philosophy, and the legitimizing processes of philosophy are, it seems to me, all interconnected. The investigation of *how* they are interconnected belongs properly to the third approach discussed in the final section of this chapter. It should be said here, however, that the seeds of the third approach are planted in the second. The third is not possible without the second being logically prior.

THROUGH THE LOOKING-GLASS

The Hatter opened his eyes very wide on hearing this; but all he *said* was, 'Why is a raven like a writing desk?' . . .
'Have you guessed the riddle yet?' the Hatter said, turning to Alice again.
'No, I give it up,' Alice replied, 'What's the answer?'
'I haven't the slightest idea,' said the Hatter.
'Nor I,' said the March Hare.
Alice sighed wearily. 'I think you might do something better with the time,' she said, 'than wasting it in asking riddles that have no answers.' (Carroll, 1972, pp. 94–7)

The third way in which one could articulate the relation between feminist theory and philosophy holds more in common with the first approach than with the second in terms of the way in which feminists working within this third approach see philosophy. In other words, the view espoused by feminists who work within this third approach is that philosophy is not neutral in character, that the problem of the relationship between women and philosophy, of how women's subjectivity is put into philosophical discourse, is not merely a problem of content. The difference between the third and the first lies not in the perception of the relation between feminism and philosophy but rather in the *response* to that situation. Whereas feminists in the first category argue that women should ignore or avoid philosophical tradition, feminists in the third argue that this tradition must be confronted. These theorists have often worked in the second approach, and have arrived at their present view because of difficulties encountered there. In a sense, feminist philosophers working in the third approach *invert* the method of feminist philosophers working in the second. Whereas, in the second approach, feminist philosophers take philosophy as the method and feminism or women as the object of study, researchers in the third category take feminist theory or a feminist perspective as their starting-point and *philosophy itself* as the object of study. This entails the creation of a situation where one can raise, as meaningful, questions pertaining to philosophical paradigms and their commitments, the effects of women's interventions into philosophy, and the processes whereby some discourses are judged legitimate, philosophically, and others not. These questions are all put into crisis, I believe, by the presence of feminist discourses in the philosophical field. They are questions that many philosophers would prefer to be left unasked. They are questions that threaten the very fabric and constitution of contemporary philosophy.

It is at the conjuncture of the three questions I raised earlier, concerning the neutrality of philosophical frameworks, the invisibility of women both as the objects of philosophical discourse and as the subjects of philosophical discourse, and the process by which philosophy legitimates itself, that the third approach lies. And it is this third approach only that can show how all three questions interconnect. By *self-consciously* demonstrating that any philosophical paradigm is *not* neutral, these feminists make themselves, both as philosophers and as women, *visible*. By making themselves visible, they in turn throw into question the legitimacy of claims and assumptions in philosophy that have been taken as axiomatic. In so far as this approach questions the very foundation and status of philosophy it also reveals the investments and concerns of philosophy. It does this by demonstrating not only *what* is excluded from a particular philosophy but also *why* it is crucial, for the very existence of that philosophy, to exclude it. In this vein, some feminists are at present engaged in projects involving the way in which the human body and sensation are treated in philosophy and the effects of this treatment on the philosophical construction of femininity (Gross, 1983; Lloyd, 1984).

In examining the history of philosophy feminists do not necessarily duplicate that history. They endeavour, one hopes, to understand its character, to listen to its 'reason' not in order to reproduce it but in order to challenge the undertones, the silences of philosophy. Both the method or framework and the content, and the connections between them, are studied. They are studied, not always for what is said but also for what is *not* said; for what *cannot* be said; examined not only in terms of the privileging of, say, Reason, but also for what is involved in the denigration of passion. Many feminists involved in projects of this kind claim that philosophy may not be able to tell us a great deal about women but it can tell us a great deal about men and male desire. The desire for objectivity, for example, is in itself a subjective drive and this subjective drive throws into question the objectivity that many philosophers claim for their accounts. The desire, which underlies the work of Descartes, for a unified and universally appropriate science, is itself in need of examination. The seventeenth-century project of subordinating ontology and metaphysics to a certain and foundational epistemology is a project that reflects social needs and desires that are a far cry from our own. The fixing of being and the mirroring conception of that being's access to the world and knowledge, so ably described by Rorty (1980), is no longer tenable or appropriate to our needs today. This shift in concern is evidenced by the stress in recent feminist philosophy, on *becoming* rather than being, on *possibilities* rather than certainty, and on meaning or *significance* rather than truth.

A common reaction of some feminists and philosophers to this cultivation of a philosophy or ambiguity entailing, as it does, the rejection of universal truths, is to accuse feminists who support this developing philosophy of being the mistresses of critique, of being merely reactive to dominant traditions in philosophy and, in this sense, of being entirely negative. This kind of response is typified by the demand put to feminist theory to show what it has to offer independently of critique, that is, a demand to inspect the theory-building capabilities of feminism. Now it seems to me that this demand is based on a misconception concerning the investments, interests, and character of the kind of feminist philosophy I have outlined in this section. In so far as this approach to philosophy has involved itself extensively in a critique of universal and totalizing forms of knowledge it is evident that it is not going to involve itself with a repetition of theory-building which aims at the formation of unilateral predictive propositions. This isn't to say that this third approach of feminists to philosophy is anti-theoretical. Rather, it indicates a commitment to a conception of theory, practice, and strategy which refutes the traditional theory/practice split. The feminist challenge to dominant philosophical pronouncements – concerning the equality of 'man', the lauding of a universal and singular rationality, and so on – is offered from an acknowledged necessary embeddedness in lived experience and is the result of the exploration of the contradictions manifest in that experience.

As recent feminist research has demonstrated (Harding and Hintikka, 1983; Finn and Miles, 1982) the predominant contemporary treatment of ontology, epistemology, ethics, and politics as separate disciplines with discrete concerns is not only unable to withstand critical scrutiny but such scrutiny, additionally, exposes the political nature of maintaining these spheres as separate (Flax, 1983, pp. 248ff). It allows, for example, free rein to the notion that a writer can be entirely objective, can transcend his political, social, and sexual identity and speak from utopia. Pointing out the necessary interconnections between ontological, epistemological, and political commitments in philosophical discourses is akin to turning over a tapestry and examining the interconnections of the threads that from the 'right' side of the fabric give the impression of

194

discrete figures and patterns. Understanding the nature and formation of those patterns and figures and their necessary interconnectedness is crucial if feminists are to grasp the way in which philosophy has constructed, and continues to construct, femininity and masculinity, Reason and Nature. It is essential, in other words, that feminists do not continue to take philosophy and its overt pronouncements at face value. I have tried to explain, in the preceding section, the ways in which this *prima facie* approach to philosophy is inadequate. The study of the underside of philosophy is characteristic of this third kind of relation between feminist theory and philosophy. What remains to be, briefly, explored is the common resistance to following the insights of this approach through to their logical conclusion. In other words, there is still a large leap to be made in terms of the way we conceptualize political struggle and action. Many feminists who would agree with the sentiments expressed in this third section still ask 'But when do we begin to produce *real* feminist theory?'; 'What is the next step – how do we get *beyond* patriarchal theory?' It is to these kinds of questions, so often heard at women's conferences and seminars, that I would like to turn.

It is in *The Principles of Philosophy* that Descartes (1970, p. 211) described philosophy as being like a tree: metaphysics being the roots that are not visible but essential, physics being the trunk, and the branches being all the other aspects of philosophy, including ethics and politics. His point in using this metaphor is that the extremities of the tree, including its fruit, cannot be understood or improved without a thorough knowledge of the tree as a complete organic system. The ethico-political theory of Descartes is notoriously spare and, according to the philosopher himself, this is because ethics and politics are, necessarily, the last objects of knowledge to be reached by reason. Put another way, if we are to understand and improve human social and political existence then we must first understand the principles of human nature, initially, as a particular and then in relation to the regulative system of Nature as a whole. This is the way that Hobbes, Spinoza, Hume, and Rousseau all proceed. The answer to the first query 'What, essentially, is a human being?' sets determining limits to what kind of social, political, and ethical organization is thought to be suitable to it. In all these theorists' work human nature is thought to have an essentially constant and universal character that is, in differing degrees, considered to be mutable – improvable or corruptible. In other words, the kind of social and political organization and the ethical and legal principles that are to govern that organization are deduced from what a human being is thought to be, what its needs, desires, capabilities, and limitations are. Once this ontological problem is fathomed the management of groups of such beings is largely a matter of deduction from these first principles. What must be kept in mind here, however, is that this mode of philosophizing involves a *formal* conception of human nature or human essence.

The introduction of the notion of a socially constructed subject, which is a notion absolutely central to feminist theory, completely undermines the coherence of the traditional approach to political philosophy and the naive mechanical and organic metaphors that accompany it. To change one's conception of what a subject is changes, necessarily, the conception of what that subject can know or become. This is one of the most important insights of feminist theory, yet it is one that many feminists have not taken account of in relation to their ethico-political stance. The scant commitment that some feminists have concerning what human being is, is incompatible with the desire of these same feminists to have and to pursue a definite ideal future. To view human being as a social product devoid of determining universal characteristics is to view its possibilities as open-ended. This is not to say that human being is not constrained by historical context or by rudimentary biological facts but rather that these factors set the outer parameters of possibility only. Within these constraints – if they can be called that – there is an almost limitless variety of possibilities. Social, political, and ethical life, in the terms of this third feminist philosophy, must be acknowledged as 'processes involved in' rather than actions that have a definite beginning and end and a clear ethos. The blueprint notion of political action is not a feminist one and is certainly not implicit in, or even consistent with, *all* feminist theory. The questions alluded to in the second section of this chapter – 'What is woman?' 'Does woman exist?' – are distinctive in their desire to capture and fix woman's being, woman's desire. They result in the destruction of the productive ambiguity of a present femininity that is lived out in a female body that for historical and socio-political reasons is at present an existence that is simultaneously extremely rich and painfully contradictory. To investigate how this lived femininity has been constructed involves living with and experimenting with these ambiguities. The notorious difficulty involved in capturing and defining femininity has been noted, negatively, throughout the history of western thought, from Aristotle to Freud. What is relatively novel is that any positivity could be attached to this ambiguity and that any theoretically coherent justification could be offered for it.

The reply of the third approach then to the riddle of the relationship between feminism and philosophy would be neither disjunctive nor conjunctive. Rather, these feminists would seek to shift the terrain and say that the riddle is Being itself – and as such it has no 'answer'. Both feminism and philosophy address this riddle – each in their own way and each with their own investments at stake. The interesting point to make here, in this third section, is that it is becoming increasingly clear that neither philosophy *nor* feminism can afford to continue to ignore each other. This may involve, for philosophy, that it accepts its ruptures, its gaps. To attempt to close the ruptures created by feminist discourses in philosophy, in order to ensure that philosophy remains intact, is not only undesirable – it is futile. These ruptures should rather be widened and welcomed *as possibilities* rather than feared as 'lacks'. Posing riddles that have no answer is something the Mad Hatter and philosophy have in common. The interrogation of philosophy, like the trial of the Mad Hatter, should be seen as providing the means to 'move beyond' some riddles but not as an end in itself – since still other riddles will pose themselves. This developing feminist philosophy involves neither the 'death' nor obsolescence of feminism or philosophy, but rather the transformation of both. The salient point here is that there cannot be an unadulterated feminist theory which would announce our arrival at a place where we could say we are 'beyond' a patriarchal theory and patriarchal experience. Nor can there be *a* philosophy which would be neutral, universal, or truly *human* in its character, thus rendering feminism redundant. Acknowledging this entails also acknowledging that a commitment to feminist politics *necessarily* involves a ceaseless critical engagement with and interrogation of our (theoretical/practical) existences.

REFERENCES

Carroll, L., *Alice in Wonderland and Through the Looking-Glass*, ed. H. Gardner (Harmondsworth: Penguin, 1972).

Daly, M., *Gyn/Ecology: The Metaethics of Radical Feminism* (Boston: Beacon Press, 1978).

d'Eaubonne, F., 'Feminism or death' in Marks and de Courtivron (eds) *New French Feminisms* (Brighton: Harvester Press, 1980).

de Beauvoir, S. *The Second Sex* (Harmondsworth: Penguin, 1975).

Descartes, R., *Philosophical Works*, vol. 1, trans. E.S. Haldane and G.R.T. Ross (London: Cambridge University Press, 1970).

Finn, G. and Miles, A. (eds), *Feminism in Canada: From Pressure to Politics* (Montreal: Black Rose Books, 1982).

Flax, J., 'Political philosophy and the patriarchal unconscious: a psychoanalytic perspective on epistemology and metaphysics', in S. Harding and M.B. Hintikka (eds) *Discovering Reality* (New York: Reidel Publishing Co., 1983).

Gross, E., 'The body of woman: psychoanalysis and Foucault', unpublished paper, 1983.

Harding, S. and Hintikka, M. (eds), *Discovering Reality: Feminist Perspectives on Epistemology, Metaphysics, Methodology and Philosophy of Science* (New York: Reidel Publishing Co., 1983).

Le Doeuff, 'Women and philosophy', *Radical Philosophy*, 17, 1977, Summer, pp. 2–11.

Lloyd, G., *The Man of Reason: 'Male' and 'Female' in Western Philosophy* (London: Methuen, 1984).

Rorty, R., *Philosophy and the Mirror of Nature* (Oxford: Blackwell, 1980).

Sartre, J.P., *Saint Genet: Actor and Martyr* (New York: Plume Books, 1964).

Sartre, J.P., *Being and Nothingness* (London: Methuen, 1977).

Solanas, V., 'The S.C.U.M. Manifesto' in B. Roszak and T. Roszak (eds) *Masculine/Feminine* (New York: Harper & Row, 1969).

Tax, M. 'Woman and her mind?' in A. Koedt, E. Levine and A. Rapone (eds) *Radical Feminism* (New York: Quadrangle Press, 1973).

Wollstonecraft, M., *A Vindication of the Rights of Woman* (New York: Norton & Co., 1975).

Part VI
PSYCHOANALYSIS AND FEMINISM

INTRODUCTION

Hazel Rowley

The place to start reading about psychoanalysis and female sexuality is Freud. His key essays on the subject were written in the 1920s and 1930s – 'Some psychical consequences of the anatomical distinction between the sexes' (1925), 'Female sexuality' (1931), and 'Femininity' (1932) – and reveal an interesting evolution in Freud's thinking: in particular he attached an increasing importance to the girl's pre-Oedipal period.

In the 1960s, at about the same time that Louis Althusser was beginning to attract attention with his 'reinterpretation' of Marx, people suddenly became interested in Lacan, who for years had been proclaiming the necessity of a 'return to Freud'. Of course, it is desirable to read some of Jacques Lacan himself before reading *about* him. The problem is that there is no obvious place to begin, no focal article on the subject of female sexuality. Secondly, Lacan's playful and allusive style, full of puns, is deliberately difficult, an attempt to reflect the obscure wanderings of the unconscious itself. And translating his punning, rhetorical style is almost impossible. However, the elusive Jacques Lacan has been pinned down, to some extent, by Juliet Mitchell and Jacqueline Rose in their book *Feminine Sexuality* (London, 1982), in which a selection of his papers on the subject are translated, with notes, and placed in historical perspective. This is a good place to start.

Ellie Ragland-Sullivan's article, although difficult if serving as an introduction to Lacan, situates his emphasis on *language* and *identification* in relation to Freud's emphasis on *myth* and *biology*. With his focus on *structure*, on the fundamental laws of language (influenced by Saussure), Lacan had some affinity with other 'structuralists' who were writing and teaching in the 1950s and 1960s – Claude Lévi-Strauss, Louis Althusser, Michel Foucault, and Roland Barthes. His anti-humanist approach to psychoanalysis could not have been more different from the 'ego psychology' dominant at the time in Anglo-American psycho-analysis.

Lacan's position within feminist theory is controversial. Many feminists dismiss him (usually along with Freud) as a 'phallocrat'. Ragland-Sullivan provides a lucid counter-position, which is useful to read before engaging with the various denunciatory positions. Her claim is that Lacan comes as close as anyone to analysing the structures underlying the patriarchal order and demystifying the basic causes of gender difference. Thus,'Lacan's thought provides a key for understanding the socialization and symbolization processes which have shaped woman's specificity through the ages.'

Ragland-Sullivan's article helps to elucidate key Lacanian terms such as the 'Mirror Stage', the 'Symbolic Order', 'Desire', and *jouissance*. Just as Juliet Mitchell does, Ragland-Sullivan insists that Lacan's analysis is not prescriptive, and therefore not ideologically unsound. For both of them, the greatest virtue of Lacan's thinking is that it avoids the pitfalls of biological essentialism – the idea that there is a true 'female nature', an 'essential woman', derived from female biology. For Lacan (and, Juliet Mitchell tries to argue, for Freud as well), man and woman are *made* in culture, not *created* in nature.

Luce Irigaray is one feminist who protests that Lacan is 'phallocentric'. Yet, says Ragland-Sullivan, it is Irigaray who is reductive, for she makes the fundamental mistake of equating gender identity with biological givens.

According to Ragland-Sullivan, Lacan's 'phallic signifier' is neutral and not intrinsically equated with the penis or with the father. If, nevertheless, the conflation constantly occurs, it is because of the unconscious associations we make, as fully acculturated members of our society. And it is this process of acculturation which interests Lacan.

As a Lacanian, Ragland-Sullivan believes that feminists who concentrate their energies on the class structure or on patriarchy *per se*, whatever that means, are fighting the wrong fight. For her, the focus of our attention should be the identifications and projections we all make in the mirror stage. This is where we come to associate the principle of 'Law and reality' with the father (men) and the principle of 'desire and subjectivity' with the mother (women). In the symbolic drama which occurs as we enter culture and language, the mother becomes 'the dark-faced part of us all . . . someone to fear, deny, ignore, fight, conquer, or conversely worship and enshrine' – all myths which have been readily conveyed as 'natural' truths.

Although Ragland-Sullivan offers a relatively clear picture of where she locates the problems for feminists, she is typically vague when it comes to questions of strategy. She herself makes the point that it is not a solution for women to live in exclusively female groups as, even then, a 'phallocratic structure' will evolve – 'because recognition and power needs inhere in the structure of the human subject itself'. Our only hope, according to her, is for gender distinctions to become more blurred, less rigid. *How* this is to happen – or what feminists must do to bring this about – is not discussed.

A number of French feminists, particularly Julia Kristéva and Luce Irigaray, have been profoundly influenced by Lacan's thinking, especially his emphasis on the role of language in psychic formation. At the same time, they find aspects of Lacan's thought quite reactionary and their aim is to subvert his authority in these areas by inverting some of his categories. Kristéva tries to undermine the supremacy of the Symbolic Order: she celebrates the 'feminine', which, for her, is not sexually specific, but simply a position of marginality to the Symbolic. Luce Irigaray and Hélène Cixous have taken more explicitly feminist positions – which is why I include them here.

Luce Irigaray attempts to undercut the mastery of 'phallocentric' discourse by asserting women's specificity. She argues, for example, that women's multiple erogenous zones – their plurality – explains the difficulty they have with masculine logic. Even if she is using female physiology as an elaborate metaphor, as some claim, she is none the less trying to subvert phallocentric oppression by emphasizing biological *difference*. And in a similar move, Hélène Cixous links woman's diffuse, polymorphous sexuality with women's language – in this case, women's writing. 'The laugh of the Medusa' (1975) virtually became a manifesto within the women's movement for *écriture féminine* (female writing).

There are obvious dangers implicit in this kind of argument. Ann Rosalind Jones, in an article well worth reading,[1] comments:

Materialist feminists . . . are suspicious of the logic through which *féminité* defines men as phallic – solipsistic, aggressive, excessively rational – and then praises women, who by nature of their contrasting sexuality, are other-oriented, empathetic, multi-imaginative. Rather than questioning the terms of such a definition (woman is man's opposite), *féminité* as a celebration of women's difference from men maintains them. It reverses the values assigned to each side of the polarity, but it still leaves man as the determining referent, not departing from the opposition male/female, but participating in it.

It is a good idea to read some critiques of the feminist celebration of sexual difference. The Marxist-feminist journal *Questions féministes* tackled the question in its first issue (1977) and the translation appears in *New French Feminisms*.[2] The section on French feminist theory in Toril Moi's book *Sexual/Textual Politics* (Methuen, 1985) is also very useful.

NOTES

1 Ann Rosalind Jones, 'Writing the body: toward an understanding of *l'écriture féminine*', *Feminist Studies*, VII, 2 (Summer 1981), pp. 247–63.
2 'Variations on common themes' (1980), in *New French Feminisms, An Anthology*, ed. Elaine Marks and Isabelle de Courtivron (Sussex: Harvester Press, 1981), pp. 212–30.

THIS SEX WHICH IS NOT ONE*

Luce Irigaray

Female sexuality has always been conceptualized on the basis of masculine parameters. Thus the opposition between 'masculine' clitoral activity and 'feminine' vaginal passivity, an opposition which Freud – and many others – saw as stages, or alternatives, in the development of a sexually 'normal' woman, seems rather too clearly required by the practice of male sexuality. For the clitoris is conceived as a little penis pleasant to masturbate so long as castration anxiety does not exist (for the boy child), and the vagina is valued for the 'lodging' it offers the male organ when the forbidden hand has to find a replacement for pleasure-giving.

In these terms, woman's erogenous zones never amount to anything but a clitoris-sex that is not comparable to the noble phallic organ, or a hole-envelope that serves to sheath and massage the penis in intercourse: a non-sex, or a masculine organ turned back upon itself, self-embracing.

About woman and her pleasure, this view of the sexual relation has nothing to say. Her lot is that of 'lack', 'atrophy' (of the sexual organ), and 'penis envy', the penis being the only sexual organ of recognized value. Thus she attempts by every means available to appropriate that organ for herself: through her somewhat servile love of the father–husband capable of giving her one, through her desire for a child–penis, preferably a boy, through access to the cultural values still reserved by right to males alone and therefore always masculine, and so on. Woman lives her own desire only as the expectation that she may at last come to possess an equivalent of the male organ.

Yet all this appears quite foreign to her own pleasure, unless it remains within the dominant phallic economy. Thus, for example, woman's auto-eroticism is very different from man's. In order to touch himself, man needs an instrument: his hand, a woman's body, language. . . . And this self-caressing requires at least a minimum of activity. As for woman, she touches herself in and of herself without any need for mediation, and before there is any way to distinguish activity from passivity. Woman 'touches herself' all the time, and moreover no one can forbid her to do

204

so, for her genitals are formed of two lips in continuous contact. Thus, within herself, she is already two – but not divisible into one(s) – that caress each other.

This auto-eroticism is disrupted by a violent break-in: the brutal separation of the two lips by a violating penis, an intrusion that distracts and deflects the woman from this 'self-caressing' she needs if she is not to incur the disappearance of her own pleasure in sexual relations. If the vagina is to serve *also*, but *not only*, to take over for the little boy's hand in order to assure an articulation between auto-eroticism and hetero-eroticism in intercourse (the encounter with the totally other always signifying death), how, in the classic representation of sexuality, can the perpetuation of auto-eroticism for woman be managed? Will woman not be left with the impossible alternative between a defensive virginity, fiercely turned in upon itself, and a body open to penetration that no longer knows, in this 'hole' that constitutes its sex, the pleasure of its own touch? The more or less exclusive – and highly anxious – attention paid to erection in western sexuality proves to what extent the imaginary that governs it is foreign to the feminine. For the most part, this sexuality offers nothing but imperatives dictated by male rivalry: the 'strongest' being the one who has the best 'hard-on', the longest, the biggest, the stiffest penis, or even the one who 'pees the furthest' (as in little boys' contests). Or else one finds imperatives dictated by the enactment of sado-masochistic fantasies, these in turn governed by man's relation to his mother: the desire to force entry, to penetrate, to appropriate for himself the mystery of this womb where he has been conceived, the secret of his begetting, of his 'origin'. Desire/need, also to make blood flow again in order to revive a very old relationship – intra-uterine, to be sure, but also pre-historic – to the maternal.

Woman, in this sexual imaginary, is only a more or less obliging prop for the enactment of man's fantasies. That she may find pleasure there in that role, by proxy, is possible, even certain. But such pleasure is above all a masochistic prostitution of her body to a desire that is not her own, and it leaves her in a familiar state of dependency upon man. Not knowing what she wants, ready for anything, even asking for more, so long as he will 'take' her as his 'object' when he seeks his own pleasure. Thus she will not say what she herself wants; moreover, she does not know, or no longer knows, what she wants. As Freud admits, the beginnings of the sexual life of a girl child are so 'obscure', so 'faded with time', that one would have to dig down very deep indeed to discover beneath the traces of this civilization, of this history, the vestiges of a more archaic civilization that might give some clue to woman's sexuality. That extremely ancient civilization would undoubtedly have a different alphabet, a different language. . . . Woman's desire would not be expected to speak the same language as man's; woman's desire has doubtless been submerged by the logic that has dominated the west since the time of the Greeks.

Within this logic, the predominance of the visual, and of the discrimination and individualization of form, is particularly foreign to female eroticism. Woman takes pleasure more from touching than from looking, and her entry into a dominant scopic economy signifies, again, her consignment to passivity: she is to be the beautiful object of contemplation. While her body finds itself thus eroticized, and called to a double movement of exhibition and of chaste retreat in order to stimulate the drives of the 'subject', her sexual organ represents *the horror of nothing to see*. A defect in this systematics of representation and desire. A 'hole' in its scoptophilic lens. It is already evident in Greek statuary that this nothing-to-see has to be excluded, rejected, from such a scene of representation. Woman's genitals are simply absent, masked, sewn back up inside their 'crack'.

This organ which has nothing to show for itself also lacks a form of its own. And if woman takes pleasure precisely from this incompleteness of form, which allows her organ to touch itself over and over again, indefinitely, by itself, that pleasure is denied by a civilization that privileges phallomorphism. The value granted to the only definable form excludes the one that is in play in female auto-eroticism. The *one* of form, of the individual, of the (male) sexual organ, of the proper name, of the proper meaning . . . supplants, while separating and dividing, that contact of *at least two* (lips) which keep woman in touch with herself, but without any possibility of distinguishing what is touching from what is touched.

Whence the mystery that woman represents in a culture claiming to count everything, to number everything by units, to inventory everything as individualities. *She is neither one nor two*. Rigorously speaking, she cannot be identified either as one person, or as two. She resists all adequate definition. Further, she has no 'proper' name. And her sexual organ, which is not *one* organ, is counted as *none*. The negative, the underside, the reverse of the only visible and morphologically designatable organ (even if the passage from erection to detumescence does pose some problems): the penis.

But the 'thickness' of that 'form', the layering of its volume, its expansion and contractions, and even the spacing of the moments in which it produces itself as form – all this the feminine keeps secret. Without knowing it. And if woman is asked to sustain, to revive, man's desire, the request neglects to spell out what it implies as to the value of her own desire. A desire of which she is not aware, moreover, at least not explicitly. But one whose force and continuity are capable of nurturing repeatedly and at length all the masquerades of 'femininity' that are expected of her.

It is true that she still has the child, in relation to whom her appetite for touch, for contact, has free rein, unless it is already lost, alienated by the taboo against touching of a highly obsessive civilization. Otherwise her pleasure will find, in the child, compensations for and diversions from the frustrations that she too often encounters in sexual relations *per se*. Thus maternity fills the gaps in a repressed female sexuality. Perhaps man and woman no longer caress each other except through that mediation between them that the child – preferably a boy – represents? Man, identified with his son, rediscovers the pleasure of maternal fondling; woman touches herself again by caressing that part of her body: her baby–penis–clitoris.

What this entails for the amorous trio is well known. But the Oedipal interdiction seems to be a somewhat categorical and factitious law – although it does provide the means for perpetuating the authoritarian discourse of fathers – when it is promulgated in a culture in which sexual relations are impracticable because man's desire and woman's are strangers to each other. And in which the two desires have to try to meet through indirect means, whether the archaic one of a sense-relation to the mother's body, or the present one of active or passive extension of the law of the father. These are regressive emotional behaviours, exchanges of words too detached from the sexual arena not to constitute an exile with respect to it: 'mother' and 'father' dominate the inter-actions of the couple, but as social roles. The division of labour prevents them from making love. They produce or reproduce. Without quite knowing how to use their leisure. Such little as they have, such little indeed as they wish to have. For what are they to do with leisure? What substitute for amorous resource are they to invent? Still . . .

Perhaps it is time to return to that repressed entity, the female imaginary. So woman does not have a sex organ? She has at least two of them, but they are not identifiable as ones. Indeed, she has many more. Her sexuality, always at least double, goes even further: it is *plural*. Is this the way culture is seeking to characterize itself now? Is this the way texts write themselves/are written now? Without quite knowing what censorship they are evading? Indeed, woman's pleasure does not have to choose between clitoral activity and vaginal passivity, for example. The pleasure of the vaginal caress does not have to be substituted for that of the clitoral caress. They each contribute, irreplaceably, to woman's pleasure. Among other caresses. . . . Fondling the breasts, touching the vulva, spreading the lips, stroking the posterior wall of the vagina, brushing against the mouth of the uterus, and so on. To evoke only a few of the most specifically female pleasures. Pleasures which are somewhat misunderstood in sexual difference as it is imagined – or not imagined, the other sex being only the indispensable complement to the only sex.

But *woman has sex organs more or less everywhere*. She finds pleasure almost anywhere. Even if we refrain from invoking the hystericization of her entire body, the geography of her pleasure is far more diversified, more multiple in its differences, more complex, more subtle, than is commonly imagined – in an imaginary rather too narrowly focused on sameness.

'She' is indefinitely other in herself. This is doubtless why she is said to be whimsical, incomprehensible, agitated, capricious . . . not to mention her language, in which 'she' sets off in all directions leaving 'him' unable to discern the coherence of any meaning. Hers are contradictory words, somewhat mad from the standpoint of reason, inaudible for whoever listens to them with ready-made grids, with a fully elaborated code in hand. For in what she says, too, at least when she dares, woman is constantly touching herself. She steps ever so slightly aside from herself with a murmur, an exclamation, a whisper, a sentence left unfinished. . . . When she returns, it is to set off again from elsewhere. From another point of pleasure, or of pain. One would have to listen with another ear, as if hearing an *'other meaning' always in the process of weaving itself, of embracing itself with words, but also of getting rid of words in order not to become fixed, congealed in them*. For if 'she' says something, it is not, it is already no longer, identical with what she means. What she says is never identical with anything, moreover; rather, it is contiguous. *It touches (upon)*. And when it strays too far from that proximity, she breaks off and starts over at 'zero': her body-sex.

It is useless, then, to trap women in the exact definition of what they mean, to make them repeat (themselves) so that it will be clear; they are already elsewhere in that discursive machinery where you expected to surprise them. They have returned within themselves. Which must not be understood in the same way as within yourself. They do not have the interiority that you have, the one you perhaps suppose they have. Within themselves means *within the intimacy of that silent, multiple, diffuse touch*. And if you ask them insistently what they are thinking about, they can only reply: Nothing. Everything.

Thus what they desire is precisely nothing, and at the same time everything. Always something more and something else besides that *one* – sexual organ, for example – that you give them, attribute to them. Their desire is often interpreted, and feared, as a sort of insatiable hunger, a voracity that will swallow you whole. Whereas it really involves a different economy more than anything else, one that upsets the linearity of a project, undermines the goal–object of a desire, diffuses the polarization of a single pleasure, disconcerts fidelity to a single discourse . . .

Must this multiplicity of female desire and female language be understood as shards, scattered remnants of a violated sexuality? A sexuality denied? The question has no simple answer. The rejection, the exclusion of a female imaginary certainly puts woman in the position of experiencing herself only fragmentarily, in the little-structured margins of a dominant ideology, as waste, or excess, what is left of a mirror invested by the (masculine) 'subject' to reflect himself, to copy himself. Moreover, the role of 'femininity' is prescribed by this masculine specula(riza)tion and corresponds scarcely at all to woman's desire, which may be recovered only in secret, in hiding, with anxiety and guilt.

But if the female imaginary were to deploy itself, if it could bring itself into play otherwise than as scraps, uncollected debris, would it represent itself, even so, in the form of *one* universe? Would it even be volume instead of surface? No. Not unless it were understood, yet again, as a privileging of the maternal over the feminine. Of a phallic maternal, at that. Closed in upon the jealous possession of its valued product. Rivalling man in his esteem for productive excess. In such a race for power, woman loses the uniqueness of her pleasure. By closing herself off as volume, she renounces the pleasure that she gets from the *non-suture of her lips*: she is undoubtedly a mother, but a virgin mother; the role was assigned to her by mythologies long ago. Granting her a certain social power to the extent that she is reduced, with her own complicity, to sexual impotence.

(Re)-discovering herself, for a woman, thus could only signify the possibility of sacrificing no one of her pleasures to another, of identifying herself with none of them in particular, *of never being simply one*. A sort of expanding universe in which no limits could be fixed and which would not be incoherence none the less – nor that polymorphous perversion of the child in which the erogenous zones would lie waiting to be regrouped under the primacy of the phallus.

Woman always remains several, but she is kept from dispersion because the other is already within her and is auto-erotically familiar to her. Which is not to say that she appropriates the other for herself, that she reduces it to her own property. Ownership and property are doubtless quite foreign to the feminine. At least sexually. But not *nearness*. Nearness so pronounced that it makes all discrimination of identity, and thus all forms of property, impossible. Woman derives pleasure from what is *so near that she cannot have it, nor have herself*. She herself enters into a ceaseless exchange of herself with the other without any possibility of identifying either. This puts into question all prevailing economies: their calculations are irremediably stymied by woman's pleasure, as it increases indefinitely from its passage in and through the other.

However, in order for a woman to reach the place where she takes pleasure as woman, a long detour by way of the analysis of the various systems of oppression brought to bear upon her is assuredly necessary. And claiming to fall back on the single solution of pleasure risks making her miss the process of going back through a social practice that *her* enjoyment requires.

For woman is traditionally a use-value for man, an exchange value among men; in other words, a commodity. As such, she remains the guardian of material substance, whose price will be established, in terms of the standard of their work and of their need/desire, by 'subjects': workers, merchants, consumers. Women are marked phallicly by their fathers, husbands, procurers. And this branding determines their value in sexual commerce. Woman is never anything but the locus of a more or less competitive exchange between two men, including the competition for the possession of mother earth.

How can this object of transaction claim a right to pleasure without removing her/itself from established commerce? With respect to other merchandise in the marketplace, how could this commodity maintain a relationship other than one of aggressive jealousy? How could material substance enjoy her/itself without provoking the consumer's anxiety over the disappearance of his nurturing ground? How could that exchange – which can in no way be defined in terms 'proper' to woman's desire – appear as anything but a pure mirage, mere foolishness, all too readily obscured by a more sensible discourse and by a system of apparently more tangible values?

A woman's development, however radical it may seek to be, would thus not suffice to liberate woman's desire. And to date no political theory or political practice has resolved, or sufficiently taken into consideration, this historical problem, even though Marxism has proclaimed its importance. But women do not constitute, strictly speaking, a class, and their dispersion among several classes makes their political struggle complex, their demands sometimes contradictory.

There remains, however, the condition of underdevelopment arising from women's submission by and to a culture that oppresses them, uses them, makes of them a medium of exchange, with very little profit to them. Except in the quasi-monopolies of masochistic pleasure, the domestic labour force, and reproduction. The powers of slaves? Which are not negligible powers, moreover. For where pleasure is concerned, the master is not necessarily well served. Thus to reverse the relation, especially in the economy of sexuality, does not seem a desirable objective.

But if women are to preserve and expand their auto-eroticism, their homo-sexuality, might not the renunciation of heterosexual pleasure correspond once again to that disconnection from power that is traditionally theirs? Would it not involve a new prison, a new cloister, built of their own accord? For women to undertake tactical strikes, to keep themselves apart from men long enough to learn to defend their desire, especially through speech, to discover the love of other women while sheltered from men's imperious choices that put them in the position of rival commodities, to forge for themselves a social status that compels recognition, to earn their living in order to escape from the condition of prostitute . . . these are certainly indispensable stages in the escape from their proletarization on the exchange market. But if their aim were simply to reverse the order of things, even supposing this to be possible, history would repeat itself in the long run, would revert to sameness: to phallocratism. It would leave room neither for women's sexuality, nor for women's imaginary, nor for women's language to take (their) place.

NOTE

* This text was originally published as 'Ce sexe qui n'en est pas un', in *Cahiers du Grif*, no. 5. English translation: 'This sex which is not one', trans. Claudia Reeder, in *New French Feminisms*, ed. Elaine Marks and Isabelle de Courtivron (New York, 1981), pp. 99–106.

JACQUES LACAN
Feminism and the problem of gender identity
Ellie Ragland-Sullivan

Lacan never tired of repeating that *Totem and Taboo* (1912) was wrong, and that the Oedipus complex was Freud's own neurosis. Lacan offered instead his own theory of the paternal metaphor and the Oedipal structure which make use of his innovative concepts of the Phallus, Castration, Desire, and *jouissance*.[1] By recasting Freud's realist picture of the Oedipal complex away from both myth and biology, Lacan introduced the concept of a structure which is formed by the intervention of a third element into the original infant–mother dyad: the Law of the Name-of-the-father. Moving from the realm of the Freudian sexual triangle to that of symbolic effect, Lacan leaves the scene of the incest taboo to dramatists and anthropologists. Sexual identity is not based on biological gender, or any other innate factor, but is learned through the dynamics of identification and language.

One finds two different systems of meaning within Lacan's epistemology, each complete in its own sphere: the one of language, and that of an unconscious discourse. In the unconscious system which Lacan calls the Other discourse, meaning does not come from substance or essence, but from structural associations and signifying effects. Within this context, not only the Oedipal myth, but myth in general is simply 'the attempt to give epic form to that which operates itself from structure'.[2] In the early 1950s Lacan used the word 'structure' to mean that which functions *like* a language: i.e. by transformations. In the same way that speech and lexicon are governed by the fundamental laws of language which Roman Jakobson names as metaphor and metonymy, Lacan has depicted an unconscious which transforms its representational networks of imagistic relations through analogous procedures of combination, condensation, substitution, and displacement.[3] In light of Lacan's structural picture of the unconscious, any direct linking of his Oedipal structure to biology through body configuration, gender, genital experience, or its 'resolution' in genital satisfaction, is a complete misinterpretation of a symbolic, representational, transformational drama.

Lacan saw the effect of the Oedipal nexus as that which decides the assumption of sex, where sex is correlated with identity rather than gender.[4] One might describe his Oedipal structure as the obligation every child is under to submit his or her sexuality to certain restrictions and to the laws of organization and exchange within a sexually differentiated group, and in this way find her or his place within that society.[5] The Oedipal crisis occurs, not because a child wants to possess its mother sexually, but when the child comprehends the sexual rules in a society. The crisis is resolved when the rules are accepted and acceded to. These rules are conveyed by what Lacan calls the Symbolic order, but by 'symbolic' he does not mean that which is representative of a second hidden thing or essence. Instead, he means that order of life which includes language, cultural codes, and conventions, and whose principal function is to differentiate one thing from another, and to mediate between non-verbal experiences – the Imaginary order of identifications – and real events – the Real. In other words, the Lacanian Symbolic order interprets, symbolizes, articulates, and universalizes both the experiential and the concrete, which it has in paradoxically circular fashion already shaped.

In a meeting of Lacan's Seminar Twenty (1972–3) he suggested that perhaps one of the women should write a book entitled *Beyond the Phallus*, ironically punning on Freud's *Beyond the Pleasure Principle* (1920). 'That would be lovely,' Lacan said, 'and it would give another consistency to the women's liberation movement. A pleasure or ecstasy (*jouissance*) beyond the phallus.'[6] Lacan's 'beyond the phallus' phrase is striking because it encapsulates the growing controversy surrounding his theories on the Phallus and Castration in their relationship to the structuring of gender identity and sexual personality. Later on, I shall consider the reasons for the seemingly ironic tone of Lacan's joke-cum-challenge. Certain feminists do not take Lacan's theories as a joke, however, and have attacked his thought, alleging him to be a phallocrat. On the contrary, I believe that Lacan's thought provides a key for understanding the socialization and symbolization processes which have shaped woman's specificity through the ages.

Lacan located the source of sexual identity in a pre-Oedipal period which occurs even earlier than the one Freud proposed. The structural cornerstones on which any identity is built are Desire and Law. In this way the roots of identity are ethical, not ontological.[7] But none of this makes sense except in light of Lacan's innovative view of human identity; what we usually call the ego or self or personality. For Lacan, identity does not derive from genetic predispositions, nor from an unfolding of neurophysiological developmental sequences; nor is it the product of a war between biological and cultural forces, nor the reflection of collective archetypes. Identity is built up as a composite of images and effects – i.e. mental representations – taken in from the outside world from the start of life, which are developed in relation to the Desire for

213

recognition and the later social requirements for submission to an arbitrary Law.

Born premature in terms of physiological functions by comparison with other animals, the human infant is more dependent on the world around it. The human neonate transcends its helplessness and insufficiencies by fusion with others, principally the main Other – usually mother – of early feeding and care.[8] In this way the (m)Other becomes the 'centre' of identity the infant lacks by serving as the mirror form with which the infant mimetically identifies. Lacan calls this period between six and eighteen months of age the mirror stage. At around eighteen months two major changes occur. The child begins to use language somewhat coherently, and also becomes aware that the father's presence – or any other third person – is a prohibiting force to the infant's merger with the (m)Other. The infant begins to perceive its own separateness from the (m)Other, only when forced to such awareness by what Lacan calls the phallic signifier or the paternal metaphor. But by 'signifier' Lacan means something different from Saussure. The Lacanian signifier resembles the Saussurian sign. The combination of sound and concept which acquire meaning in relation to other sounds and concepts – articulated speech in other words – is what Lacan means by signifier. By signified he refers to the cumulative effects caused by the signifiers that are repressed into the unconscious, but later surface as the fixed identity themes of a person's being.[9] The phallic signifier of difference imposes a sense of limitations and 'self'-boundaries on a mirror-stage psychic illusion of symbiotic wholeness. At the same time the phallic signifier introduces the possibility for reflective self representation through naming.[10] Playing on the French words non and nom, Lacan says that the father's Name appears to mean 'no'. Language then works to reinforce the phallic injunction to differentiation by offering substitutive possibilities in compensation for the loss of natural spontaneity. Culture has, thus, begun to impose itself on nature.

The learning of psychic differentiation from the (m)Other is so painful that Lacan describes the experience as Castration; i.e. the infant feels incomplete, broken, an *hommelette*.[11] But one must not take this term literally. No incest wish is being punished here by fear of organ loss. The fear is more global; fear of loss of 'self'-continuity. Paradoxically, language both creates an unconscious space in being – a permanent sense of loss or Otherness – by introducing a deferral of 'lived' experience, but also becomes a mechanism for helping human beings to master their own incompleteness. The infant represses the pain of separation, and also internalizes the phallic signifier. The residue of this drama is what Lacan has named Desire: a structural inadequacy in the human subject which drives individuals to strive forever, to seek new ways to compensate for the elemental loss of a psychic illusion of unity. People, language itself, material goods, meaning and belief systems, all play substitutive roles in displacing the lost object(s) along a signifying chain of Desire. Lacan equates Desire with libido, but locates the source as a lack of the Other – a lack which seeks to overcome itself – rather than in biological or sexual drive.[12] As individuals become ever further alienated into the objectifying rules and norms of language, codes, and social laws, and ever further away from the pre-Oedipal dyadic sense of oneness, they feel a want-in-being (*manque-à-être*) which is neither existential, nor real, nor metaphysical, nor material. It is a 'subversion of the human subject which makes him or her aim, not at renunciation or repression, but at the realization of Desire, in other words, at the refinding of a pre-social self.'[13]

By a 'subversion' of the subject Lacan means that the unconscious experiences of fusion and separation – Desire and Law – circumscribe consciousness and language, and thereby subvert perception and intentionality from the domain of objectivity and willed action to that of structural effect and dictate. The conscious, speaking subject seeks the roots of its own unconscious formation by the mere fact of using language, but more specifically through the whole symbolic system of substitution. The goal sought is a repetition, the replacement of the pleasure (*jouissance*) in the illusion of wholeness which was characteristic of the pre-phallic period. *Jouissance*, a word which Lacan recommends that one not even translate into English, means orgasm, or the purely sexual release of tension experienced in *plaisir*.[14] Abstractly speaking, *jouissance* becomes the temporary pleasure afforded by the recognition of others, substitutes for the original Other. But substitutes are of necessity imperfect, for the gap or lack in being *is* the unconscious which, by definition, is unknown.

In direct contradiction to the prevalence of ego psychologies in Anglo-American thought, Lacan shows the human subject as neither unified, whole, nor autonomous. Split between language and individuality, between 'saying' and 'being', the subject is operated by the structures of Desire and Law which are both explicable in mathematical terms. The mirror-stage duality of mother – infant symbiosis is experienced by the infant as a singularity or unity, and is only perceived as the dyad it actually is from the perspective of Oedipal triangularity. This humble mother–infant–father drama places the foundation of human ontology on a structural split. It introduces a permanent drive towards identification with, and recognition from, others – in an effort to deny the unwelcome insights of the tenuousness of being, with their implicit intimations of death, i.e. a gap in being; an identity composed of fragments. The human tendency to seek unities through love, meaning, belief, and so on, derives from the mirror-stage experience of taking on an alien identity and Desire as our own and then repressing it. The paradoxically opposite and equally strong tendency is to strive for difference in order to bow to the forces which first divided the subject along lines of social and personal parts. Such structural underpinnings denote the Imaginary order of identification and homogeneity, and the Symbolic order of individuation and heterogeneity. These conflictive inclinations will always delimit human behaviour to unitary strivings and binary displacements and substitutions.

Although the specific meanings attached to the structures of Desire and Law vary according to personal experience and historical context, the experiences themselves shape both History and personal trajectory. The 'enemy' which feminists must confront, then, is neither class-structure, not patriarchy *per se*, but the mirror-stage process by which a human subject takes on its essential form and fixations in a mathematically formalizable equation. In so far as the primordial sensation of sameness is attached to the (m)Other, Desire – cum lack – is elementally linked to the female. In so far as the secondary experience of individuation or difference is attached to the father, Law is linked to the male. Freud's error, according to Lacan, was to mistake this symbolic, structural drama for a biologically based, natural one.

. . .

One of the most prolific French feminist writers on the contemporary scene is Luce Irigaray. Like the philosopher Gilles Deleuze, and the psychoanalyst Félix Guattari, Irigaray sees the Lacanian Symbolic order as enemy territory, ruled by phallocrats, patriarchs, and pederasts. It is an order to be resisted if women are to gain the freedom of their own specificity. But Irigaray reads Lacan ideologically and substantively, and therefore accuses him of making prescriptive statements. By equating the phallic signifier with patriarchy, she substantivizes the concept biologically such that Phallus = penis = male. But she only harks back to older biological determinisms by implying that males and females have 'natural' psychic attributes in keeping with gender. By failing to see that the phallic signifier is intrinsically neutral, meaningless in its own right, and only takes its power from associations catalysed in the Oedipal drama, Irigaray does not understand that Lacan is describing first causes, not approving them.

In *Speculum de l'autre femme* (1974) Irigaray accuses psychoanalysis of a 'masculine bias', of being arrested in the phallic phase, and equating female sexuality with motherhood.[15] In *Ce Sexe qui n'en est pas un* (1977) she portrays Lacan as a profiteering cynic who gains pleasure, power, and love from being a Master.[16] In her rejection of the Lacanian theory of a phallic fixing of a child's sexual destiny, Irigaray treats the mirror stage as implicitly male. His mirror becomes the most recent version of a philosophical topos whose *raison d'être* is to valorize sameness and visibility, she says.[17] In Lacan's case the standard of sameness is the Phallus. Irigaray asks: '*And as far as the organism is concerned, what happens when the mirror reveals nothing to see?* No sex, for example, as is the case for the little girl.'[18] Although Irigaray offers no 'other' perception in *Speculum*, she does advance some ideas of her own in *Ce Sexe*. She concludes that Lacan's theory of a phallic fixing of sexual identity is homosexual in its exclusion of otherness, with heterosexuality merely as a mediate homosexual form in its exchange of women between men. As a foil to a phallic sexual economy, she proposes woman's subtlety and pliancy, her 'feeble resistance'.[19]

What I find particularly disturbing in Irigaray's analysis is her 'resistance' to getting Lacan 'right'. Because she misreads Lacan, she misses the chance to use his theories to either transcend his own limitations (as other feminists have done with Freud), or to make sense of suggestions that Lacan has purposely left unresolved. In her depiction of the Lacanian mirror stage as the earliest in a series of historical stages which oppresses women, Irigaray reduces this stage to the literal and biological. In fact, Lacan's mirror-stage concept is a metaphor for a mimetic process which occurs in inter-social relations with or without a mirror. Initially, the mirror stage refers to the representation of a visual, corporal unity with which the infant identifies, in contrast to the inner tumult felt because of motor-skill and neurological prematuration at birth and for some months after. In the first six months of life, Lacan hypothesizes that infants merge perceptually with images and objects in the outside world, actually become them in their elemental fantasies. Lacan denotes this primordial perception by Frege's mathematical 0. When the infant identifies with the human form – its (m)Other's and its own in a mirror – it has passed cognitively from 0 to 1. But by identifying a centre of unity outside itself, by taking an-Other to be itself, human perception of difference starts out based on a lie – on a disjunction or asymmetry – whose later effects range from the production of a double as in the *Doppelgänger* phenomenon, to a bodily disintegration such as that depicted by Hieronimus Bosch's figures.[20] In adult life, the repressed mirror-stage structure functions dynamically to diffract the supposed unity of the speaking subject, and keeps people from feeling 'one' with themselves. And this victimization by an-Other discourse which serves as the repressed centre of being, haunts males, as well as females.

Irigaray's confusion of the fixing of a Gestalt during the six- to eighteen-month mirror-stage period, with the phallic fixing of sexual identity which occurs after the mirror stage, blinds her to what I find most important for feminist theory: that Lacan's epistemology comes the closest of any to demystifying the basic causes and differences of sexual personality. His description of the structures underlying the patriarchal order is certainly not an ideological support for maintaining that order. The essential drama is one of structural effect. The confusion of sexual organs and gender is a secondary occurrence, which is solidified and substantified in language, enshrined in myth, and passed on as 'natural' truth.

. . .

The French philosopher Jean-Marie Benoist has described the phallic or Oedipal function as a semantico-syntactic operator of Desire. As the absent – i.e. figurative or metaphorical – operator of the unconscious, the phallic signifier traps the subject in the Symbolic, teaches the limit of Desire, and permits any triangular social configuration to symbolize itself (Benoist, pp. 226–8). It also coincides with the learning of language, thereby linking *logos* to Desire and Law. The Oedipal complex which Freud defined as the organized ensemble of loving and hostile desires felt by the child towards her or his parents, has been recast by Lacan to account for the evolution that little by little substitutes the father for the mother. This is what Irigaray refers to as the phallic fixing of sexual identity. In the summary of French psychoanalyst Serge Leclaire, the mother is taken as the central and primordial character in the complex, and the father as the principal and ultimate reference. The mirror-stage identification with a unified, corporal image of 'self' corresponds more or less to identification with the (m)Other's body. Gradually, the child identifies as well with the object of the (m)Other's Desire. Wishing to be all for her, the child wants to be the signifier of her Desire: i.e. the Phallus in the symbolic and signifying sense of that which replaces lack.[21] For from an Imaginary perspective, the Phallus is the signifier of the lack inherent in Desire. In this context, the first signified for an infant is the paternal metaphor. But since a child does not know what the (m)Other's Desire really is, the first and only real and concrete signifier is the child's Desire to fuse with – i.e. please – the (m)Other. Thus, children quickly detach themselves from any primal identification with whatever will replace the (m)Other's lack, for they see that despite their efforts to be what (m)Other wants, she still remains dissatisfied. This fact points a child towards otherness, i.e. the referentiality of the father. And so the first metaphorical or 'pure' signifier is the Name-of-the-father which spells out prohibition, separation, difference, compromise, i.e. Castration. At this stage, the (m)Other is the mediator who opens the way to permit the birth of Desire and Law: the child cannot fill all her wants. In this phase, the child learns the relation of the (m)Other to the father's name. In the third phase, the father's real sexual organ is equated with having the Phallus or not; i.e. with being lacking or not. The psychic evolution of the Oedipal complex is an identificatory reshaping of the subject, then, which is complete when the child fixes a sexual identity by identifying either with the (m)Other or the father. The gender complications of this drama mean that when a child renounces identification with the possibility of being 'all' for Mama, that concern is transferred into making social sense of gender difference (Schneiderman, *Returning*, pp. 121–2).

. . .

Even though the Lacanian Phallus does not refer to the real father, or to the biological organ, this term does underline the idea that the real father, the penian part-object, and the phallic differential function are confused in language. An identificatory logic locates the phallic signifier at the origin of culture, and arbitrarily links the male – *qua* father – to the principles of Law and reality, setting him in opposition to the mother-linked principles of Desire and subjectivity. The Shakespearean ontological crisis of being could be understood in Lacanian terms as a completion of the sentence as 'to be or not to be, the Phallus'. The historical plight of woman has been the linguistic and representational misunderstanding which translates 'be' as 'have' and Phallus as penis.[22] In defence of the theory that there is no natural causality to sexual identity, Lacan says that man and woman exist as pure signifiers, the nature of things being the nature of words (*Séminaire* XX, p. 68). But Lacan does not mean that words make up the unconscious discourse in any transparent or one-to-one way.

The influence of modern linguistics on Lacan's thought is well known. Saussure taught that language is an ever-flowing, referential, differential, arbitrary system. Lacan adds to this what Saussure's theory lacks: a context. Language is not, as Freud believed, a set of simply received sounds. It is an all-encompassing network whose effects create impressions and reactions, and later attribute meanings and labels, which ultimately link up with mirror-stage networks of perceptual images and relations.

. . .

We see that for Lacan language is not a static, transparent medium through which to unveil hidden meanings. Nor will its depths be plumbed by a proper clarification of all its potential codes and organizatory mechanisms. Nor is it merely a series of untruths, awaiting Derridean deconstruction. Language is a dense and opaque body which struggles to embody Real and Imaginary experiences and symbols, which it can only ever approximate because of its intrinsically representational and deferred nature. Thus, while philosophers place themselves in conscious thought and language, seeing themselves as its correlate, Lacan situates himself within unconscious meaning which makes normative language 'mean' more than it says. He speaks of the efforts of the unconscious to both know and deny its own messages and structures through the material elaborations of conscious language systems. Under Lacan's moulding hands, language can no longer be seen as a pristine means to translation of thought, but has itself become the 'royal road' to the unconscious, and a paradoxical bridge back to consciousness. What the French psychoanalyst offers feminist theory, then, is a picture of the place of man and woman within a history of structuration, symbolization, and meaning (*Séminaire* XX, p. 69).

. . .

In scrutinizing woman's history of oppression I would offer the concept of a double Castration. At the level of primary Castration, both males and females experience loss, and gain an unconscious and a social personality. At a secondary level, this structural drama is substantivized, interpreted, explained. Since the (m)Other within is the dark-faced part of us all, the idea of unseen dominance or secret power is displaced onto woman. She becomes someone to fear, deny, ignore, fight, conquer, or conversely worship and enshrine. Whether extolled or denigrated, people indirectly take a position towards their own unconscious truths in their fundamental stance towards woman. The myths that have grown up to elaborate this symbolic drama are then propounded as 'natural' truths, finding their validity in theology, biology, genetics, science, politics, economics, mythology, and so on.

One can well understand that feminists who take Lacan's ideas at face value would reject his argumentation as finalistic and deterministic. I find, on the contrary, the theoretical basis for a continued feminist rewriting of the Other's discourse and Desire, one which prescribes change in light of informed comprehension of structural cause and effect. I would make a distinction here between femininity and feminism, however. I see femininity as allying itself with the archaic corporal (m)Other, as well as the (m)Other as a principle of loss. In this picture masculinity becomes a flight from the feminine, a rejection of the pain of loss and Castration. At the same time, the mirror-stage (m)Other remains as an internalized principle of sensuality and corporal experience, thus raising the issue of female sexuality to a problematic level for both men and women. Whether woman is feared as a seductress, sought as a sex object, or idealized as a mother, her *primary* value is supposed to reside in her physical being. The pervasiveness of the equation of the feminine with the sexual explains, in part, why feminists threaten the very sexual economy on which gender identity is established.

. . .

Lacan maintained that one of the many functions of language is to compensate for psychic division undergone through the Oedipal split. Although there is not a one-to-one link between conscious and unconscious 'language', a person's unconscious experiences will later govern their use of language in an invisible intentionality. For example, a person who identifies with phallic forces will use language to represent his or her ego on the slope of the master: one who bases authority on 'knowing'. The hysteric, on the contrary, poses the very question of being by addressing her or his discourse to the master (*Séminaire* XX, 'A Jakobson'). Although the intentionality which informs these discourse structures is not sex-linked, the patriarchal order tends to make masters of men, and hysterics of women. But, by master, Lacan does not think of one who does 'know'. He describes a discourse based on ignorance and opinion, one which masks the truth of the unconscious. By denying Castration, the master discourse perpetuates the denial and suppression of the split in the subject, and thereby retains an unchallenged belief in conscious autonomy, and unity of being. Lacan locates the hysteric's discourse close to the analyst's, that is, close to the search for meaning in terms of the truths of the unconscious. Whether master, hysteric, analyst, or academic, people speak to master the signifiers hidden in the discourse of the Other. In this sense, to speak risks making oneself visible at the level of unconscious intentionality. Discourse-wise, anatomical difference *is* a correlative of different uses of language, then. That is, gender characterizes itself by specific modes of entry into general discourse as a positioning of oneself towards the paternal metaphor. It should not be surprising, from this point of view, that many feminist literary critics have found that women writers 'speak' a different language from their male counterparts.[23] At a macro-level, however, I would contend that literature itself – not literary criticism – is a subversion of the phallic order, and as such is on a feminine and hysterical slope.

There is no 'beyond the phallus', then, if one means beyond differentiation, society, language, Law, and reality. The Symbolic order keeps its subjects from plunging headlong into incestuous lures and hallucinatory desires, psychosis being total submersion in the Imaginary order of the Other. Primary Castration, seen as differentiation from the (m)Other, is unavoidable and universal if people are to live in sanity. Secondary Castration attributes meaning to this drama in terms of gender difference. Generally speaking, men set out on a quest to try to be the Phallus, to embody power and prestige. And women try to marry as high up the phallic ladder as possible. Yet, no one can be the Phallus, for it is only ever a signifier: something that represents a subject for another signifier. For men as well as women, the climb to power – whether directly held or held by association – entails compromise, submission, and association.

The Symbolic order codes and linguistic descriptions change all the time. As new economic and historical realities continue to reflect the change in sex roles, and in gender possibilities, the secondary meanings attached to Castration mirror new realities. Such changes bring many questions to mind. If the mirror-stage separation trauma were to be less gender-related, what impact would this have on sexual identity? Would the Oedipal drama come to centre on individual, as opposed to sexual, differences? Can loss ever *not* be associated with the (m)Other unless we live in a *1984*-type fantasy world? Lacan has never said, as Freud did, that female sexuality is an outcome of thwarted phallic strivings. Nor does Lacan attribute female gender specificity, as did Heinz Kohut, to a natural biological development. Instead, it is to the double effects of Castration on women that he points to, first through separation, and then through an arbitrary linking of power-penis-Phallus, and conversely, loss-no penis-Castration.

. . .

. . . In Lacan's own theoretical terms, feminist power would lie in the direction of disrupting the history of Other repetition, of sowing disunity among standard social codes, practices, and linguistic commonplaces, as well as by altering the structure of object relations. Irigaray's effort to create a language according to what she calls the 'laws of the feminine' is certainly one kind of step in that direction. But it is Lacan's thought which gives us the basis of a new theory on which to continue rewriting our history.

In conclusion, I submit that feminist efforts to change the social, linguistic order encounter a circular dilemma. Although mirror-stage identification and phallic differentiation are not biologically determined along sexual lines, their effects are predictable. If Lacan is right, then we know what must be restructured. And it is not by overthrowing patriarchy *cum* capitalism that human beings will gain the freedom of Desire which Deleuze and Guattari foretell, nor that feminists will eradicate phallocractic – i.e. power-based – values even if they live in exclusively female groups. For any group evolves its own phallocratic structure, because recognition and power needs inhere in the structure of the human subject itself. Within a Lacanian context, then, there can be no tomorrow of communist egalitarianism which will eradicate power structures, and no Utopia where woman's superior values will replace man's tarnished ones. But there can be a tomorrow where differentiations are made along more equitable lines; a tomorrow that eschews the gender rigidities that gave rise to the mammocratic woman whose power was no less than her phallocratic husband's, even though devious means were required. As gender distinctions become ever more blurred, both sexes will attenuate their own future disillusionments by understanding the complexity of the quadrature of the human subject in its relationship to society, and its inherently paradoxical strivings.

NOTES

1 Elisabeth Roudinesco, *Un Discours au réel: théorie de l'inconscient et politique de la psychanalyse* (Paris: Maison Marne, 1973), p. 200 (*Séminaire inédit de Jacques Lacan, 1970*).
2 Jacques Lacan, *Le Séminaire* (1954–1955), *Livre II, Le Moi dans la théorie de Freud et dans la technique de la psychanalyse* (Paris: Seuil, 1978), p. 51.
3 Jacques Lacan, 'Of structure as an inmixing of an otherness prerequisite to any subject whatever', in *The Structuralist Controversy*, ed. Richard Macksey and Eugenio Donato (Baltimore: The Johns Hopkins Press, 1975), pp. 187–8.
4 Jacques Lacan, *Le Séminaire* (1953–1954), *Livre I, Les Ecrits techniques de Freud* (Paris: Seuil, 1975), p. 80.
5 Anika Lemaire, *Jacques Lacan*, trans. D. Macey (Boston: Routledge & Kegan Paul, 1977), p. 81.
6 Jacques Lacan, *Le Séminaire* (1972–1973), *Livre XX, Encore* (Paris: Seuil, 1975), p. 69.
7 Jacques Lacan, *Le Séminaire* (1964), *Livre XI, Les Quatre Concepts Fondamentaux de la Psychanalyse* (Paris: Seuil, 1973), p. 35.
8 Fitzhugh Dodson, *Tout se joue avant six ans*, trans. and ed. Robert Laffont (Verviers, Belgium: Marabout Service, 1970), p. 38. Dodson recounts the

experiment conducted by Frederick II of Prussia. In trying to discover the 'original' language of humanity – Greek or Latin? – Frederick II isolated several newborns and prohibited their nurses from speaking to them. He hoped to learn which language was innate when the infants eventually spoke. Although the infants were physically well cared for, they did not live long enough to speak. All died of unknown causes.

9 Lacan has reformulated Saussure's concept of the sign in which the signified (concept) is superior to the signifier (sound or form) in determining meaning. Lacan has equated the signified with the unconscious, and the signifier with articulated language. But, by making the unconscious the superior meaning system above and beyond linguistic meaning, Lacan has reversed Saussure's order.

10 Anthony Wilden, *The Language of the Self* (Baltimore: The Johns Hopkins Press, 1968), p. 186. Wilden refers here to Lacan's unedited *Séminaire* (1956), *Livre IV*.

11 Lacan created the word *hommelette* to describe the dual nature of the human ego, broken into two halves like the egg which makes the omelette.

12 Jacques Lacan, 'The signification of the phallus', in *Ecrits: A Selection*, trans. Alan Sheridan (New York: W.W. Norton & Co., Inc., 1977), p. 287.

13 Fredric Jameson, 'Marxism, psychoanalytic criticism and the problem of the subject', *Yale French Studies, Literature and Psychoanalysis*, Nos. 55/56 (1977), p. 395.

14 Stuart Schneiderman, *Returning to Freud: Clinical Psychoanalysis in the School of Lacan*, selections ed. and trans. Stuart Schneiderman (New Haven: Yale University Press, 1980), p. vii (translator's preface).

15 Luce Irigaray, *Speculum de l'autre femme* (Paris: Minuit, 1974).

16 Luce Irigaray, *Ce Sexe qui n'en est pas un* (Paris: Minuit, 1977). In one of the chapters entitled 'Cosi fan tutti' Irigaray compares Lacan to Don Alfonso from Mozart's opera by the same name. Don Alfonso wins money by betting on a permanent *malentendu* between the sexes. Cf. Jane Gallop, 'Impertinent questions: Irigaray, Sade, Lacan', *Sub-Stance*, No. 26 (1980).

17 Naomi Schor, '*Eugénie Grandet:* mirrors and melancolai', unpublished paper, given in January of 1981, at the University of Vermont, French Department. Forthcoming in a volume *The m(O)ther Tongue: Essays in Feminist Psychoanalytic Literary Interpretation*, eds M.S. Gohlke, S.A. Garner, C. Kahane.

18 Luce Irigaray, 'La "Mécanique" des fluides', *L'Arc: Jacques Lacan*, 58, No. 1 (1974), 55. Irigaray's quotation refers to Lacan's essay 'Le stade du miroir', in the *Ecrits* (Paris: Seuil, 1966).

19 Irigaray, *Ce Sexe*. In a chapter entitled 'Quand nos lèvres se parlent' Irigaray urges women to combat phallocracy by resisting phallic militancy. She praises woman's subtlety as a strategy (p. 214).

20 Jean-Marie Benoist, *La Révolution structurale* (Paris: Denoël/Gonthier, 1980), p. 213.

21 Jacques Lacan, 'La Signification du phallus', *Ecrits II* (Paris: Editions du Seuil, 1971), p. 113.

22 In Sheridan's translation of 'The signification of the phallus' (*Ecrits*, 1977) Lacan says that the relations between the sexes are actually governed by a 'to seem' which replaces the 'to have' [the Phallus]. The 'to seem' covers the confusion of the phallic signifier with the phallic organ, in order to protect it on the male side, and to mask its lack on the female side, and which projects the ideal or typical manifestations of each sex (p. 289).

23 Sandra M. Gilbert and Susan Gubar, *The Madwoman in the Attic: The Woman Writer and the Nineteenth-Century Literary Imagination* (New Haven: Yale University Press, 1979).

24 Heinz Kohut, *The Search for the Self: Selected Writings of Heinz Kohut: 1950–70*, 2 vols, ed. Paul H. Ornstein (New York: International Universities Press, 1978), p. 228.

THE LAUGH OF THE MEDUSA*

Hélène Cixous

I shall speak about women's writing: about *what it will do*. Woman must write her self: must write about women and bring women to writing, from which they have been driven away as violently as from their bodies – for the same reasons, by the same law, with the same fatal goal. Woman must put herself into the text – as into the world and into history – by her own movement.

The future must no longer be determined by the past. I do not deny that the effects of the past are still with us. But I refuse to strengthen them by repeating them, to confer upon them an irremovability the equivalent of destiny, to confuse the biological and the cultural. Anticipation is imperative.

. . .

I write this as a woman, towards women. When I say 'woman', I'm speaking of woman in her inevitable struggle against conventional man; and of a universal woman subject who must bring women to their senses and to their meaning in history. But first it must be said that in spite of the enormity of the repression that has kept them in the 'dark' – that dark which people have been trying to make them accept as their attribute – there is, at this time, no general woman, no one typical woman. What they have *in common* I will say. But what strikes me is the infinite richness of their individual constitutions: you can't talk about *a* female sexuality, uniform, homogeneous, classifiable into codes – any more than you can talk about one unconscious resembling another. Women's imaginary is inexhaustible, like music, painting, writing: their stream of phantasms is incredible.

. . .

It is time to liberate the New Woman from the Old by coming to know her – by loving her for getting by, for getting beyond the Old without delay, by going out ahead of what the New Woman will be, as an arrow quits the bow with a movement that gathers and separates the vibrations musically, in order to be more than her self.

I say that we must, for, with a few rare exceptions, there has not yet been any writing that inscribes femininity, exceptions so rare, in fact,

224

that, after ploughing through literature across languages, cultures, and ages,[1] one can only be startled at this vain scouting mission. It is well known that the number of women writers (while having increased very slightly from the nineteenth century on) has always been ridiculously small. This is a useless and deceptive fact unless from their species of female writers we do not first deduct the immense majority whose workmanship is in no way different from male writing, and which either obscures women or reproduces the classic representations of women (as sensitive – intuitive – dreamy, etc.).[2]

Let me insert here a parenthetical remark. I mean it when I speak of male writing. I maintain unequivocally that there is such a thing as *marked* writing; that, until now, far more extensively and repressively than is ever suspected or admitted, writing has been run by a libidinal and cultural – hence political, typically masculine – economy; that this is a locus where the repression of women has been perpetuated, over and over, more or less consciously, and in a manner that's frightening since it's often hidden or adorned with the mystifying charms of fiction; that this locus has grossly exaggerated all the signs of sexual opposition (and not sexual difference), where woman has never *her* turn to speak – this being all the more serious and unpardonable in that writing is precisely *the very possibility of change*, the space that can serve as a springboard for subversive thought, the precursory movement of a transformation of social and cultural structures.

Nearly the entire history of writing is confounded with the history of reason, of which it is at once the effect, the support, and one of the privileged alibis. It has been one with the phallocentric tradition. It is indeed that same self-admiring, self-stimulating, self-congratulatory phallocentrism.

. . .

To write. An act that will not only 'realize' the decensored relation of woman to her sexuality, to her womanly being, giving her access to her native strength; it will give her back her goods, her pleasures, her organs, her immense bodily territories which have been kept under seal; it will tear her away from the super-egoized structure in which she has always occupied the place reserved for the guilty (guilty of everything, guilty at every turn: for having desires, for not having any; for being frigid, for being 'too hot'; for not being both at once; for being too motherly and not enough; for having children and for not having any; for nursing and for not nursing . . .) – tear her away by means of this research, this job of analysis and illumination, this emancipation of the marvellous text of her self that she must urgently learn to speak. A woman without a body, dumb, blind, can't possibly be a good fighter. She is reduced to being the servant of the militant male, his shadow. We must kill the false woman who is preventing the live one from breathing. Inscribe the breath of the whole woman.

225

It is by writing, from and toward women, and by taking up the challenge of speech which has been governed by the phallus, that women will confirm women in a place other than that which is reserved in and by the symbolic, that is, in a place other than silence. Women should break out of the snare of silence. They shouldn't be conned into accepting a domain which is the margin or the harem.

Listen to a woman speak at a public gathering (if she hasn't painfully lost her wind). She doesn't 'speak', she throws her trembling body forward; she lets go of herself, she flies; all of her passes into her voice, and it's with her body that she vitally supports the 'logic' of her speech. Her flesh speaks true. She lays herself bare. In fact, she physically materializes what she's thinking; she signifies it with her body. In a certain way she *inscribes* what she's saying, because she doesn't deny her drives the intractable and impassioned part they have in speaking. Her speech, even when 'theoretical' or political, is never simple or linear or 'objectified', generalized: she draws her story into history.

It is impossible to *define* a feminine practice of writing, and this is an impossibility that will remain, for this practice can never be theorized, enclosed, coded – which doesn't mean that it doesn't exist. But it will always surpass the discourse that regulates the phallocentric system; it does and will take place in areas other than those subordinated to philosophico-theoretical domination. It will be conceived of only by subjects who are breakers of automatisms, by peripheral figures that no authority can ever subjugate.

Hence the necessity to affirm the flourishes of this writing, to give form to its movement, its near and distant byways. Bear in mind to begin with (1) that sexual opposition, which has always worked for man's profit to the point of reducing writing, too, to his laws, is only a historico-cultural limit. There is, there will be more and more rapidly pervasive now, a fiction that produces irreducible effects of femininity. (2) That it is through ignorance that most readers, critics, and writers of both sexes hesitate to admit or deny outright the possibility or the pertinence of a distinction between feminine and masculine writing. It will usually be said, thus disposing of sexual difference: either that all writing, to the extent that it materializes, is feminine; or, inversely – but it comes to the same thing – that the act of writing is equivalent to masculine masturbation (and so the woman who writes cuts herself out a paper penis); or that writing is bisexual, hence neuter, which again does away with differentiation. To admit that writing is precisely working (in) the in-between, inspecting the process of the same and of the other without which nothing can live, undoing the work of death – to admit this is first to want the two, as well as both, the ensemble of the one and the other, not fixed in sequences of struggle and expulsion or some other form of death but infinitely dynamized by an incessant process of exchange from one subject to another. A process of different subjects knowing one another and beginning one another anew only from the living boundaries of the other: a multiple and inexhaustible course with millions of encounters and transformations of the same into the other and into the in-between, from which woman takes her forms (and man, in his turn; but that's his other history).

In saying 'bisexual, hence neuter', I am referring to the classic conception of bisexuality, which, squashed under the emblem of castration fear and along with the fantasy of a 'total' being (though composed of two halves), would do away with the difference experienced as an operation incurring loss, as the mark of dreaded sectility.

To this self-effacing, merger-type bisexuality, which would conjure away castration (the writer who puts up his sign: 'bisexual written here, come and see', when the odds are good that it's neither one nor the other), I oppose the *other bisexuality* on which every subject not enclosed in the false theatre of phallocentric representationalism has founded his/her erotic universe. Bisexuality: that is, each one's location is self (*répérage en soi*) of the presence – variously manifest and insistent according to each person, male or female – of both sexes, non-exclusion either of the difference or of one sex, and, from this 'self-permission', multiplication of the effects of the inscription of desire, over all parts of my body and the other body.

Now it happens that at present, for historico-cultural reasons, it is women who are opening up to and benefiting from this vatic bisexuality which doesn't annul differences but stirs them up, pursues them, increases their number. In a certain way, 'woman is bisexual'; man – it's a secret to no one – being poised to keep glorious phallic monosexuality in view. By virtue of affirming the primacy of the phallus and of bringing it into play, phallocratic ideology has claimed more than one victim. As a woman, I've been clouded over by the great shadow of the sceptre and been told: idolize it, that which you cannot brandish. But at the same time, man has been handed that grotesque and scarcely enviable destiny (just imagine) of being reduced to a single idol with clay balls. And consumed, as Freud and his followers note, by a fear of being a woman! For, if psychoanalysis was constituted from woman, to repress femininity (and not so successful a repression at that – men have made it clear), its account of masculine sexuality is now hardly refutable; as with all the 'human' sciences, it reproduces the masculine view, of which it is one of the effects.

Here we encounter the inevitable man-with-rock, standing erect in his old Freudian realm, in the way that, to take the figure back to the point where linguistics is conceptualizing it 'anew', Lacan preserves it in the sanctuary of the phallos (ϕ) 'sheltered' from *castration's lack*! Their

227

'symbolic' exists, it holds power – we, the sowers of disorder, know it only too well. But we are in no way obliged to deposit our lives in their banks of lack, to consider the constitution of the subject in terms of a drama manglingly restaged, to reinstate again and again the religion of the father. Because we don't want that. We don't fawn around the supreme hole. We have no womanly reason to pledge allegiance to the negative. The feminine (as the poets suspected) affirms: 'And yes,' says Molly, carrying *Ulysses* off beyond any book and towards the new writing; 'I said yes, I will Yes.'

The Dark Continent is neither dark nor unexplorable. – It is still un-explored only because we've been made to believe that it was too dark to be explorable. And because they want to make us believe that what interests us is the white continent, with its monuments to Lack. And we believed. They riveted us between two horrifying myths: between the Medusa and the abyss. That would be enough to set half the world laughing, except that it's still going on. For the phallologocentric sub-lation[3] is with us, and it's militant, regenerating the old patterns, anchored in the dogma of castration. They haven't changed a thing: they've theorized their desire for reality! Let the priests tremble, we're going to show them our sexes!

Too bad for them if they fall apart upon discovering that women aren't men, or that the mother doesn't have one. But isn't this fear convenient for them? Wouldn't the worst be, isn't the worst, in truth, that women aren't castrated, that they have only to stop listening to the Sirens (for the Sirens were men) for history to change its meaning? You only have to look at the Medusa straight on to see her. And she's not deadly. She's beautiful and she's laughing.

Men say that there are two unrepresentable things: death and the feminine sex. That's because they need femininity to be associated with death; it's the jitters that give them a hard on! for themselves! They need to be afraid of us. Look at the trembling Perseuses moving backward towards us, clad in apotropes. What lovely backs! Not another minute to lose. Let's get out of here.

Let's hurry: the continent is not impenetrably dark. I've been there often. I was overjoyed one day to run into Jean Genet. It was in *Pompes funèbres*.[4] He had come there led by his Jean. There are some men (all too few) who aren't afraid of femininity.

Almost everything is yet to be written by women about femininity: about their sexuality, that is, its infinite and mobile complexity, about their eroticization, sudden turn-ons of a certain miniscule-immense area of their bodies; not about destiny, but about the adventure of such and such a drive, about trips, crossings, trudges, abrupt and gradual awaken-ings, discoveries of a zone at one time timorous and soon to be forthright. A woman's body, with its 1,001 thresholds of ardour – once, by smashing yokes and censors, she lets it articulate the profusion of meanings that run through it in every direction – will make the old single-grooved mother-tongue reverberate with more than one language.

We've been turned away from our bodies, shamefully taught to ignore them, to strike them with that stupid sexual modesty; we've been made victims of the old fool's game: each one will love the other sex. I'll give you your body and you'll give me mine. But who are the men who give women the body that women blindly yield to them? Why so few texts? Because so few women have as yet won back their body. Women must write through their bodies, they must invent the impregnable language that will wreck partitions, classes, and rhetorics, regulations and codes, they must submerge, cut through, get beyond the ultimate reserve-discourse, including the one that laughs at the very idea of pronouncing the word 'silence', the one that, aiming for the impossible, stops short before the word 'impossible' and writes it as 'the end'.

Such is the strength of women that, sweeping away syntax, breaking that famous thread (just a tiny little thread, they say) which acts for men as a surrogate umbilical cord, assuring them – otherwise they couldn't come – that the old lady is always right behind them, watching them make phallus, women will go right up to the impossible.

If woman has always functioned 'within' the discourse of man, a signifier that has always referred back to the opposite signifier which annihilates its specific energy and diminishes or stifles its very different sounds, it is time for her to dislocate this 'within', to explode it, turn it around, and seize it; to make it hers, containing it, taking it in her own mouth, biting that tongue with her very own teeth to invent for herself a language to get inside of. And you'll see with what ease she will spring forth from that 'within' –the 'within' where once she so drowsily crouched – to overflow at the lips she will cover the foam.

A feminine text cannot fail to be more than subversive. It is volcanic; as it is written it brings about an upheaval of the old property crust, carrier of masculine investments, there's no other way. There's no room for her if she's not a he. If she's a her-she, it's in order to smash everything, to shatter the framework of institutions, to blow up the law, to break up the 'truth' with laughter.

NOTES

* Translated by Keith Cohen and Paula Cohen.
1 I am speaking here only of the place 'reserved' for women by the Western world.
2 Which works, then, might be called feminine? I'll just point out some examples: one would have to give them full readings to bring out what is

229

pervasively feminine in their significance. Which I shall do elsewhere. In France (have you noted our infinite poverty in this field? – The Anglo-Saxon countries have shown resources of distinctly greater consequence), leafing through what's come out of the twentieth century – and it's not much – the only inscriptions of femininity that I have seen were by Colette, Marguerite Duras, . . . and Jean Genet.

3 Standard English term for the Hegelian *Aufhebung*, the French *la relève*.

4 Jean Genet, *Pompes funèbres* (Paris, 1948), p. 185 [privately published].

Part VII

BIOLOGY AND FEMINISM

INTRODUCTION

Gisela Kaplan and Lesley Rogers

Any movement intent on changing the status of women in society has invariably involved challenge to the predominant notions of the male–female differences and the role of biology in determining differences between the sexes. Such challenges have been met by conservative reactions which have called upon theories of biological determinism of sex differences in behaviour, in order to justify the inequalities between men and women. During the 1970s and 1980s, we have seen the proliferation and increasing popularity of so-called scientific theories claiming that human behaviours, including those that differ between the sexes, races, and classes, are determined by biology.

There has been confusion of theoretical constructs with the biological facts. The article by Bleier points out that the values and biases of individual scientists influence the methodologies which they use, the data that they accept or reject in substantiating their theories, and the way in which they interpret any given set of data. Scientific data have frequently been manipulated to strengthen the belief in biological differences between the sexes. The mid-1970s, with the publication of E.O. Wilson's *Sociobiology: A new Synthesis* (Harvard University Press: Cambridge, Mass., 1975), saw the formation of an area of biology that claims that a large range of human behaviours is genetically determined. In sociobiological thinking, biological explanations subsume sociological explanations. As Bleier discusses, sociobiological theories have been used as counter-arguments to the feminist movement. They have been taken up in support of the racist and sexist platforms of many neo-fascist organizations. The biological-determinist position sees either that there is no real possibility for change in society, or that change can occur only through reform or re-education against women's 'biological nature'.

Some feminists have been influenced by, and have adopted, theories of biological determinism of sex differences in behaviour. One such position has involved the celebration of women's feminine virtues endowed by their biology. Adherents of this ideology have argued for the superiority of women. The liberal application of this ideology is to argue for 'equality with difference'; the radical position is to argue for complete

233

separatism based on the assumption that the 'feminine' character has little chance of blossoming in patriarchal society. A less extreme position, but one also based on biological determinism, is that there are biologically based differences between the sexes which however do not justify social inequalities. As Bleier so clearly states, the ultimate effectiveness of movements is weakened if they rely on biological determinist theories as these theories are seriously flawed and scientifically meaningless. The rest of Bleier's book discusses the scientific fallacies of some of these theories. The introductory section presented for reading here provides an overview, and it will hopefully encourage reading of other chapters in Bleier's most excellent book.

The article by Star addresses more specifically some of the contradictions of reasoning in research on sex differences in behaviour and the extent to which these sex differences are determined by differences in the asymmetry of functions of the left and right hemispheres. Star examines the way in which cultural, religious, and mythical ideas of the past have shaped present thinking about left and right, the former being associated with negative attitudes and the latter with positive. She suggests that some of these deep-seated attitudes have entered into scientific theories which attempt to link sex differences in behaviour to differences in the degree of left–right asymmetry in the organization of the brain. As the article explains, there are two quite contradictory beliefs in this area. The coexistence of these two opposites can occur as long as supporting evidence for either is lacking. Each of these theories has similar social implication, in that they both attempt to tie sex differences in behaviour to a biological cause. It must be stressed that in neither case has this cause been proven, or indeed tested.

While new means of measuring levels of brain activity in humans have become possible since the publication of Star's article (e.g. PET scans, radioactive marking of active neurones), no one has yet published any data reporting sex differences in asymmetry of neural activity. Even if such sex differences are found, this would not tell us whether they are biologically or culturally (environmentally) determined, or, perhaps more likely, result from a complex interaction of both biology and environment. Such experiments could document differences if they occur, but not reveal the cause of these differences.

Since the publication of the article by Star, Geschwind and his colleagues have put forward and popularized a theory according to which male superiority on mathematical tasks results from a greater asymmetry between the hemispheres. This, in turn, is supposed to stem from a retarding action of the male sex hormone, testosterone, on development of the left hemisphere. Such a one-way path of causation, as hypothesized, from genes to sex hormone levels, to brain asymmetry, and, finally, to complex cognitive behaviour is, putting it politely, too simplistic an explanation. In our chapter we quoted examples of environmental influences on the levels of sex hormones for the purpose of showing that, even if it were proven that males have retarded development of the left hemisphere, the causal arrow between this factor and the level of testosterone could point in either direction. So far the only evidence for testosterone affecting the development of asymmetry in the brain has come from a study by Zappia and Rogers (1987) using chickens.[1] However, even in this species, the environmental influence of light also influences the development of asymmetry. A one-way causality showing biological determinism of brain asymmetry does not exist. Scientists can postulate theories of causation to explain the correlative evidence available for the human species, but these theories do not have scientific substance until they are proven, no matter how many textbooks, journal papers, or popular articles are published. Their danger lies in the fact that pseudo-scientific explanations of sex differences so readily support preconceived notions and that they reinforce these ideologies even in the absence of evidence. Indeed, there seems to be no limit to the bizarre development of such theorizing by some members of the scientific and, in particular, the medical professions. Witness, for example, a recent postulate that there may be more left-handed individuals who have AIDS (Geschwind, N. and Galaburda, A.M., *Cerebral Lateralization* (Bradford Books, MIT Press, Cambridge, Mass., 1987), pp. 175–6). These two authors had previously suggested that lowered levels of testosterone decrease the body's immune responses. Based on a single study using rats they suggest that stress of the mother during pregnancy causes a temporary rise in testosterone in the male foetus. This, on the one hand, causes more retardation of the left hemisphere and more left-handedness, and, on the other hand, in later life it causes rebound lower levels of testosterone and homosexuality. (We must add that any link between lowered levels of testosterone in the adult and homosexuality has never been established, and any link between maternal stress and homosexuality of the offspring has been suggested only by Dörner using rats in dubious, uncontrolled experiments; see Geschwind and Galaburda, p. 175.) Geschwind and Galaburda then link the raised levels of testosterone to lowered immune responsiveness and therefore increased susceptibility to AIDS. Hence, the convoluted 'logic' linking left-handedness to homosexuality and, within the homosexual population, left-handed individuals to being at greater risk of contracting AIDS! This is why, they say, female prostitutes (presumably right-handed?) have a lower incidence of AIDS.

We hope this last example will clinch our point that a scientific hypothesis can follow and reinforce social and political attitudes and as such, without supporting evidence, it can be published in all its bizarre nakedness. It is up to those of us who seek genuine, and not pseudo-scientific evidence to strip these hypotheses bare of flights of imagination and political purpose by critical examination of their logic and their supporting evidence. There is no simple biological explanation for behaviour and social differences between the sexes as many scientist and other supporters of the status quo would have us believe.

NOTE

1 J.V. Zappia and L.J. Rogers (1987), 'Sex differences and reversal of brain asymmetry by testosterone in chickens', *Behavioural Brain Research* (23), 261–7.

THE POLITICS OF RIGHT AND LEFT
Sex differences in hemispheric brain asymmetry

Susan Leigh Star

In vertebrates, the brain is divided into two halves – right and left – which in humans are thought to be specialized for different functions. Broadly speaking, some verbal and mathematical abilities are mostly controlled/processed through the left side of the brain, and musical ability, intuition, and spatial/Gestalt perception through the right side of the brain. This specialization is called *hemispheric asymmetry*, or *cerebral lateralization*. However, it should be noted that the left side of the brain receives messages predominantly from the *right* side of the body, whose movements it controls, and the right side of the brain monitors the sensations and controls the movements of the *left* half of the body.

There is a growing body of research asserting sex differences in the extent to which the left and right hemispheres contribute to brain functioning. Given the technical nature of research, 'translation' and popularization to make it understandable are needed and have already begun. But both the academic research and its popularizations present dangers of concern to women.

Popularizations of current research on brain asymmetry rely heavily upon cultural stereotypes about left and right, mixed with eastern and western myths about yin/yang and left/right. Robert Ornstein, a major figure in both the research on brain asymmetry and its popularizations, draws upon the old Buddhist literature about yin and yang and left/right to emphasize his points about left brain and right brain functions. In so doing, he condones and reifies many traditional stereotypes of 'masculine' and 'feminine' and extends their use into 'scientific' research.[1] Unfortunately, he is not unique in doing so.

Both Hinduism and Buddhism have posited different functions for the right and left *sides* of the body. The left side is named dark, mysterious, sinister, and feminine; the right side is seen as light, logical, and masculine. The Buddhist version says that the two sides of the body contain different types of energy, yin (left) and yang (right).

Such mythologies have found their way into the west as well. For example, the famous Osgood Semantic Differential Test, given in the late

237

1950s to a group of college students, showed the following common associations with left and right:

The Left was characterized as bad, dark, profane, female, unclean, night, west, curved, limp, homosexual, weak, mysterious, low, ugly, black, incorrect, and death, while the Right meant just the opposite – good, light, sacred, male, clean, day, east, straight, erect, heterosexual, strong, commonplace, high, beautiful, white, correct. . . .[2]

Contemporary research suggests an association of left brain activity with verbal activity and rational, linear thinking; and right brain activity with emotions, musical ability, Gestalt (holistic) ways of thinking, as well as with certain kinds of spatial ability. It is important to stress that phrases such as 'left brain activity' do not necessarily imply exclusiveness, but may merely indicate an asymmetry in the activities of the two hemispheres that can be monitored electrically by recording brain waves, also called the electroencephalogram or EEG. Thus the left side of the brain has been identified through EEG studies as more active during speech. So scientists, like the myth-makers who came before them, have associated *sides* with *functions*, a phenomenon they refer to as lateralization.

However, linking 'feminine' and 'masculine' to these functions is a false and stereotyped addition. Often it is based on faulty methodology, sometimes on guesswork, both readily obscured by the technical language in which research findings are recorded. But unfortunately the (il)logic of patriarchy generates a dualism that equates women with the dark, mysterious, evil side of things, or else with the weaker, more emotional, less logical, and less masterful side.

SEX DIFFERENCES RESEARCH

Before beginning a detailed analysis of the research and issues surrounding differences in brain asymmetry, several important issues must be raised about all sex differences research.

1 In any research on sex differences, one must consider the possibility that potentials have been squelched in women by cultural stereotyping. Where biology is invoked to support such stereotypes, that 'biology' should be critically and politically examined, particularly its language and research methods. In this area, it seems useful for feminists to unravel old myths and cultural stereotypes that have no factual basis by using counter-examples and exposing the political and other biases of the research.

2 A more fundamental theoretical problem with sex differences research is that its basic orientation is towards *differences*. By searching these

out it magnifies them and often obscures the fact that they may be the conveniently stereotyped extremes of broadly overlapping potentialities and functions. Research on sex differences therefore has often served further to stereotype and oppress women. The unstated biases that consistently inform this research are self-fulfilling: researchers find what they expect and interpret their findings in traditional ways. Pseudo-scientific 'proof' marching under the banner of 'science' only strengthens old stereotypes.

3 One of the key ways in which this stereotyping has been perpetuated has been to confuse nature with nurture: anything that can be found to have a biological *correlate* is interpreted as innate. Patriarchal science conveniently equates biological sex differences with innateness, and innateness with genetic predetermination (or tendencies/capacities with nature/function). Where biological correlates of sex differences are found, we must ask if they are a reflection of socialization – and if they could be a useful way to *examine* socialization (and implicitly, to counteract negative socialization). For example, if women's biceps muscles are less developed than men's, to what extent is this due to intrinsic biological differences and to what extent to differences in patterns of physical exercise of girls and boys from earliest infancy? One way of raising this issue is to ask: do we *somatize* our oppression? Rather than assuming that our bodies determine our social state, we must also consider how our social state shapes facets of our physical being, making both, therefore, changeable.

BRAIN ASYMMETRY

What then should we accept as true about right and left brain differences? A specialization of functions seems to exist in each hemisphere of the brain. It follows therefore that if one side of the brain is damaged, the other side cannot always fill in or take over. A common example of this is a bloodclot in the brain, a 'stroke': if a stroke victim loses control over the movements of one side of the body, or over speech or other functions, the uninjured part of the brain does not take over immediately (although relearning is possible in varying degrees, depending on the extent and location of the damage).

Lateralization (asymmetry of brain function) is not as rigid in young children as in adults, though it appears to be fairly complete at 5 years of age – which is relatively late in the course of human brain development. Before this age, damage to either hemisphere often results in the other assuming the functions of the injured one. After 5, major damage to one hemisphere can lead to permanent loss of ability.[3]

Initial studies on hemispheric asymmetry began with the work of

Roger Sperry in the early 1960s. He and his co-workers studied surgical patients with severe epilepsy who have had their *corpora callosa* (the nerves and other tissue connecting the two halves of the brain) severed in the (successful) attempt to control seizures. As a result, these people had two separately functioning brain systems – their right hand literally did not know what the left was doing. By presenting the two sides of the brain with a variety of stimuli, Sperry was able to generalize about the types of functions that the two hemispheres perform separately. He concluded that the left brain determines logical thought, most speech, mathematical ability, and 'executive' decisions, while the right brain rules spatial ability, emotions, and intuitions. But even at this level, there was stereotyping: the left brain was called the 'major lobe' in the literature[4] – despite the fact that the two lobes are of equal size and the same functional differences were observed in both sexes. The right brain was called minor and was perceived to be a 'passive, silent passenger who leaves the driving of behaviour mainly to the left hemisphere'.[5]

Although Sperry found a clear-cut dichotomy between left and right brain functions, he and later investigators recognized that in normal, uninjured individuals the two hemispheres were interdependent and that right brain functions were no less significant or complex than those of the left brain. However the strict equation of spatial ability with right hemisphere functions and of verbal ability with the left, combined with the tenet that it is most efficient to use one side at a time, formed the basis for most subsequent theories about sex differences in asymmetry. Thus did theory become 'fact' that was subsequently used to build new theories.

Despite the demonstrated interplay between the left and right halves of the brain, verbal and spatial abilities had been so firmly identified with sides of the brain that many experimenters simply equated superior verbal ability with 'left brain dominance' and superior spatial ability with 'right brain dominance' without recording EEGs (brain waves) or performing any other physiological measurements to determine which half in fact was active during the specific tasks. Therefore, most of the major hypotheses about sex differences in hemispheric asymmetry are inferred from differences in performance on specific verbal and spatial tasks and are based on little or no direct physiological measurements. At least four highly questionable assumptions underlie later experimenters' conclusions:

1 that certain tests (ranging from college board scores to various 'spatial tasks') actually measure verbal or spatial ability;
2 that this measured verbal or spatial ability is the same as that which Sperry (and later, others) deduced from the surgically 'split-brain', epileptic individuals;

3 that all spatial tasks 'activate' the right brain and verbal tasks the left brain; and perhaps most importantly,

4 that differences in performance on tests are due to differences in intrinsic brain lateralization rather than to differences in prior training or experience, or differences in response to specific test situations.

Eleanor Maccoby and Carol Jacklin give an excellent summary of the problems with the first assumptions in their book on sex differences.[6] There are serious questions about whether the verbal and spatial tasks/tests actually measure ability, as well as problems regarding sex differences in the taking and administering of these tests. For example, a female taking a 'spatial' test from an older male researcher in a laboratory coat may well score lower than her male-aged peer for reasons other than intrinsic ability.

Assumption 2 is just that – an assumption. There is no way to be sure whether superior scores on college board vocabulary tests indicate greater left hemisphere dominance. Yet this assumption is rarely questioned in the literature.

Assumption 3 is especially tenuous when one looks at the variety of tasks that are categorized as 'spatial'. Everything from fine discrimination tests and detailed tasks to mechanical, manipulative tasks is grouped under 'spatial' and is assumed to be associated with right brain activity – an association initially never tested with EEG measurements.

The final assumption, though rarely questioned, is clearly dubious in view of sex differences in training, especially for spatial and mechanical tasks.

The literature on brain asymmetry presents a classic case of sexist language, sexist interpretation of biological findings, and an interesting reflection of male-centred valuation. *Many of the observed sex differences can be easily attributed to socialization or faulty methodology . . . and these are often the sex differences that are interpreted in the literature as 'male superiority'* (e.g. male 'superiority' on spatial tasks for which boys traditionally have been trained).

The 'Levy–Sperry Hypothesis' and the 'Buffery–Gray Hypothesis' have been the two most widely discussed and believed theories about sex differences in brain asymmetry. They are both based on alleged sex differences in spatial and verbal tasks, and represent two entirely different reasonings from the same set of 'facts': Levy and Sperry say that women are inferior on spatial tasks because of a *lesser degree of lateralization*; Buffery and Gray say that they are superior on verbal tasks because female brains are *more lateralized*!

THE LEVY–SPERRY HYPOTHESIS

Levy and Sperry begin their reasoning by noting that females perform poorly on certain tests for spatial abilities, and that left-handed men perform poorly on the same tests. Left-handers, they state, perform poorly on these tasks because of 'cross-talk' from their left hemispheres while performing the tasks: they are said to be less lateralized.[7] The authors argue that the superiority of right-handed males in such spatial tasks is due to a *greater* lateralization of the two hemispheres; Levy states that 'it might be that female brains are similar to those of left-handers in having less hemispheric specialization than male right-handers' brains.'[8] She and Sperry also draw a further analogy between females and left-handers: they state that in left-handers language is mediated by both sides of the brain (whereas in right-handers it is a left brain function) and that the language component in the right hemisphere of left-handers (which is absent in right-handers) is what interferes with 'pure' right-hemisphere performance on spatial tasks. (In fact, it is *not* true that left-handers usually have bilateral language representation.)[9] From this Levy and Sperry generalize to females who, they assume, also have bilateral representation for language, and they conclude that this is why females as a group perform more poorly on spatial tasks.

A number of researchers have already begun to accept their *hypothesis as fact*, and are using it to interpret further findings, although the problems with it are legion. Levy and Sperry do not address training and socialization as possible factors in performance of spatial tasks. They do not verify their assumption that the tests measure the degree of hemisphere specialization. And they do not address the critical fact that females consistently perform better than males on tests of *verbal* ability, a fact that would seem to contradict their assumption that females have bilateral language representation (which, by their reasoning, should make their verbal abilities *poorer*). Rather, they seem more interested in explaining male *superiority* on spatial tasks, whatever contortions of logic this might demand.

THE BUFFERY–GRAY HYPOTHESIS

Buffery and Gray examine the same test scores as Levy and Sperry, which show that males perform better at certain spatial tasks; but unlike Levy and Sperry, they also take into account female verbal superiority.

To explain how both apparent superiorities could exist, Buffery and Gray construct the following hypothesis. They postulate that in males, linguistic and visuo-spatial abilities are represented in both hemispheres, whereas in females they are separated into the left and right hemispheres respectively. (Thus for Buffery and Gray, females are *more* lateralized than males, exactly opposite to Levy and Sperry's conclusion.) Buffery and Gray then assert that bilateral representation is most efficient for visuo-spatial tasks – a direct contradiction of most theories – because they require a global, holistic perception. Hence males, with less lateralization than females, perform better on visuo-spatial tests. Then, with a confounding leap in logic, they assert that verbal tasks 'require *more* lateralization', since they are more 'specific' and 'delicate' and 'localized' than spatial tasks. Hence women, with greater lateralization than men, perform better at verbal tasks.

There are three serious problems with their hypothesis. The first is that attributing a more global or Gestalt perception to the spatial tasks that have been used in these cases requires a bit of imagination. One test used, for instance, is the rod and frame test – the ability in a dark room to adjust a movable glowing rod within a tilted frame to a vertical position. Another tests the ability to distinguish pictures of familiar objects within a camouflaging background. The ability to take a figure out of its background context is called field independence and is used as an example of 'spatial ability'.

In these sorts of test females, on average, are less able to separate a figure from its immediate context, and are therefore said to be more field-dependent than males.[10] From this it would appear that *females* are the ones who exhibit Gestalt perception (right brain), yet this is attributed to *men* in the attempt to explain their supposedly superior spatial ability.

But a more blatant contradiction emerges from the Buffery–Gray theorizing. They casually mention that

> male superiority on visual tasks only appears when manipulation of spatial relationships is involved. On tasks which depend for their execution principally on the discrimination and/or comparison of fine visual detail, the direction of the sex differences is reversed. Thus women are better than men on . . . a *number* of other tests of visual matching and visual search. . . . (emphasis mine)[11]

Thus, the *only* tasks that show men more able are tests of manipulation of the environment or of some part of it. The equation of this with spatial ability, not to mention its high valuing, reflects the respect accorded the skill of manipulation in this society.

Buffery and Gray end the above quote with: 'Thus women are better than men on . . . a number of other tests of visual matching and visual search *which are predictive of good performance on clerical tasks*'! (emphasis mine).[12]

Finally, Buffery and Gray, like Levy and Sperry, never verify the brain activity they associate with particular tasks. They *postulate* that men are less lateralized than women; they *postulate* that verbal skills require greater lateralization, and visuo-spatial skills less lateralization. But they never measure with brain wave recordings (EEGs) or other tests the actual brain activity of males or females during the performance of any of these tasks.

EEG STUDIES ON SEX DIFFERENCES IN BRAIN ASYMMETRY

In recent experiments Davidson and Schwartz have recorded the EEGs of men and women performing different tasks.[13] They find that right-handed females show greater brain asymmetry than males on self-generated tasks and can also control the *amount* of asymmetry more precisely. For example, when women are asked to perform a 'right brain' task, such as whistling, they use more of their right brains and less of their left brains then do men. This is also true for left brain tasks. When asked (after prior training) to produce more or less asymmetry in either direction, females are much better at both tasks.

Another task was to produce an internal state of high emotion or a non-emotional state at different times. This was done by either reliving a situation of intense anger, or by thinking of some nondescript topic. During the emotional tasks, females showed more right-hemisphere activity than males; during the non-emotional tasks, they showed *less*. *Males showed no shift in asymmetry between the two emotional conditions*. So, females showed greater shifts in asymmetry between emotional tasks and non-emotional tasks than did males in this study.

The third task involved biofeedback training to enable people to control the amount of hemispheric asymmetry they were producing and to produce asymmetry at will. Females were better at producing greater asymmetry, even to the degree of using *only* one side of their brains. There were no sex differences when people were asked to use both sides of the brain simultaneously.

Davidson *et al.* generate the following sets of hypotheses on the basis of their work:

1 They characterize the 'male' way of *feeling* as much more analytical, more 'left brain', while females may typically process emotions in a more global and Gestalt-like manner. In other words, during these experiments males were unable to produce a right brain emotional state without left brain interference.

2 When asked to think about something without emotion, males were less able to do so than females. This provides an interesting twist to the traditional stereotype that women's 'emotional' way of thinking clouds their rationality.

3 Females have better control over the direction of their EEG asymmetry than do males – i.e. they can utilize *either* hemisphere more precisely depending on appropriateness.

Another piece of information directly relates to the nature/nurture question and brain asymmetry, although at this time its significance is not clear. In a study in which the brains of 100 newborn infants were measured at autopsy, Witelson and Pallie reported that female infants have a significantly larger left temporal planum – the portion of the left brain that is primarily responsible for speech – than do male infants, in proportion to their total brain size.[14]

INTERPRETATIONS FROM A FEMINIST PERSPECTIVE

What seems most clear from the studies I have examined is that the imputation of male superiority on 'visual-spatial' tasks, used as the basis for most of the theorizing about brain asymmetry, is a shaky and artifact-laden generalization. Most of the test results can probably be attributed to training or socialization, and do not necessarily reflect inborn differences in brain functioning. Furthermore, even if men's superiority were a proven fact, which it is not, the significance of the 'visuo-spatial tasks' is questionable. What these researchers seem to be saying is that on tests of 'spatial skill' men are better at manipulating the environment, except when 'focused, delicate' spatial skills are required. Manipulation of the environment is not necessarily a desirable skill, nor is the ability to take things out of context (field independence).

For feminists, our central concern must be to eliminate patriarchal mechanisms that have blocked the expression *and validation* of language and spatial/environmental skills in women, and to encourage the development of those skills in the holistic manner of which we seem to be capable. There is no more poignant expression of the way in which women's capabilities have been distorted by socialization than the above quote about clerical abilities from Buffery and Gray. Similarly, the numerous adages about women's 'excessive talkativeness' attest to the way in which our verbal abilities are often devalued.

New research paradigms are emerging in the areas of brain research and in other types of work in psychophysiology. Some questions that feminist researchers need to ask are:

- What, if anything, do different ways of processing thought tell us about our potential and our socialization?
- How can we use our ability to feel deeply and think clearly in an integrated way?
- What kinds of spatial abilities do we want to develop and validate for ourselves? How can we strengthen the value of non-manipulative environmental skills?
- How can we enhance the optimal use of *all* our mental potentialities and skills?

One thing that emerges from the data is that men seem to have difficulty in employing their right cerebral hemispheres in a focused way or for the execution of any but manipulative spatial tasks. Yet researchers have interpreted the test results to mean that men are superior in 'spatial ability'.

We are dealing with two contradictory stereotypes: men are linked with the right brain because of their supposed superior spatial abilities, women with the left brain because of superior verbal scores. Yet men are also stereotyped as 'more analytic' (or 'logical') which is said to be a left brain skill. Complex and circuitous arguments are required to come up with 'superior spatial ability' while leaving the myth of men's razor-sharp intellect intact.

Hemispheric asymmetry research at present is only a small part of the brain research that is being done on sex differences. But it is an extremely important part – both in itself and as an example of what can happen when psychological research is poorly designed and/or over-interpreted.

There is a strong relationship between attempts to dichotomize right brain/left brain ways of perceiving, thinking, feeling, and being in relation to the environment, and the dualistic social system summarized by the term patriarchy. In spite of the complex and often contradictory nature of the literature on left and right brain functioning, men's dominance in the social and economic spheres has been linked simplistically to their capacities for linear (left brain) thinking.

This point of view is unfortunately adopted by some feminists in their condemnations of male dominance. For example, in her article in *Amazon Quarterly*, Gina writes:

So dualism resides in the very brain. The ways of perceiving that came to be grouped in the left hemisphere are the tools men used to take control of the planet. Linear thinking, focused narrowly enough to squeeze out human or emotional considerations, enabled men to kill . . . with free consciences. Propositional thinking enables men to ignore the principles of morality inherent in all the earth's systems, and to set up instead their own version of right and wrong which they could believe as long as its logic was internally consistent. . . . All ways of perceiving that threatened the logical ways with other realities were grouped together on the other (right) side of the brain and labelled 'bad'. The separation of 'good' and 'bad' qualities into left and right sides of the brain, and the universally constant valuation of qualities, can be seen in every patriarchal culture through its attitudes towards left and right-handedness. . . .[15]

Thus Gina, in turn, introduces a dualism that *rejects* as male our ability to use the tools of intellectual reasoning and logic. This, too, is dangerous for it perpetuates stereotypic masculine/feminine dualities in an even subtler way by attributing them to the same person. Women's left brains are not precarious, 'male' places to be visited but not dwelt in. The dangers of greatest concern to women are that:

1 researchers (men or women who unquestioningly accept their androcentric education) characterize women's and men's abilities on the basis of wrong research results and unfounded interpretations;
2 these interpretations are already often uncritically accepted as true, and thus form the grid through which we then formulate further experiments and interpret their results;
3 interpretations favourable to women are not drawn out of the data;
4 some feminists are reacting to the popularizations of 'left brain'/'right brain' thinking by misguidedly urging women to 'reclaim our right brains', which shortchanges what women can do.

What is required is not the patching together of 'left brain' with 'right brain' qualities to form a pseudo-whole. Rather, the precise use of *all* our skills is what we should consider ideal.

NOTES

I would like to thank Artemis March and Richard Davidson for their help and advice.

The writing of this paper was partially supported by a Public Health Service training grant from the Human Development and Aging Program, University of California, San Francisco, No. AG00022–10 5TO1

1 Note here that it is 'feminine' and 'masculine' – not female and male. This subtlety allows for a woman to be called masculine (or a male, feminine) if she exhibits behaviour *a priori* classified as masculine. This reification eventually leads to the nonsensical concept of androgyny – two socially-created halves joined to make a 'natural' whole.
2 W. Domhoff, 'But why did they sit on the king's right in the first place?', *The Nature of Human Consciousness*, ed. R. Ornstein (San Francisco: W.H. Freeman, 1973).
3 One of the many unknowns in the field is why the capacity to utilize either hemisphere for specific functions is lost after this age. In the research in this area, two intriguing findings are: a) the critical age for lateralization is later with lower socio-economic status, and b) females throughout life appear to retain more capacity for an undamaged right hemisphere to take over speech in the case of damage to the left hemisphere. For information on lateralization and socio-economic status, see E.E. Maccoby and C. Jacklin, (eds), *The Psychology of Sex Differences* (Stanford: Stanford University Press, 1974), p. 126. Information on females and lateralization was originally taken from an article, gina, 'Rosy Rightbrain's exorcism/invocation', *Amazon Quarterly*, 2, 4 (1974). Richard Davidson, a researcher in the area, agreed in conversation that it was correct. See also, H. Lansdell, *American Psychologist*, 16, 448 (1961); and *Journal of Abnormal Psychology*, 81, 255 (1973). A thorough recent review of sex differences in brain asymmetry can be found in H. Fairweather, 'Sex differences in cognition', *Cognition*, 4 (1976), pp. 231–80.

4 R.W. Sperry, 'The great cerebral commissure', *Scientific American* (January 1964), pp. 42–52; R.W. Sperry, 'Split brain approach to learning problems', *The Neurosciences: A Study Program*, G.C. Quarton *et al.* (eds) (New York: Rockefeller, 1967); J. Levy-Agresti and R.W. Sperry, 'Differential perceptual capacities in major and minor hemispheres', *Proc. Nat. Acad. Sci.*, U.S., 61, p. 1151 (1968).

5 R.W. Sperry, 'Lateral specialization in the surgically separated hemispheres', *The Neurosciences: Third Study Program*, F.O. Schmitt and R.T. Wardon (eds) (Cambridge, Mass.: MIT Press, 1974).

6 Maccoby and Jacklin, *The Psychology of Sex Differences*, pp. 125–7.

7 I have not yet found out whether EEG studies have been done on left-handers to determine if they *are* less lateralized during these tests or if this is another example of reasoning back from performance. It occurred to me while writing this that there could be a significant training factor involved with the performance of spatial tasks for left-handers, since many tools, games, and everyday spatial tasks are designed for right-handers. For example, my sister, who is left-handed, was poorer at performing the spatial task of cutting things out of paper with scissors – until she was given a special pair of left-hander's scissors, and my left-handed grandmother taught her to use them, after which she could perform the task with ease.

8 J. Levy, 'Lateral specialization of the human brain: behavioural manifestations and possible evolutionary basis', *The Biology of Behavior*, J.A. Kiger, Jr (ed.) (Corvallis: Oregon State University Press, 1972), p. 174.

9 J. Marshall, 'Some problems and paradoxes associated with recent accounts of hemispheric specialization', *Neuropsychologia*, 11 (1973), pp. 463–70.

10 Lauren Gibbs, 'Sex differences in the brain: questions of scientific research', mimeographed (Cambridge, Mass.: Harvard University Department of Psychology and Social Relations, 1976):

> "Dependence-independence" are highly charged words in our society with strong value and sex referents. Independence is a prized character trait and associated with "masculinity", while dependence, a "feminine" trait, is despised. The unqualified use of these terms encourages continued acceptance of destructive male–female stereotypes and goals (less rigid reliance on the isolated self and less blocking out of context might be useful to our society) . . .

11 W. Buffery and J. Gray, 'Sex differences in the development of spatial and linguistic skills', in *Gender Differences: Their Ontogeny and Significance*, C. Ounsted and D.C. Taylor (eds) (Edinburgh: Churchill Livingstone, 1972), p. 127.

12 The use of the word 'predictive' here is interesting – it is an adjective with a deleted agent. This means that unmasked questions are implicit in the word, such as *who* predicts, for *whom*, and *why*? For a linguistic analysis of 'scientific' terminology like this, which deletes agent, subject, and motivation, see Julia Stanley, 'Passive motivation', *Foundations of Language*, 13 (1975), pp. 25–39.

13 R.J. Davidson and G.E. Schwartz, 'Patterns of cerebral lateralization during cardiac biofeedback versus the self-regulation of emotion: sex differences', *Psychophysiology*, 13 (1976), pp. 62–8.

14 Witelson and Pallie, 'Left hemisphere specialization for language in the newborn', *Brain*, 96 (1973), pp. 641–6.

15 Gina, 'Rosy Rightbrain'. See also Dorothy Lee, 'Codifications of reality: lineal and nonlineal', in Ornstein (ed.), *The Nature of Human Consciousness* for a description of a somewhat alternative culture.

248

SCIENCE AND GENDER

Ruth Bleier

GLOBAL POLITICS AND BIOLOGICAL DETERMINISM

The underlying scientific issue in evaluating any theory of biological determinism is the feasibility of isolating biological from learned influences in the determination of physical characteristics, behaviours, social relationships, and social organization. The effort to separate genetic and environmental influences continues to plague thinking in many fields. Yet it represents a false dichotomy that does not reflect biological processes, but like other dualisms I shall discuss later, may serve reactionary social and political purposes in certain social-scientific contexts, like the sociobiological discourse on human nature and female and male natures.

The evident lack of scientific usefulness of the gene–culture dichotomy is belied by the penetration of these ideas into all of the social sciences and by the massive media exposure that sociobiology has received as a scientific 'breakthrough' in major newspapers, television, radio, and popular weekly and monthly magazines. A front-page article in the *New York Times* announced the 'revolutionary' implications of Wilson's first book before it appeared (Alper, Beckwith, and Miller 1978). Socio-biologists Irven DeVore and Robert Trivers have made a film (*Sociobiology: Doing What Comes Naturally*) and a science curriculum (*Exploring Human Nature*), which have been incorporated into high school science courses throughout the country. Articles have appeared in *Home and Garden, People, Time, Psychology Today*, the *New York Times Sunday Magazine*, the *Boston Globe*, and the *National Observer* (Lowe, 1978, p. 124). *Newsweek* (18 May 1981) carried profiles of a woman and a man on its cover and the bold-face caption, 'The sexes; how they differ and why'. Its message about biologically determined sex differences in ability and achievement reached a quarter of a million *Newsweek* subscribers. Through its reproduction in the *Reader's Digest* (September 1981), 31 million more readers in sixteen languages were reached.

If this amount of attention, which also includes the continuing production by sociobiologists of new books that say nothing new and are aimed

249

at the lay public, is being paid to a question with neither intrinsic scientific or intellectual merit nor hope of definitive proof, we can suspect that it is a question of great political, social, or economic merit and most likely all three. It seems, then, important to explore the circumstances that can help to explain why a significant part of the biological and social scientific enterprise is devoted to the teasing out and measurement of gender or sex differences, in efforts to find genetic, hormonal, or other biological bases of behaviours and characteristics that are claimed to be differentiated by sex. Who cares and why? How do reputable scientists come to advance or support theories of human behaviours and social organization on the basis of scientific assumptions and methods so flimsy that they would be unacceptable to themselves and to the scientific community if the studies were in their own fields of expertise, such as entomology (Wilson's field)? The answers are many and complex and require analysis at levels from the most personal to the more universal. As I have already suggested, we need to look to a patriarchal social, political, and economic system that gains much in power, privileges, and profits for itself and for individual men from the subordinate position of women and now finds itself faced with the first serious historic threat to its dominance. The women's movement and feminist scholarship can create revolutionary changes in our political/social/economic system and in the entire body of human knowledge and epistemology – and there is no end in sight. Even for those participating, the potential is awesome; to those on the outside who see or believe themselves to be, sooner or later, the losers, that potential, as well as today's realities, may be intolerable to contemplate.

Wilson and other sociobiologists deny that sociobiological theories have 'a reactionary political message' or can be 'construed as a support of the status quo' (Wilson, 1978, pp. 292–3) or that they can be held responsible for the abuse and misinterpretation of their conclusions. There are, however, innumerable examples of the explicitly sociological and political content of sociobiologists' writings as it is incorporated in their underlying assumptions, their perceptions and descriptions of human behaviours and social relationships, and the conclusions they draw within their logical system. It is, after all, making a particular political analysis to say that male aggressivity and dominance over women, territoriality and xenophobia (that is, national chauvinism and racism), conformity and indoctrinability, are innate human traits, specifically because such assertions withdraw these issues from the political arena. The claim makes these issues biological rather than sociological, even though claims for the innateness of these and other human characteristics are not supported by evidence, but are inferences drawn from fallacious analogies, speculations, subjective belief, and illogical thought processes. Thus, they are not scientific assertions. Such explanations are very soothing to some liberal humanists, which many scientists and academicians believe themselves to be, who decry injustice and inequalities but are relieved of the necessity of action, since wars, oppression, and discrimination are natural and inevitable. Biological determinist theories are, in addition, uncritically embraced as self-confirming by all who prefer and defend the status quo and welcome its legitimization by science.

Biological determinists may appear to be apolitical because they carefully avoid discussion or recognition of any political, cultural, or social factors that could account for the presumably innate characteristics that interest them, just as they avoid acknowledgement of the existence of any class or group that oppresses others or controls and manipulates the media (which account for a major share of the 'trait' for *indoctrinability*), or benefits from oppressing, exploiting, or controlling. Ignoring political and social factors in analysing the origins of political and social relationships is, in fact, taking a very specific political position under the guise of science: it is not only useless but biologically hazardous to do social 'tampering' and to have political programmes that fly in the face of our genetically programmed natures. And indeed, sociobiologists are sometimes explicit in that conclusion:

It's time we started viewing ourselves as having biological, genetic and natural components to our behavior, and that we start setting up a physical and social world to match those tendencies. (Trivers, from film, *Sociobiology: Doing What Comes Naturally*)

When 'those tendencies' are defined to be male aggressivity, female passivity, dominance hierarchies, sex roles, territoriality, racism, xenophobia, competitiveness, and conformity and are the descriptive litany of behaviours and relationships that exist in the particular social orders of which we are a part, it takes no imagination to see how sociobiological views can form, unchanged, the ideological base for any conservative or reactionary political programmes.

And indeed they do. The extreme right in France and the openly fascist National Front in Britain have embraced Wilson's sociobiological views as the scientific basis for their racist, sexist, and antisemitic programmes.

Against this destructive theory [Marxism], we racialists declare that man and society are the creation of his biological nature. We insist not only that genetic inheritance determines inequality – not social environment – but that social organisation and behaviour themselves are essentially the product of our biological evolution. . . . The theory that behaviour and social organisation are determined to a crucial extent by genetic inheritance is now central to that most progressive branch of the biological sciences call 'sociobiology'. (Verrall, 1979, p. 10)

251

While sociobiologists themselves acknowledge the racist and chauvinist implications that could be drawn from their interrelated theories of altruism, kin selection, and inclusive fitness,[1] the spokesmen for the National Front translate these theories explicitly into their outspokenly racial programme:

Of a far greater significance is the basic instinct common to all species to identify only with one's like group; to in-breed and to shun out-breeding. In human society this instinct is *racial* and it – above all else – operates to ensure genetic survival. (Verrall, 1979, p. 11)

This statement did not require any tortured extrapolation from the claim of the sociobiologist, W.D. Hamilton: 'I hope to produce evidence that some things which are often treated as purely cultural in man – say racial discrimination – have deep roots in our animal past and thus are quite likely to rest on direct genetic foundations' (1975, p. 134). National Front theorists have revived nineteenth-century brain science in support of racism: 'We all know that differences between races in the capacity for rational thought are explained by inherited differences in the physical structure of the brain' (Verrall, 1979, p. 10). They also spell out the implications of sociobiological research on sex differences, stating that the obvious existence of male dominance and aggression and of female passivity and domesticity in the animal world

quickly demonstrate that 'feminist' talk of sexual roles being condi-tioned by society itself is the most puerile Marxist rubbish. Sexual and other behaviour differs between man and woman simply because of differences in male and female hormone secretions. . . . This is why men and women think and behave differently. (ibid., p. 10)

While scientists, in this case, are one step removed from the reac-tionary political applications of their biological determinist theories, supplying only the ideological underpinnings, this was not always the case. As early as 1895 German scientists and physicians were formulating theories of 'racial hygiene' (also known as *eugenics*) and suggesting medical practices that could weed out the poor, feeble-minded, criminal, and other biological 'misfits' who threatened Nordic superiority (Proctor, 1982). Their Society for Racial Hygiene became one of the more impor-tant biomedical societies in Germany. Along with racist social anthropo-logists, it welcomed the rise of Hitler, who could implement its policies wholesale. By 1938, the medical wing of the Nazi party, the National Socialist Doctors' Association, had a membership of over 30,000 doctors, about 60 per cent of all practising physicians. Laws for the sterilization or 'mercy killings' of institutionalized 'misfits' were passed and carried out, claiming hundreds of thousands of victims. The Nuremberg and Buchenwald trials finally revealed the role of physicians and scientists in the experimentations, carried out in Nazi concentration camps to the endpoint of death, on Jews, women, homosexuals, Poles, and others considered to be biological inferiors.

Biological determinist thinking is also an important part of the philosophy underlying the political programme of the New Right in the United States today, expressed in its efforts to reinforce the patriarchal family and reinstate it as women's exclusive sphere by withdrawing programmes for social welfare, removing women from the labour force, and bringing their sexuality and reproductivity more fully under state and male control (Eisenstein, 1982). Woman is to be legally defined and socially confined as mother, reproducer, and nurturer; dependent and subordinate.

While it may be argued that scientists cannot be held responsible for all of the uses to which their published scientific work is put or for distortions it may suffer, they *are* responsible for the quality of the work they publish, for the honesty and validity of the questions they ask, the reliability of the data and the assumptions they use, the methodology and logic by which they pass from premises to conclusions, and the breadth or open-mindedness of their interpretations and conclusions. Thus, by choosing public and political arenas to aggressively propagate their ideas and by violating basic tenets of scientific methodology and integrity, sociobiologists have made unfounded theories accessible for use and abuse by reactionary political ideologists. The European and American political Right has not had to distort either the words or the implications of sociobiological writings in order to make them relevant as scientific justification for New Right political ideology.

BIOLOGICAL DETERMINISM IN FEMINIST THOUGHT

Finally, it must also be acknowledged that biological determinists or sociobiological assumptions either implicitly or explicitly underlie, in varying degrees, a broad spectrum of feminist thoughts and writings that includes both lesbian separatists and liberal reformers in the United States, psychoanalytic and Marxist essentialists in France, and some American academicians who are engaged in the critical reinterpretation of traditional scholarship in their fields of sociology, biology, and psychology. Their writings represent a range of views. These include the position that gender differences are deep and irreconcilable, and that women's characteristics and temperaments are superior and should be celebrated. Another, probably more pervasive and heterogeneous position holds that though there are biologically based gender differences, they do not imply superiority or inferiority nor do they justify inequities in social, economic, and political policy and practice. Rather they call for public education and reform of sexist policies, laws, and practices.

My argument is not against having a range of programmes and

253

approaches generated by a variety of viewpoints; the effectiveness of any movement for social and political change can only be enhanced by its capacity to encompass such a range (i.e. by its capacity to include people holding a variety of ideas and preferences for political and social styles, tactics, and strategies). However, the ultimate effectiveness of movements and programmes can only be weakened if they rely upon theories of biological determinism. This is both because such theories are seriously flawed and basically scientifically meaningless and because essentialist thinking (i.e. belief in the existence of an ultimate essence within each of us that does not change) has always functioned as a central feature of ideologies of oppression. The 'voice of the natural', to use Barthes' phrase, has always been a voice for the status quo (Sturrock, 1979, p. 60). That is, essentialism is flawed because it presents a limited and limiting perspective on nature and human potentialities and because it is a poor strategy, a view expressed as well by the Combahee River Collective. 'As Black women we find any type of biological determinism a particularly dangerous and reactionary basis upon which to build a politic' (Hull et al., 1982, p. 17). It is always used by ruling orders as a justification for their seizure or possession of power and control. Questions of biological difference are raised for political reasons and frequently are given legitimacy by being posed as scientific issues. We may indeed value the characteristics that in our western societies are associated with femaleness – and, indeed, *need* to celebrate them, since they seem to be the only force standing in the way of our society's plunge into self-destruction – but we need not justify them as natural, biological, or innate. That we start learning our characteristics and temperaments from the time of birth already burdens them with the possibility of more permanence than is good for our biological potentialities for development, growth, and change. The chance of liberating ideas lies not with trying to turn traditional or misogynist or racist ideologies 180 degrees around and in our favour, but in turning them under completely, destroying their roots. We cannot replace one false illusion with another when our central task is demystification and when our power to transform lies in clear-eyed knowledge and an appreciation of complexity, integration, and change.

Since in this paper I go beyond a critique of biological determinist theories to offer alternative interpretations and contradictory evidence, I actually engage in the very activity I warn readers to question, if not distrust. Put differently, I present 'facts' to refute 'facts', which I claim have been made (up) in the interests of the dominant group – white men. I offer feminist interpretations to replace patriarchal interpretations, which I say reflect the ideology, desires, and necessities of a particular interest group. I am indeed caught in my own trap!

But perhaps I am not. As I shall try to maintain throughout my work,

I see any theory – feminist or patriarchal – as flexible and open to change. In fact, as a scientist and a political being, my 'mind lingers with pleasure' when I encounter theories that allow for constant change, interaction, contradiction, ambivalence. They have always appealed to me enormously. I have interpreted my own experimental research results accordingly and have been much more interested in the work of those scientists whose work is motivated by a desire to demonstrate the flexibility rather than the biological limits and rigidity of the brain and its resulting behavioural possibilities.

Holding a view or a philosophy of flux in science is in harmony with a philosophical position that endorses political movements and attitudes that aim at social change by means of opposition to prevailing opinion and the status quo. But I maintain that the revolutionary force and the open spirit of enquiry that underlies any striving for change is no more 'partisan' or 'biased' than so-called objective philosophical and intellectual positions. But as it actively aims for change, it opposes the Powers That Be. Feminism is a prime example: it posits that women are oppressed and it openly works for social change. It is developing a profound philosophical world view that will point to change in all systems based upon racial, class, and sexual oppression.

I would argue that the nature of my world view, as it influences my approach in this book, is its own justification. That is, while biological determinists – in the face of overwhelming contradictions – assert the genetic, hormonal, and evolutionary determinism of human nature and our behaviours, it is my aim to describe all those myriad contradictions that make such theories totally inadequate as explanations of behaviours and forms of social relationships. Even if some of the 'facts' I cite in support of my arguments are disputable, I shall have made the case – and I hope convincingly so – that there is no simple 'truth' as sociobiologists and other supporters of the status quo would have us believe. In the absence of clear paths to truth and social justice, the one hope for bringing about change for the better lies in the capacities of the human brain to make it possible to break out of the cultural constraints that some human beings have constructed to the detriment of others.

NOTES

1 The presumably genetically based tendency to help relatives who carry some of your own genes, since that enhances your own reproductive fitness; that is, it enhances the survival in others of genes identical to some of your own.

REFERENCES

Alper, J., Beckwith, J., and Miller, L., 'Sociobiology as a political issue', in A. Caplan (ed.), The Sociobiology Debate (New York: Harper & Row, 1978).

Barash, D., *Sociobiology and Behavior* (New York: Elsevier, 1977).

Barash, D., *The Whisperings Within* (New York: Harper & Row, 1979).

Chamberlin, T., 'The method of multiple working hypotheses', *Science* (1965), 148, pp. 754–9 (old series, 1890, 15, 92).

Combahee River Collective, 'A black feminist statement', in G.T. Hull, P.B. Scott, and B. Smith (eds), *But Some of Us are Brave* (Old Westbury: The Feminist Press, 1977).

Cravens, H., *The Triumph of Evolution* (Philadelphia, Pa: University of Pennsylvania Press, 1978).

Eisenstein, Z., 'The sexual politics of the new right: Understanding the crisis of liberalism for the 1980s', *Signs* (1982), 7, pp. 567–88.

Fee, E., 'Nineteenth-century craniology: the study of the female skull', *Bulletin of the History of Medicine* (1979), 53, pp. 415–33.

Hamilton, W., 'Innate social aptitudes of man: an approach from evolutionary genetics', in R. Fox (ed.), *Biosocial Anthropology* (New York: Wiley, 1975).

Haraway, D., 'The biological enterprise: sex, mind, and profit from human engineering to sociobiology', *Radical History Review* (1979), 20, pp. 206–37.

Hillman, J., *The Myth of Analysis* (Evanston: Northwestern University Press, 1972).

Kuhn, T., *The Structure of Scientific Revolutions*, 2nd edition (Chicago: University of Chicago Press, 1970).

Lowe, M., 'Sociobiology and sex differences', *Signs* (1978), 4, pp. 118–25.

Merchant, C., *The Death of Nature, Women, Ecology, and the Scientific Revolution* (New York: Harper & Row, 1980).

Osler, M., 'Apocryphal knowledge: the misuse of science', in M. Hanen, M. Osler, and R. Weyant (eds), *Science, Pseudoscience and Society* (Waterloo: Wilfrid Laurier University Press, 1980a).

Osler, M., 'Sex, science, and values: a critique of sociobiological accounts of sex differences', *Proceedings third annual meeting Canadian Research Institute for the Advancement of Women* (1980b), pp. 119–24.

Proctor, R., 'Nazi science and medicine', *Science for the People* (1982), 14, pp. 15–20.

Shields, S., 'Functionalism, Darwinism, and the psychology of women. A study in social myth', *American Psychologist* (1975), 30, pp. 739–54.

Sturrock, J., 'Roland Barthes', in J. Sturrock (ed.), *Structuralism and Since* (Oxford: Oxford University Press, 1979).

Verrall, R., 'Sociobiology: the instincts in our genes', *Spearhead* (1979), 127, pp. 10–11.

Wilson, E.O., *Sociobiology: the new synthesis* (Cambridge, Mass.: Harvard University Press, 1975).

Wilson, E.O., *On Human Nature* (Cambridge, Mass.: Harvard University Press, 1978).

Part VIII

RELIGION

INTRODUCTION

Marie Tulip

Feminists have had a complex and changing relation to patriarchal religion over the past twenty years: some have seen the church as irredeemably sexist and have moved outside it, either to reject religion altogether or, like Mary Daly, to discover in 'the becoming of women' a spiritual Otherworld of spinning and sparking. Others, like Rosemary Radford Ruether and Elisabeth Schüssler Fiorenza, have stayed inside the Christian tradition, working to transform the patriarchal church from within. And others, through experience of their own which they identify as religious, or through appropriating the ancient traditions of Goddess religion or witchcraft, have begun to create new ways for women to find their religious power, autonomy, and identity.

Two of the most significant feminist theologians of the 1970s were Mary Daly and Rosemary Ruether, both from a Catholic tradition, both American, and both writing at the creative edge of feminist thought. Daly's *Beyond God the Father* (Boston: Beacon Press, 1973) still stands as a comprehensive and radical critique of patriarchal religion and all its secular derivatives. Rejecting the Father God and the oppressive authoritarianism of human fathers, Daly sees the huge energy which is released in women bonding together for sisterhood as an ontological spiritual revolution that will transform human consciousness. To what she sees as the 'passive' ethic of obedience in Christianity, she opposes a new ethics of existential courage, a reclaiming of the right to name the self, the world, and 'ultimate meaning and reality, which some would call God'. Although, with existential hope, Daly sees the Second Coming as female, in *Gyn/Ecology* (Boston: Beacon Press, 1978), she deepens her critique of patriarchy to an horrific account of the destruction of women, and moves out beyond 'the boundary' to an abstract Otherworld from which to explore female possibility.

Rosemary Ruether, in contrast, stays firmly within the Judaeo-Christian tradition and works to transform the sexist structures of this world. She is not concerned so much with ontology and questions of being and nothingness, like Daly, as with liberation theology and trans-forming oppressor/oppressed relationships to create a new community of

259

justice and peace. In the 1970s, Ruether wrote several books on dualism, particularly sexual dualism, which she sees as the basis for the oppression of women and all other forms of domination. She locates the origin of dualism in prehistoric times, in the fear of sexuality leading to alienation from the body, and the consequent flight of the male from body, sex, the earth to mind, spirit, sky, from chaos and contingency to order and control, from a cyclical organic religious world to a historical dualistic world of hierarchical oppression by race, class, sex, militarism, and the domination of nature.

Ruether's lecture, 'Renewal or new creation? Feminist spirituality and historical religion' (included here), while it comes from a later phase of her work, in the mid-1980s, gives an indication of the wide historical and cultural sweep of her style, and her continuing emphasis on the prophetic-liberating principle as crucial to the Judaeo-Christian tradition, particularly as she extends it to the liberation of women and of our whole culture from patriarchal oppression. She sees that all the religions are androcentric (Christianity, Judaism, Islam, Buddhism, and Hinduism) and says feminists must begin analysing whether and how women can appropriate the androcentric stories and traditions of the patriarchal religions in such a way as to empower and affirm women as subjects of their own histories. And as well as seeking to transform the Judaeo-Christian tradition, this lecture shows how Ruether is now moving into a new interest in contemporary story as a revelatory form through which primary religious vision finds expression today. This leads her to a sort of feminist religious solidarity with women from quite different feminist religious traditions who are telling new stories, such as Starhawk from the tradition of Wicca.

It must be said that Ruether's suspicion of ancient Goddess religion as basically androcentric is not shared by other feminists like Carol Christ who claim this tradition as enriching for women today. Ruether speaks mainly of a later patriarchalized version of it, within history, but her scepticism carries over into prehistoric times despite the work of respected anthropologists like Marija Gimbutas whose research gives clear evidence of the religious and social power of women in Goddess-worshipping societies.

Where Daly and Ruether situated themselves as critical presences outside the patriarchal centres of scholarship, Elisabeth Schüssler Fiorenza puts women at the centre of her analysis. Rather than a tradition of patriarchal dominance with women silenced or at the margins, she sees the history of women in patriarchal society and church as a long history of struggle. Her major work, *In Memory of Her: A Feminist Theological Reconstruction of Christian Origins* (New York: Crossroad, 1983), is both a closely reasoned work of innovative feminist methodology and a meticulous reconstruction of early Christian history.

Fiorenza shows early Christianity as a 'discipleship of equals' in which women played a central role. Through historical research and also by reading the silences in androcentric texts, Fiorenza reconstructs the communities as they must have been before they were recorded by male writers, from an androcentric perspective, and before the process had begun of their compromising accommodation to the patriarchal codes of the first century.

Feminist biblical scholars now agree that it is not just the interpretation of the Bible that has a male bias, but the Bible itself is a male book – written by men, from an androcentric perspective, in a patriarchal culture. Fiorenza's response is a new feminist hermeneutics that starts with a hermeneutics of suspicion, and goes on to develop a hermeneutics of remembrance, of proclamation, and of creative actualization. Fiorenza situates herself and her work very strongly and clearly in the community of women and it is to women that she sees herself as accountable, not to the academy. To her, the place of revelation and grace, and the basis for a feminist hermeneutics, is not the Bible or the tradition of the patriarchal church or in any particular principle but in the community of women and the lives of women who live the 'option for our women selves' (Fiorenza, 1985, p. 128).[1] Fiorenza shows that the Bible and the biblical tradition have always had both a liberating and an oppressive power, and it is communities of women that have the authority to interpret it through a process of critical evaluation.

Ruether and Fiorenza and the early Daly all at times argue that it is important for feminists to transform patriarchal religious language, symbols, and structures because otherwise their destructive power will continue to silence and oppress all women. Other feminists reject the traditional religions and are exploring new ways of expressing the religious dimension of their lives through analysing aspects of their own experience and the religious experience of other women, past and present.

Women's spirituality, including Goddess religion and the Old Religion or Wicca, casts a very wide net and links up with other disciplines such as healing, depth psychology, poetry, and art. There is a huge outpouring of writing and action exploring women's new spiritual relation to ourselves and the universe outside the patriarchy, going back into ancient history and archaeology, and rediscovering and recreating women's whole constantly interrupted heritage. When women identify with old traditions such as Goddess religion or witchcraft it is not with the aim of going back nostalgically to a bygone matriarchal fantasy world or an ancient authority pattern, but to find a symbol system that can be used to displace the deep-rooted and pervasive male symbols in ourselves and our culture and give women access to their own power and identity.

In discussing how the Goddess symbol functions to empower women today, Carol Christ, in her essay reprinted here, focuses on four areas which, in the many various approaches, are among the most important in any feminist religious understanding of the world: the legitimacy of female power as a beneficent and independent power; affirmation of the female body and the life cycle expressed in it, its connections with nature, and acceptance of ageing and death as well as life; the positive valuation of female initiative and will; and the celebration of women's bonds to each other, as mothers and daughters, co-workers, sisters, friends, and lovers, together with women's culture and heritage. In the four areas, Christ says the 'mood' created by the symbol of the Goddess is one of positive joyful celebration and affirmation of female freedom and independence.

Women do not yet have an adequate language for our new experience of ourselves and the world. But as we struggle to transform the languages of patriarchal religions such as Christianity and Judaism, or to appropriate old religions like Goddess religion and Witchcraft, or to find new ways of resolving this dialectic relation between language and our experience as women, there is emerging a detailed reflection on women's culture and experience in conversation and stories and theological writing from which knowledge of our religious selves is being glimpsed and shared.

NOTE

1 E.S. Fiorenza, 'The will to choose or to reject: continuing our critical work', in L.H. Russell (ed.), *Feminist Interpretation of the Bible*, Oxford and New York: Blackwell, 1985.

BREAD NOT STONE

The challenge of feminist biblical interpretation

Elisabeth Schüssler Fiorenza

Who of you if their children ask for bread would give them a stone?
(Matthew 7:9)

. . . It is like leaven which a woman took and hid in three measures
of meal till it was all leavened. (Luke 13:21)

Bakerwoman God
Strong, brown Bakerwoman God . . .
Bread well kneaded
by some divine and knotty
pair of knuckles,
by your warm earth hands . . .[1]

In an essay entitled 'Notes toward finding the right question', the Jewish
writer Cynthia Ozick asks whether in the present discussion on 'the relation of women to the Jewish Way' the right question to ask is 'theological'. She argues that the status of the Jewish woman is not
'theological' but sociological. To change women's status in Judaism does
not require changing 'one iota of the status of Jewish belief'.[2] Only at
the end of the essay does her doubt appear in the question 'What if?':

So the question arises: if, in the most fundamental text and texture of
Torah, the lesser status of women is not worthy of a great 'Thou shalt
not,' . . . then perhaps there is no essential injustice, then perhaps the
common status of women is not only sanctioned, but in fact divinely
ordained?[3]

In responding to Ozick's essay, the Jewish feminist theologian Judith
Plaskow argues that the 'right question' is indeed theological in the
strictest sense of the word. The issues raised by Jewish feminism reach
beyond *halakha*. They demand a new understanding of the Torah, God,
and Israel. They ask for the acknowledgement of the 'profound injustice
of Torah itself', for the reception of female God-language and symbols,
and finally for a new understanding of the community of Israel that
would allow women to name their own religious experiences and to

263

articulate their own theological interpretations.[4]

The essays in the book *Bread Not Stone* (Boston, 1984) centre around the same feminist theological questions and challenges that confront not only Judaism but also Christianity. I have focused on problems concerned with the Bible and biblical interpretation in Church and academy. In this way I seek to develop a feminist biblical hermeneutics, that is, a theory, method, or perspective for understanding and interpretation. In doing so I also seek to contribute to the feminist articulation of a new scholarly paradigm of biblical interpretation and theology. Feminist theology begins with the experiences of women, of women-church. In our struggle for self-identity, survival, and liberation in a patriarchal society and Church, Christian women have found that the Bible has been used as a weapon against us but at the same time it has been a resource for courage, hope, and commitment in this struggle. Therefore, it cannot be the task of feminist interpretation to defend the Bible against its feminist critics but to understand and interpret it in such a way that its oppressive and liberating power is clearly recognized.

A feminist hermeneutics cannot trust or accept Bible and tradition simply as divine revelation. Rather it must critically evaluate them as patriarchal articulations, since even in the last century Sarah Grimké, Matilda Joslyn Gage, and Elizabeth Cady Stanton had recognized that biblical texts are not the words of God but the words of *men*.[5] This insight particularizes the results of historical-critical scholarship that the Bible is written by human authors or male authors. This critical insight of a feminist hermeneutics has ramifications not only for historical scholarship but also for our contemporary political situation because the Bible still functions today as a religious justification and ideological legitimization of patriarchy.

To speak of power is to speak of political realities and struggles although we might not be conscious of this when we speak of the power of the Word. The Bible is not simply a religious but also a profoundly political book as it continues to inform the self-understandings of American and European 'secularized' societies and cultures. Feminist biblical interpretations therefore have a critical political significance not only for women in biblical religion but for all women in western societies.

The Bible is not only written in the words of men but also serves to legitimate patriarchal power and oppression in so far as it 'renders God'[6] male and determines ultimate reality in male terms, which make women invisible or marginal. The interconnection between androcentric language and patriarchal power becomes apparent when we remember that in 1850 an Act of Parliament was required to prohibit the common use of *they* for sex-indeterminable references and legally to insist that *he* stood for *she*.[7] At a time when patriarchal oppression is on the rise again in American society and religion, the development of a feminist biblical hermeneutics is not only a theological but also a profoundly political task.

The controversies that have surrounded a feminist interpretation ever since Elizabeth Cady Stanton planned and edited *The Woman's Bible* indicate that such a feminist challenge goes to the roots of religious patriarchal legitimization.[8] The recent, often violent, and seemingly irrational reactions to the *Inclusive Language Lectionary* amply prove this critical political impact of feminist biblical interpretation.[9] Writing in the *Washington Post* James J. Kilpatrick makes his point succinctly: 'It is probably a waste of time, energy, and indignation to denounce the latest efforts to *castrate* the Holy Bible, but vandalism of this magnitude ought not to go unremarked' [emphasis added].[10]

If language determines the limits of our world, then sacred androcentric, that is, grammatically masculine, language symbolizes and determines our perception of ultimate human and divine reality. Those who protest an inclusive language translation as the 'castration' of Scripture consciously or not maintain that such ultimate reality and authority are in the words of Mary Daly 'phallocentric'.

From its inception feminist interpretation of Scripture has been generated by the fact that the Bible was used to halt the emancipation of slaves and women.[11] Not only in the last century but also today patriarchal right-wing forces in society lace their attacks against women's rights and freedoms in the political, economic, reproductive, intellectual, and religious arenas with biblical quotations and appeals to scriptural authority.[12] In countless pulpits and fundamentalist television programmes, such patriarchal attacks are proclaimed as the Word of God while the feminist struggle for women's liberation is denounced as 'godless humanism' that undermines the 'American family'. Yet the political right does not simply misquote or misuse the Bible as a Christian feminist apologetics seeks to argue.[13] It can utilize certain scriptural texts because they *are* patriarchal in their original function and intention.

Feminist interpretation therefore begins with a hermeneutics of suspicion that applies to both contemporary androcentric interpretations of the Bible and the biblical texts themselves. Certain texts of the Bible can be used in the argument against women's struggle for liberation not only because they are patriarchally misinterpreted but because they are patriarchal texts and therefore can serve to legitimate women's subordinate role and secondary status in patriarchal society and church. While some of us have maintained that feminists must abandon the Bible and biblical religion, here I seek to argue why feminists cannot afford to do so. We have to reclaim biblical religion as our own heritage because 'our heritage is our power'.[14] At the same time I insist that such a reclaiming of our heritage can only take place through a critical process of feminist assessment and evaluation.

Reclaiming the Bible as a feminist heritage and resource is only possible because it has not functioned only to legitimate the oppression of *all* women: freeborn, slave, black and white, native American, European and Asian, immigrant, poor, working-class and middle-class, Third World and First World women. It has also provided authorization and legitimization for women who have rejected slavery, racism, anti-Semitism, colonial exploitation, and misogynism as unbiblical and against God's will. The Bible has inspired and continues to inspire countless women to speak out and to struggle against injustice, exploitation, and stereotyping. The biblical vision of freedom and wholeness still energizes women in all walks of life to struggle against poverty, unfreedom, and denigration. It empowers us to survive with dignity and to continue the struggle when there seems to be no hope for success.[15]

A critical feminist hermeneutics of liberation therefore seeks to develop a critical dialectical mode of biblical interpretation that can do justice to women's experiences of the Bible as a thoroughly patriarchal book written in androcentric language as well as to women's experience of the Bible as a source of empowerment and vision in our struggles for liberation. Such a hermeneutics has to subject biblical texts to a dialectical process of critical readings and feminist evaluations. In order to do so it insists that *the* litmus test for invoking Scripture as the Word of God must be whether or not biblical texts and traditions seek to end relations of domination and exploitation.

In short, if we claim that oppressive patriarchal texts are the Word of God then we proclaim God as a God of oppression and dehumanization. The question is indeed 'theological' in the strictest sense of the word, requiring not only a new naming of God but also a new naming of Church and its use of Scripture. Such a process of naming transforms our metaphor of Scripture as 'tablets of stone' on which the unchanging word of God is engraved for all times into the image of bread that nurtures, sustains, and energizes women as people of God in our struggles against injustice and oppression.

II

The hermeneutical centre of such a feminist biblical interpretation, I therefore argue here, is the *ekklesia gynaikon* or women-church, the movement of self-identified women and women-identified men in biblical religion. When as a Christian I use the expression *women-church*, I do not use it as an exclusionary but as a political-oppositional term to patriarchy. It thus becomes necessary to clarify here in what way I use the term *patriarchy* as an heuristic category. I do not use the concept in the loose sense of 'all men dominating all women equally', but in the classical Aristotelian sense. *Patriarchy* as a male pyramid of graded subordinations and exploitations specifies women's oppression in terms of the class, race, country, or religion of the men to whom we 'belong'.

This definition of patriarchy enables us to use it as a basic heuristic concept for feminist analysis, one that allows us to conceptualize not only sexism but also racism, property-class relationships, and all other forms of exploitation or dehumanization as basic structures of women's oppression.

Although public life and political self-determination were restricted in Athenian democracy to the freeborn propertied male heads of patriarchal households and reserved in the patriarchal church for ordained males, I understand women-church as the dialogical community of equals in which critical judgement takes place and public freedom becomes tangible. Women-church seeks to realize the fullest meaning of the Greek New Testament notion of *ekklesia* as the public assembly of free citizens who gather in order to determine their own and their children's communal, political, and spiritual well-being. The synagogue or church of women is the gathering of all those women and men who empowered by the Holy Spirit and inspired by the biblical vision of justice, freedom, and salvation continue against all odds the struggle for liberation from patriarchal oppression in society and religion. As such the feminist movement in biblical religion is not just a civil rights but also a liberation movement. Its goal is not simply the 'full humanity' of women, since humanity as we know it is male-defined. The goal is women's (religious) self-affirmation, power, and liberation from all patriarchal alienation, marginalization, and exploitation.

Therefore, like other liberation theologies, feminist theology explicitly takes an advocacy position. But it articulates this advocacy position differently for women and for men. Whereas in a feminist conversion *men* must take the option for the oppressed and become women-identified, in such a conversion *women* must seek to overcome our deepest self-alienation. Since all women are socialized to respect and to identify with men, our position of advocacy must be articulated not as an 'option for the oppressed' but as self-respect and self-identification *as women* in a patriarchal society and religion.

While feminist theory advocates for men a 'theology of relinquishment',[16] it articulates for women a theology of 'self-affirmation'. The more we identify as women and in a feminist process of conversion overcome our patriarchal self-alienation, the more we will realize that our alienation from other women – the separation between white and black women, middle-class and poor women, native American and European women, Jewish and Christian women, Protestant and Catholic women, nun-women or clergy-women and laywomen, lesbian and heterosexual women, First World and Third World women – is in the words of Adrienne Rich 'a separation from ourselves'.[17]

The patriarchal dehumanization and victimization of the 'poorest and most despised women on earth' exhibits the full death-dealing power of patriarchy, while their struggles for liberation and their courage to survive is the fullest experience of God's grace in our midst. The *locus* of divine revelation and grace is therefore not simply the Bible or the tradition of a patriarchal church but the 'church of women' in the past and in the present. God's nurturing presence 'reveals' its power in the struggles of all women who seek to live 'the option for our women selves' in a patriarchal society and religion. Conversely, the 'option for our women selves' is the 'option for the most oppressed women' and the commitment to their struggles. Such an option allows us 'to find God in ourselves' and 'to love Her fiercely, to love Her fiercely'.[18]

The spiritual authority of women-church rests on the experience of God's sustaining grace and liberating presence in the midst of our struggles for justice, freedom, and wholeness of all. It rests not simply on the 'experience of women' but on the experience of women struggling for liberation from patriarchal oppression:

> The dream of freedom for oneself in a world in which all women are free emerges from one's life experience in which one is not free, precisely because one is a woman. The liberation of women is thus not an abstract goal . . . but is the motive for that process. Individual freedom and the freedom of all women are linked when one has reached the critical consciousness that we are united first in our unfreedom.[19]

A feminist critical theology of liberation, therefore, must reject all religious texts and traditions that contribute to 'our unfreedom'. In a public feminist critical discourse this theology seeks to evaluate *all* biblical texts, interpretations, and contemporary uses of the Bible for their contribution to the religious legitimization of patriarchy as well as for their stand toward patriarchal oppression. A feminist critical theology of liberation therefore develops a hermeneutics of critical evaluation rather than one of correlation.[20]

What leads us to perceive biblical texts as oppressive or as providing resources in the struggle for liberation from patriarchal oppression or as models for the transformation of the patriarchal church into women-church is not a revealed principle or a special canon of texts that can claim divine authority. Rather it is the experience of women struggling for liberation and wholeness. In so far as biblical texts remember the struggles of our foremothers and forefathers against patriarchal oppression and their experience of God's sustaining presence, they can become paradigmatic for women-church and 'inspire' our own struggles and visions of life.

I have therefore proposed that we understand the Bible as a structuring prototype of women-church rather than as a timeless archetype, as an open-ended paradigm that sets experience in motion and structures transformations. Rather than reducing the biblical multiformity and richness of experience to abstract principles or impulses to be applied to new situations, I suggest the notion of a historical prototype open to its own critical transformation.

This notion of the Bible as a formative root-model of women-church allows us to explore models and traditions of emancipatory praxis as well as of patriarchal oppression. It allows us to reclaim the whole Bible, not as a normative immutable archetype, but as an experiential authority that can 'render God' although it is written in the 'language of men'. It allows us to reclaim the Bible as enabling resource, as bread not stone, as legacy and heritage, not only of patriarchal religion but also of women-church as the discipleship of equals. The perception of the Bible as a historical prototype provides women-church with a sense of its ongoing history as well as its Christian identity.

In short, through a process of critical evaluation as well as structural and creative transformation the Bible can become Holy Scripture for women-church. In so far as the interpretive model proposed here does not identify biblical revelation with androcentric texts and patriarchal structures, it maintains that such revelation is found among the discipleship community of equals in the present and in the past.[21] Since the model proposed here locates revelation, not in androcentric texts, but in the experience of God's grace and presence among women struggling for liberation from patriarchal oppression and dehumanization, this model requires a feminist critical hermeneutics of the Bible in the context of women-church.[22]

III

A feminist reading of the Bible requires both a transformation of our patriarchal understandings of God, Scripture, and the church and a transformation in the self-understanding of historical-critical scholarship and the theological disciplines.

Such an attempt encounters resistance from two groups. Women often consider theoretical and methodological discussions as a male 'trip', as a flight from practical engagement and political activism. While this certainly can be the case, I would nevertheless argue that feminists cannot afford to be anti-intellectual. Since 'knowledge is power', women have to become involved in the production and distribution of knowledge. Women's systemic exclusion from scholarship and intellectual influence is an important aspect of our powerlessness. This is especially true in theology, since women only recently gained access to the academic disciplines of theology. Even theologically trained women are more hesitant to enter a critical theological discussion than to share their religious experiences and spiritual insights.

I have therefore begun to use technical theological terms such as hermeneutics in order to elaborate in lectures and workshops the concept of theology-anxiety by analogy with the notion of maths-anxiety, into which women are systematically socialized.[23] The following two reactions, which I recently received after a lecture on feminist hermeneutics before an audience of ministers and theology students, will illustrate my point. First, although I had spoken about theology anxiety, explaining how the 'power of theological naming' was stolen from us, one of the few male participants complimented me on my rigorous, intellectual approach but counselled that I should not use difficult theological terms such as *hermeneutics* because 'women do not have the sophistication to understand them'. Later, a woman participant related that in her senior year at college she wrote a paper for a seminar on the Old Testament in which she used the word *hermeneutics*. To her surprise the professor had circled the word in red ink and written in the margin: 'What a fancy word! Please use simpler terms.' After listening to my elaborations on how women are kept from theological thinking, she understood for the first time why she had been censured, although the literature she had consulted had used the term frequently.

The second group that finds it difficult to accept that feminist studies in general and feminist theology in particular seek to effect a paradigm shift in the academic disciplines comprises established members of the academy. Feminist theology is often tolerated as a 'woman's affair' or as supplementary to male scholarship, but not as a different perspective and method for doing theology. Women in the academy are seen as 'competent' scholars when we adopt the investigative methods and theoretical frameworks of our male mentors. Women scholars are expected to gather 'data', faithfully to apply standard methods, or to do routine research in insignificant areas, but not to cut new paths, to establish new theoretical frameworks, or to write ground-breaking works, works that will change the discipline. The feminist sociologist Dorothy Smith describes this experience:

> The universe of ideas, images and themes – the symbolic modes which are the general currency of thought – have been either produced by men or controlled by them. Insofar as women's work and experience has been entered into it, it has been on terms decided by men and because it has been approved by men.[24]

In her book *Women and Ideas and What Men Have Done to Them* the Australian feminist scholar Dale Spender seeks to recover the lost intellectual history of women from Aphra Behn to Adrienne Rich. She argues that the invisibility of women, the absence of women's intellectual voice, the experience that every feminist work has been received as if it emerged from nowhere, is fundamental to the perpetuation of patriarchal

power. Women thinkers and artists disappear from the historical consciousness not only of men but also of women, because patriarchy
demands that any articulation of the central problem of male power that
confronts women should remain invisible and unreal.

As this book demonstrates for centuries women have been challenging
men, and men have used punitive measures against them; for centuries
women have been claiming that the world and men look very different
from the perspective of women. Far from being an unusual claim, it is
a common assertion of women of the past and a familiar issue in contemporary feminism that women's meanings and values have been
excluded from what have been put forward as society's meanings and
values.[25]

Needless to say, women-church's values and visions have also been
excluded from the church's or God's values and words. Feminist theology
seeks to interrupt this theological and spiritual patriarchal silencing of
women. It listens carefully to women's spiritual and religious experiences
in order to define new theoretical frameworks and approaches that would
allow us to bring women's patriarchal silences 'into speech',[26] and to
make our values, insights, and visions integral to the theological discourse
of the church.

A comparison with a recent philosophical work on the present intellectual discourse on hermeneutics might help to situate the discussions and
proposals. In *Beyond Objectivism and Relativism: Science, Hermeneutics,
and Praxis*, Richard Bernstein points out that in contrast with European
scholars, Anglo-American thinkers have become interested in hermeneutics
only during the past decade or so. Analysing the contributions of
Gadamer, Habermas, Kuhn, Rorty, and Arendt to the 'new conversation'
about human rationality, he develops a complex argument that challenges
the dichotomy between objectivism and relativism.

Rather than seeking ultimate foundations and a 'fixed Archimedean
point' on which to secure our thoughts, beliefs, and actions, these thinkers
attempt to overcome the either/or of objectivism and relativism in a
practical-moral concern for ways in which we can foster a 'reawakening
consciousness of solidarity'. Bernstein points out that we encounter in their
arguments something like a circle that can be compared to the hermeneutical circle. Dialogical communities that can foster solidarity, freedom, and
public discourse presuppose incipient forms of such communal life.

There is no guarantee . . . no 'logic of history' that must inevitably lead
to dialogical communities that embrace all of humanity in which reciprocal judgment, practical discourse, and rational persuasion flourish. If
anything we should have learned how much the contemporary world
conspires against it and undermines it.

Bernstein therefore concludes that it is not

> sufficient to come up with some new variations of arguments that will show, once and for all, what is wrong with objectivism and relativism, or even open up a way of thinking that can move us beyond objectivism and relativism; such a movement gains 'reality and power' only if we dedicate ourselves to the practical task of furthering the type of solidarity, participation, and mutual recognition that is founded in dialogical communities.[27]

A comparison with Bernstein's proposal underlines three important contributions that the critical feminist hermeneutics developed in these essays can make to the general discussion of biblical hermeneutics. The chapters in this book diagnose that biblical interpretation and theology are caught in the same Cartesian anxiety and either/or of objectivism and relativism. I have argued therefore that rather than seek a 'revealed' Archimedean point in the shifting sand of biblical-historical relativity – be it a liberating tradition, text, or principle in the Bible – a feminist critical hermeneutics has to explore and assess whether and how Scripture can become an enabling, motivating resource and empowering authority in women's struggle for justice, liberation, and solidarity.[28]

Moreover, Bernstein recognizes that much of humanity has been and still is systematically excluded from participating in such dialogical communities. But he does not develop this insight as a critical impulse for practical discourse. By making women the subjects of biblical interpretation and critical theological evaluation, a feminist critical hermeneutics takes the experience of women's exclusion and invisibility as its critical point of departure. Finally, whereas such dialogical communities remain for Bernstein a *telos* that he cannot name concretely and identify historically, I have put forward women-church as the dialogical community that is incipiently given but still needs to be realized in feminist conversion and historical struggle for liberation from patriarchal oppression.

Although a critical feminist hermeneutics must seek to transform the discipline of biblical scholarship and theology, its primary commitment is not to the academy but to women-church and to all women struggling for dignity, self-affirmation, survival, and freedom in cultural and societal patriarchy. Its primary questions and problems are not those of the academy but those of women-church. Its validity and impact will depend on how much it is able to reclaim the Bible as a resource for women-church. In order to do our work feminist scholars and students of the Bible must therefore heed the warning of the feminist poet and social activist Renny Golden in 'Academic Women':

Rainbow fish precious, picked from the catch.
You swim through their corridors, upstream.
You've done their task and ours,
double labor familiar as laundry.
We quote from your books,
claim you before men
who tell our bodies they're all we got.
Sisters, light dazzles when it's pure.
Beacons: remember you illumine someone's way.
Their seduction is naming you stars . . .
brilliant, singular, without purpose.

When you speak of the common woman, the poor woman
get the accent right.
Consider the net enfolding you.
Outside we are thousands.
Unless you swim in our waters,
you'll miss depth.
From time to time you will have to mention us,
but you won't get it right.[29]

NOTES

1 Alla Bozarth Campbell, *Womanpriest* (New York: Paulist Press, 1978), pp. 217f.
2 Cynthia Ozick, 'Notes toward finding the right question', in Susan Heschel (ed.), *On Being a Jewish Feminist: A Reader* (New York: Schocken Books, 1983), p. 142.
3 ibid., p. 144.
4 Judith Plaskow, 'The right question is theological', in ibid., p. 231.
5 For the importance of Gage's thought, see especially Sally Roesch Wagner, 'Introduction', in Matilda Joslyn Gage, *Woman, Church, and State* (Watertown, Mass.: Persephone Press, 1983), pp. xv–xxxix.
6 Cf. the helpful review and discussion of different theological models of revelation (especially chapter 12, 'The Bible: document of revelation'), in Avery Dulles, *Models of Revelation* (Garden City, NY: Doubleday, 1983). Dulles only mentions but does not elaborate the model of liberation theology, and does not consider the paradigm of feminist theology.
7 Cf. Dale Spender, *Man-Made Language* (London and Boston: Routledge and Kegan Paul, 1980), p. 150.
8 Elizabeth Cady Stanton (ed.), *The Original Feminist Attack on the Bible: The Woman's Bible* (1895; New York: Arno Press, 1974), with Barbara Welter's introduction.
9 Cf. especially Susan Brooks Thistlewaite, 'Opening the mail which did not tick', *Review of Books and Religion* 12/6 (1984), pp. 6–8.
10 James J. Kilpatrick, 'God is not a chairperson', *Washington Post* (21 October 1983). Positively, the *Inclusive Language Lectionary* has rekindled interest in textual criticism and biblical translation.

11 Angelina E. Grimké, 'An appeal to the Christian women of the South', *Anti-Slavery Examiner* I/2 (1836), pp. 16–26, argued that in God's eyes slavery was sin and the laws keeping slaves in bondage were man-made. Because of the attacks of the press and the clergy against them as women who spoke up, both Grimké sisters were drawn more deeply into the struggle for women's rights. One of the signs is Sarah Grimké, *Letters on the Equality of the Sexes and the Condition of Women* (Boston, Mass.: Isaac Knapp, 1838). Cf. Judith A. Sabrosky, *From Rationality to Liberation: The Evolution of Feminist Ideology* (Westport, Conn.: Greenwood Press, 1979). See also the review of opposing interpretations of the slave and women passages in the New Testament by Willard Swartley, *Slavery, Sabbath, War, and Women: Case Studies in Biblical Interpretation* (Philadelphia, Pa.: Herald Press, 1983).

12 Cf. Charlene Spretnak, 'The Christian Right's "Holy War" against feminism', in *The Politics of Women's Spirituality* (Garden City, NY: Doubleday, Anchor Books, 1982), pp. 470–96; Shirley Rogers Radl, *The Invisible Woman: Target of the Religious Right* (New York: Delta Books, 1983).

13 See for instance my discussion of 'the defence of Paul', in *In Memory of Her: A Feminist Theological Reconstruction of Christian Origins* (New York: Crossroad, 1983), pp. 8–10, and the theological rationalizations of the household code texts discussed in chapter 7, pp. 251–84.

14 This expression is taken from Judy Chicago, *The Dinner Party: A Symbol of Our Heritage* (Garden City, NY: Doubleday, Anchor Books, 1979). See also Gustavo Guttierez, *The Power of the Poor in History: Selected Writings* (Maryknoll, NY: Orbis Press, 1983), especially chapter 7, 'Theology from the underside of history'.

15 Cf. Andrea Dworkin, 'Antifeminism', *Trivia* 2 (1983), pp. 6–36, who concludes her analysis with this question:

'Can a political movement rooted in a closed system – with no support among power-based movements – break that closed system apart? Or will the antifeminism of those whose politics are rooted in sex-class power and privilege always destroy movements for the liberation of women? Is there a way to subvert the antifeminism of power-based political programs or parties – or is the pleasure and profit in the subordination of women simply too overwhelming, too great, too marvelous to allow for anything but the political defense of that subordination (antifeminism)?

It is my contention here that a critical feminist interpretation of the Bible can contribute to such a 'subversion of antifeminism' by denying any divine-religious authority to the biblical 'subordination' passages and by 'envisioning' and 'building up' women-church as the discipleship community of equals that from 'within' will contribute to break open the closed patriarchal systems of church and society.

16 I have borrowed this expression from Marie Augusta Neal, although she uses it in a different context and sense. Cf. her *A Socio-Theology of Letting Go* (New York: Paulist Press, 1977).

17 Adrienne Rich, 'Disloyal to civilization: feminism, racism, gynephobia (1978)', in *On Lies, Secrets, and Silence* (New York: Norton, 1979), p. 307.

18 Ntozake Shange's ending chorus *For Colored Girls Who Have Considered Suicide When the Rainbow Is Enuf* is often quoted by religious feminists. But it must not be overlooked that such an affirmation is only possible through the naming of sexist-racist oppressions. Anne Cameron, *Daughters of Copper Woman* (Vancouver: Press Gang Publishers, 1981), ends her record of stories about a secret society of native Vancouver Island women with a poem that

concludes in a similar vein: 'I have been searching Old Woman and I find her in mySelf' (p. 150).

19 Marcia Westkott, 'Women's studies as a strategy for change: between criticism and vision', in Gloria Bowles and Renate Duelli Klein (eds), *Theories of Women's Studies* (London and Boston: Routledge and Kegan Paul, 1983), p. 213.

20 Cf. for example Anne Carr, 'Is a Christian feminist theology possible?', *Theological Studies* 43 (1982), pp. 279–97, and now also Rosemary Radford Ruether, 'Feminist interpretation: a method of correlation', in L. Russell (ed.), *Feminist Interpretation of the Bible* (Philadelphia, Pa: Westminster Press, forthcoming). For a discussion of such a method of correlation in contemporary theology see David Tracy, 'Particular questions with general concerns', in Leonard Swidler (ed.), *Consensus in Theology* (Philadelphia, Pa: Westminster Press, 1980), pp. 33–9, and for a critical evaluation see Francis Schüssler Fiorenza, *Foundational Theology: Jesus and the Church* (New York: Crossroad, 1984), pp. 276–84.

21 My position is often misunderstood as postulating a period of equality in the earliest beginnings of the Church, which very soon was superseded by the patriarchal form of Church. My point, however, is not only that the 'discipleship of equals' preceded the 'patriarchalization' of church but also that it was repressed rather than replaced. Although the discipleship community of equals or women-church was submerged and often oppressed by ecclesiastical patriarchy, it has never ceased to exist. Rather than conceptualize church history as a history of decline (or progress, depending on the point of view), I conceptualize it as a history of struggle. In so far as the Bible is the model for both women-church *and* patriarchal Church, it is also the paradigm of this struggle.

22 Mary Ann Tolbert, 'Defining the problem: the Bible and feminist hermeneutics', in *Semeia: The Bible and Feminist Hermeneutics* 28 (1983), p. 123, seems to assume that I propose a reconstruction of the earliest egalitarian period of early Christianity as the basis of faith. I hope it has become clear that this is not the case. Although I share Bultmann's programme of *Sachkritik*, I do not share his neo-orthodox existentialist position or his method of demythologization. I completely agree with Tolbert that the biblical texts cannot be 'depatriarchalized' (in analogy to demythologized). At the same time I cannot accept the first part of Tolbert's suggestion that a feminist hermeneutics must seek 'to understand the same God as enemy and friend, as tormentor and saviour'. Her additional phrase 'to read the same Bible as enslaver and liberator, that is the paradoxical challenge of feminist biblical hermeneutics' (p. 126) restates my own position. My argument has been precisely that God and the Bible cannot be commensurate if we take the feminist hermeneutical insight seriously that the Bible is 'man-made', written in androcentric language, and rooted in patriarchal cultures and religions.

23 In lectures and conversations, Mary Elizabeth Hunt first has suggested this analogy between maths anxiety and theology anxiety.

24 Dorothy Smith, 'A peculiar eclipsing: women's exclusion from man's culture', *Women's Studies International Quarterly* 1/4 (1978), p. 281.

25 Dale Spender, *Women of Ideas and What Men Have Done to Them: From Aphra Behn to Adrienne Rich* (London: ARK Paperbacks, 1982), p. 8.

26 See especially the influential contribution of Nelle Morton, 'The rising women's consciousness in a male language structure', in *Women and the Word: Toward a Whole Theology* (Berkeley, Calif.: GTU, 1972), pp. 43–52.

27 Richard J. Bernstein, *Beyond Objectivism and Relativism: Science,*

Hermeneutics, and Praxis (Philadelphia, Pa: University of Pennsylvania Press, 1983), p. 231.

28 The 'true' answer to this question cannot be substantiated by hermeneutic-theological theory but must be validated in the emancipatory praxis of women-church. Feminist theology is a second-order reflection.

29 Renny Golden and Shelia Collins, *Struggle Is a Name for Hope: Poetry*, Worker Writer Series 3 (Minneapolis, 1983), p. 20.

RENEWAL OR NEW CREATION?

Feminist spirituality and historical religion

Rosemary Radford Ruether

More than a century ago, Karl Marx described religion as the opiate of the people. What he meant by that famous phrase was that religion was a tool of the ruling classes that served to pacify oppressed people and alienate them from their own critical responses to unjust social systems. Religion sacralizes the existing social order as an expression of the will of God. It deflects the protest of the oppressed into pipe-dreams of another world transcendent to their own. What Marx hoped to accomplish by his critique of religion was to de-alienate the protest and hopes from their sublimated or transcendental expression in religious visions of redemption, and bring them back to earth, where they could fuel real struggle against social evil and real efforts to transform life on earth.

WAS RELIGION EVER WOMEN-CENTRED?

If the industrial proletariat of Marx's day could be seen as the victims of the religious opiate, then women can be seen as perhaps doubly the victims of religious pacification. All the major historical religions – not only Christianity, but also Islam, Judaism, Buddhism, and Hinduism – have been male-dominated in religious leadership and have promoted systems of religious law and symbolism that marginalize women. I believe this is also true of earlier forms of religion, which Judaism and Christianity have called 'pagan' (a word that means 'religion of the country-people', although it has been construed by Jews and Christians to mean a worshipper of false or evil powers). In the texts, rituals, and oral traditions with which I am familiar, namely, the ancient Greek and Near Eastern materials, these religions also appear to be essentially androcentric.

Some contemporary feminists have assumed that these non-biblical religions were feminist because they contain female personification of deity. But the presence of goddesses in a religion does not necessarily mean that that religion is genuinely gynecentric, that is, defined and led by women and upholding full female personhood. Christianity, too, has a powerful female figure that functions as an object of devotion: the

Virgin Mary. But that female cult object served overwhelmingly to sacralize the auxiliary and submissive role of the female vis-à-vis male humanity and the male God. Figures such as Isis, Astarte, Athena, or other Goddesses from classical antiquity have elements of power and autonomy that have been repressed in the more patriarchalized Virgin Mary. Yet they too seem to function as part of an androcentric world-view, that is to say, a world where the Goddess as mother, sister, or spouse functions to rescue and establish male kingly power, rather than to uplift the power of women.

It has been sometimes argued that this patriarchalized version of goddess religion is a later stratum and conceals the earlier, truly gynecentric form of these religions. But if we have no archaeological or textual survivals of these religions and no living community that represents them, we have no way of knowing whether such earlier levels existed or not. This question is still open, as far as I am concerned. What has not been proved is that there was once upon a time a great era, during which women were either equal or dominant in society, a dominance expressed in a genuinely gynecentric religion.

Religions of the Greek and ancient Near Eastern world from pre-Christian antiquity show clear elements of androcentrism. For example, followers of the sacred mysteries of Eleusis, the only mystery religion in antiquity to lift up the mother–daughter relationship (through the celebration of the finding of the raped daughter by her Goddess mother), nevertheless were led by hereditary colleges of male priests. It is also important to remember that these ancient Goddess cults were originally civic and political in nature. In Pharaonic Egypt, the great Goddess Isis' role as rescuer of Osiris from the dead and as mother of Horus was central to the foundations of kingly power. Isis attracted many female adherents, although not necessarily more in number than her male devotees. And although women were priestesses in all periods, they held secondary rank compared with male priestly roles. The focus on Isis as the central figure in the cult seems only to have increased in the Hellenistic period, when the connection of the Isis cult with the reigning Pharaoh disappeared, and it became a mystery religion of personal salvation.

In fact, the more one studies different religious traditions and their early roots, the more one is tempted to suggest that religion itself is essentially a male creation. Could it be that the male, marginalized from direct participation in the great mysteries of gestation and birth, asserted his superior physical strength to monopolize leisure and culture and that he did so by creating ritual expressions that duplicated female gestating and birthing roles so as to transfer power of these primary mysteries to the male? If so, it would perhaps explain why mother Goddess figures predominate in early religion yet do not function to give women power.

> **Creation of a truly just and harmonious society still eludes us, as much as it eluded the ancient peoples who awaited a messianic intervention of God. We still have not solved the root problem of sin, which is the desire for domination.**

This ritual sublimation of female functions, as a transfer of spiritual power over life to males, is continued in Christianity. Its central mysteries in baptism and the eucharist duplicate female roles in gestation, birth, and nourishment but give power over the spiritualized expression of these functions not only to males, but to males who eschew sex and reproduction.

In the ancient Near Eastern, Greco-Roman, Judaeo-Christian, and modern developments of religious traditions, there seem to me to be three stages of androcentric use of religion. In the first stage, the male sublimates female procreative functions into a great Mother Goddess, situates himself as the son and beloved of this Mother Goddess, and is rescued from death and enthroned as king through the power of the Mother. One finds this pattern in ancient Near Eastern myths and rites of Innana, Ishtar, Anath, and Isis, and remnants of it remain in Christian Mariology.

In the second stage, the great Mother is dethroned and subordinated as the creaturely Mother Earth and Church, created and ruled over by a Father God, who now assumes transcendence outside of and above the cosmos. Here the female becomes the symbol of that which is to be dominated, ruled over, and ultimately shunned by transcendent, spiritual male mind.

In the third stage, the male leadership class emancipates itself from religious tutelage and assumes direct power over the cosmos through science, while relegating religious piety to a private world identified with women. Thus in classical patriarchal religion, i.e. Orthodox Judaism and Islam, males dominated not only the priesthoods and teachers but even the required prayers, relegating women to the margins. Now, in privatized religions, women monopolize the practices of the religion, while the official leadership and teaching authority remain vested in a male clerical class.

FEMINIST APPROPRIATION OF RELIGIOUS TRADITIONS

This evaluation of major known religions as androcentric is not an argument against feminists who prefer to explore non-biblical religions, such as Buddhism or Goddess traditions from the ancient Near East, Greece, or the Germanic world, rather than the dominant religion of American society, i.e. Christianity. There may be stories and symbols in such traditions that appeal deeply to those who have been alienated from the patriarchalism of the dominant biblical religions. Such explorations are, in my view, fully legitimate from the point of view of religious authenticity. But whether one seeks to be a feminist within the religious traditions of Judaism, Christianity, or Islam, or within Buddhism, or through a renewed encounter with Isis and Ishtar, one is still faced with somewhat parallel problems of androcentrism. The dominant priesthood was male. The female divine symbols, where they exist, generally have played an auxiliary role to male social power.

Thus, whatever elements of a particular religious tradition appear to be positive for women have to be analysed carefully for their androcentric import. One must ask how the story or symbol can be translated from its androcentric context into a context that is interpreted from the side of female experience and that will affirm the empowerment of women as subjects of their own histories. Feminists today have to ask, first of all, whether religion or spirituality is what they should be about at all. What function can it play that enhances a liberationist transformation of history, rather than another escapism? Is the new preoccupation with feminist spirituality simply another expression of that bourgeois religiosity that directs women's energies inward while males run the outer world?

Second, we have to ask how stories and symbols drawn from past religious traditions can be translated from their androcentric form into one defined by and for women (although not necessarily against men, i.e. not necessarily a female reversal of androcentrism). Third, we need to ask at what point we should go beyond reinterpretation of past traditions to the generation of new stories and rituals from our own experience, and what norms we can use to discern the good from the destructive in such new story-telling and ritual-making. Finally, we might ask whether such feminist restatements of older traditions must proceed along separate paths, corresponding roughly to the religious divisions of male culture, or whether feminists engaged in religious critique and revisioning can begin to come together on some new synthesis of perspectives traditionally set against each other.

ELEMENTS OF HEBREW RELIGION

Now I wish to trace these four steps of feminist critique and revisioning from the context of the Christian interpretation of biblical religion. Christian tradition appropriates and builds on the Jewish religious tradition embodied in Hebrew scripture. So it is appropriate to start by asking what distinctive expressions of religion are found in Hebrew scripture.

Feminist critique of Yahwist religion has focused on the patriarchal ordering of society and the imaging of deity in terms of patriarchal leadership roles, such as King, Warrior, Shepherd (a kingly title), and Judge. These aspects of Hebrew religion are, however, parallel to patterns also found in ancient Near Eastern religions. To imagine that the Jews invented patriarchalism and patriarchal religion to suppress a matriarchal faith of other Near Eastern people is historical myopia. I agree with Judith Ochshorn[1] that the rejection of polytheism for monotheism strengthens patriarchalism to the extent that the one God is presumed to be male and represented by males, thus setting up the hierarchy of God over human as analogous to male over female. But Hebrew monotheism leaves open the alternative possibility: that the one God is beyond gender and is imaginable as both male and female. One finds some female imagery for God in Hebrew scripture and Jewish tradition.

Moreover, the distinctive elements of Hebrew faith do not lie primarily in the strengthening of patriarchalism. Characteristic of Hebrew religion is the shift from mythically to historically rooted religion. Babylonian and Canaanite religion focused on stories that represent mythical primordial events (such as the slaying of Tiamat, personifying primal chaos, by Marduk, representing human order in the city-state) or the recurring cycles of drought and rain, death and renewal in nature. But in the stories of Anath and Baal, the Hebrew tradition recalls the liberation of Israel from bondage in Egypt, the giving of the the Law in the desert, and the trek through the wilderness to the promised land. When the festivals of the nature cycle are taken over into the Hebrew liturgical year they are overlaid with new interpretation drawn from these historical commemorations.

These historical paradigms function not simply as ritual *mimesis* but also as spurs to historical action. 'Because these things happened to you, you shall or shall not do certain things.' Historical precedent became ethical paradigm for living historically in community. As developed in the prophets, one also sees emerging in Hebrew religion a social shift in the function of religion over against royalist religion that serves to sacralize existing systems of power and wealth. True, the prophets also assume that kings represent the deity, as keepers of the social order. But they can call to account kings who fail in these tasks, particularly when kings do not protect the weakest members of society: the poor, widows, and orphans. Rapacious economic power, which inflates prices and steals the subsistence of the poor, is placed under divine judgment.

THE PROPHETIC PARADIGM – THEN AND NOW

This social shift of religion from panegyric of the powerful, in the name of the gods, to social criticism and calling the powerful to account is of great significance. It laid the basis for the language of social criticism and historical transformation in those cultures that trace their roots to

281

the Bible. The prophetic paradigm not only criticized unjust and oppressive power but also criticized the use of religion to sacralize such oppressive power. This shift in the social location of religion is the root of the Marxist critique of religion. Both the prophets and the gospels decry the use of law or ritual to create a privileged priestly or scribal elite and to institutionalize forms of cult regarded as salvific in themselves, without regard to social concern for justice and mercy. This critique of religion is not directed at paganism but at the Jewish temple or scribal leadership itself. It is a self-criticism that aims at the renewal of the ethical content of religious practice.

The prophetic paradigm also contains the language of radical social transformation. God is seen as active in history, overthrowing oppressors, bringing into being a new social order of justice and mercy. Hope is directed towards an historical future, when the wrongs of the present system will be righted. Modern social movements of liberation draw on this prophetic paradigm, even if in secular form. They also, however, restate the prophetic paradigm in the framework of a modern recognition that social structures are human creations. Ancient societies assumed that existing social systems were part of the order of the cosmos, so they could only be changed by an intervention of the God who created the world, recreating the cosmos itself. Humans could only wait for such transformative intervention of God into history to create a new heaven and earth. They might hasten the day by ethical obedience, but they could not really transform these systems themselves.

Modern social movements are born in the new consciousness that institutions like kingship, feudal hierarchy, and slavery are human creations that violate justice, i.e. the true nature of things. The concept of 'nature' ceases to be used to justify these social systems; it refers rather to an ideal of original equality in light of which these social hierarchies are judged as unjust. Humans in history are thus empowered to change such systems themselves. Yet creation of a truly just and harmonious society still eludes us, as much as it eluded the ancient peoples who awaited a messianic intervention of God. We still have not solved the root problem of sin, which is the desire for domination.

Feminism, too, is a restatement of the prophetic paradigm in its modern form, in the context of women's oppression and hope for liberation. We too cry against oppression and stand in judgement of religious systems that justify oppression. But unlike in ancient Hebrew prophecy, it is the patriarchal oppression of women that is decried and the liberation of women that is envisioned. Hebrew prophetic criticism remained confined to the concerns of oppressed males in an oppressed nation, vis-à-vis the powerful males of this society or of the imperial powers that surrounded Israel. Although it might seek to alleviate the oppression of slaves or women in the patriarchal family, prophetic critique did not originate from these groups nor did it express a consciousness of patriarchy itself as contrary to justice or to God's will.

Modern social movements, such as liberalism or socialism, or black and Third World liberation movements, also have tended to express the concerns of oppressed males. While they might assail monarchy, feudalism, bourgeois class hierarchy, slavery, and racism, they tended to continue the assumption that the subordination of women was part of an unchangeable 'order of nature'. Feminism extends modern revolutionary consciousness by naming patriarchy as a human (male) construct and an expression of unjust power that distorts the true nature and capacities of women and also of men, turning gender relationality into domination and subordination. Patriarchy is named as something that both can be changed and should be changed.

Feminism thus can appropriate the biblical prophetic paradigm as a root of feminism only by a radical recontextualization, applying the critique of oppression and of alienated religion, and the claims of future hope, to questions of patriarchy and the liberation of women – issues not addressed by the ancient authors. That is, of course, also true of all modern liberation theologies. Not only do these modern liberation theologies assume a human origin and control over the social systems in a way that goes beyond ancient consciousness. They also apply this language to questions, such as racial oppression of American blacks or Latin American victims of monopolistic capitalism, not literally addressed in the Bible. Such application of ancient language to modern issues is not historical exegesis, but analogical *midrash*, in which ancient paradigms are retold in the context of modern issues and modern consciousness. Again, the same is true of any sermonic application of ancient stories, although historical exegesis may be useful to delineate the ancient meaning and context and thus to make more appropriate its translation to the modern analogate. This should be quite obvious but it has been concealed by the modern preoccupation with historical meaning as the only legitimate exegesis.

RETELLING OLD STORIES

Feminist use of the prophetic paradigm therefore has to be clearer that it is not simply exegeting the ancient text. It is retelling the story in new ways. Latin American liberation theologians can imagine that when they take a text about the oppression of the poor the word *poor* in antiquity meant something similar to their critique of poverty in Latin America. Black theologians have used texts about the elect nation for enslaved black people in America and imagined that they are talking about something similar to an ancient Israel as an elect nation. But feminists can have no such illusions of liberal continuity. When we apply language about oppression and liberation to patriarchy and to women, feminist hermeneutics claims the power to retell the story in new ways, a power that has not been owned by other liberation theologies.

One fairly familiar way of retelling old stories consists in a careful study of the original context of the biblical story and a recontextualization of it in a parallel contemporary setting. For example, in a paper that I wrote in 1983 on feminist hermeneutics, I studied the Lukan account of Jesus' commentary on the text of Isaiah 61:1–2, which appears in Luke 4:17–27. In that paper I noted that the Lukan Jesus himself radically revised the meaning of the text as it was spelled out in Isaiah 61:5–7. In the Isaiah text, 'good news to the poor, liberty to the captives' was understood to mean that a dejected and captured Israel would triumph over its foes, the gentile nations around it: 'Strangers will become your servants and you will eat the wealth of nations.' In Luke, Jesus rejects the understanding of this text as national triumph. Instead, he uses it to direct a rebuke against the ethnocentric complacency of the synagogue by declaring that the lepers and widows from among the despised gentile people around Israel will hear God's Word and be healed and that the people of the synagogue will remain closed to it.

A contemporary feminist liberation *midrash* on this text might use it similarly to critique the sexism and class bias of the affluent church. It might suggest that bag ladies and homeless people in their midst are the special objects of God's love and care, while they, the self-righteous church people, fall under divine judgement for their hardness of heart to the poor. This kind of claiming and retelling of biblical stories depends on discerning a liberationist intention in the original story and recontextualizing that liberationist element, while avoiding any tendency to import a Christian chauvinism that would scapegoat the Jewish people as the butt of the story.

Another way of retelling traditional stories consists of studying stories that have a specifically misogynist intent, in order to turn those stories inside out and release the power of women that is being repressed through the old story. A brilliant example of this type of *midrash* is found in Judith Plaskow's retelling of the Lilith story.[2] The rabbinic commentary on Lilith conflates the two creation stories of Genesis 1 and 2. It supposes that Adam, prior to Eve, must have had a wife who was created from the earth at the same time as he. But this earlier wife, Lilith, refused to lie under Adam, and when he complained to God about her, she left him and went out into the waterless places. There she became a demoness who haunts male wet dreams and threatens newborn babies.

Plaskow retold the story of Lilith and Eve by making Lilith represent the repressed power and autonomy of women, which is feared by patriarchy and driven out beyond the boundaries of patriarchal culture. There it is demonized by telling women fearful tales of monstrous viragos who come to a bad end. The 'return of Lilith' in Plaskow's *midrash* is the story of women's reappropriation of their own repressed potential by a reconciliation and consciousness-raising session between Lilith and Eve.

NEW VISIONS, NEW STORIES

A third way of telling new stories plumbs the dimension of primary religious experience, which I would call 'revelation'. This way goes beyond simply retelling old stories through study and discussion. It assumes that revelation, in the sense of primary religious vision, happens today and is not confined to some privileged period of the past. In other words, the Holy Spirit is present and is not simply the tool of historical institutional structures. Most of these primary visions remain private, and only occasionally are they shared in such a way as to take on the function of a communal paradigm that expresses a new consciousness among a community that is being born. Religious feminism is generating many new visions of this kind today, some of which are taking hold as new communal paradigms.

One such new paradigm that is in the process of being born is the image of the Christa or the crucified woman. There has been a remarkable proliferation of such images of crucified women as statues and paintings recently. Whenever they have been publicized in the Christian community, a storm of hostile protest has risen. The usual argument is to say that Jesus was a male, and so one cannot represent the crucified as a woman. But the vicious level of the protest clearly goes beyond a mere statement of historical fact. What is being challenged is the concept that the suffering of a male God is redemptive for both men and women, while the sufferings of women are regarded not only as non-redemptive, but as pornographic. Images of tortured women abound in male sexual fantasy as objects of sadism. Thus to suggest that the image of a tortured woman represents the presence of redemptive divine power jars the patriarchal mentality deeply and is experienced as blasphemy against the sacred.

It is not at all clear how salutary it is for women to claim this image of the crucified to interpret their own sufferings under patriarchy. The image of Christ's crucifixion has for so long functioned as a tool of passive acceptance of victimization that for most people, women especially, it has lost its meaning as divine presence in human suffering that empowers the explosive protest against and overthrow of unjust powers that proliferate violence and victimization. Mary Daly, in her book, *Gyn/Ecology*,[3] tells a story of women's victimization through a long history of sexual surgery, rape, and battering. Women's history becomes an extended crucifixion story. This story of torture is intended to generate women's anger and, in that sense, the power to overthrow patriarchy. But tortured women remain only victims. One experiences no depth of divine presence in female suffering itself.

A story told by a woman in a class I taught recently on women and violence dramatizes this deeper appropriation of women's suffering in what I would call primary religious vision. The woman told the story of how she had been raped by an unknown man in a woods and experienced her own death, believing that he would kill her. When he departed and she found herself still alive, she experienced herself as surrounded by a vision of God as a crucified woman. This filled her with a sense of relief, since she knew she would not have to tell a male God that she had been raped. God was a woman who knew what it was like to be raped.

Her story astonished and compelled us. Like all primary religious visions, it went beyond mere interpretation or theological restatement. It welled up from a depth of inarticulated female experience, disclosing many dimensions of meaning. But what is stated primarily in this vision is that the divine is present precisely where the divine has never been allowed to be present in patriarchal religion, in female sexual victimization by men. The divine is present here, not as representative of the male victimizer but on the side of the female victim, one with the female victim, as one who knows this anguish, who is part of it, and who also heals women and empowers them to rise from the dead and live again beyond the grasp of this destructive violence.

WOMEN-CHURCH: AN EMERGING SYNTHESIS?

How have women begun to claim their power to do feminist *midrash*, to recast traditional stories in feminist retelling, and to communicate new primary visions as collective paradigms? I believe their power to do so is being claimed in the women-church movement. The women-church movement represents women's spirituality moving from the secondary level of theological critique of patriarchal symbols to the primary level of liturgical *mimesis* of religious experience. Here women not only claim the right to preach, that is, to interpret traditional texts. They also claim the right to write the texts, to generate the symbols and stories out of their own religious experience. Feminists of Christian tradition here no longer petition the patriarchal church to respond to women's call to ministry, and for inclusive language and relevant practice. Rather, they depart from the institutional turf controlled by the patriarchal church to engage in building alternative communities of worship and mutual support, where one is free to shape the language, community dynamics, and practice in a way as fully expressive of women's vision of redemption from patriarchy as we can imagine.

Such feminist liturgies and communities, rising from women of

Christian heritage, parallel the feminist *minyan* movement among Jewish feminists, where women take power not only to be a *minyan* for prayer but also to shape the language of prayer itself. Parallels also exist with feminist liturgies that are an integral part of neo-pagan gatherings. Priestesses of the Wicca movement, such as Starhawk in her book *The Spiral Dance*,[4] lay out a pattern of feminist ritual that focuses on the planetary cycles of the year and the rhythms of the female body. Their ritual casts circles of power for women and men beyond patriarchy, heals the wounds of the present system, and sends magical power of collective intention to blast the works of patriarchal violence.

Significant differences exist between neo-pagan and biblically based feminists, as well as between Jewish and Christian feminists, that call for serious and objective discussion. For example, there seem to me fundamental differences between how one relates to myth as distinct from history,[5] and how one understands the relationship of one's community to a historical tradition. Also different are the interpretation of ritual as magic and the understanding of prayer and ritual as response to divine initiative. There also seem to me to be basic differences in the perception of human nature and its relation to non-human nature or the cosmos around us, as well as how one defines the causes of evil and the basis of a struggle against evil.

I do not believe it has been possible to discuss these issues in a meaningful way because there is too much sense of hurt and threat on both sides. Questions are interpreted as attacking and attempting to discredit one or another, rather than seeking a fuller vision of what we are doing. Yet it is also the case that many in the Christian feminist context, and perhaps the Jewish as well, are adopting elements from the neo-pagan movement into their own liturgical work as helpful contributions, even though these critical questions of anthropology, divine-human relationship, and historical accountability remain unresolved. Thus a feminist liturgy with recognizably Christian elements, such as reflections on biblical texts and blessing and sharing bread and wine, might also use a guided meditation from Diane Mariechild's *Mother Wit*.[6] A cloning liturgy, done to celebrate the seventieth birthday of long-time Grail member, Janet Kalven, might adopt from Wicca the casting of the circle of power as a way of gathering the liturgical community. The Feminist Spiritual Community of Portland, Maine, is an example of a liturgical community that bridges the Christian and pagan spiritualities. Founded with a grant from the United Church of Christ, this group has developed into a community that claims three distinct circles of feminist spirituality: the circle of Sophia (Judaeo-Christian), the circle of Isis (Wicca), and the circle of Great Spirit (Native American). Each circle explores liturgies in their own tradition and then presents them to the whole community, which presently consists of about sixty regular members and a larger circle of occasional participants.

This practical eclecticism indicates that such Jewish and Christian feminists stand on a boundary, facing two directions, and refuse to opt simply for one against the other. On the one hand, they affirm a responsibility to their historic faith communities. Despite all the patriarchal elements, they claim the essentially liberationist message of their tradition and seek to translate its riches into expressions liberating for women. They also call these communities themselves to recognize feminist restatement as an authentic future of their own best insights. In this way they also insist on remaining rooted in real historical communities and traditions. They do not want to float in a rootless world of fantasy.

At the same time, these Jewish and Christian feminists are open to new possibilities, generated from new religious experience, which may derive from an imaginative recapturing either of repressed options of human religious history or even of options that never really were but were only hinted at in early human beginnings. It is these options of primary religious imagination that are being explored particularly by neo-pagan women.

Perhaps what is in the process of being born through this dialectic is a feminist re-synthesis of the various layers of the religious tradition itself, finding a new point of integration between

1 religion based on mimetic experiencing of the rhythms of nature;
2 religion shaped by historical responsibility and the striving for obedience to law, in order to create a just society, and
3 religion shaped by ecstatic encounter with redemption from historical ambiguity and a proleptic entrance into the blessedness of harmonious integration of human history and nature.

One of the barriers to positive encounter between these various approaches to religion lies in the biblical concept of historical revelation, which suggests that Judaism rises above and supersedes paganism. Christianity took this over and saw itself as rising above and superseding both Judaism and paganism. The new religious perspective situates itself against the old as superior to inferior, truth to falsehood, authentic knowledge of the divine against idolatry. Neo-paganism perhaps has a reversed version of this pattern when it sees itself as representing an original good state of humanity and its harmony with nature, over against Judaism and Christianity, which are seen as expressions of a fall into alienation and patriarchal oppression, a variant of the Paradise–Fall myth of Christianity.

There may be elements of truth in both these myths of historical relationship, the first seeing the gains in the new religious point of view and the second seeing the losses. I believe that there were indeed both gains and losses in this history of shifts of religious perspective. While historical faith gains a new sense of human autonomy and ethical responsibility, it also tends to lose a sense of respect for our integration into the cycles of nature and thus to set the stage for a destructive relationship between humans (ruling-class males) and dominated nature. For such faith, dominated nature tends to include women and dominated races and non-human nature.

Christianity, while moving to a new universalism and an anticipation of the eschatological, lost respect for the particularities of people and place and fell into an ahistorical spiritualism that negated the need for social ethics as part of the redemptive task. I see this dialogue between Judaeo-Christian traditions and neo-pagan religion as a new opportunity to get beyond these classical ways of setting religious options against each other as truth and falsehood, anticipation and fulfillment. It is an opportunity to recapitulate this whole historical journey and to seek a new dynamic integration of the cyclical, the historical, and the eschatological.

As feminist theology finds itself on the boundary, facing both towards a reinterpretation of past historical tradition and also forward to the creation of new possibilities, it will find itself already involved in a dynamic re-synthesis of this journey. This seems to me evident in the spontaneous interaction of these three dimensions of our religious tradition. It remains, however, for us to become more consciously reflective and theological about this process. There needs to be more reflective analysis of what it is we are doing in this project and of how we can become genuinely accountable to the past, to each other as women and also as men and women, and to a just and sustainable future for all of earth's beings.

NOTES

1 See Judith Ochshorn, *The Female Experience and the Nature of the Divine* (Bloomington, Ind.: Indiana University Press, 1981).
2 Judith Plaskow, 'The coming of Lilith: toward a feminist theology', in *Womanspirit Rising*, Plaskow and Christ (eds), (NY: Harper & Row, 1989), pp. 198–209.
3 *Gyn/Ecology: The Metaethics of Radical Feminism* (Boston, Mass.: Beacon Press, 1979).
4 Starhawk, *The Spiral Dance: Re-birth of the Ancient Religion of the Goddess* (NY: Harper & Row, 1979).
5 The point is not to set history against myth, but to analyse these as different ways of relating to primal paradigms.
6 *Mother Wit: A Feminist Guide to Psychic Development* (Trumansburg, NY: Crossing Press, 1981).

WHY WOMEN NEED THE GODDESS
Phenomenological, psychological, and political reflections

Carol P. Christ

At the close of Ntosake Shange's stupendously successful Broadway play
'For Colored Girls Who Have Considered Suicide When the Rainbow Is
Enuf', a tall beautiful black woman rises from despair to cry out, 'I
found God in myself and I loved her fiercely'.[1] Her discovery is echoed
by women around the country who meet spontaneously in small groups
on full moons, solstices, and equinoxes to celebrate the Goddess as
symbol of life and death powers and waxing and waning energies in the
universe and in themselves.[2]

> It is the night of the full moon. Nine women stand in a circle, on a
> rocky hill above the city. The western sky is rosy with the setting sun;
> in the east the moon's face begins to peer above the horizon. . . . The
> woman pours out a cup of wine onto the earth, refills it and raises it
> high. 'Hail, Tana, Mother of mothers!' she cries. 'Awaken from your
> long sleep, and return to your children again!'[3]

What are the political and psychological effects of this fierce new love
of the divine in themselves for women whose spiritual experience has
been focused by the male God of Judaism and Christianity? Is the
spiritual dimension of feminism a passing diversion, an escape from
difficult but necessary political work? Or does the emergence of the
symbol of Goddess among women have significant political and psychological ramifications for the feminist movement?

To answer this question, we must first understand the importance of
religious symbols and rituals in human life and consider the effect of
male symbolism of God on women. According to anthropologist Clifford
Geertz, religious symbols shape a cultural ethos, defining the deepest
values of a society and the persons in it. 'Religion,' Geertz writes, 'is a
system of symbols which act to produce powerful, pervasive, and long-
lasting moods and motivations'[4] in the people of a given culture. A
'mood' for Geertz is a psychological attitude such as awe, trust, and
respect, while a 'motivation' is the *social* and *political* trajectory created
by a mood that transforms mythos into ethos, symbol system into social
and political reality. Symbols have both psychological and political

290

effects, because they create the inner conditions (deep-seated attitudes and feelings) that lead people to feel comfortable with or to accept social and political arrangements that correspond to the symbol system.

Because religion has such a compelling hold on the deep psyches of so many people, feminists cannot afford to leave it in the hands of the fathers. Even people who no longer 'believe in God' or participate in the institutional structure of patriarchal religion still may not be free of the power of the symbolism of God the Father. A symbol's effect does not depend on rational assent, for a symbol also functions on levels of the psyche other than the rational. Religion fulfils deep psychic needs by providing symbols and rituals that enable people to cope with limit situations[5] in human life (death, evil, suffering) and to pass through life's important transitions (birth, sexuality, death). Even people who consider themselves completely secularized will often find themselves sitting in a church or synagogue when a friend or relative gets married, or when a parent or friend has died. The symbols associated with these important rituals cannot fail to affect the deep or unconscious structures of the mind of even a person who has rejected these symbolisms on a conscious level – especially if the person is under stress. The reason for the continuing effect of religious symbols is that the mind abhors a vacuum. Symbol systems cannot simply be rejected, they must be replaced. Where there is not any replacement, the mind will revert to familiar structures at times of crisis, bafflement, or defeat.

Religions centred on the worship of a male god create 'moods' and 'motivations' that keep women in a state of psychological dependence on men and male authority, while at the same legitimating the *political* and *social* authority of fathers and sons in the institutions of society.

Religious symbol systems focused around exclusively male images of divinity create the impression that female power can never be fully legitimate or wholly beneficent. This message need never be explicitly stated (as, for example, it is in the story of Eve) for its effect to be felt. A woman completely ignorant of the myths of female evil in biblical religion none the less acknowledges the anomaly of female power when she prays exclusively to a male God. She may see herself as like God (created in the image of God) only by denying her own sexual identity and affirming God's transcendence of sexual identity. But she can never have the experience that is freely available to every man and boy in her culture, of having her full sexual identity affirmed as being in the image and likeness of God. In Geertz's terms, her 'mood' is one of trust in male power as salvific and distrust of female power in herself and other women as inferior or dangerous. Such a powerful, pervasive, and long-lasting 'mood' cannot fail to become a 'motivation' that translates into social and political reality.

In *Beyond God the Father*, feminist theologian Mary Daly detailed the psychological and political ramifications of father religion for women. 'If God in "his" heaven is a father ruling his people,' she wrote,

then it is the 'nature' of things and according to divine plan and the order of the universe that society be male dominated. Within this context, *a mystification of roles* takes place: The husband dominating his wife represents God 'himself'. The images and values of a given society have been projected into the realm of dogmas and 'Articles of Faith', and these in turn justify the social structures which have given rise to them and which sustain their plausibility.[6]

Philosopher Simone de Beauvoir was well aware of the function of patriarchal religion as a legitimater of male power. As she wrote,

Man enjoys the great advantage of having a god endorse the code he writes; and since man exercises a sovereign authority over women it is especially fortunate that this authority has been vested in him by the Supreme Being. For the Jew, Mohammedans, and Christians, among others, man is Master by divine right; the fear of God will therefore repress any impulse to revolt in the downtrodden female.[7]

This brief discussion of the psychological and political effects of God religion puts us in an excellent position to begin to understand the significance of the symbol of Goddess for women. In discussing the meaning of the Goddess, my method will first be phenomenological. I will isolate a meaning of the symbol of the Goddess as it has emerged in the lives of contemporary women. I will then discuss its psychological and political significance by contrasting the 'moods' and 'motivations' engendered by Goddess symbols with those engendered by Christian symbolism. I will also correlate Goddess symbolism with themes that have emerged in the women's movement, in order to show how Goddess symbolism undergirds and legitimates the concerns of the women's movement, much as God symbolism in Christianity undergirded the interests of men in patriarchy. I will discuss four aspects of Goddess symbolism here: the Goddess as affirmation of female power, the female body, the female will, and women's bonds and heritage. There are, of course, many other meanings of the Goddess that I will not discuss here.

The sources for the symbol of the Goddess in contemporary spirituality are traditions of Goddess worship and modern women's experience. The ancient Mediterranean, pre-Christian European, native American, Mesoamerican, Hindu, African, and other traditions are rich sources for Goddess symbolism. But these traditions are filtered through modern women's experiences. Traditions of Goddesses, subordination to Gods, for example, are ignored. Ancient traditions are tapped selectively and eclecticly, but they are not considered authoritative for modern consciousness. The Goddess symbol has emerged spontaneously in the

292

dreams, fantasies, and thoughts of many women around the country in the past several years. Kirsten Grimstad and Susan Rennie reported that they were surprised to discover widespread interest in spirituality, including the Goddess, among feminists around the country in the summer of 1974.[8] *WomanSpirit* magazine, which published its first issue in 1974 and has contributors from across the United States, has expressed the grass roots nature of the women's spirituality movement. In 1976, a journal, *Lady Unique*, devoted to the Goddess emerged. In 1975, the first women's spirituality conference was held in Boston and attended by 1,800 women. In 1978, a University of Santa Cruz course on the Goddess drew over 500 people. Sources for this essay are these manifestations of the Goddess in modern women's experiences as reported in *WomanSpirit*, *Lady Unique*, and elsewhere, and as expressed in conversations I have had with women who have been thinking about the Goddess and women's spirituality.

The simplest and most basic meaning of the symbol of Goddess is the acknowledgement of the legitimacy of female power as a beneficent and independent power. A woman who echoes Ntosake Shange's dramatic statement, 'I found God in myself and I loved her fiercely', is saying 'Female power is strong and creative'. She is saying that the divine principle, the saving and sustaining power, is in herself, that she will no longer look to men or male figures as saviours. The strength and independence of female power can be intuited by contemplating ancient and modern images of the Goddess. This meaning of the symbol of Goddess is simple and obvious, and yet it is difficult for many to comprehend. It stands in sharp contrast to the paradigms of female dependence on males that have been predominant in western religion and culture. The internationally acclaimed novelist Monique Wittig captured the novelty and flavour of the affirmation of female power when she wrote, in her mythic work *Les Guerillères*,

> There was a time when you were not a slave, remember that. You walked alone, full of laughter, you bathed bare-bellied. You say you have lost all recollection of it, remember . . . you say there are no words to describe it, you say it does not exist. But remember. Make an effort to remember. Or, failing that, invent.[9]

While Wittig does not speak directly of the Goddess here, she captures the 'mood' of joyous celebration of female freedom and independence that is created in women who define their identities through the symbol of Goddess. Artist Mary Beth Edelson expressed the political 'motivations' inspired by the Goddess when she wrote,

> The ascending archetypal symbols of the feminine unfold today in the psyche of modern Every woman. They encompass the multiple forms

of the Great Goddess. Reaching across the centuries we take the hands of our Ancient Sisters. The Great Goddess alive and well is rising to announce to the patriarchs that their 5,000 years are up – Hallelujah! Here we come.[10]

The affirmation of female power contained in the Goddess symbol has both psychological and political consequences. Psychologically, it means the defeat of the view engendered by patriarchy that women's power is inferior and dangerous. This new 'mood' of affirmation of female power also leads to new 'motivations'; it supports and undergirds women's trust in their own power and the power of other women in family and society.

If the simplest meaning of the Goddess symbol is an affirmation of the legitimacy and beneficence of female power, then a question immediately arises, 'Is the Goddess simply female power writ large, and if so, why bother with the symbol of Goddess at all? Or does the symbol refer to a Goddess "out there" who is not reducible to a human potential?' The many women who have rediscovered the power of Goddess would give three answers to this question:

1 The Goddess is divine female, a personification who can be invoked in prayer and ritual;
2 the Goddess is symbol of the life, death, and rebirth energy in nature and culture, in personal and communal life; and
3 the Goddess is symbol of the affirmation of the legitimacy and beauty of female power (made possible by the new becoming of women in the women's liberation movement).

If one were to ask these women which answer is the 'correct' one, different responses would be given. Some would assert that the Goddess definitely is *not* 'out there', that the symbol of a divinity 'out there' is part of the legacy of patriarchal oppression, which brings with it the authoritarianism, hierarchicalism, and dogmatic rigidity associated with biblical monotheistic religions. They might assert that the Goddess symbol reflects the sacred power within women and nature, suggesting the connectedness between women's cycles of menstruation, birth, and menopause, and the life and death cycles of the universe. Others seem quite comfortable with the notion of Goddess as a divine female protector and creator and would find their experience of Goddess limited by the assertion that she is not *also* out there as well as within themselves and in all natural processes. When asked what the symbol of Goddess means, feminist priestess Starhawk replied, 'It all depends on how I feel. When I feel weak, she is someone who can help and protect me. When I feel strong, she is the symbol of my own power. At other times I feel her as the natural energy in my body and the world.'[11] How are we to evaluate such a statement? Theologians might call these the words of a sloppy thinker. But my deepest intuition tells me they contain a wisdom that western theological thought has lost.

To theologians, these differing views of the 'meaning' of the symbol of Goddess might seem to threaten a replay of the trinitarian controversies. Is there, perhaps, a way of doing theology, which would not lead immediately into dogmatic controversy, which would not require theologians to say definitively that one understanding is true and the others are false? Could people's relation to a common symbol be made primary and varying interpretations be acknowledged? The diversity of explications of the meaning of the Goddess symbol suggests that symbols have a richer significance than any explications of their meaning can express, a point literary critics have long insisted on. This phenomenological fact suggests that theologians may need to give more than lip service to a theory of symbol in which the symbol is viewed as the primary fact and the meanings are viewed as secondary. It also suggests that a *thea*logy[12] of the Goddess would be very different from the *theo*logy we have known in the west. But to spell out this notion of the primacy of *symbol* in thealogy in contrast to the primacy of the *explanation* in theology would be the topic of another paper. Let me simply state that women, who have been deprived of a female religious symbol system for centuries, are therefore in an excellent position to recognize the power and primacy of symbols. I believe women must develop a theory of symbol and thealogy congruent with their experience at the same time as they 'remember and invent' new symbol systems.

A second important implication of the Goddess symbol for women is the affirmation of the female body and the life cycle expressed in it. Because of women's unique position as menstruants, birthgivers, and those who have traditionally cared for the young and the dying, women's connection to the body, nature, and this world has been obvious. Women were denigrated because they seemed more carnal, fleshy, and earthy than the culture-creating males.[13] The misogynist anti*body* tradition in western thought is symbolized in the myth of Eve who is traditionally viewed as a sexual temptress, the epitome of women's carnal nature. This tradition reaches its nadir in the *Malleus Maleficarum (The Hammer of Evil-Doing Women)*, which states, 'All witchcraft stems from carnal lust, which in women is insatiable'.[14] The Virgin Mary, the positive female image in Christianity, does not contradict Christian denigration of the female body and its powers. The Virgin Mary is revered because she, in her perpetual virginity, transcends the carnal sexuality attributed to most women.

The denigration of the female body is expressed in cultural and religious taboos surrounding menstruation, childbirth, and menopause in women. While menstruation taboos may have originated in a perception of the awesome powers of the female body,[15] they degenerated into a simple perception that there is something 'wrong' with female bodily functions. Menstruating women were forbidden to enter the sanctuary in ancient Hebrew and pre-modern Christian communities. Although only Orthodox Jews still enforce religious taboos against menstruant women, few women in our culture grow up affirming their menstruation as a connection to sacred power. Most women learn that menstruation is a curse and grow up believing that the bloody facts of menstruation are best hidden away. Feminists challenge this attitude to the female body. Judy Chicago's art piece 'Menstruation Bathroom' broke these menstrual taboos. In a sterile white bathroom, she exhibited boxes of *Tampax* and *Kotex* on an open shelf, and the wastepaper basket was overflowing with bloody tampons and sanitary napkins.[16] Many women who viewed the piece felt relieved to have their 'dirty secret' out in the open.

The denigration of the female body and its powers is further expressed in western culture's attitudes towards childbirth.[17] Religious iconography does not celebrate the birthgiver and there is no theology or ritual that enables a woman to celebrate the process of birth as a spiritual experience. Indeed, Jewish and Christian traditions also had blood taboos concerning the woman who had recently given birth. While these religious taboos are rarely enforced today (again, only by Orthodox Jews), they have secular equivalents. Giving birth is treated as a disease requiring hospitalization, and the woman is viewed as a passive object, anaesthetized to ensure her acquiescence to the will of the doctor. The women's liberation movement has challenged these cultural attitudes, and many feminists have joined with advocates of natural childbirth and home birth in emphasizing the need for women to control and take pride in their bodies, including the birth process.

Western culture also gives little dignity to the postmenopausal or ageing woman. It is no secret that our culture is based on a denial of ageing and death, and that women suffer more severely from this denial than men. Women are placed on a pedestal and considered powerful when they are young and beautiful, but they are said to lose this power as they age. As feminists have pointed out, the 'power' of the young woman is illusory, since beauty standards are defined by men, and since few women are considered (or consider themselves) beautiful for more than a few years of their lives. Some men are viewed as wise and authoritative in age, but old women are pitied and shunned. Religious iconography supports this cultural attitude towards ageing women. The purity and virginity of Mary and the female saints is often expressed in the iconographic convention of perpetual youth. Moreover, religious mythology associates ageing women with evil in the symbol of the wicked old witch. Feminists have challenged cultural myths of ageing women and have urged women to reject patriarchal beauty standards and to celebrate the distinctive beauty of women of all ages.

The symbol of Goddess aids the process of naming and reclaiming the female body and its cycles and processes. In the ancient world and among modern women, the Goddess symbol represents the birth, death, and rebirth processes of the natural and human worlds. The female body is viewed as the direct incarnation of waxing and waning, life and death, cycles in the universe. This is sometimes expressed through the symbolic connection between the twenty-eight-day cycles of menstruation and the twenty-eight-day cycles of the moon. Moreover, the Goddess is celebrated in the triple aspect of youth, maturity, and age, or maiden, mother, and crone. The potentiality of the young girl is celebrated in the nymph or maiden aspect of the Goddess. The Goddess as mother is sometimes depicted as giving birth, and giving birth is a symbol for all the creative, life-giving powers of the universe.[18] The life-giving powers of the Goddess in her creative aspect are not limited to physical birth, for the Goddess is also seen as the creator of all the arts of civilization, including healing, writing, and the giving of just law. Women in the middle of life who are not physical mothers may give birth to poems, songs, and books, or nurture other women, men, and children. They too are incarnations of the Goddess in her creative, life-giving aspect. At the end of life, women incarnate the crone aspect of the Goddess. The wise old woman, the woman who knows from experience what life is about, the woman whose closeness to her own death gives her a distance and perspective on the problems of life, is celebrated as the third aspect of the Goddess. Thus, women learn to value youth, creativity, and wisdom in themselves and other women.

The possibilities of reclaiming the female body and its cycles have been expressed in a number of Goddess-centred rituals. Hallie Mountainwing and Barby My Own created a summer solstice ritual to celebrate menstruation and birth. The women simulated a birth canal and birthed each other into their circle. They raised power by placing their hands on each other's bellies and chanting together. Finally they marked each other's faces with rich, dark, menstrual blood saying, 'This is the blood that promises renewal. This is the blood that promises sustenance. This is the blood that promises life.'[19] From hidden dirty secret to symbol of the life power of the Goddess, women's blood has come full circle. Other women have created rituals that celebrate the crone aspect of the Goddess. Z. Budapest believes that the crone aspect of the Goddess is predominant in the autumn, especially at Halloween, an ancient holiday. On this day, the wisdom of the old woman is celebrated, and it is also recognized that the old must die so that the new can be born.

The 'mood' created by the symbol of the Goddess in triple aspect is one of positive, joyful affirmation of the female body and its cycles and acceptance of ageing and death as well as life. The 'motivations' are to overcome menstrual taboos, to return the birth process to the hands of women, and to change cultural attitudes about age and death. Changing cultural attitudes towards the female body could go a long way towards overcoming the spirit–flesh, mind–body dualisms of western culture, since, as Ruether has pointed out, the denigration of the female body is at the heart of these dualisms. The Goddess as symbol of the revaluation of the body and nature thus also undergirds the human potential and ecology movements. The 'mood' is one of affirmation, awe, and respect for the body and nature, and the 'motivation' is to respect the teachings of the body and the rights of all living beings.

A third important implication of the Goddess symbol for women is the positive valuation of will in a Goddess-centred ritual, especially in Goddess-centred ritual magic and spell-casting in womenspirit and feminist witchcraft circles. The basic notion behind ritual magic and spell-casting is energy as power. Here the Goddess is a centre or focus of power and energy; she is the personification of the energy that flows between beings in the natural and human worlds. In Goddess circles, energy is raised by chanting or dancing. According to Starhawk,

> Witches conceive of psychic energy as having form and substance that can be perceived and directed by those with a trained awareness. The power generated within the circle is built into a cone form, and at its peak is released – to the Goddess, to re-energize the members of the coven, or to do a specific work such as healing.[20]

In ritual magic, the energy raised is directed by will power. Women who celebrate in Goddess circles believe they can achieve their wills in the world.

The emphasis on the will is important for women, because women traditionally have been taught to devalue their wills, to believe that they cannot achieve their will through their own power, and even to suspect that the assertion of will is evil. Faith Wildung's poem 'Waiting', from which I will quote only a short segment, sums up women's sense that their lives are defined not by their own will, but by waiting for others to take the initiative.

> Waiting for my breasts to develop
> Waiting to wear a bra
> Waiting to menstruate
>
> Waiting for life to begin, Waiting –
> Waiting to be somebody
>
> Waiting to get married
> Waiting for my wedding day
> Waiting for my wedding night
>
> Waiting for the end of the day
> Waiting for sleep. Waiting . . . [21]

Patriarchal religion has enforced the view that female initiative and will are evil through the juxtaposition of Eve and Mary. Eve caused the fall by asserting her will against the command of God, while Mary began the new age with her response to God's initiative, 'Let it be done to me according to thy word' (Luke 1:38). Even for men, patriarchal religion values the passive will subordinate to divine initiative. The classical doctrines of sin and grace view sin as the prideful assertion of will and grace as the obedient subordination of the human will to the divine initiative or order. While this view of will might be questioned from a human perspective, Valerie Saiving has argued that it has particularly deleterious consequences for women in western culture. According to Saiving, western culture encourages males in the assertion of will, and thus it may make some sense to view the male form of sin as an excess of will. But since culture discourages females in the assertion of will, the traditional doctrines of sin and grace encourage women to remain in their form of sin, which is self-negation or insufficient assertion of will.[22] One possible reason the will is denigrated in a patriarchal religious framework is that both human and divine will are often pictured as arbitrary, self-initiated, and exercised without regard for other wills.

In a Goddess-centred context, in contrast, the will is valued. *A woman is encouraged to know her will, to believe that her will is valid, and to believe that her will can be achieved in the world*, three powers traditionally denied to her in patriarchy. In a Goddess-centred framework, a woman's will is not subordinated to the Lord God as king and ruler, nor to men as his representatives. Thus a woman is not reduced to waiting and acquiescing in the wills of others as she is in patriarchy. But neither does she adopt the egocentric form of will that pursues self-interest without regard for the interests of others.

The Goddess-centred context provides a different understanding of the will than that available in the traditional patriarchal religious framework. In the Goddess framework, will can be achieved only when it is exercised in harmony with the energies and wills of other beings. Wise women, for example, raise a cone of healing energy at the full moon or solstice when the lunar or solar energies are at their high points with respect to the earth. This discipline encourages them to recognize that not all times are propitious for the achieving of every will. Similarly, they know that spring is a time for new beginnings in work and love, summer a time for producing external manifestations of inner potentialities, and fall or winter times for stripping down to the inner core and extending roots. Such awareness of waxing and waning processes in the universe discourages arbitrary ego-centred assertion of will, while at the same time encouraging the assertion of individual will in co-operation with natural energies and the energies created by the wills of others. Wise women also have a tradition that whatever is sent out will be returned and this reminds them to assert their wills in co-operative and healing rather than egocentric and destructive ways. This view of will allows women to begin to recognize, claim, and assert their wills without adopting the worst characteristics of the patriarchal understanding and use of will. In the Goddess-centred framework, the 'mood' is one of positive affirmation of personal will in the context of the energies of other wills or beings. The 'motivation' is for women to know and assert their wills in co-operation with other wills and energies. This, of course, does not mean that women always assert their wills in positive and life-affirming ways. Women's capacity for evil is, of course, as great as men's. My purpose is simply to contrast the differing attitudes towards the exercise of will *per se*, and the female will in particular, in Goddess-centred religion and in the Christian God-centred religion.

The fourth and final aspect of Goddess symbolism that I will discuss here is the significance of the Goddess for a revaluation of woman's bonds and heritage. As Virginia Woolf has said, 'Chloe liked Olivia', a statement about a woman's relation to another woman, is a sentence that rarely occurs in fiction. Men have written the stories, and they have written about women almost exclusively in their relations to men.[23] The celebrations of women's bonds to each other, as mothers and daughters, as colleagues and co-workers, as sisters, friends, and lovers, is beginning to occur in the new literature and culture created by women in the women's movement. While I believe that the revaluing of each of these bonds is important, I will focus on the mother–daughter bond, in part because I believe it may be the key to the others.

Adrienne Rich has pointed out that the mother–daughter bond, perhaps the most important of woman's bonds, 'resonant with charges . . . the flow of energy between two biologically alike bodies, one of which has lain in amniotic bliss inside the other, one of which has labored to give birth to the other',[24] is rarely celebrated in patriarchal religion and culture. Christianity celebrates the father's relation to the son and the mother's relation to the son, but the story of mother and daughter is missing. So, too, in patriarchal literature and psychology the mothers and the daughters rarely exist. Volumes have been written about the Oedipal complex, but little has been written about the girl's relation to her mother. Moreover, as de Beauvoir has noted, the mother–daughter relation is distorted in patriarchy because the mother must give her daughter over to men in a male-defined culture in which women are viewed as inferior. The mother must socialize her daughter to become subordinate to men, and if her daughter challenges patriarchal norms, the mother is likely to defend the patriarchal structures against her own daughter.[25]

These patterns are changing in the new culture created by women in which the bonds of women to women are beginning to be celebrated. Holly Near has written several songs that celebrate women's bonds and women's heritage. In one of her finest songs she writes of an 'old-time woman' who is 'waiting to die'. A young woman feels for the life that has passed the old woman by and begins to cry, but the old woman looks her in the eye and says, 'If I had not suffered, you wouldn't be wearing those jeans/Being an old-time woman ain't as bad as it seems.'[26] This song, which Near has said was inspired by her grandmother, expresses and celebrates a bond and a heritage passed down from one woman to another. In another of Near's songs, she sings of 'a hiking-boot mother who's seeing the world/For the first time with her own little girl.' In this song, the woman tells the drifter who has been travelling with her to pack up and travel alone if he thinks 'travelling three is a drag' because 'I've got a little one who loves me as much as you need me/And darling, that's loving enough.'[27] This song is significant because the mother places her relationship to her daughter above her relationship to a man, something women rarely do in patriarchy.[28]

Almost the only story of mothers and daughters that has been transmitted in Western culture is the myth of Demeter and Persephone, which was the basis of religious rites celebrated by women only, the Thesmophoria, and later formed the basis of the Eleusian mysteries, which were open to all who spoke Greek. In this story, the daughter, Persephone, is raped away from her mother, Demeter, by the God of the underworld. Unwilling to accept this state of affairs, Demeter rages and withholds fertility from the earth until her daughter is returned to her. What is important for women in this story is that a mother fights for her daughter and for her relation to her daughter. This is completely different from the mother's relation to her daughter in patriarchy. The 'mood' created by the story of Demeter and Persephone is one of celebration of the mother–daughter bond, and the 'motivation' is for mothers and daughters to affirm the heritage passed on from mother to daughter and to reject the patriarchal pattern where the primary loyalties of mother and daughter must be to men.

The symbol of Goddess has much to offer women who are struggling to be rid of the 'powerful, pervasive, and long-lasting moods and motivations' of devaluation of female power, denigration of the female body, distrust of female will, and denial of the women's bonds and heritage that have been engendered by patriarchal religion. As women struggle to create a new culture in which women's power, bodies, will, and bonds are celebrated, it seems natural that the Goddess would re-emerge as symbol of the new-found beauty, strength, and power of women.

NOTES

This essay, which was the keynote address at the University of California at Santa Cruz Extension conference 'The Great Goddess Re-emerging' in the spring of 1978, appeared in slightly different form in *Heresies*, Spring, 1978, and is reprinted with permission of *Heresies*.

1 From the original cast album, Buddah Records, 1976.
2 See Susan Rennie and Kristen Grimstad, 'Spiritual explorations cross-country', *Quest* I (4) (1975), pp. 49–51; and *WomanSpirit* magazine.
3 See Starhawk, 'Witchcraft and women's culture', in *Womanspirit Rising* (New York: Harper & Row, 1979).
4 'Religion as a cultural system', in William L. Lessa and Evon V. Vogt (eds), *Reader in Comparative Religion*, 2nd edn (New York: Harper & Row, 1972), p. 206.
5 Geertz, p. 210.
6 Boston, Mass.: Beacon Press, 1974, p. 13, italics added.
7 *The Second Sex*, trans. H.M. Parshleys (New York: Alfred A. Knopf, 1953).
8 See Grimstad and Rennie (1975).
9 *Les Guerillères*, trans. David LeVay (New York: Avon Books, 1971), p. 89. Also quoted in Morgan MacFarland, 'Witchcraft: the art of remembering', *Quest*, I (4) (1975), p. 41.
10 'Speaking for Myself', *Lady Unique*, I (1976), p. 56.
11 Personal communication.
12 A term coined by Naomi Goldenberg to refer to reflection on the meaning of the symbol of Goddess.
13 This theory of the origins of the western dualism is stated by Rosemary Ruether, in *New Woman: New Earth* (New York: Seabury Press, 1975), and elsewhere.
14 Heinrich Kramer and Jacob Sprenger (New York: Dover, 1971), p. 47.
15 See Rita M. Gross, 'Menstruation and childbirth as ritual and religious experience in the religion of the Australian Aborigines', in *The Journal of the American Academy of Religion*, 45 (4) (1977) Supplement, pp. 1147–81.
16 *Through the Flower* (New York: Doubleday & Company, 1975), plate 4, pp. 106–7.
17 See Adrienne Rich, *Of Woman Born* (New York: Bantam Books, 1977), chs. 6 and 7.
18 See James Mellaart, *Earliest Civilizations of the Near East* (New York: McGraw-Hill, 1965), p. 92.
19 Barby My Own, 'Ursa major: menstrual moon celebration', in Anne Kent Rush (ed.), *Moon, Moon* (Berkeley, Calif., and New York: Moon Books and Random House, 1976), pp. 374–87.
20 Starhawk, in *Womanspirit Rising* (New York: Harper & Row, 1979), pp. 259–68.
21 In Judy Chicago, pp. 213–17.
22 'The human situation: a feminine view', in *Journal of Religion*, 40 (1960), pp. 100–12.
23 *A Room of One's Own* (New York: Harcourt Brace Jovanovich, 1928), p. 86.
24 Rich, p. 226.
25 De Beauvoir, pp. 448–9.
26 'Old-time woman', lyrics by Jeffrey Langley and Holly Near, from *Holly Near: A Live Album*, Redwood Records, 1974.
27 'Started out fine', by Holly Near from *Holly Near: A Live Album*.
28 Rich, p. 223.

Part IX
RADICAL FEMINISM

INTRODUCTION

Robyn Rowland and Renate D. Klein

When we wrote the chapter on radical feminism for the companion volume to this book, *Feminist Knowledge: Critique and Construct*, we found a richness in the radical feminist analysis of women's experience of patriarchy and in the development of theory which relates to the lived lives of women; a fearlessness in facing the terror of physical violence towards women; an unashamed love for women, individually and as a group; and a grappling with the difficult issues of difference and diversity among women.

We found radical feminism to be an extensive theory and summarized it in the following way: radical feminism contends that the oppression of women is the first and primary oppression. It is a woman-centred interdependent theory and practice, which takes its starting-point from women's lived experience, making the personal political. It maintains that men oppress women through patriarchy, a system of structures, institutions, and ideology created by men in order to sustain and recreate male power and female subordination.

While recognizing and accepting differences between women, radical feminism holds the oppression of women to be universal, crossing race and class boundaries, so that 'sisterhood' becomes an empowering concept. It does not neglect these differences, but incorporates them as important in defining the nature of women's oppression as women.

Radical feminism has focused on male power at significant sites for women. It has stressed women's control of our bodies as crucial to liberation, giving rise to analysis and action within the women's health movement, in the naming and analysis of violence against women, and in an analysis of sexuality and the imposition of heterosexuality as an institution. The family has been seen as tying women to compulsory heterosexuality, economic dependence, and a patriarchal ideology of motherhood which is alienating and self-destroying.

Radical feminism has also stressed the importance of creating and sustaining women's culture in its various forms, as a political act. And it emphasizes women's resistance to patriarchy currently and historically.

We were initially asked to select readings for this volume which were difficult to obtain in print and which would represent aspects of radical feminism. We have found this a difficult task because of the breadth of work available. So we have chosen some historical documents that capture the passion and commitment of the beginning of the most recent wave of radical feminism, and some pieces that encapsulate dilemmas or represent values within radical feminism. Of necessity, we have had to leave out some of the better-known writers and activists whose work is readily available.

The authors are English, American, and Australian, following the selection of material we used to write the book chapter. The pieces do not cover all the concerns of radical feminism, neglecting here important issues such as race, motherhood, the family, women's health, and women's creativity.

Feminist Practice. Notes from the Tenth Year is a booklet that is difficult to obtain now, so we have selected some pages from this in order to show radical feminists grappling with issues of socialism and class, and reinforcing the political nature of radical feminist theory and practice. The introductory paper 'We are the feminists that women have warned us about' expresses what these English women saw as the basic principles of women's liberation from a radical feminist perspective. These political values are still firmly in place within the platform of radical feminism over ten years later. It is interesting that it concludes with a determination 'to enjoy ourselves while we do it', because humour, laughter, dance, and song have always been a part of radical feminism. The enjoyment of women together is essential in building a life that can deal with the atrocities of patriarchal violence, still *live* in the world, love, and go on resisting.

An Australian, Susan Hawthorne, writes 'In defence of separatism'. This is an extract from an Honours thesis, written in 1976, and develops the rationale for separatism. More importantly, it differentiates between separatism and segregation, an important delineation, pointing out the empowering qualities of separatism and its various representations. Her delineation of the varieties of separatism which feminism encompasses is very important in that it does not define it as exclusivity.

Charlotte Bunch, an American radical feminist has made an important contribution to radical feminism and it is difficult to select from her writings. Her recent book *Passionate Politics, Essays 1968–1986. Feminist Theory in Action* (New York: St Martin's Press, 1987) shows the range of her work. This early piece of hers selected here, 'Not for lesbians only', is contained within another classical radical feminist book, *Building Feminist Theory. Essays from Quest* (New York and London: Longman). Given initially as a speech in 1975, it discusses the important process of a development of The Furies, a radical feminist collective, and Bunch's own development into lesbianism. It contains her important contribution to an analysis of heterosexuality. But it also shows the radical feminist grappling with class analysis and the way class is seen to be an integral element within patriarchy.

We wanted to reprint some pieces from the landmark volume *Radical Feminism* edited by Ann Koedt, Ellen Levine, and Anita Rapone (New York: Quadrangle, 1973) because this book is virtually unobtainable now. Yet it is a classic text, which represents very clearly the expansive nature of radical feminist thought in the period of the late 1960s and early 1970s. The book begins by tracing historically the tradition of radical feminism, and covers issues of sexual independence, violence, housework, marriage and the family, lesbianism, consciousness-raising, and political action, and the creative analysis by radical feminism of literature. 'The myth of the vaginal orgasm' by Ann Koedt is an exemplary piece of radical feminist work from that period, attacking the dogma of Freud and encouraging women to seek their own definitions of sexual pleasure. It still seems surprisingly and refreshingly relevant today. It is too easy to forget the chains of inherited, repressed, and anti-women sexuality which formed the consciousness of the 1960s, and how difficult and radical it was publicly and privately to break these chains.

Mary Daly's work could not be given adequate coverage in our chapter on radical feminism, yet within the movement she has been a guiding theoretician, attacking the language of patriarchy, documenting man's violence towards women, and spinning a new way of Being for women with authentic Self. In this early piece, 'The spiritual dimension of women's liberation', she attacks the phallocentric nature of Christianity and its institutionalized oppression of women. She outlines what is very important to radical feminists, but often neglected by their critics: the sense of spiritual connection with the Self and other women, which situates radical feminism within a value system predicated on feeling and spirit and the relationship of sisterhood – not a false 'brotherhood'.

Janice Raymond's work on friendship between women, exemplified in her book *A Passion for Friends. Toward a Philosophy of Female Affection* (Boston, Mass.: Beacon Press, 1986), has been important in reclaiming the history of women's relationships with other women; in renaming the bonds that women have been told are 'unnatural' and do not exist; and in analysing the way patriarchy attempts to break these bonds and negate them. This article, 'The visionary task: two sights-seeing', is an excellent summary of her thesis and a search for true connection between women, not a false sentimentality. She explains her development of the term Gyn/affection, her rejection of the vision of women as victims, and the hope that a renewed valuing of affection among women will continue its place in the long history of women's resistance to patriarchy.

It is appropriate, we feel, that the readings finish with one that stresses the interrelationship of theory and practice, love, friendship, and women's united resistance.

WE ARE THE FEMINISTS THAT WOMEN HAVE WARNED US ABOUT*

Jessica York, Diana Leonard, Corine Liensol, Gail Chester, Jane Warrick, Amanda Sebestyen, Rob Henderson, and Reema Pachachi

It used to be that no self-respecting women's liberation group could organize or write anything without introducing itself, so that other women could identify the women involved and have a better way of locating and judging what they were saying. But lately this has gone out of fashion. . . .

However, we do want to start by saying something about ourselves: who we are, how we came together, what we've been discussing together and would like to discuss with a wider group, and, finally, where we hope to be going. We know, of course, that what we select to say about ourselves and our political position is only a partial picture, but we hope it's an honest start.

The group that produced these papers for a day workshop at the White Lion Free School, London, in April 1979, started after the National WL conference in Birmingham in 1978, out of a sense of desperation at feeling that none of the most evident and vocal factions at the plenary represented the politics of very many women in Women's Liberation.

Our first occasional meetings were of a slightly changing group of friends who wanted to sort out afresh what was positive about our politics and to be supportive of each other. It was a period when some of us who were very committed to the movement and had been active in it for a long time were feeling in need of reassurance that there was some point in going on.

Gradually the group developed, with the addition of some women we hadn't known before but who were interested in what was being said, and a few of the original participants dropping out. Our main concern has been with discussing what is happening in the movement and trying to analyse together the strengths and weaknesses of the changes we can see. We are all agreed that we would call ourselves radical feminists and that we want to do something about the fact that we feel our politics have been lost, have become invisible, in the present state of the WLM.

We feel that this was partly radical feminism's own fault, for in England we have not written much for ourselves, concentrating on action, and so been defined (maligned?) by others by default.

We feel that radical feminism has been *a*, if not *the*, major force in the WLM since the start, but as factions started to emerge it has rarely been women who called themselves radical feminists who have defined radical feminism. For a long time it was used as a term of abuse to corral those aspects of WL which frightened those concerned with male acceptability, those aspects which most threatened their image of respectability. Radical feminists became a corporate object of derision which these women and men could then dissociate themselves from. (Nowadays this mantle has fallen onto the Revolutionary Feminists and radical feminism is either hooked onto revolutionary feminism or ignored completely.)

Because of the fluid nature of our group, not everyone who remains involved felt able actively to contribute to organizing the day conference. But those of us who wrote papers and booked the venue felt that a day meeting was a way of beginning to reassert some of the important principles of WL which we feel are being ignored, glossed over, or seen as no longer necessary – with dire consequences.

Those of us responsible for the meeting – Jessica York, Diana Leonard, Corine Liensol, Gail Chester, Jane Warrick, Amanda Sebestyen, Rob Henderson, and Reema Pachachi – are from various backgrounds (classes, colours, and sexualities), have varying life styles (living alone, in groups, with and without children) and have been in the WLM from 10 months to 10 years. We are variously currently active in women's groups at work, in the Women's Research and Resources Centre and its publications group, in the Spare Rib Collective, the Reclaim the Night support group, Women Against Imperialism, the British Sociological Associations's women's caucus, feminist publishing, Women in Print, and a women's band. None of us are in a political party.

So what do we see as the basic principles of WL? And how do we see ourselves as differing from others? The latter is difficult, because no tendency in the WLM has *a* set, agreed, rigid line (there are no cadres) *and* lines change. (For instance, some of the papers produced for the recent socialist feminist conference – March 1979 – adopted what we see as radical feminist attitudes, many of which socialist feminists as a whole, and especially those in aligned left groups, were openly despising two years ago.)

Well, after discussion, here are some of the principles of WL from the earliest days which we still think very important:

309

– All women share a common oppression. The main difference between women and men (apart from genitals) is that women have a specific oppression in which men are the oppressors. Men do not share that oppression with women, rather they benefit from it.

– The Women's Liberation Movement has to be independent from men. A women's movement has to work out its own independent political strategy. There can be no men in the movement in any way.

– Only people who suffer from an oppression are able to talk about it: only they can describe the experience and only they can produce analyses which do not pull their punches.

– The 'personal is political' means that our different personal experiences have a link: the oppression of all women. In WL groups we pool our experiences to find their common roots in our common oppression. This process is called consciousness-raising. It is not to be confused with therapy, which aims to provide individual solutions to individual problems.

– Consciousness-raising cannot be outgrown; it must remain the basis of all our theory and practice.

– Small local CR groups, where women can create trust and solidarity, are the microcosm of the way we want to change society. Each woman must be assumed to be able to take responsibility.

– Our personal ambitions include changing the whole of our individual lives. No change is so trivial or so fundamental that it must wait till after The Revolution.

– But we also know that the political is not personal: there can be no one liberated woman. There is no 'liberated lifestyle' because: No woman is free until all of us are free.

– We have been divided so long, sisterly solidarity is important, especially in relation to men. This means always taking the woman's side, and not being dismissive of each other. It means recognizing that when women do things that maintain their oppression, we are not collaborating or being stupid, but just trying to get by as best we may in the given situation. (This is the 'pro-woman line'.)

– We reject hierarchy and the 'star' system. No one person or group can speak for the movement.

– Our principal concern in political action is not with changing laws but with agit-prop and grass-roots organizing. It is definitely not about getting other people to change things *for* us; it is about being strong enough through collective action to force changes to be made.

– Whatever we do we mean to enjoy ourselves while we do it.

NOTE

* This title refers back to a famous phrase by Robin Morgan 'We are the women that men have warned us about' in her paper of 1970 called 'Goodbye To All That . . .'

IN DEFENCE OF SEPARATISM

Susan Hawthorne

SEPARATISM

Separatism is a politically[1] motivated strategy for empowering women and undermining patriarchy. It varies in its manifestations within women's lives, and includes the following:

1 Valuing dialogue with other women, e.g. in consciousness-raising groups, study groups, or political action groups.
2 Engaging in political or social action with other women, e.g. abortion action groups, rape crisis groups, newsletter collectives.
3 Partaking in social gatherings in which only women participate, e.g. parties, women's dances. (Remember how women's dances challenged our ideas about what it was to have a good time – and that it was possible to do so without men around?)
4 Working in an environment which is run by and for women, e.g. women's health centres, women's publishing, unemployment centres for young women.
5 Becoming woman-identified, giving emotional support to women, and involving oneself in sexual relations with women (and moreover refusing to support men in any of the above ways), e.g. lesbianism or celibacy.
6 Participating in groups with other women that are concerned with women's creativity, e.g. theatre groups, writing workshops, art exhibitions, music groups.
7 Living in an all-women environment and having no contacts with any men. This is usually understood to be the standard separatist position. In fact, it is a fairly extreme position and only possible for a limited number of women. Those for whom it is most feasible are those who live in all-women communities in the country. Nevertheless many urban women do manage to limit their contacts with men sufficiently to enable them to live a strongly separatist lifestyle. Although it is not a position that all women will choose to engage in, it is important that feminists endorse it. The importance of separatist communities or households lies in the visible proof it gives to other women that women

do not need men for social, financial, and physical support.
8 Lesbian separatists may also choose not to have contact with heterosexual women in one or more of the above areas.

The forms of separatism listed above need not occur in this order, this
is not a hierarchical list whereby one can measure one's level of feminist
commitment. But it is important to recognize that separatism is a
strategy engaged in by every feminist. It is a fundamental element of all
feminist philosophy. The crucial factor in a separatist philosophy is that
women do not need men, and that this may be displayed in any or all
of the above ways. We, as women, can show that we are capable of
being self-sufficient, whether it be in the political, emotional, physical,
cultural, or spiritual sphere.

Separatism is also justifiable on the grounds that it challenges the
structures in this society which maintain women's oppression.

POWER

Separatism is an instance of women taking power into our own hands,
but it is sometimes confused with the oppressive tool, segregation.

The chief differences between the two is how they are used, and by
whom, and for what purposes. Segregation is used by the economically
dominant group as a means of control, i.e. to maintain and perpetuate
a given economic, political and social stratification system. Whereas
separatism is used by the economically disadvantaged in order to
radically alter existing political, social and economic arrangements.[2]

Segregation is an instance of coercive power, a manifestation of domination. Separatism is a means of fighting oppression, a withdrawal of
support or action, and potentially a strategy of liberation. Both are
powerful political devices. The distinction is in terms of who is initiating
the separation and for what purpose. From the point of view of the
oppressed, separatism is voluntary, segregation is involuntary. As Lucia
Valeska writes: 'It is differential treatment (legal and illegal) that created
the situation and it will, of necessity, be differential treatment that gets
us out of it'.[3] By living all or part of our lives separate from men we
are able to build up our strengths in an environment which is not
sexist,[4] and in which there is no systematic advantage or disadvantage
with regard to power, for any one group. I am not claiming that all-
women environments are always positive and supportive, but rather, that
the power relations are not institutionalized and inevitable, or at the
mercy of a man's 'good will'.

OPPRESSION

Identification with the oppressor can create the illusion of powerfulness. In order to break through this illusion it is necessary first to recognize our own value, and second, to come to value other women. This is more likely to occur if we operate in separatist structures.

As we experiment with the different degrees of separatism outlined above, we are able, at least potentially, to discard the internalized and oppressive male value system. For example, consciousness-raising groups enabled us to value both our own and other women's experiences of the world. This in turn has enabled many women to speak out publicly against the male value-system which does not take seriously the views of women on such matters as rape, wife-beating, and pornography.

The more extreme separatist position, whereby women decide to live in an environment where men never intrude, challenges many assumptions about women's dependency on men. Women prove that they do not need men in any aspect of their lives, and that they are capable of being self-sufficient. This is a radical departure from patriarchal thinking and is, I think, essential if we are to claim liberation for ourselves as a real possibility.

It has been argued that separatism is unrealistic and counter-productive to women's liberation on the grounds that the world is made up of both men and women (and in that order) and that if women are to be liberated, men too must be. Virginia Held, for instance, rejects separatism on the grounds that:

> If one seeks the transformation of society into a community of equals ... separatism is not ... an answer ... if women refuse to let themselves love men, they betray the goal of a society in which power is not the ultimate arbiter.[5]

The charge that separatism is counter-productive comes from those, like Held, who claim that men will change if women are nice to them; or from those who think that separatism causes divisiveness between women because non-separatist women will be alienated from feminism, and thus our effectiveness as a political movement will be decreased.

The former claim, made by Held, accompanies the suggestion that women should engage in 'experiments in love' with men, in order to quicken the actualization of love between women and men. And though she admits that such attempts may be costly to women, to attempt and fail is better than not attempting at all.

Despite this recommendation by Held, she does, nevertheless, recognize that in doing so 'women will have to accept a kind of schizophrenic existence'[6] in order to love and fight the oppressor simultaneously. She fails to see that by questioning romantic love between women and men, and by considering other modes of relating, this 'schizophrenic existence' could be avoided. Moreover as Sara Ann Ketchum and Christine Pierce state, men 'might work faster if women pulled out on them'.[7] The latter recommendation is politically and strategically more likely to be successful given the inequitable distribution of power at present.

The claim that separatism causes divisiveness between women is, I suggest, due to internalization of the oppressors' values. Internalization results in the oppressed denigrating any actions of their own that are not supported by the existing societal structures. It is unlikely that men or patriarchal institutions will support separatism. For instance, Mihailo Markovic calls it 'a specific form of sexism, a female chauvinism that consists in expressing resentment, hostility and even hatred for the opposite sex'.[8] He fails to notice the institutionalized misogyny of patriarchy which is manifested by men in such acts of hatred as wife-beating, rape, and pornography, not to mention foot-binding, clitoridec-tomy, and suttee.[9] Markovic goes on to say that 'every individual must be free to choose the most suitable form of her/his sexual life and at the same time must respect the freedom of others'.[10] Compulsory hetero-sexuality has successfully prevented women from having precisely that freedom of choice.[11] Some women will also refuse to support separatism. For instance, one collective of writers has expressed the view that:

> Separatism is not a political reality because women must eat and work and have shelter and they do have children. Furthermore it is inherently a romantic or idealistic red herring, because all women will never leave the system or stop relating to men . . .[12]

Women's liberation has always encouraged minimal separatism, which, however, is not as effective as more radical separatism since a lot of time and energy continues to be expended on supporting men, male values, and patriarchal institutions. However, I have not advocated complete separatism for all women, rather I suggest that feminists recognize the level of separatism in which they are prepared to engage. I am also recommending that most women, and all feminists, be consciously separatist in some aspect(s) of their lives that are relevant to the goals of women's liberation. No group seeking liberation ever has a primary commitment to the 'liberation' of the oppressor – their liberation is a consequence that follows if and only if the oppressed first liberate themselves. Women working together are better able to achieve these goals than if we work with the oppressor, since the 'liberation' of men from their dominance is not our responsibility.

315

DOMINATION

Separatism leads to a questioning of some fundamental aspects of our lives, including romantic love, heterosexuality, male domination, and ultimately patriarchy itself.

Separatism threatens those who accept these as valid or given, since it clearly challenges the reality of male domination. Separatists reject the structure of power inherent in patriarchal society. We reject not only the fact that it is in male hands, but also the formalized and hierarchical shape that that power has. It is in men's interests to maintain the present power structure, and due to the effects of domestication, internalization of male values, and identification with men, some women will continue to believe in the maintenance of these structures.

It is in our interests to change the balance of power and to change the shape of power in this society. That is, we are not satisfied with reforms that allow more women to become oppressive through entry into male power structures.

LESBIAN FEMINISM

Adrienne Rich writes:

Lesbian existence comprises both the breaking of a taboo and the rejection of a compulsory way of life. It is also a direct or indirect attack on male right of access to women. But it is more than these, although we may first begin to perceive it as a form of nay-saying to patriarchy, an act of resistance.[13]

And:

we can say that there is a nascent feminist political content in the act of choosing a woman lover or life partner in the face of institutionalized heterosexuality. But for lesbian existence to realize this political content in an ultimately liberating form, the erotic choice must depend and expand into conscious woman-identification – into lesbian/feminism.[14]

A lesbian feminist analysis challenges the institution of heterosexuality as a crucial support of patriarchy. It does so by challenging the validity of the heterosexual model. Proponents of the analysis recognize the importance of woman-identification and the potential that women have to act as a cohesive political group in changing the nature and structure of our society. By challenging the validity of the heterosexual model, lesbian feminists challenge the distribution of power and identify the institution of heterosexuality as oppressive. The recognition of woman-identification is central in repudiating the long-term effects of women's oppression.

316

Long-term effects of the institution of heterosexuality include the domination of our minds by a particular world-view: the one developed by men that prevents women from developing our own vision of what is possible. The result of this is a limited conception of how relationships function. The norm in heterosexual relationships is that they function in such a way as to benefit the male partner. Finally, the lesbian feminist analysis recognizes the importance of women as a force for political and social change.

Lesbian feminism and separatism meet at many points. As noted previously, however, there are degrees of separatism, and many lesbian feminists do, in fact, incorporate separatism into their daily lives. By rejecting heterosexuality we are excluding men from an important part of our lives. By excluding men we change the shape of relationships, since the distribution of power is not *systematically* weighted in favour of one party.

The outcome of such relationships is an increase in freedom, freedom to love, freedom to think thoughts that leap beyond the bounds of patriarchy, freedom to construct new futures, and freedom to dream. For as Susan Griffin writes: 'when one dreams of a new world, this world immediately becomes possible'.[16]

Separatism allows us to not only dream of new worlds, but also to experiment in incorporating them into our daily existence.

NOTES

1 The political basis of separatist strategies is extremely important, since without it tea parties, 'ladies auxiliaries', etc., would be included as separatist acts. These clearly do not play a part in the liberation of women.

2 Lucia Valeska, 'On the future of female separatism', *Quest*, Vol. 1, No. 1, p. 6.

3 ibid., p. 6.

4 Margaret Small, 'Lesbians and the class position of women', in Nancy Myron and Charlotte Bunch (eds), *Lesbianism and the Women's Movement* (Baltimore, Md: Diana Press, 1975), p. 58.

5 Virginia Held, 'Marx, sex, and the transformation of society', *The Philosophical Forum*, Vol. V, Nos 1-2 (1973-4), cited in Sara Anne Ketchum and Christine Pierce, 'Sex objects sexual partners and separatism', paper read at the August 1975 meeting on Philosophical Aspects of Feminism of the Annual Conference of the Australian National University Philosophy Society, Canberra, p. 11.

6 ibid., p. 176.

7 Ketchum and Pierce, op. cit. (1975), p. 15.

8 Mihailo Markovic, 'Women's liberation and human liberation', *Philosophical Forum*, Vol. V, Nos 1-2 (1973-4), p. 165.

9 See Mary Daly, *Gyn/Ecology: The Metaethics of Radical Feminism* (Boston, Mass.: Beacon Press, 1978).

10 Markovic, op. cit. (1973-4), p. 165.

11 See Adrienne Rich, *Compulsory Heterosexuality and Lesbian Existence* (London: Onlywomen Press, 1981).
12 Barb W., Zelda D., Joan R., and Anna C., 'Women's liberation: the problems and the potential' (Melbourne, 1976), p. 7.
13 Rich, op. cit. (1981), p. 21.
14 ibid., p. 31.
15 See Dale Spender, *Man Made Language* (London: Routledge and Kegan Paul, 1981), ch. 3; and Dale Spender, *Men's Studies Modified* (Oxford: The Athene Series, Pergamon Press, 1981).
16 Susan Griffin, *Rape: The Power of Consciousness* (New York: Harper and Row, 1979), p. 25.

NOT FOR LESBIANS ONLY

Charlotte Bunch

I am listed in your programme as Charlotte Bunch-Weeks, a rather ominous slip of the tongue (or slip in historical timing) that reflects a subject so far avoided at this conference that I, for one, want to talk about.

Five years ago, when I *was* Charlotte Bunch-Weeks, and straight, and married to a man, I was also a socialist feminist. When I left the man and the marriage, I also left the newly developing socialist feminist movement – because, for one reason, my politics then, as now, were inextricably joined with the way I lived my personal, my daily life. With men, with male politics, I was a socialist; with women, engaged in the articulation of women's politics, I became a lesbian feminist – and, in the gay–straight split, a lesbian feminist separatist.

It's that gay-straight split that no one here seems to want to remember – and I bring it up now, not because I want to relive a past painful to all concerned, but because it is an essential part of our political history which, if ignored, will eventually force lesbians to withdraw again from other political women. There were important political reasons for that split, reasons explicitly related to the survival of lesbians – and those reasons and the problems causing them are still with us. It is important – especially for political groups who wish to give credence and priority to lesbian issues – to remember why separatism happened, why it is not an historical relic but still vital to the ongoing debate over lesbianism and feminism.

In my personal experience, I, and the other women of The Furies collective, left the women's movement because it had been made clear to us that there was no space to develop a lesbian feminist politics and lifestyle without constant and non-productive conflict with heterosexual fear, antagonism, and insensitivity. This was essentially the same experience shared by many other lesbian feminists at about the same time around the country. What the women's movement could not accept then – and still finds it difficult to accept – is that lesbianism is political: this is the essence of lesbian feminist politics. Sounds simple. Yet most feminists still view lesbianism as a personal decision or, at best, as a civil rights concern or a cultural phenomenon. Lesbianism is more than a question of civil rights and culture, although the daily discrimination against lesbians is real and its alleviation through civil libertarian reforms is important. Similarly, although lesbianism is a primary force in the emergence of a dynamic women's culture, it is much more. Lesbian feminist politics is a political critique of the institution and ideology of heterosexuality as a cornerstone of male supremacy. It is an extension of the analysis of sexual politics to an analysis of sexuality itself as an institution. It is a commitment to women as a political group, which is the basis of a political/economic strategy leading to power for women, not just an 'alternative community'.

There are many lesbians still who feel that there is no place in socialist feminist organizations in particular, or the women's movement in general, for them to develop that politics or live that life. Because of this, I am still, in part, a separatist; but I don't want to be a total separatist again; few who have experienced that kind of isolation believe it is the ultimate goal of liberation. Since unity and coalition seem necessary, the question for me is unity on what terms, with whom, and around what politics? For instance, to unify the lesbian feminist politics developed within the past four years with socialist feminism requires more than token reference to queers. It requires an acknowledgement of lesbian feminist analysis as central to understanding and ending women's oppression.

The heart of lesbian feminist politics, let me repeat, is a recognition that heterosexuality as an institution and an ideology is a cornerstone of male supremacy. Therefore, women interested in destroying male supremacy, patriarchy, and capitalism must, equally with lesbians, fight heterosexual domination – or we shall never end female oppression. This is what I call 'the heterosexual question' – it is *not* the lesbian question.

Although lesbians have been the quickest to see the challenge to heterosexuality as a necessity for feminists' survival, straight feminists are not precluded from examining and fighting against heterosexuality. The problem is that few have done so. This perpetuates lesbian fears that women remaining tied to men prevent them from seeing the function of heterosexuality and acting to end it. It is not lesbianism (women's ties to women) but heterosexuality (women's ties to men), and thus men themselves, which divides women politically and personally. This is the 'divisiveness' of the lesbian issue to the women's movement. We won't get beyond it by demanding that lesbians retreat, politics in hand, back into the closet. We shall only get beyond it by struggling over the institutional and ideological analysis of lesbian feminism. We need to discover what lesbian consciousness means for any woman, just as we struggle to understand what class or race consciousness means for women of any race or class. And we must develop strategies that will destroy the political institutions that oppress us.

It is particularly important for those at this conference to understand that heterosexuality – as an ideology and as an institution – upholds all those aspects of female oppression discussed here. For example, heterosexuality is basic to our oppression in the workplace. When we look at how women are defined and exploited as secondary, marginal workers, we recognize that this definition assumes that all women are tied to men. I mention the workplace because it upset me yesterday at the economics panel that no one made that connection; and further, no one recognized that a high percentage of women workers are lesbians and therefore their relationship to, and attitudes towards, work are fundamentally different from those assumed by straight workers. It is obvious that heterosexuality upholds the home, housework, the family as both a personal and economic unit. It is apparently not so obvious that the whole framework of heterosexuality defines our lives, that it is fundamental to the negative self-image and self-hatred of women in this society. Lesbian feminism is based on a rejection of male definitions of our lives and is therefore crucial to the development of a positive woman-identified identity, of redefining who we are supposed to be in every situation, including the workplace.

What is that definition? Basically heterosexuality means men first. That's what it's all about. It assumes that every woman is heterosexual; that every woman is defined by and is the property of men. Her body, her services, her children belong to men. If you don't accept that definition, you're a queer – no matter whom you sleep with; if you do not accept that definition in this society, you're queer. The original imperialist assumption of the right of men to the bodies and services of women has been translated into a whole variety of forms of domination throughout this society. And as long as people accept that initial assumption – and question everything *but* that assumption – it is impossible to challenge the other forms of domination.

What makes heterosexuality work is heterosexual privilege – and if you don't have a sense of what that privilege is, I suggest that you go home and announce to everybody that you know – a room-mate, your family, the people you work with – everywhere you go – that you're a queer. Try being a queer for a week. Do not walk out on the street with men; walk only with women, especially at night, for example. For a whole week, experience life as if you were a lesbian, and I think you will know what heterosexual privilege is very quickly. And, hopefully, you will also learn that heterosexual privilege is the method by which women are given a stake in male supremacy – and that it is therefore the method by which women are given a stake in their own oppression. Simply stated, a woman who stays in line – by staying straight or by refusing to resist straight privileges – receives some of the benefits of male privilege indirectly and is thus given a stake in continuing those privileges and maintaining their source – male supremacy.

Heterosexual women must realize – no matter what their personal connection to men – that the benefits they receive from men will always be in diluted form and will ultimately result in their own self-destruction. When a woman's individual survival is tied to men, she is at some intrinsic place separated from other women and from the survival needs of those other women. The question arises not because of rhetorical necessity – whether a woman is personally loyal to other women – but because we must examine what stake each of us has in the continuation of male supremacy. For example, if you are receiving heterosexual benefits through a man (or through his social, cultural, or political systems), are you clear about what those benefits are doing to you, both personally and in terms of other women? I have known women who are very strong in fighting against female job discrimination, but when the battle closes in on their man's job, they desert that position. In universities, specifically, when a husband's job is threatened by feminist hiring demands, I have seen feminists abandon their political positions in order to keep the privileges they receive from their man's job.

This analysis of the function of heterosexuality in women's oppression is available to any woman, lesbian or straight. Lesbian feminism is not a political analysis 'for lesbians only'. It is a political perspective and fight against one of the major institutions of our oppression – a fight that heterosexual women can engage in. The problem is that few do. Since lesbians are materially oppressed by heterosexuality daily, it is not surprising that we have seen and understood its impact first – not because we are more moral, but because our reality is different – and it is a *materially* different reality. We are trying to convey this fact of our oppression to you because, whether you feel it directly or not, it also oppresses you; and because if we are going to change society and survive, we must all attack heterosexual domination.

CLASS AND LESBIANISM

There is another important aspect of lesbian feminism that should be of interest to a socialist feminist conference: the connection between lesbianism and class. One of the ways that lesbianism has affected the movement is in changing women's individual lives. Those of us who are out of the closet have, in particular, learned that we must create our own world – we haven't any choice in the matter because there is no institution in this society that is created for us. Once we are out, there is no place that wholeheartedly accepts us. Coming out is important, partly because it puts us in a materially different reality in terms of what we have to do. And it is the impact of reality that moves us (or anyone) to understand and change. I don't believe that idealism is the primary force that moves people; necessity moves people. And lesbians who are out are moved by necessity – not by choice – to create our own world. Frequently (and mistakenly), that task has been characterized as cultural. While the culture gives us strength, the impetus is always economic: the expression of necessity is always material. For middle-class women this is especially true – lesbianism means discovering that we have to support ourselves for the rest of our lives, something that lower- and working-class women have always known. This discovery makes us begin to understand what lower- and working-class women have been trying to tell us all along: 'What do you know about survival?'

I heard a lot about class analysis when I was in the Left, and some of it was helpful. But it wasn't until I came out as a lesbian and had to face my own survival on that basis – as an outlaw, as a woman alone – that I learned abut class in my own life. Then I learned what the Left had never taught me – what my middle-class assumptions were and the way in which my background crippled me as a woman. I began to understand how my own middle-class background was holding me back personally and the ways in which middle-class assumptions were holding back the growth of our movement. Class affects the way we operate every day – as has been obvious in much of what has happened in this conference. And theories of class should help us understand that. The only way to understand the function of class in society, as far as I'm concerned, is to understand how it functions right here, on the spot, day to day, in our lives.

Another way in which class consciousness has occurred in the lesbian community – and I want to acknowledge it because it is frequently one of the things kept locked in the bedroom closet – is the cross-class intimacy that occurs among lesbians. This intimacy usually leads to an on-the-spot analysis of class oppression and conflict based on the experience of being hit over the head with it over and over again. Understand that I am not advising every middle-class woman to go out and get herself a lower-class lesbian to teach her about class-in-the-raw; but also understand that I am saying that there's no faster way to learn how class functions in our world.

Cross-class contact occurs all the time in the lesbian community, frequently without any self-conscious politics attached to it. For example, in lesbian bars, a political process that is often misinterpreted as a purely social process is going on in women's lives. Because there are no men in that environment, the conflicts around class and race – those issues basic to women's survival – become crystal clear, if you understand them not in rhetorical or theoretical terms but in the ways that women's lives are interacting with each other. This is one reason why a lot of class analysis, particularly the practical kind, has come out of the lesbian feminist movement – analysis based on our experience of class contact and conflict, our recognition of it, and our integration of its meanings in the way we live our lives. This material experience of class realities produces real commitment to struggle and to the class question not out of idealism but as integral to our survival. Idealism can be abandoned at any time. Survival cannot.

I want to be clear about what it is that I am *not* saying. I am not saying that all lesbians are feminists; all lesbians are not politically conscious. I am saying that the particular material reality of lesbian life makes political consciousness more likely; we can build on the fact that it is not in the interests of lesbians to maintain and defend the system as it is.

I am also *not* saying that the only way to have this political analysis is to be a lesbian. But I *am* saying that so far most of the people with lesbian feminist politics who have challenged heterosexuality are lesbians. But ours is not the only way, and we've got to make it not the only way. We, as lesbians, are a minority. We cannot survive alone. We will not survive alone. But if we do not survive, the entire women's movement will be defeated and female oppression will be re-enacted in other forms. As we all understand survival more clearly we see that the politics and analysis of women's oppression coming out of the lesbian's life experience has got to be integrated into the politics of socialist feminism and the rest of the women's movement.

It is not okay to be queer under patriarchy – and the last thing we should be aiming to do is make it okay. Nothing in capitalist-patriarchal America works to our benefit, and I do not want to see us working in any way to integrate ourselves into that order. I'm not saying that we should neglect work on reforms – we must have our jobs, our housing, and so forth. But in so doing we must not lose sight of our ultimate goal. Our very strength as lesbians lies in the fact that we are outside patriarchy; our existence challenges its life. To work for 'acceptance' is to work for our own disintegration and an end to the clarity and energy we bring to the women's movement.

It is not okay, and I do not want it ever to be okay, to be queer in patriarchy. The entire system of capitalism and patriarchy must be changed. And essential to that change is an end to heterosexual domination. Lesbians cannot work in movements that do not recognize that heterosexuality is central to all women's oppression; that would be to work for our own self-destruction. But we can coalesce with groups that share the lesbian feminist analysis and are committed to the changes essential for our survival. This is the basis upon which we can begin to build greater unity and a stronger, more powerful feminist movement.

NOTE

This paper is an expanded and revised version of a speech given at the Socialist Feminist Conference, Antioch College, Yellow Springs, Ohio, 5 July 1975. Many of the ideas expressed about lesbian feminist politics were first developed several years ago in The Furies. Nevertheless, I am continually discovering that most feminists, including many lesbians, have little idea what lesbian feminist politics is. This speech takes those basic political ideas and develops them further, particularly as they relate to socialist feminism.

THE MYTH OF THE VAGINAL ORGASM

Anne Koedt

Whenever female orgasm and frigidity are discussed, a false distinction is made between the vaginal and the clitoral orgasm. Frigidity has generally been defined by men as the failure of women to have vaginal orgasms. Actually the vagina is not a highly sensitive area and is not constructed to achieve orgasm. It is the clitoris which is the centre of sexual sensitivity and which is the female equivalent of the penis.

I think this explains a great many things: first of all, the fact that the so-called frigidity rate among women is phenomenally high. Rather than tracing female frigidity to the false assumptions about female anatomy, our 'experts' have declared frigidity a psychological problem of women. Those women who complained about it were recommended psychiatrists, so that they might discover their 'problem' – diagnosed generally as a failure to adjust to their role as women.

The facts of female anatomy and sexual response tell a different story. Although there are many areas for sexual arousal, there is only one area for sexual climax; that area is the clitoris. All orgasms are extensions of sensation from this area. Since the clitoris is not necessarily stimulated sufficiently in the conventional sexual positions, we are left 'frigid'.

Aside from physical stimulation, which is the common cause of orgasm for most people, there is also stimulation through primarily mental processes. Some women, for example, may achieve orgasm through sexual fantasies, or through fetishes. However, while the stimulation may be psychological, the orgasm manifests itself physically. Thus, while the cause is psychological, the *effect* is still physical, and the orgasm necessarily takes place in the sexual organ equipped for sexual climax – the clitoris. The orgasm experience may also differ in degree of intensity – some more localized, and some more diffuse and sensitive. But they are all clitoral orgasms.

All this leads to some interesting questions about conventional sex and our role in it. Men have orgasms essentially by friction with the vagina, not the clitoral area, which is external and not able to cause friction the way penetration does. Women have thus been defined sexually in terms of what pleases men; our own biology has not been properly analysed.

Instead, we are fed the myth of the liberated woman and her vaginal orgasm – an orgasm that in fact does not exist.

What we must do is redefine our sexuality. We must discard the 'normal' concepts of sex and create new guidelines that take into account mutual sexual enjoyment. While the idea of mutual enjoyment is liberally applauded in marriage manuals, it is not followed to its logical conclusions. We must begin to demand that if certain sexual positions now defined as 'standard' are not mutually conducive to orgasm, they no longer be defined as standard. New techniques must be used or devised which transform this particular aspect of our current sexual exploitation.

FREUD – A FATHER OF THE VAGINAL ORGASM

Freud contended that the clitoral orgasm was adolescent and that upon puberty, when women began having intercourse with men, women should transfer the centre of orgasm to the vagina. The vagina, it was assumed, was able to produce a parallel, but more mature, orgasm than the clitoris. Much work was done to elaborate on this theory, but little was done to challenge the basic assumptions.

To appreciate fully this incredible invention, perhaps Freud's general attitude about women should first be recalled. Mary Ellman, in *Thinking About Women*, summed it up this way:

> Everything in Freud's patronizing and fearful attitude toward women follows from their lack of a penis, but it is only in his essay *The Psychology of Women* that Freud makes explicit . . . the deprecations of women which are implicit in his work. He then prescribes for them the abandonment of the life of the mind, which will interfere with their sexual function. When the psychoanalyzed patient is male, the analyst sets himself the task of developing the man's capacities; but with women patients, the job is to resign them to the limits of their sexuality. As Mr. Rieff puts it: For Freud, 'Analysis cannot encourage in women new energies for success and achievement, but only teach them the lesson of rational resignation.'

It was Freud's feelings about women's secondary and inferior relationship to men that formed the basis for his theories on female sexuality.

Once having laid down the law about the nature of our sexuality, Freud not so strangely discovered a tremendous problem of frigidity in women. His recommended cure for a woman who was frigid was psychiatric care. She was suffering from a failure to adjust mentally to her 'natural' role as a woman. Frank S. Caprio, a contemporary follower of these ideas, states:

> whenever a woman is incapable of achieving an orgasm via coitus,

provided the husband is an adequate partner, and prefers clitoral stimulation to any other form of sexual activity, she can be regarded as suffering from frigidity and requires psychiatric assistance. (*The Sexually Adequate Female*, p. 64)

The explanation given was that women were envious of men – 'renunciation of womanhood'. Thus it was diagnosed as an anti-male phenomenon.

It is important to emphasize that Freud did not base his theory upon a study of women's anatomy, but rather upon his assumptions of woman as an inferior appendage to man, and her consequent social and psychological role. In their attempts to deal with the ensuing problem of mass frigidity, Freudians embarked on elaborate mental gymnastics. Marie Bonaparte, in *Female Sexuality*, goes so far as to suggest surgery to help women back on their rightful path. Having discovered a strange connection between the non-frigid woman and the location of the clitoris near the vagina,

it then occurred to me that where, in certain women, this gap was excessive, the clitoridal fixation obdurate, a clitoridal–vaginal reconciliation might be effected by surgical means, which would then benefit the normal erotic function. Professor Halban, of Vienna, as much a biologist as a surgeon, became interested in the problem and worked out a simple operative technique. In this, the suspensory ligament of the clitoris was severed and the clitoris secured to the underlying structures, thus fixing it in a lower position, with eventual reduction of the labia minora. (p. 148)

But the severest damage was not in the area of surgery, where Freudians ran around absurdly trying to change female anatomy to fit their basic assumptions. The worst damage was done to the mental health of women, who either suffered silently with self-blame, or flocked to psychologists looking desperately for the hidden and terrible repression that had kept from them their vaginal destiny.

LACK OF EVIDENCE

One may perhaps at first claim that these are unknown and unexplored areas, but upon closer examination this is certainly not true today, nor was it true even in the past. For example, men have known that women suffered from frigidity often during intercourse. So the problem was there. Also, there is much specific evidence. Men knew that the clitoris was and is the essential organ for masturbation, whether in children or adult women. So, obviously women made it clear where *they* thought their sexuality was located. Men also seem suspiciously aware of the clitoral powers during 'foreplay', when they want to arouse women and produce the necessary lubrication for penetration. Foreplay is a concept created for male purposes, but works to the disadvantage of many women, since as soon as the woman is aroused the man changes to vaginal stimulation, leaving her both aroused and unsatisfied.

It has also been known that women need no anaesthesia inside the vagina during surgery, thus pointing to the fact that the vagina is in fact not a highly sensitive area.

Today, with extensive knowledge of anatomy, with Kelly, Kinsey, and Masters and Johnson, to mention just a few sources, there is no ignorance on the subject. There are, however, social reasons why this knowledge has not been popularized. We are living in a male society which has not sought change in women's role.

ANATOMICAL EVIDENCE

Rather than starting with what women *ought* to feel, it would seem logical to start out with the anatomical facts regarding the clitoris and vagina.

The clitoris

This is a small equivalent of the penis, except for the fact that the urethra does not go through it as in the man's penis. Its erection is similar to the male erection, and the head of the clitoris has the same type of structure and function as the head of the penis. G. Lombard Kelly, in *Sexual Feeling in Married Men and Women*, says:

> The head of the clitoris is also composed of erectile tissue, and it possesses a very sensitive epithelium or surface coating, supplied with special nerve endings called genital corpuscles, which are peculiarly shaped for sensory stimulation that under proper mental conditions terminates in the sexual orgasm. No other part of the female generative tract has such corpuscles. (Pocketbooks, p. 35)

The clitoris has no other function than that of sexual pleasure.

The vagina

Its functions are related to the reproductive function. Principally, 1) menstruation, 2) receive penis, 3) hold semen, and 4) birth passage. The interior of the vagina, which according to the defenders of the vaginally caused orgasm is the centre and producer of the orgasm, is

> like nearly all other internal body structures, poorly supplied with end

organs of touch. The internal entodermal origin of the lining of the vagina makes it similar in this respect to the rectum and other parts of the digestive tract. (Kinsey, *Sexual Behavior in the Human Female*, p. 580)

The degree of insensitivity inside the vagina is so high that: 'Among the women who were tested in our gynecologic sample, less than 14% were at all conscious that they had been touched' (Kinsey, p. 580).

Even the importance of the vagina as an *erotic* centre (as opposed to an orgasmic centre) has been found to be minor.

Other areas

Labia minora and the vestibule of the vagina. These two sensitive areas may trigger off a clitoral orgasm. Because they can be effectively stimulated during 'normal' coitus, though infrequently, this kind of stimulation is incorrectly thought to be vaginal orgasm. However, it is important to distinguish between areas that can stimulate the clitoris, incapable of producing the orgasm themselves, and the clitoris:

Regardless of what means of excitation is used to bring the individual to the state of sexual climax, the sensation is perceived by the genital corpuscles and is localized where they are situated: in the head of the clitoris or penis. (Kelly, p. 49)

Psychologically stimulated orgasm

Aside from the above-mentioned direct and indirect stimulations of the clitoris, there is a third way an orgasm may be triggered. This is through mental (cortical) stimulation, where the imagination stimulates the brain, which in turn stimulates the genital corpuscles of the glans to set off an orgasm.

WOMEN WHO SAY THEY HAVE VAGINAL ORGASMS

Confusion

Because of the lack of knowledge of their own anatomy, some women accept the idea that an orgasm felt during 'normal' intercourse was vaginally caused. This confusion is caused by a combination of two factors. One, failing to locate the centre of the orgasm, and two, by a desire to fit her experience to the male-defined idea of sexual normalcy. Considering that women know little about their anatomy, it is easy to be confused.

Deception

The vast majority of women who pretend vaginal orgasm to their men are faking it to 'get the job'. In a best-selling Danish book, *I Accuse*, Mette Ejlersen specifically deals with this common problem, which she calls the 'sex comedy'. This comedy has many causes. First of all, the man brings a great deal of pressure to bear on the woman, because he considers his ability as a lover at stake. So as not to offend his ego, the woman will comply with the prescribed role and go through simulated ecstasy. In some of the other Danish women mentioned, women who were left frigid were turned off sex and pretended vaginal orgasm to hurry up the sex act. Others admitted that they had faked vaginal orgasm to catch a man. In one case, the woman pretended vaginal orgasm to get him to leave his first wife, who admitted to being vaginally frigid. Later she was forced to continue the deception, since obviously she couldn't tell him to stimulate her clitorally.

Many more women were simply afraid to establish their right to equal enjoyment, seeing the sexual act as being primarily for the man's benefit, and any pleasure that the woman got as an added extra.

Other women, with just enough ego to reject the man's idea that they needed psychiatric care, refused to accept their frigidity. They wouldn't accept self-blame, but they didn't know how to solve the problem, not knowing the physiological facts about themselves. So they were left in a peculiar limbo.

Again, perhaps one of the most infuriating and damaging results of this whole charade has been that women who were perfectly healthy sexually were taught that they were not. So, in addition to being sexually deprived, these women were told to blame themselves when they deserved no blame. Looking for a cure to a problem that has none can lead a woman on an endless path of self-hatred and insecurity. For she is told by her analyst that not even in her one role allowed in a male society – the role of a woman – is she successful. She is put on the defensive, with phoney data as evidence that she'd better try to be even more feminine, think more feminine, and reject her envy of men. That is, shuffle even harder, baby.

WHY MEN MAINTAIN THE MYTH

Sexual penetration is preferred

The best physical stimulant for the penis is the woman's vagina. It supplies the necessary friction and lubrication. From a strictly technical point of view this position offers the best physical conditions, even though the man may try other positions for variation.

The invisible woman

One of the elements of male chauvinism is the refusal or inability to see women as total, separate human beings. Rather, men have chosen to define women only in terms of how they benefited men's lives. Sexually, a woman was not seen as an individual wanting to share equally in the sexual act, any more than she was seen as a person with independent desires when she did anything else in society. Thus, it was easy to make up what was convenient about women; for on top of that, society has been a function of male interests, and women were not organized to form even a vocal opposition to the male experts.

The penis as epitome of masculinity

Men define their lives primarily in terms of masculinity. It is a universal form of ego-boosting. That is, in every society, however homogeneous (i.e. with the absence of racial, ethnic, or major economic differences) there is always a group, women, to oppress.

The essence of male chauvinism is in the psychological superiority men exercise over women. This kind of superior–inferior definition of self, rather than positive definition based upon one's own achievements and development, has of course chained victim and oppressor both. But by far the most brutalized of the two is the victim.

An analogy is racism, where the white racist compensates for his feelings of unworthiness by creating an image of the black man (it is primarily a male struggle) as biologically inferior to him. Because of his position in a white male power structure, the white man can socially enforce this mythical division.

To the extent that men try to rationalize and justify male superiority through physical differentiation, masculinity may be symbolized by being the *most* muscular, the most hairy, having the deepest voice, and the biggest penis. Women, on the other hand, are approved of (i.e. called feminine) if they are weak, petite, shave their legs, have high soft voices.

Since the clitoris is almost identical to the penis, one finds a great deal of evidence of men in various societies trying either to ignore the clitoris and emphasize the vagina (as did Freud) or, as in some places in the Middle East, actually performing clitoridectomy. Freud saw this ancient and still practised custom as a way of further 'feminizing' the female by removing this cardinal vestige of her masculinity. It should be noted also that a big clitoris is considered ugly and masculine. Some cultures engage in the practice of pouring a chemical on the clitoris to make it shrivel up into 'proper' size.

It seems clear to me that men in fact fear the clitoris as a threat to masculinity.

Sexually expendable male

Men fear that they will become sexually expendable if the clitoris is substituted for the vagina as the centre of pleasure for women. Actually this has a great deal of validity if one considers *only* the anatomy. The position of the penis inside the vagina, while perfect for reproduction, does not necessarily stimulate an orgasm in women because the clitoris is located externally and higher up. Women must rely upon indirect stimulation in the 'normal' position.

Lesbian sexuality could make an excellent case, based upon anatomical data, for the irrelevancy of the male organ. Albert Ellis says something to the effect that a man without a penis can make a woman an excellent lover.

Considering that the vagina is very desirable from a man's point of view, purely on physical grounds, one begins to see the dilemma for men. And it forces us as well to discard many 'physical' arguments explaining why women go to bed with men. What is left, it seems to me, are primarily psychological reasons why women select men at the exclusion of women as sexual partners.

Control of women

One reason given to explain the Middle Eastern practice of clitoridectomy is that it will keep the woman from straying. By removing the sexual organ capable of orgasm, it must be assumed that her sexual drive will diminish. Considering how men look upon their women as property, particularly in very backward nations, we should begin to consider a great deal more why it is not in men's interest to have women totally free sexually. The double standard, as practised, for example, in Latin America, is set up to keep the woman as total property of the husband, while he is free to have affairs as he wishes.

Lesbianism and bisexuality

Aside from the strictly anatomical reasons why women might equally seek other women as lovers, there is a fear on men's part that women will seek the company of other women on a full, human basis. The recognition of clitoral orgasm as fact would threaten the heterosexual *institution*. For it would indicate that sexual pleasure was obtainable from either men *or* women, thus making heterosexuality not an absolute, but an option. It would thus open up the whole question of *human* sexual relationships beyond the confines of the present male–female role system.

REFERENCES

Alfred C. Kinsey, *Sexual Behavior in the Human Female* (Pocketbooks, 1953).

Marie Bonaparte, *Female Sexuality* (Grove Press, 1953).

Albert Ellis, *Sex Without Guilt* (Grove Press, 1958 and 1965).

G. Lombard Kelly, *Sexual Feelings in Married Men and Women* (Pocketbooks, 1951 and 1965).

Mette Ejlersen and Chr. Erichsens Forlag, *I Accuse (Jeg Anklager)* (1968).

Frank S. Caprio, *The Sexually Adequate Female* (Fawcett Gold Medal Books, 1953 and 1966).

Mary Ellman, *Thinking About Women* (Harcourt, Brace & World, 1968).

Masters and Johnson, *Human Sexual Response* (Little, Brown, 1966).

THE SPIRITUAL DIMENSION OF WOMEN'S LIBERATION

Mary Daly

Women who are committed to achieving liberation and equality often turn away from organized religion, seeing it either as irrelevant or as a stubborn and powerful enemy, placing obstacles to all they seek to attain. Having been turned off by institutional religion they choose to leave it behind and forget it, except when it really shows muscle – as in the struggle over abortion laws. Some, on the other hand, have opted to continue their relationship with church or synagogue in the hope of changing sexist beliefs, laws, and customs in those institutions. The second choice is based upon a conviction that there are important values transmitted through these institutions that make it worth the pain and effort of staying in and fighting the system.

These are personal choices and no one can set down hard-and-fast rules for everyone to follow. However, it is important that women be aware of the issue of religion. First of all, it is necessary to understand institutional religion's role in the oppression of women, which it continues to exercise in this culture whether they personally relate to it or not. Second, women should be sensitive to the fact that the movement itself is a deeply spiritual event which has the potential to awaken a new and post-patriarchal spiritual consciousness.

INSTITUTIONALIZED CHRISTIANITY AND THE OPPRESSION OF WOMEN

The Judaic-Christian tradition has been patriarchal down through the millennia, although sometimes this has been modified or disguised.[1] The Bible reflected the oppressed condition of women in ancient times. In the Decalogue of the Old Testament a man's wife is listed among his possessions, along with his ox and his ass. The biblical story of Eve's birth, which has been called the hoax of the ages, fixed woman's place in the universe. The story of the Fall of Adam and Eve perpetuated the myth of feminine evil, giving a powerful image of woman as temptress – a dominant theme in western culture for thousands of years. In the New Testament, the Apostle Paul put women in their place: veiled, silent, and subordinate. In the early centuries of Christianity the Fathers of the Church classified women as fickle, shallow, garrulous, weak, and unstable. In the Middle Ages, Thomas Aquinas decreed that they are misbegotten males, and theologians dutifully taught this for centuries.

In the modern period popes and theologians greeted the first wave of feminism with the double-talk of the feminine mystique: women should be equal but subordinate. On childbirth, Pope Pius XII pontificated: 'She loves it [the child] the more, the more pain it has cost her.' Today, some liberal Catholic and Protestant theologians admit that sexism exists in the churches but show little inclination to do anything about it. All of this, of course, is in blatant contradiction to Christian teaching about the worth and dignity of every human person.

Although there have been outstanding 'exceptional women' in every period of Christian history, their existence has had almost no effect upon the official ideology and policies of the churches. This fact can be understood when it is realized that the Judaic-Christian tradition has functioned to legitimate male-dominated society. The image of God as exclusively a father and not a mother, for example, was spawned by the human imagination under the conditions of patriarchal society and sustained as plausible by patriarchy. Then, in turn, the image has served to perpetuate this kind of society by making its mechanisms for the oppression of women appear right and fitting. If God in 'his' heaven is a father ruling 'his' people, then it is in the 'nature' of things and according to divine plan and the order of the universe that society should be male-dominated. Within this context a mystification of roles takes place: the husband dominating his wife can feel that he represents God himself. A theologian such as Karl Barth could feel justified in writing that woman is 'ontologically' subordinate to man.

It might seem that intelligent people do not really think of God as an old man with a beard, but it is quite possible for the mind to function on two different and even contradictory levels at the same time. For example, many speak of God as spirit and at the same time, on the imaginative level, envisage 'him' as male. The widespread concept of the Supreme Being has been a not very subtle mask of the divine father figure, and it is not too surprising that it has been used to justify oppression, especially that of women, which is said to be 'God's plan'.

In the third chapter of Genesis:
'And thy desire shall be thy husband
and he shall rule over thee . . .'

Doctrines about Jesus also have often reflected a kind of phallic obsession. Some theologians have argued that since Jesus was male and called only males to become apostles, women should not be ordained. The doctrine of a unique 'incarnation' in Jesus reinforced the fixed idea of patriarchal religion that God is male and male is God. So also did the image of the Virgin kneeling in adoration before her own Son. The mechanism that can be seen in all of this is the familiar vicious circle in which the patterns of a particular kind of society are projected into the realm of religious beliefs and these in turn justify society as it is. The belief system becomes hardened and functions to resist social change, which would rob it of its plausibility. (In a matriarchal or a diarchal society, what credibility would the image of a divine patriarch have?)

Patriarchal religion tends to be authoritarian. Given the fact that the vicious circle is not foolproof, there is always the possibility that beliefs may lose their credibility. For this reason they are often buttressed by notions of 'faith' that leave no room for dissent. For example, the believer is often commanded to assent blindly to doctrines handed down by authority (all male). The inculcation of anxieties and guilt feelings over 'heresy' and 'losing the faith' has been a powerful method used by institutional religion to immunize itself from criticism. Women especially have been victimized by this.

Traditional Christian ethics also have been to a great extent the product and support of sexist bias. Much of the theory of Christian virtue appears to be the product of reactions on the part of men – probably guilt reactions – to the behavioural excesses of the stereotypic male. There has been theoretical emphasis upon charity, meekness, obedience, humility, self-abnegation, sacrifice, service. Part of the problem with this moral ideology is that it became generally accepted not by men but by women, who have hardly been helped by an ethic which reinforced their abject situation.

This emphasis upon the passive virtues, of course, has not challenged exploitativeness, but supported it. Part of the whole syndrome has been the reduction of hope to passive expectation of a reward from the divine Father for following the rules. Love or charity has been interpreted to mean that people should turn the other cheek to their oppressors. Within the perspective of such a privatized morality, 'sin' often becomes an offence against those in power, or against 'God' – the two being more or less equated. The structures of oppression are not seen as sinful.

It is consistent with all of this that the traditional Christian moral consciousness has been fixated on the problems of reproductive activity to a degree totally disproportionate to its feeble concern for existing human life. The deformity of perspective was summed up several years ago in Archbishop Robers' remark that 'if contraceptives had been dropped over Japan instead of bombs which merely killed, maimed, and shriveled up thousands alive, there would have been a squeal of outraged protest from the Vatican to the remotest Mass center in Asia.' Pertinent also is Simone de Beauvoir's remark that the Church has reserved its uncompromising humanitarianism for man in the foetal condition.

But I suffer not a woman to teach, nor to usurp authority over the man but to be in silence; for Adam was first formed, then Eve; and Adam was not deceived, but the woman being deceived, was in the transgression.

(Timothy 1, 2:12–14)

Although both of these remarks are directed at the Catholic Church, the same attitudes are widespread in Protestantism. Many theologians today do, of course, acknowledge that this passive and privatized morality has failed to cope with structures of oppression. However, few seriously face the possibility that the roots of this distortion are deeply buried in the fundamental and all-pervasive sexual alienation which the women's movement is seeking to overcome.

THE SPIRITUAL POTENTIAL OF THE MOVEMENT

As the women's revolution begins to have an effect upon the fabric of society, beginning to transform it from patriarchy into something that never existed before – into a diarchal situation that is radically new – it will, I think, become the greatest single challenge to Christianity to rid itself of its oppressive tendencies or go out of business. Beliefs and values that have held sway for thousands of years will be questioned as never before. The movement, if it is true to its most authentic and prophetic dimensions, is possibly also the greatest single hope for the survival and development of authentic spiritual consciousness over against the manipulative and exploitative power of technocracy.

The caricature of a human being which is presented by the masculine stereotype depends for its existence upon the acceptance by women of the role assigned to them – the eternal feminine. By becoming whole persons women can generate a counterforce to the polarization of human beings into these stereotypes, forcing men to re-examine their own self-definition. This movement towards the becoming of whole human beings, to the degree that it succeeds, will transform the values and symbols of our society, including religious symbols.

The women's liberation movement is a spiritual movement because it aims at humanization of women and therefore of the species. At its core it is spiritualized in the deepest sense of the word, because it means the self-actualization of creative human potential in the struggle against oppression. Since the projections of patriarchal religion serve to block the dynamics of creativity, self-actualization, and authentic community by enforcing reduction of people to stereotyped roles, the challenge to patriarchy which is now in its initial stages is a sign of hope for the emergence of more genuine religious consciousness. The becoming of women may not be only the doorway to deliverance from the omnipotent Father in all of his disguises, but, to many, also a doorway *to* something, namely, to a more authentic search for transcendence, that is, for God.

Women's liberation is an event that can challenge authoritarian, exclusivist, and non-existential ideas of faith and revelation. Since women have been extra-environmentals, that is, since we have not been part of the authority structure which uses 'faith' and 'revelation' to reinforce the mechanisms of alienation, our emergence can unmask the idolatry often hidden behind these ideas.

The head of every man is Christ; and the head of every woman is man. . . .

(Corinthians, 1, 11:3)

There could result from this becoming of women a remythologizing of western religion. If the need for parental symbols of God persists, something like the Father–Mother God of Mary Baker Eddy will be more acceptable to the new woman and the new man than the Father God of the past. A symbolization for incarnation of the divine presence in human beings may continue to be needed in the future, but it is highly unlikely that women or men will find plausible that symbolism which is epitomized in the Christ–Mary image. Perhaps this will be replaced by a bisexual imagery which is non-hierarchical.

The becoming of women can bring about a transvaluation of values. Faith can come to be understood in a non-authoritarian and universalist sense. Hope, rather than being restricted to expectation of rewards for conformity, can come to be experienced and understood as creative, political, and revolutionary. Love will mean uniting to overcome oppression. It will be understood that the most loving thing one can do for the oppressor is to fight the oppressive situation that destroys both the oppressor and the oppressed. Suffering, which has been so highly esteemed in Christianity, will be seen as acceptable not when abjectly and submissively endured, but when experienced in the struggle for liberation.

And if they will learn anything, let them ask their husbands at home; for it is a shame for women to speak in church.

(Corinthians 1, 14:35)

The ethic emerging in the struggle has as its main theme not prudence but existential courage. This is the courage to risk economic and social security for the sake of liberation. It means not only risking the loss of jobs, friends, and social approval, but also facing the nameless anxieties encountered in new and uncharted territory. There is the anxiety of meaninglessness that can be overwhelming at times when the old simple meanings, role definitions, and life expectations have been rooted out and rejected openly, and a woman emerges into a world without models. There is also the anxiety of guilt over refusing to do what society demands, an anxiety that can still hold a woman in its grip long after the guilt has been recognized as false. To affirm oneself and one's sisters in the face of all this requires courage.

Likewise, ye wives, be in subjection to your own husbands . . .
(Peter 1, 3:1)

Such courage expresses itself in sisterhood, which is not at all merely the female counterpart of brotherhood. Sisterhood is a revolutionary fact. It is the bonding of those who have never bonded before, for the purpose of overcoming sexism and its effects, both internal and external. It is the coming together of those who are oppressed by sexual definition. The Christian churches have been fond of preaching the 'brotherhood of man', which included women incidentally, as baggage. However, the concept has never been realized because brotherhood in patriarchy, despite frequent attempts to universalize the term, is exclusive and divisive. 'Brother' means us versus them. It begins by excluding women as 'the other' and continues its divisiveness from there, cutting off 'the other' by familial, tribal, racial, national, economic, and ideological categories.

Women are learning to be aware that brotherhood, even when it attempts to be universal, means a male universalism. The churches, the peace movement, the New Left, for the most part fail to notice the need for change in the situation of the more than 50 per cent female membership of the groups to which they would extend their brotherhood.

The 'sisterhoods' of patriarchal society have really been mini-brotherhoods, following male models and serving male purposes. The religious sisterhoods within the Catholic Church, for example, have been male-dominated according to canon law. These communities, though they have offered an alternative to marriage and attracted some gifted women, have used the word 'sister' in an elitist and divisive sense and have supported the ideology of sexism.

The sisterhood of women's liberation involves a strategic polarization for the sake of women's internal wholeness or oneness, because as in the case of all oppressed groups, women suffer from a duality of consciousness. We have internalized the image that the oppressor has of us and are therefore divided against ourselves and against each other by self-hatred. We can only overcome this by bonding with each other.

Sisterhood implies polarization also for the sake of political oneness, to achieve liberation. However, its essential dynamic is directed to overcoming the stereotypes that reduce people to the role of 'the other'. That is, it points towards a unity deeper than most theologians are capable of envisaging, despite the great amount of ink that has been spilled on the subject of 'the bonds of charity'.

Sisterhood is an event that is new under the sun. It is healing, revolutionary, and revelatory – which is what Christian brotherhood was claimed to be but failed to be. It is at war with the idols of patriarchal religion, but it is in harmony with what is authentic in the ideals of the religious traditions. In this sense, the movement in its deepest dimension is itself both anti-Church and Church. It has the potential to release the authentic values that have been distorted and suppressed by the sexism of synagogue and church.

NOTE

1 A documented historical study and criticism of this can be found in my book, *The Church and the Second Sex* (New York: Harper and Row, 1968).

THE VISIONARY TASK
Two sights-seeing
Janice Raymond

SYNOPSIS

The essential feminist tension is dual-vision, i.e. living in the world as men have fabricated it while creating the world as women imagine it could be. Dissociation from, assimilation to, and victimism in the world are three different forms of worldlessness to which women have been subject. All three militate against a vision of female friendship, which locates women in the world. The author argues for a hopeful vision and reality of female friendship that avoids a misplaced optimism, shallow sentimentalism, and disillusioned pessimism about the possibilities of friendship among women.

The possibilities of female friendship are founded on vision. Today, vision is all the more important to talk about when the fabric of friendship among women seems often rent by disagreements, disruptions, and dissensions.

There are many ways to speak about vision. Every meaning of vision, however, is possessed of a certain tension. This tension is linguistically present in its dual dictionary definition, but it is also experienced in any attempt to live out a vision. At one and the same time, vision is 'the exercise of the ordinary faculty of sight' and 'something which is apparently seen otherwise than by ordinary sight'. Another way of phrasing this is to ask how indeed it is possible to see with the ordinary faculty of sight, that is, to maintain a necessary realism about the conditions of existence, *and* to see beyond these conditions, that is, to overleap reality. Or, how do women live in the world as men have defined it while creating the world as women imagine it could be?

An undivided vision is based on two sights-seeing – near- and far-sightedness. In my opinion, this dual vision is the *essential tension* of feminism. Feminists must learn to live in and with that tension. This means not being crushed by the *contrast* between what the world is and the way it ought to be.

The state of female atrocity, or all of the ways in which women have been oppressed, abused, and rendered invisible under patriarchy, presents one view of women. The state of female friendship presents another. If women do not have a vision of female friendship, if women do not come to realize how profound the possibilities are of being for each other, as well as how buried these possibilities have been for us, I believe there is no true realism about the possibilities of feminism itself.

Dual vision poses a tension but not a contradiction. Realism about the conditions of man-made existence must be illuminated by a vision of feminist imagination. And the feminist visionary task must root itself in the real world else, like an electrical charge that has no ground, its energy becomes diffuse and dispersed in all directions (Hynes, 1981).

Hannah Arendt wrote:

Humanity in the form of fraternity invariably appears historically among persecuted peoples and enslaved groups . . . it is often accompanied by so radical a loss of the world, so fearful an atrophy of all the organs with which we orient ourselves in a world common to ourselves and others and going on to the sense of beauty or taste, with which we love the world. (Arendt, 1968, p. 13)

Using the example of sisterhood instead of fraternity, we can apply these words to the situation of women under patriarchy. Feminist literature, theory, and action have emphasized the ideal of sisterhood as a collective response to women's oppression. Different schools of feminism have stressed the political nature of feminism and the necessity to build a strong solidarity of sisterhood.

Indeed sisterhood is powerful, but perhaps not powerful enough when it comes to the visionary task of which I speak. To resist the state of atrocity that men have perpetrated against women may generate sisterly solidarity, but it may not provide anything beyond the communion of resistance. It may not provide, as Arendt says, 'a world common to ourselves and others and going on to the sense of beauty or taste, with which we love the world', and I would add, 'are happy in it'.

At the same time that feminism is a political reality, it is also a way of life full of struggle, risk, *and promise*, the promise of *happiness in this world*. Organized sisterhood against the conditions of female oppression and the feminist struggle against all states of female atrocities serve as a powerful bulwark against the forces and structures of patriarchy. But a purely political feminism accentuating only conflict and resistance bears too similar a resemblance to religious eschatologies which would have women believe that true happiness is achievable only in the life to come.

Women must reject the sentimentality and false vision of patriarchal romanticism precisely because men have dreamed false dreams for women. This does not mean that women should reject vision. It does not mean that women will shape our own vision so that we will not only enable our freedom but create the conditions of female friendship.

In order to move beyond oppression and the struggle and conflict that inescapably accompany resistance to oppression, there must be a vision of 'moreness'. Let it not be misunderstood that in advocating a movement 'beyond' struggle, I mean one that leaves the struggle behind. Rather one revivifies the struggle hopefully by a moreness that enriches female life and living. Friendship invigorates the reality of feminist resistance with this moreness. It augments sisterhood with spirit, thereby infusing feminist solidarity with an energy or vital force of affection.

Affection is a carefully chosen word in my discussion of vision and female friendship. The more commonly understood meaning of affection is a feeling, emotion, fondness, attachment, and love for another. There is another meaning of affection, however, that conveys more than personal movement of person to person. Affection in this sense means the state of influencing, acting upon, moving, and impressing, and of being influenced, acted upon, moved, and impressed. I maintain that women who affect other women stimulate response and action; bring about a change in living; stir and arouse emotion, ideas, and activities that defy dichotomies between the personal and political aspects of affection.

Elsewhere, I have suggested a new word, *Gyn/affection*, to describe this personal and political movement of women towards each other (Raymond, 1982). I define Gyn/affection a a synonym for female friendship, but it has a distinct meaning context of its own. The basic meaning of Gyn/affection is that women affect, stir, and arouse each other to full power through friendship. One task of feminism has been to show that 'the personal is political'. Female friendship gives integrity to that claim. The word Gyn/affection is meant to reunite the political and personal aspect of friendship.[1]

Sisterhood signals the kind of political community that is and has to be possible among women who are not necessarily friends. None of us is beyond sisterhood because feminist resistance to all forms of female oppression is ongoing. However, sisterhood and friendship have a richer meaning when they are brought together, that is when political sisterhood proceeds from a shared affection, vision, and spirit, and when friendship has a more expansive political effect. We need to create a feminist politics based on friendship, and we need a philosophy of friendship that is realized in personal and socio-economic power for women. A genuine friendship goes beyond the Self's relations with other Selves to the society in which the female Self is allowed to grow. Thus the active and dynamic expression of female friendship involves more than feeling. It means the sharing of a common life and participation in a common world.

Worldliness and friendship must be intimately linked in the lives of

344

women today who live with the basic tension that feminism presents – that of acting in a world that men have fabricated while yearning to go beyond it. Alice Walker has eloquently described the lucidity she experienced when her daughter told her that 'there's a *world* in your eye' (Walker, 1983, p. 393).[2] There must be a world in each of our eyes.

More than most philosophers, Hannah Arendt has discussed the concept of *worldliness*. Arendt's notion of worldliness, originally analysed in the context of the history of the Jews and of Judaism, has much pertinence for feminist worldliness.[3] Because women have been the eternal victims of male cruelty and injustice; because survival has been the key focus of female existence and feminist political thought; because women have almost everywhere lacked involvement in and control over the political world in which we have lived; and because the world is man-made, many women have developed a *worldlessness* by *dissociation* from the world. Women in general have assumed this worldlessness almost by default, that is, by virtue of the passive positions most women have been forced into throughout history and in almost every culture. Other women, such as some feminist separatists, have made dissociation from the world a political ideal and reality. The difficulty in both cases is that when women make dissociation the basis for survival or for affinity, many come to conceive of their existence as independent from the rest of the world. Philosophically, this can make women very narrow in vision; politically it can make them very vulnerable. Even radical and voluntary dissociation from the world, originally undertaken as a necessary and daring political stance, can culminate in women developing a worm's-eye view of the world and being more exposed to attack than ever before. The more women dissociate from the world, the further removed are women from a definite share of what should be a common world. This is the condition of any group within any diaspora, whether scattered voluntarily or forcibly. A Gyn/affective friendship cannot exist under these conditions of worldlessness.

On the other hand, the dissociation from the world that is not chosen for consciously defined feminist reasons – in other words, that experienced by women in general whose apprehension of the world is derivative from husbands or other men – is reinforced by these women's lack of knowledge that women are a common people. In contrast to other oppressed groups, women do not possess the past of a cohesive and self-conscious community with its own political traditions, philosophical vitality, and history. Or should I say that this past is one that most women know little about? The rootlessness of women in their own group identity contributes more than anything to the worldless, unrealistic, and unpolitical perception that many women have.

Female friendship – not just any kind of friendship – but the Gyn/affection of which I have spoken, is one way to rootedness, to the grasp of reality that women need, and to the experience of our own history. Female friendship, of this nature, orients women to the world, not as persons but *as women*. To paraphrase Arendt, when one is oppressed as a woman, one must respond as a woman. Female friendship cannot arise in a context where women have 'the great privilege of being unburdened by care for the world' (Arendt, 1978, p. 27), because Gyn/affection is a political virtue with a political effect.

Any strong and vital reality of female friendship cannot be created within a dissociated enclave of women who have little knowledge of or interest in the wider world. Female friendship is strongest and most effective when it takes shape *within an enclave of women who are located in the world* by virtue of their thinking and action and who do not dissociate from the world or from each other. The feminist task of 'reconstituting the world', to use Adrienne Rich's phrase (1978), can only come about in a worldly context and in struggle against the forces that threaten us. Reconstituting the world means reconstituting our lost bonds with our Gyn/affective Selves and with others like our Selves. Strong friendships with strong women shape the world as women imagine it could be, while permitting women to move with worldly integrity in the world men have made.

The opposite of dissociation is *assimilation* to the world. This is another posture that many women have assumed as a location in the world. Assimilation is the stance of a woman who desires to succeed in the world of men and who forgets, or constantly tries to ignore, the fact of her femaleness. The assimilationist strives to lose her female identity, or to go beyond it, or to be regarded *as a person* in a world that grants the status of persons only to men. Realism, survival, worldliness are all acquired by assimilation to the male dominant world on its own terms.

Assimilation spells the end of any strong reality of female friendship even before it begins. For the assimilationist, men and/or male-defined structures are what counts. As women assimilate, they are reluctantly accepted into the ranks of male society mainly as exceptions and only in so far as they do not interfere with the homo-relational bonds[4] that men have established. In order to become part of the male dominant society, women have to believe (or pretend) that they are both persons and women, in the ways that men have defined both for women. What is demanded of assimilationist women by the male dominant world is that they behave in ways that distinguish them from ordinary women, e.g. they are encouraged to be bright, articulate, upwardly mobile professionals, but, at the same time, they must exhibit acceptable manners and modes of man-made femininity, e.g. charming behaviour, wearing feminine clothing or make-up. The complicated psychology learned well by the assimilationist woman is how to *be* and *not be* a woman, or how to be the woman that men still recognize as their own creation while avoiding the woman who recognizes her Self and other women who are Self-defined.

Assimilation fosters private solutions. Everything is reduced to personal self-propulsion. It is a forward self-propulsion that does not depend on authentic Self-definition, Self-movement, and certainly not on Gyn/affection. Thus it locates women in an isolated sphere of action that is built upon a pseudo-individualism. For the assimilationist, the world becomes anywhere that is accessible to any 'rational' person without questioning the boundaries of the terrain or one's location within them. This world becomes an inauthentic one for women not by virtue of the *fact* that it is man-made but because that fact is not doubted and defied.

In a society that is not only hostile to women, but pervaded by what Andrea Dworkin has named woman-hating (1974), it is possible to assimilate only by assimilation to anti-feminism also. Explicitly or implicitly, assimilationists disidentify with other women, whether they are in the company of men or women, or both. The irony of this is that both men and women will always perceive them first and foremost as women. It is unfortunate that assimilationists do not recognize, or ignore, this basic fact, wishing it will go away, when it never will.

The road to assimilation is the road to conformism: a conformism very often creating new stereotypes that assume shape under the guise of liberation and 'new woman' rhetoric, but conformism none the less. Thus what we witness is a brand of assimilationism that often displays the verbiage and outward life-style of liberation. Assimilationists frequently view their freedom as an emancipation from the world of traditional women, as well as from the world of feminist women. Sometimes, they exaggerate declarations that they are not feminists, or they take pains to proclaim that they have moved beyond feminism. In the latter case, many women have taken the term *post-feminist* as a badge of maturity. The irony of such disidentifications with feminism is that often assimilationist women engage in quite extraordinary activities that *are* feminist in the sense that these endeavours require unconventional capabilities, courage, determination, and persistence. One also thinks of women scientists, truck drivers, welders, and presidents of colleges who are not only very excellent at what they do, but very often more astute and humane than men in the same fields. However, many of these women, when asked, would deny any kind of woman-identification in a strong sense of the phrase. Assimilationist women want no social roots in any community of women. Hetero-relations become their guiding ethic.[5] Their emancipation is their assimilation. Hence assimilation, like dissociation, leads to a worldlessness that constricts rather than constructs female friendship.

In addition to assimilation and dissociation, *victimism* is a third posture that women have assumed towards the world. I use the word to describe women whose primary female or feminist identity seems to be grounded in women's shared state of having been victimized by men. In relationships with each other, such women emphasize their heritage of shared pain, although the ways in which various women have been victimized differs by age, class, race, and other factors.

I am not trying to minimize the pain of women's victimization by men in a patriarchal culture. It is extremely important that women understand and act on the full picture of female oppression. However, one-dimensional emphasis on the state of atrocity can have the unintended effect of stressing that what women have in common is only, or mostly, our shared pain. Such a perspective, as reflected in women's relationships, in women's sharing of experiences, and in feminist literature and activism, can also create the impression that because women have been historically bound to and by men, that woman is *for man*, no matter how she might have to be forced to do his bidding.

Victimism drives women further away from strong female friendships by obscuring the historical reality that women have been and can be *for women* in other than sisterly suffering ways. Among many feminists, the emphasis on victimism bolsters the conviction that female friendship can only arise negatively, that is, because men are so bad, and/or in reaction to the atrocities promoted by a woman-hating culture. Here female friendship seems spawned by the results of the oppression of women. Thus in a better world, presumably one in which men were good, female friendship might not be necessary.

It is obvious that feminist analysis and action has to be well acquainted with the varieties of male terrorism perpetrated against women. It should be as obvious that a vision of Gyn/affection is a vital counterpart to the reality of women as abused, battered, and killed. Sustained and one-dimensional emphasis on victimism, however, reduces the history of women to an eternal state of atrocity over which women have never exerted any counter-control. While it is necessary for women to recognize the prevalence and the longevity of anti-feminism across historical ages and cultural lines, the imperative for such recognition should not lead women to the conclusion that the force of anti-feminism is almost natural and without end – so overwhelming that any will to feminist action is lost.

Ultimately what victimism does is negate Self-definition and Self-responsibility in the world. When women do not define themselves beyond the role of sufferer, then women will settle for the world as men have made it. Victimism means annihilation by the world. It makes women world-sufferers rather than world-makers. It establishes women in the world negatively. Women's commonality is reduced to our shared oppression. There is the unstated, and hopefully unintended, premise that feminists might lose their feminist identity if anti-feminism disappeared from the world.

348

Women have indeed been broken by men. Yet men would make the case that it is they who have been damaged by women. For example, they blame mothers who gave them too much or too little attention, or wives who dominate or are too dependent. Men have always claimed the wounded role. The overcoming of brokenness by women, as well as the rejection of men as broken creatures in need of women's restorative power, is necessary to the process of female friendship.

Women, as a people, cannot be held together nor move in the world linked primarily by a common enemy or by a negative identity of oppression. Only within the framework of female friendship can a woman live as a woman, working for a reconstituted world, without exhausting herself in the struggle against woman-hating, and without despairing at the enormity of the task.

This issue has been entitled 'Rethinking Sisterhood: Unity in Diversity'.* Much emphasis in recent years of feminist writing and activity has been on the necessity to recognize and accept the diversity of women's lives and life experiences. Race, class, age, sexuality have all been in the forefront of this focus. Sometimes diversity has turned divisive. My work is meant to convey a sense of *hope* about the possibilities of friendship among women. It is not a naive hope, but one that has been tempered by a diversity that has often turned divisive, as well as by a myriad of other obstacles to Gyn/affection that women have experienced in the 'maturity' of feminist movement. All of us, in our relationships with women, have met with a host of stumbling-blocks: unfulfilled expectations, betrayal, lack of real caring, and the wall of entrenched differences between friends that becomes insurmountable. Dissociation, assimilation, and victimism have worked in their own ways to erase female friendship.

While it is not my intention to romanticize the subject of female friendship, I am calling for the regaining of hope about the present and future of friendship. This hope is grounded in several things: the reality of friendship that lives in my Self and in other women; the fact that women have been each other's best friends, relatives, faithful companions, emotional and economic supporters, and faithful lovers in all times and places; the continuity and consistency of these woman-to-woman affinities that veritably have formed historical and cultural traditions of female friendship in all epochs and cultures.

Hope is not necessary when things go smoothly, when there is a euphoria about the possibilities of women together as there was in the first stages of this particular wave of feminism. Many women have come through the feminism of the 1960s and early 1970s jaded, 'turned off', or disillusioned by other women. Women who 'should have been different' turned out to be 'just as bad, if not worse than men'. Both hope and friendship are easy when things proceed well. Hope is hard to hold but is no less called for when things are not as good as we expected them to be, when sisterhood does not seem as powerful as it once was, or as once we felt it to be. Yet the failures of friendship can never destroy the presence of its past in our lives, and certainly not its possibilities.

A hopeful vision of female friendship is not based on some ontological essence of female energy and vitality that women naturally possess by virtue of a more refined capability for love, caring, and respect for others. Rather it is anchored in the historical and cultural facts of what women have created for our Selves in spite of the state of female atrocity. The obstacles to female friendship and the divisiveness that often attends diversity serve as correctives to a shallow sentimentalism about women's affinities with women. Such difficulties remind us that to ground Gyn/affection in an ontological capability of women to bond with each other is a false optimism that will betray itself.

Misplaced optimism and shallow sentimentalism are two sides of a similar coin. Another position to be avoided is pessimism about women's ability to originate and sustain Gyn/affection. Relationships disintegrate. Violence against women issues in horizontal violence among women. Even something like the defeat of the ERA (for the moment) may dull the spirit of women working together to achieve simple and concrete goals for their Selves and other women. In the 'maturity' of feminist life and living, old directions are questioned.

A feminist vision realistically accepts these facts of worldly existence. Seeing with 'the ordinary faculty of sight', or being in the world as men have created it, is to know that the possession of vision will not make such facts disappear. Yet the same vision when it sees 'something which is apparently seen otherwise than by ordinary sight' knows that such realism is not the whole perspective. Simultaneously two sight-seeing is needed. Vision, near- and far-sightedness, is neither false optimism nor disillusioned pessimism. But vision is imperative to build Gyn/affection. Female friendship alone cannot vanquish the oppression of women, nor can it guarantee that friendship lasts forever. But it can create and sustain hope in the midst of all the factors that militate against Gyn/affection.

NOTES

1 The classical Greek philosophical tradition on friendship taught that friendship had a public nature. It was, in fact, the basis of the *polis*. Aristotle, for example, held that friendship fastened the moral and political fibres of the state together, and that friendship and justice coalesce. Of course, the citizens of this *polis* were all male. Women had no civic status, and therefore friendship *and* politics were affairs between men.

2 In her essay, 'Beauty: When the other dancer is the Self', Walker tells the story of her eye, wounded in early girlhood by a copper pellet from her brother's 'BB' gun. She trenchantly portrays years of feeling shame and ugliness, and the changes such feelings produced in a young life against the

backdrop of her mother's and sister's refrain, 'You did not change'. Only when her almost three-year-old daughter declares 'Mommy, there's a world in your eye' much later in Walker's life does the latter make peace with both her outer and inner vision. Rebecca's insight is no mere metaphor. It has significance for the visionary task of all women. It succinctly states the tension between the near- and far-sightedness with which my essay is concerned.

3 I am enormously indebted to Arendt's development of the typologies of dissociation and assimilation, and have drawn on many of her ideas in this section.

4 The fact, prevalence, and power of male homo-relations is disguised by such man-to-man rapport being institutionalized in every aspect of an apparently hetero-relational culture. It is women who bear the burden of living out the hetero-relational imperative. In truth, this is a male homo-relational society that is built on male–male relations, transactions, and bonding at all levels. See again, Raymond (1982).

5 I use the word *hetero-relations* to express the wide range of affective, social, political, and economic relations that are ordained between men and women by men. The literature, history, philosophy, and science of patriarchy have reinforced the supposedly mythic and primordial relationship of *woman for man* (Raymond, 1982).

REFERENCES

Arendt, Hannah, *Men in Dark Times* (New York: Harcourt, Brace & World, 1968).

Arendt, Hannah, *The Jew as Pariah: Jewish Identity and Politics in the Modern Age*, Feldman, Ron (ed.) (New York: Grove Press, 1978).

Dworkin, Andrea, *Woman Hating* (New York: E.P. Dutton, 1974).

Hynes, H. Patricia, *Conversation* (Mass.: Montague, 1981).

Raymond, Janice G., 'A genealogy of female friendship', *Trivia: A Journal of Ideas*, I (1) (1982), pp. 5–26.

Rich, Adrienne, 'Natural resources', in *The Dream of a Common Language, Poems 1974–1977* (New York: Norton, 1978).

Walker, Alice, *In Search of Our Mother's Gardens* (New York: Harcourt Brace Jovanovich, 1983).

* See acknowledgements for details.

Part X

SOCIALIST FEMINIST INTERVENTIONS

INTRODUCTION

Louise C. Johnson

The task of selecting a representative collection of socialist feminist theorizing is an impossible one. The task of collecting a few statements that exemplify a set of arguments is, however, more feasible. The arguments to be developed here use two extracts: Barbara Taylor (1980), 'Lords of creation: Marxism, feminism and "utopian" socialism' and Mia Campioni and Elizabeth Grosz [Gross] (1983) 'Love's labours lost: Marxism and feminism'. Each is designed to complement a more extensive commentary on socialist feminist theoretical interventions in the companion volume *Feminist Knowledge: Critique and Construct*.

The arguments revolve around the nature of the Marxist tradition, which socialist feminists inhabit, critique, and reconstruct. The British historian, Barbara Taylor,[1] sees the pre-Marxist phase of utopian socialism as producing a set of ideas and practices which had women's oppression as a central focus. This was a focus displaced by the ascendancy of Marxism as the dominant socialist orthodoxy – an orthodoxy that rendered 'The Woman Question'[2] peripheral. As someone still within – if critical of – the subsequent Marxist tradition, Taylor interprets this shift in terms of its historical context. But as a socialist and a feminist, her criteria for evaluating this tradition are based on how those within it consider or marginalize the position of women. On these grounds Marxism is found wanting, but not rejected.

The character and consequences of this legacy from the emergent phase of the Marxist tradition is explored in more detail by the Australian philosophers, Mia Campioni and Elizabeth Grosz.[3] In this examination, their position is less as loyal adherents to Marxism and more as feminists reconsidering that tradition. It is from this perspective that they evaluate recent socialist history and theoretical statements on 'The Woman Question'. Marxism is seen as the only radical alternative to capitalism both practically and theoretically. As such, they argue, Marxists share many phallocentric assumptions with bourgeois theory. Being the primary oppositional discourse but sharing many assumptions with patriarchal theorizing, means that Marxism both dominates over and arbitrates within the theoretical field. Marxism sets the rules for

355

radical political practice in such a way as to delegitimize the theoretical and pragmatic claims of feminism. Socialist feminism 'remains locked in a paradox as a *feminist* position unless it can somehow develop a radically *woman-centred* version of "socialism" which entails "seeing women first"' (p. 357). The vehicle for moving beyond Marxism involves seizing the principle of historical materialism and moving its foundations from economic ones to those of the sexually differentiated body. It is from a recognition of the lived oppressions and autonomy of women's bodies that further theoretical critiques and reconceptualizations can be built.

New socialist feminisms thereby emerge, not from further interventions into Marxist theory, but from an historical materialism built on women's bodies and lived realities. The move is from critique, to reformulation, to massive reconceptualization.[4]

In the rest of this introduction, the selected readings will be used to illustrate further the boundary transgressions which are reconstructing socialist feminist interventions in which Marxism itself is redefined, as is the socialist feminism loyal to it. These traditions are also used to affirm new possibilities for the future. The argument proceeds in three parts:

1 The assumption of hegemony by Marxism;
2 The theoretical problems of such dominance for socialist feminism;
3 New possibilities for socialist feminism.

MARXIST HEGEMONY

The socialist tradition predates Marxism and, for Barbara Taylor, utopian socialism is the beginning of the 'democratic-communist project' (p. 355) to liberate women and men from oppressions. She sees in the theory and practices of Owenism a major concern for the place of patriarchy in sustaining capitalism. Capitalism for utopian socialists was not an 'economic order dominated by a single, class-based division, but an arena of multiple antagonisms and contradictions . . . living in the hearts and minds of women and men as well as in their material circumstances' (p. 352). The atomized, economistic, competitive individual at the centre of bourgeois culture – and some later Marxist analyses of it – for the Owenites: 'was the product of a patriarchal system of psycho-sexual relations. Building an alternative . . . would involve not merely the transfer of economic power from one class to another, but a wholesale transformation of personal life' (p. 353). Robert Owen's utopian socialism, designated as 'unscientific' by Marx and Engels, is supplanted by their 'scientific socialism'. With this shift, for Taylor, the centrality of women's oppression to the theorization of capitalist social relations by socialists, disappears.

The Owenite emphasis on the universal, trans-class character of 'male supremacy' . . . disappeared, to be replaced with dogmatic assertions of sexual equality within the proletariat, calls for sex unity in the face of the common class enemy, and a repudiation of organized feminism as bourgeois liberal deviationism. (pp. 351–2)

Marxism thereby subsumes 'The Woman Question' under the Class Question. Why this occurs and comes to be the dominant version of socialism which feminists confront in the 1960s is explained by Taylor in terms of historical context. In the early years of industrialization, she argues, it was easier to envisage a very different world and to fight the very process of proletarianization. In contrast, by the 1850s, working people were a dominant reality and it was as proletarians that they were to be organized. Campioni and Grosz offer a different interpretation, seeing in the triumph of Marxism the reassertion of male political and theoretical authority. Borne by masculinist theoreticians, revolutionary party members, trade unionists, and academics, Marxist theoretical dominance was assured by means of their power. For Campioni and Grosz, another element in maintaining Marxist hegemony was the adoption of common assumptions on the nature of truth, reality, and reason and a sharing of organizational forms such as planned, effective social organization and respect for law and order with the very bourgeois order it condemned.

CONSEQUENCES OF MARXIAN HEGEMONY FOR SOCIALIST FEMINISM

As the dominant oppositional discourse with a great deal of power, Marxism becomes the standard against which all other revolutionary discourses are compared and found wanting. All other forms of political struggle or theorization are thereby incorporated as variants; as a part of the Marxist project (the classic example being the domestic labour debate); or seen as impurities and therefore unworthy; or counter-revolutionary, to be condemned and discarded. Marxism as the arbiter dismisses claims of an autonomous feminist position and political practice.

Such a dismissal also follows from a strict definition of the legitimate discursive field of socialist feminism by Marxist theory. With concepts such as 'class', 'labour', and 'alienation' based on productive wage-labour, women become theoretically and politically relevant only when they inhabit the male world of paid work. Since the revolutionary objective is defined as the reorganization of productive relations, issues of male power in reproduction, sexuality, or the family, became private matters and explicable solely in terms of the interests 'capital' has in maintaining them.

357

It was against such practical and theoretical marginalization that socialist feminism emerged in the 1970s. And in their theorizations of reproduction, women's domestic and paid work, the family and the state, Marxism was critiqued and the reformulation begun. But for Campioni and Grosz these contributions were primarily to Marxism. As a result socialist feminist innovations tended to strengthen rather than fundamentally challenge Marxism's 'globalizing and reductionist tendencies' (p. 362). They continue: 'The potential explanatory power of the conceptual tools feminisms may possess as an *alternative*, not a *complement* to Marxism are effectively denied in order that Marxism's hegemony may be salvaged' (p. 362). Theoretical unity is achieved through domination and incorporation. It is therefore in relation to Marxism that socialist feminisms are defined and given a coherent history. Fragmentary and non-unified theoretical and practical struggles are deplored as weaknesses, while the imposed and accepted taxonomy limits the possibilities of what socialist feminism can be and is.

SOCIALIST FEMINIST POSSIBILITIES

Despite the power of feminist critiques of Marxism, the tradition remains present, if only as something from which socialist feminism is differentiated. Historically, it was from within the ranks and theorizations of the tradition that socialist feminism emerged and proceeded to pose new challenges to Marxists and to Marxism by prioritizing *feminist* over Marxist concerns.

One of the decisive moments in contemporary socialist feminism is the critical scrutiny of Marxism itself – its epistemological and ontological premises, as well as its status as a discourse whose practitioners hold power, gendered and therefore *interested* positions. All of these components of Marxism are thereby opened to re-evaluation and elements are taken only when they are of use to *feminist* concerns. Thus historical materialism, the importance of contradiction, and utopianism, are all seized as analytical tools.

The fundamental break with the Marxist tradition then becomes the assumption of a women-centred position. It is from this perspective that all of Marxism is to be critically reconsidered. If socialist or socialist feminist concepts or analysis are unable to centralize sexual difference, then they become highly suspect and are to be rejected. As to how any further analysis is to proceed, Marxism and its obverse – bourgeois ideologies – remain the touchstones. But they no longer have the status of the subject, but of the object in the dichotomous, value-loaded logic of A/not A, male/not male (female), Marxism/not Marxism. For now the logic is feminist/not feminist or, more accurately and radically, *feminisms/phallocentrism*. Within this conceptually separatist realm,

358

rights to autonomy, difference, plurality, fluidity, and specificity are affirmed. Alliances and affinities are effected to seize, analyse, and transform the various bodily and imaginative spaces inhabited by women in the integrated circuit of contemporary patriarchal capitalism.

The selected readings are vehicles for the elaboration – but also a questioning – of this argument. Two very different statements from different cultures in addressing divergent topics do not, indeed cannot, 'represent' socialist feminism. They are not presented here to do so, but rather to offer observations and challenges and new possibilities for the further critical evaluation of socialist feminist discursive interventions.

NOTES

1 At the time of writing this article, first published in the *New Statesman* (March 1980), Barbara Taylor had left her native Canada to research nineteenth-century utopian socialism in Britain (the results of which appeared in 1983 as *Eve and the new Jerusalem*, Virago) and described herself as active in the women's liberation movement.

2 With the assumption of theoretical hegemony by Marxism within socialist theorizing, sexual difference and oppression was consigned to the marginal status of 'The Woman Question' to be considered primarily in relation to the practically and theoretically more important 'Class Question'.

3 At the time of writing, both occupied untenured jobs within the breakaway radical part of Sydney University's philosophy department.

4 Details of the second phase of this movement – of the critique and reformulation of Marxist concepts – appear in the companion volume: *Feminist Knowledge: Critique and Construct* (Gunew (ed.), London: Routledge, 1990).

LORDS OF CREATION
Marxism, feminism, and 'utopian' socialism
Barbara Taylor

Exactly a century ago Engels consigned the ideas and hopes of the first British socialists, the Owenites, to a utopian prehistory of scientific socialism, a period of 'crude theories' and 'grand fantasies' which had to be superseded by historical materialism before the communist struggle could be waged on a sound, scientific basis. Here I want to suggest that it is time this evaluation was reassessed, and that an important beginning point for this reassessment is one aspect of Owenite policy on which they sharply differed from their Marxist successors: the issue of women's emancipation.

The Owenites' commitment to feminism was part of the general humanist outlook which Engels later identified as a key feature of all utopian thought: the 'claim to emancipate . . . all humanity at once' rather than 'a particular class to begin with'. The goals were spelled out in detail: with the establishment of a worldwide network of Communities of Mutual Association, all institutional and ideological impediments to sexual equality would disappear, including oppressive marriage laws, privatized households, and private ownership of wealth. The nuclear family (which was held to be responsible not only for the direct subordination of women to men but also for the inculcation of 'competitive' ideology) would be abolished and replaced by communal homes and collective child-rearing. This transformation in living conditions would allow a new sexual division of labour to be introduced: housework ('domestic drudgery') would be performed on a rotational basis (either by men or by children of both sexes) with 'the most scientific methods available', leaving women time to participate in all other aspects of community life, from manufacturing and agricultural labour to government, office, and educational and cultural activities. With childcare collectivized and all economic pressures removed, marriage would become a matter of 'romantic affection' only to be entered into by mutual agreement and dissolved by mutual choice. Or as one leading socialist feminist told an Owenite congress in 1841, 'when all should labour for each, and each be expected to labour for the whole, then would woman be placed in a position in which she would not sell her liberties and her finest feelings . . .'

Alongside these revolutionary hopes went a whole series of lesser reform proposals, including demands for immediate changes in the marriage laws to allow civil marriage and divorce, support for the female franchise (the Owenites frequently criticized the Chartists for excluding women from the suffrage demands), and campaigns to extend education for women and girls. Many of the women who agitated for these reforms were lower-middle class, but as the popular base of the movement expanded they were joined by a small number of working-class feminists, particularly during the general union phase of Owenism in 1833–4, when a number of women's trade unions were formed.

These unions sometimes became centres of lively feminist discussion, encouraged by the Owenite newspaper, *The Pioneer*, which opened a 'Woman's Page' to carry letters from female trade unionists on subjects like equal pay and the right to equal employment. The problem of sex prejudice within the radical working class itself was a common theme. 'The working men complain that the masters exercise authority over them; and they maintain their right to associate, and prescribe laws for their own protection', ran one 'Woman's Page' editorial at the height of the trade union agitation, 'but speak of any project which will diminish the authority of the male, or give him an equal, where once he found an inferior, and then the spirit of Toryism awakes . . . ' When it comes to women, another woman wrote, all men are aristocrats, whatever their class. 'Can it be right, can it be just . . . that woman should be thus trampled on and despised by those who style themselves the lords of creation?' she demanded, going on to add that in her view:

nothing short of a total revolution in all present modes of acting and thinking among all mankind, will be productive of the great change so loudly called for by [women's] miserable state; and there is certainly no system so . . . likely . . . as that proposed by the benevolent Owen, of community property and equality of persons, in which all are *free and equal*. . . . Indeed, I am confident that if women really understood the principles and practice of Socialism, there would not be one who would not become a devoted Socialist.

These were indeed, as Engels later said of the utopian outlook as a whole, 'stupendously grand thoughts'; but were they only that? Before going on to consider this question in greater detail, it is worth reminding ourselves that what he and later Marxists offered instead was a wholly different account of gender/class relations, one in which sexism was reduced to a bourgeois property relation, and thereby evacuated from the working-class struggle. The Owenite emphasis on the universal, trans-class character of 'male supremacy' (their own term) disappeared, to be replaced with dogmatic assertions of sexual equality within the proletariat, calls for sex unity in the face of the common class enemy,

361

and a repudiation of organized feminism as bourgeois liberal deviationism. The vision of a reorganized sexual and family existence which
had been so central to Owenite thinking was increasingly pushed to the
far side of a socialist agenda whose major focus became an economic
revolution which would automatically liberate the whole of the working
class. This is something of a caricature, since so many staunch sexual
egalitarians were to be found in the ranks of later Marxist organizations,
but even the bravest of them rarely flouted an orthodoxy in which the
Woman Question was subsumed under the Class Question. 'It is not
women's petty interests of the moment that we should put in the fore-
ground,' Clara Zetkin told a cheering audience of fellow Social
Democrats in 1896, 'our task must be to enroll the modern proletarian
woman in the class struggle.'

There was more separating these two ways of thinking about women's
oppression than merely the alleged gap between an immature, voluntarist
utopianism and a mature, scientific socialism. The movement from
Owenism to Marxism meant the repudiation of an independent feminist
platform within socialist politics. Why was the struggle against sexual
oppression an integral part of the early socialist strategy?

For the Owenites, unlike later Marxist theorists, capitalism was not
simply an economic order dominated by a single, class-based division,
but an arena of multiple antagonisms and contradictions, each of them
living in the hearts and minds of women and men as well as in their
material circumstances. The very term which they used to describe this
society – 'the competitive system' – indicated the style of their critique,
which moved freely between an economic analysis of workers' exploitation, a moral condemnation of selfish individualism, and a psychological
account of the 'dissocial impulses' which were being bred not only in
factories and workshops, but in schools, churches, and – above all – in
the home where, in the words of William Thompson, 'the uniform
injustice . . . practised by man towards woman, confounds all notions of
right and wrong . . .'

> Every family is a centre of absolute despotism where of course
> intelligence and persuasion are quite superfluous to him who has only
> to command to be obeyed: from these centres, in the midst of which
> all mankind are now trained, spreads the contagion of selfishness and
> the love of domination through all human transactions . . .

The psychological underpinnings of the competitive system, in other
words, were habits of domination and subordination formed within the
most intimate areas of human life. The enslavement of women by men
deformed human character and strangled human potential to the point
where social hierarchy became generally accepted as both natural and
inevitable. Having been trained to mastery within the family, men took

this self-seeking mode into public life as well: *homo economicus*, atomized, competitive individual at the centre of bourgeois culture, was the product of a patriarchal system of psychosexual relations.

Building an alternative to this crippling style of social existence would involve not merely the transfer of economic power from one class to another, but a wholesale transformation of personal life in which all 'artificial' divisions of wealth and power would be supplanted by the organic bonds of communal fellowship. Within each co-operative community women and men would learn new ways of living and loving together. This project, which seemed so 'phantastical' to later Marxists, was absolutely central to the early socialist strategy. For how could 'social sentiment' defeat the 'competitive spirit' unless competition was uprooted from the most intimate areas of life? 'Where does freedom begin, unless in the heart?' For the Owenites, like the earlier Puritan reformers and all the Romantics of the period, it was the establishment of a correct order in sexual relations which was the key to general moral reorganization. Communism found its first and foremost expression in the liberated male–female relation. Feminism was therefore not merely an ancillary feature of the socialist project, but one of its key motivating impulses.

Why did Owenism develop in this way? If, as I have suggested, later Marxist thinkers took a different view of the Woman Question, how and why did all this difference arise?

Owenism developed in a period of rapid social transition, when both class and gender relations were being sharply transformed by new patterns of work and family life. Most early socialists were craftworkers or small tradespeople for whom the 1830s and 1840s represented a period of extended economic and social crisis: the crisis which produced a modern working class. At the most general level, early socialism represented a systematic struggle against these critical developments, and an attempt to reroute them in a new, progressive direction. Unlike later socialist movements, in which working people organized as proletarians, the Owenites were organizing against the process of proletarianization, believing that through economic co-operation and the remoulding of human character they could effectively short-circuit capitalist social relations.

But if in the 1830s plans to establish a new world outside the range of capitalist control still seemed a viable option, by the 1880s, when the second phase of British socialism began, there was far less 'outside' to go to, and working-class organizations which developed within the boundaries of their proletarian status had their ability to see past those boundaries correspondingly reduced. The experience of living within capitalism wore down the socialist imagination, and the effects of this erosion were felt at the theoretical level as well. 'At any point after

1850,' Edward Thompson has written, 'Scientific Socialism had no more need for Utopias (and doctrinal authority for suspecting them). Speculation as to the society of the future was repressed, and displaced by attention to strategy' (Postscript to *William Morris*, 1976, p. 787). The result for British revolutionary Marxists was a systematic denial of the necessary visionary element within socialist consciousness, ending all too often in what William Morris described as a 'sham, Utilitarian Socialism' divested of any genuine libertarian aims, or what his twentieth-century disciple, Thompson, has characterized as:

> the whole problem of the subordination of the imaginative utopian faculties within the later Marxist tradition: its lack of moral self-consciousness or even a vocabulary of desire, its inability to project any images of the future or even its tendency to fall back in lieu of these upon the utilitarian's early paradise – the maximization of economic growth. (ibid, p. 792)

The decline of a genuine feminist vision within British revolutionary movements was one measure of this loss. As the older dream of emancipating 'all humanity at once' was displaced by the economic struggle of a single class, so women and women's interests were pushed to one side. This occurred in two ways.

First, the strategic shift away from the struggle against proletarianization to the proletarian struggle meant the political marginalization of all those who were not, scientifically speaking, proletarians. If the Owenites had cast their net too wide in hoping to attract 'all classes of all nations' to the co-operative cause, Marxism, with its insistence that there was only one route to communism and only one group who would walk it – organized productive workers – tightened the net to the point where only a minority of women were drawn into it, even on a class basis. When combined with a low level of female employment in the most highly organized industrial sectors, this made the fight for socialism seem pretty much a masculine affair. Women Marxists who challenged this situation did so not on the grounds that there was a separate women's cause to be fought alongside and within the class movement, but that women (at least working women) had a right to stand alongside their menfolk in the common cause. The Woman Question which displaced earlier socialist-feminism within late nineteenth-century Marxism was concerned not with the question of how to make a revolution which would free women as a sex, but how to shape women for the class revolution. 'What do women have to do?' Eleanor Marx demanded in 1892, 'we will organize – not as "women" but as *proletarians* . . . for us there is nothing but the working-class movement.'

Second, this contraction of the socialist struggle pushed a whole range of issues beyond the boundaries of revolutionary politics. Since it was no longer the total reformation of women and men which was at stake, but simply the reorganization of productive relations, all questions connected to reproduction, marriage, or personal existence became converted from central problems of strategy to merely private matters. 'I have been told that at the meetings arranged for reading and discussing with working women, sex and marriage problems come first,' Lenin scolded Clara Zetkin in their famous dialogue. 'I could not believe my ears when I heard that. The first state of proletarian dictatorship is battling with the counter-revolutionaries of the whole world . . . and active communist women are busy discussing sex problems.' Not all British revolutionaries, even Leninist ones, shared this attitude, but those who held out against it tended to be a beleaguered minority, particularly in this century. It is thus not surprising to find that when socialist-feminists began to organize in the 1970s, it was with the slogan 'the personal is political' that they mounted their first challenge to the male-dominated Left. The issues had never disappeared; it was just that the voices which could raise them had been long suppressed.

The present must always condescend to the past, and from our vantage point there is indeed a great deal in the thinking of the pre-Marxian socialist which seems theoretically naive and strategically implausible. It is not necessary to deny this, however, in order to suggest that the wholesale dismissal of utopian socialism by later Marxist socialists revealed certain limitations in their own thinking as well: a narrowing of both means and ends which has had serious consequences for the libertarian cause in general and for the liberation of women in particular. Socialist-feminists look back to the Owenites, then, not out of nostalgia for a transition long past, but as a way of tracing the beginnings of a democratic-communist project which is still very much our own, and with which we are still struggling to redefine the ends of modern Marxist movements. For, after all, what count as utopian answers depends on who is raising the questions.

The original version of this paper did not contain reference details in footnotes. Readers are directed to the author's book-length study: B. Taylor, *Eve and the New Jerusalem: Socialism and Feminism in the Nineteenth Century*, London: Virago, 1983.

LOVE'S LABOURS LOST
Marxism and feminism
Mia Campioni and Elizabeth Grosz

Marxism and feminism bear a difficult relation to one another. The relation has been conceptualized as a union, a marriage – however shaky,
a mutually supportive intermingling of theories and modes of practice.
Feminism, it was argued, stood to offer Marxism an account of sexual
oppression while Marxism, in turn, purported to offer feminism a theory
of political struggle and change. More recently, however, strains between
these two political movements have moved discussion away from the
ideal of a happy union towards a debate between potentially antagonistic
participants. A debate between Marxism and feminism has emerged
manifested *within* feminism as a debate between socialist feminism and
other feminisms. The question is which position is politically and
theoretically adequate, or which provides the most exhaustive explanations of women's social relations in modern western cultures; and hence
which position is more radical and effective in presenting strategies for
political change.

Socialist feminists have argued against what they label as 'radical
feminism' on philosophical as well as political grounds. Theories that
take women, their bodies, sexualities, and consciousness as primary, or
which regard patriarchy – the systematic domination of men over women
– as the foundation of all social power are variously declared
individualist, subjectivist, humanist, functionalist, essentialist, naturalist,
and reductionist from a Marxist or socialist perspective. These feminists'
positions are supposed to neglect the primacy of the historico-political
determination of women's oppression in favour of such 'natural' or
ahistorical concepts/categories as 'men' and 'women'. Yet rarely if ever
has the socialist/Marxist perspective been scrutinized in terms of *its*
epistemological and ontological premises. The impact of historical
materialist and scientific socialist presumptions on feminisms, including
socialist feminism has so far remained outside of debate.

Our aim in this paper is to examine some of the central philosophical
and theoretical presuppositions Marxism makes – about the subject, abut
the nature of reality and knowledge in so far as these have direct even
if unrecognized consequences for the development and growth of

366

feminist theories. We will not be directing our critical analysis at any particular version of Marxism but at a number of shared presuppositions that any form of Marxism typically adopts. While it is clear that no single version or variant of Marxism necessarily maintains every presupposition we discuss, nevertheless we claim that every version maintains at least some of these theoretical allegiances. Although there are many Marxisms and socialisms, our aim here is not a detailed textual analysis of one or several positions but a general analysis of Marxism's broad presuppositions and some of the political effects these presuppositions lead to in relation to feminist theory.

Our position is that Marxist concepts of the subject, reality, and reason are phallocentric.[1] This phallocentrism is not eradicated or removed simply by admitting to charges of 'sex-blindness', by adding women's oppression to a whole set of other oppressions. Rather, it needs to be located at the very epistemological and ontological foundations of the Marxist position. As a consequence, we believe that socialist feminism remains locked in a paradox as a *feminist* position unless it can somehow develop a radically *woman-centred* version of 'socialism' which entails 'seeing women first', conceptualizing a space which allows women to be considered autonomous shapers and creators of meaning.[2] Whether it is at all possible to realign the Marxist battery of concepts to accommodate sexual difference is a problem that socialist feminism must work out for itself.

This article assesses some of the philosophical assumptions upon which Marxism, as a Master-knowledge of history and society bases itself. In doing so it addresses not just the theoretical principles involved but also some of the political strategies to which these principles give rise. The discussion divides into three parts. The first examines Marxism's dominance of the left intellectual and political field. The second identifies some of the traditional philosophical assumptions it shares in common with 'bourgeois' theory, particularly the uses made of notions of reason, the subject–object relation, reality and truth, and the relationship between theory and practice. The final part offers analysis of some of the effects of Marxism's philosophical adherences and closures on other modes of radical thought, drawing mainly on the case of feminism. This entails scrutiny of the adequacy of Marxist concepts of subjectivity, and its positions on power and the sexually differentiated body, the struggles for equality versus the right to difference in feminisms.

In addressing ourselves broadly to Marxism or Marxist feminism, we wish to counter two common strategies adopted by Marxists to evade criticism. The first is to separate out 'Marxism' from 'socialism'. While many criticisms of Marxism are justified, so it is argued, they do not apply to *this* (i.e. socialist) version. This tactic accommodates criticism by indefinitely altering and reworking secondary hypotheses, Marxism's 'outer shell', such as centralism and the unity of organization, the primary position of the proletariat, definitions of classes, functions of the state; meanwhile, more primary hypotheses, its 'central core', like the primacy of material production/reproduction, the concept of class, the capitalist state as the locus of power and, more importantly, the unitary goal of Socialist Revolution, are left intact. The second tactic seems a standard mode of reply to criticisms posed to Marxist theory by the existence of so-called socialist systems (USSR, Eastern Europe, China, Cuba, etc.), which has been to produce or invent *another* Marxism, which is always elsewhere. This form is immune to criticism because it always posits a different form of state or social organization, one not yet in existence, one always other to the view that is criticized.[3]

MARXISM AND THE POLITICAL FIELD

In its position as *the* radical political theory, Marxism maintains a position of power which remains largely unrecognized and which negatively affects its relations to other left political positions. This kind of dominance within left-wing politics is the result of its usually unacknowledged connections to existing institutions and bodies of authority as well as to its modes of operation within left circles. Its strategies seem dual. On the one hand, they can be regarded as institutional and based on acquiring recognition and status from institutional bodies and established agencies of power. On the other hand, they are defensive/offensive in relation to other forms of left politics. This involves the controlling, labelling, and classification of theoretical positions other than Marxism. In defending itself, Marxism criticizes other theories which are then discarded as unworthy or incorporated as part of its project.

At the level of theory, politics, and organization, Marxism shares many characteristics with the very system it claims to challenge. Rather than being radically 'other', Marxism is virtually the alter-ego, the inversion around a shared axis of its capitalist counterpart. Capitalism and socialism are perhaps two sides of the same coin. This is evident in the way in which Marxism shares with the bourgeois order it condemns, a belief in certain essential values for effective social organization. These shared values include: respect for law and order, planned organization, the need for accurate prediction, policy-making, and planning, the need for enlightened leadership, full development of productive capacities, the need for social unity, belief in progress and evolution. As well, it shares: an ideal of society as a unitary totality, a concept of universal (equal) subjectivity, the idea that global explanations are superior to particularized or local explanations, a unitary view of truth, reason, reality, and causality as ultimate neutral and objective principles in knowledge. Where Marxism is indeed a radical opposite of bourgeois thought is in its methods – as well as its prescription for how to define or express these values, and for whom.

The first form of institutional support for Marxism thus comes from holding a set of values and interests in common with traditional modes of thought. Second, within existing institutions of power and authority, the position of Marxism can be characterized as one with considerable recognition. Its place in institutions of learning, in the circuits of publications, in trade unions, political parties and movements, and in various cultural and political organizations suggests it has an 'honourable' place within capitalism as an acknowledged, even if not admired adversary. Within the university structure, Marxism has a position comparable to the official trade union movement.[4] It is acknowledged as the 'official enemy' of capitalism occupying a position that is representative of all radical politics. This has the effect of reducing all other forms of struggle for change to variants, impurities, or counter-revolutionary positions within a primary political schema, thereby keeping them in check. Marxism may be criticized, but it is also engaged with as a worthy adversary to bourgeois theory. The extent to which Marxism has become respectable and recognized in universities as *the* rival scientific knowledge to bourgeois forms of thought is also indicated by the number of senior academics who are Marxists, the number of courses in Marxist and Marxist-related areas, the recommended reading lists in areas of Marxist expertise in the humanities[5] – particularly in education, law, psychology, sociology, urban studies, history, geography, and languages. Third, apart from its network of institutional supports, Marxism, as a conceptual system, shares another common history with conventional thought, and even the understanding provided by common sense. Importantly, in relation to our arguments here, Marxism shares with bourgeois thought a *universal* representation of humanity that is in fact masculine. It is phallocentric and ignores sexual specificity because of its complicity in a shared set of assumptions that mark all socio-political thought hitherto: that the norm of humanity is best represented by 'man'. Marxism shares with bourgeois thought the strategy of defining women only in relation to male norms. Given this common set of assumptions and methods, it is not surprising that the superiority of Marxism over feminism can be asserted as a natural fact, since for most women it is extremely difficult to articulate *ourselves* as the norm of judgements and values – to develop a woman-centred concept of ourselves and our world. It is largely because of this shared mode of dominant thinking that Marxism has been unable to claim itself indispensable to feminism. In reinterpreting and redirecting feminist thought and practice according to its *a priori* framework, it simply reflects and reproduces already customary ways of conceptualizing women as incomplete, lacking.[6]

Women are considered only in relation to men, hence there is an emphasis on issues reflecting this assumption in Marxist theory: reproduction, the family, women and work, sexuality. The question of the relationship between Marxism and feminism implies a symmetry between competing but equal politico-theoretical frameworks, but in fact Marxism more often relates to feminism as a form of Master-knowledge, a form of theoretical domination that creates subjugated/subjected knowledges and perpetuates the silence that has robbed women of their history and culture. In establishing its position as the leader of radical politics, Marxism seizes for itself a substantial technique for control – the power of definition. It assumes both the power of self-definition and the power of definition over the whole political field, including other forms of left-wing politics. In this way, Marxism reduces the specificity, aims, and struggles of different groups so that they are commensurate with Marxist criteria and therefore able to be judged by them. This tendency abounds in the fields of women's struggles, anti-racism, anti-heterosexism. It reduces these struggles so that they are all instances of one struggle – the one Marxism guides. For example, attempts are made to reduce abortion, childbirth, rape, prostitution, and pornography to class issues or to capitalist financial interests, sexuality, and male domination to the bourgeois family, marriage, monogamy, private property, and state control. All issues raised by the power relations between men and women are claimed to be ultimately explicable in terms of the interests capital has in upholding them. Capitalism is ultimately shown to bear an intrinsic and essential relation to patriarchy, and hence its overthrow is supposed to rob the latter of its crucial material base.[7] With respect to the 'issue' of heterosexism, that institution employed to ensure men's continual access to women, this is only ever acknowledged if, once again, it can be argued that compulsory heterosexuality serves capitalism, not all men.[8] In this context, we need to examine more closely the continual dismissal by Marxists of attempts to theorize the origins of patriarchy by reference to myths, religion, prehistoric arte-facts, modes of symbolic exchange, and kinship categories.[9] Similarly, questions about an inherent ethnocentrism of western culture with its paranoid adherence to materialism and anti-spiritualism, as well as its naive belief in a scientific progress synonymous with control over nature, are more often than not rephrased in terms of greedy commercial interests. In this way, the evils of white society are reduced to results of imperialism, which has the effect of implying that Marxists are natural anti-racists.[10] These are just a few examples of the globalizing/reduc-tionist tendency in Marxism that enables it to subsume many different struggles and aims under its umbrella. Marxism is thus able to install itself as a Master-knowledge of the left, relegating other forms of knowledge and struggle to a secondary or auxiliary position. Marxism is nevertheless able to utilize the 'inputs' of such knowledges very ably to expand its grip on the political field. By adding 'women's issues', anti-racism, anti-heterosexism to its agenda in the manner we have outlined, it is able to cover an ever wider terrain.

In this way, Marxism exerts a power over other radical struggles that seems only marginally better than the oppressive situations it purports to challenge. Instead of Marxism assuming a position of support and recognition *vis-à-vis* other radical struggles, it declares a partnership in which *it* decrees the conditions of interaction. It utilizes a power to direct 'autonomous' struggles along its path. In any partnership, Marxism is in fact prioritized and taken as the position from which one can ultimately evaluate the other partner, and the partnership as a whole. In this relation, the 'junior partner' has to avow its own *insufficiency* to be accorded a place, 'marginal' movements are put into the position of having to prove their radical credentials – their 'faith' or 'belief' in radical social change as determined by Marxism. On the other hand, they are also required to admit their ignorance and their need to embrace a more comprehensive and challenging theory. Without Marxist guidance, other theories are regarded as confused, inconsistent, ahistorical, romantic, or naive; as lacking objectives and 'adequate explanatory tools', hence co-optable.

In acting as Master-knowledge, Marxism takes the position of the subject, the knower, and its radical 'partner', such as feminism, is assigned the role of object of knowledge. Marxism, in other words, delegates to itself the right of definition and analysis. It establishes grades of judgement, imposes dichotomous categories over a field of differences, defines key concepts and issues, and determines the criteria of intelligibility by which it can reduce its partner to one of two positions. Either the other valiantly tries to insert herself, her struggles, her knowledges within the master paradigm, expending all energy in the process; or, alternatively, finds herself relegated to the status of heretic, playing the role of hysterical other to the cool of Marxist reason, thereby apt to be ridiculed, or simply refused a hearing.

The debate between Marxism and other radical movements has thus been a one-sided communication of directives and truths. In refusing to acknowledge the self-sufficiency, the difference of other theories and struggles which may fall outside its paradigm, Marxism effectively acts as a form of control on those movements. By prioritizing Marxist principles which assume the right to decide which issues, goals, and modes of action are appropriate, the very autonomy of other struggles is absorbed and transformed into a form accommodating Marxism.

What is conveniently overlooked is that all of these concepts and principles may prove to mean quite different things from a *feminist perspective*; that is to say, one that takes women's social relations *qua* women as primary. Moreover these criticisms and evaluations only gain a status *within* Marxist discourse, yet this discourse is not open to serious questioning when confronted with the theoretical innovations and developments feminisms have to offer. The potential explanatory power of the conceptual tools feminisms may possess as an *alternative, not a complement* to Marxism are effectively denied in order that Marxism's hegemony may be salvaged. We would not want to detract from the importance of contributions made by Marxist-feminists in extending Marxism's scope to analyses of women's oppression under capitalism, particularly in areas that Marxism has previously ignored or under-developed such as the family, women, and labour, and women's relation to the state. We would argue, however, that these contributions are also continually fuelling Marxist systems of interpretation, strengthening their globalizing and reductionist tendencies. Moreover, it prevents a thorough examination of the presumed ability of Marxism indefinitely to extend itself beyond the parameters of its original paradigm and of its investments in exerting power over fields of feminist thinking and action. The right to intervene and dominate in this field is simply asserted by pointing to Marxism as the more complete theory of society with an established tradition in political thinking. That this more complete theory of society reflects primarily masculine views and interests defining women with respect to their place in a male world and in accordance with how they complement men, is underestimated in favour of pointing out links with capitalist interests.

The effect of this paradigm on the field of women's struggles is that priorities and evaluations imported from Marxism are imposed on diverse and complex variants of feminism, reducing them to terms oppositional to Marxism. The many differences between and within feminisms are often written off by homogenizing them into neat units of 'otherness' such as 'radical feminism', 'bourgeois feminism', or 'lesbian separatism'. This often serves to relegate those outside the Marxist framework to the role of adversary to true, social, revolutionary change and, by extension, to that of objective supporter of capitalism and thus of continued oppression and exploitation. This binary logic, the logic of either/or (if you are not for us you must be against us) imputes that not to be a Marxist implies not being able to achieve one's own aim – the liberation of women from male domination – let alone being incapable of explaining the 'larger, more important' issues of social power.

This practice of transforming difference into dichotomous opposition is a significant political strategy. By representing itself simply as a neutral mode of dividing and distinguishing differences as natural opposites, Marxism denies any complicity in the very construction of the dichotomy, let alone its investment in the primacy of one of the terms of the dichotomy at the expense of the other. Dichotomies divide a disparate field according to one value and judge initially non-comparable others on

372

the basis of that value. Male/female becomes male/non-male. The logical form A/not A, the general form of a philosophically dichotomous structure, demonstrates clearly the primacy accorded to A as the positive, affirmative term, and characteristic value governing the field of the dichotomy.

This practice of privileging one of the two terms, defining the second as an absence of the first, is also a favourite mode of description of Marxism, for example, such opposites as public/private, political/psychological, objective/subjective, economic/ideological, production/reproduction, class/sex all implicitly prioritize the left term at the expense of the right. This tactic establishes a veneer of objectivity and naturalness which serves to disguise the political values which the dichotomy actually wields.[11] In general then, dichotomous thinking reduces multiplicity and plurality of levels and positions to a single oppositional norm. The claim for the appropriateness of this mode of dividing up the world lies in the belief in a singular explanatory paradigm and a universal homogenized politics to combat all the particular expressions of an oppressive social system by giving them an underlying or central cause such as the exploitation of the proletariat by capital.[12]

One of the major effects of Marxism's institutional position and its modes of definition of itself and others, is an insidious politics of representation. In presenting itself as a form of knowledge, Marxism claims to be able to explain the real conditions of existence beyond lived experience. What is to be considered real is defined as that which is outside of experience, independent of one's perceived place in the social formation and beyond the surface manifestations of everyday life. Knowledge of these real conditions which is considered a prerequisite to viable and effective political action – is possible only if one submits oneself to the central tenets of the Marxist understanding of reality. Marxism articulates what the worker or the oppressed cannot know or say. It speaks on behalf of those who cannot speak because they lack the capacity for synthesizing particularities into a systematic whole. It is never made clear, however, why this need for totalizing is a need of the oppressed; rather, it seems to function as a need for the intellectual (who is usually white, middle-class, and male) to think in terms of universals and totalities.[13] The fact that their 'real interests' are not always directly perceived as such by the oppressed, is explained by terms like 'political apathy', 'false consciousness', 'self-interest(!)', 'ideology', or more recently and rather inappropriately, 'the unconscious'. There is, however, no *a priori* correspondence between those represented and their representatives, between the objects and the subjects of knowledge, although this is what Marxism assumes when it judges itself to be the true representative of the masses (whoever is included in this category).

It is a reduction of difference and specificity to sameness by means of its implicit concepts of truth, reality, and rationality that allows Marxism to intervene, impose its judgements, and claim to represent all other struggles. One of the ways in which Marxism attempts this reduction is in its representation of a common enemy: the macrolithic system of capitalism. While this common enemy may well exist for all such groups it is unwarranted to conclude that its operations and effects are all the same for all groups.[14] To posit patriarchy as 'the enemy' as feminism does offers Marxism a chance to co-opt or appropriate its aims and goals by making patriarchy the inevitable double of capitalism.[15]

Marxism suggests not only a common enemy, it also involves a commonness of interests and a shared stake in struggles. These positions become subsumed under Marxism's primacy and their particularity, specificity, and appropriateness in context is ignored. All positions are levelled with respect to each other, they all become variations or trends of the same thing, different struggles against a common enemy. These other struggles are seen to be tinged with features of the very system they challenge and are seen as incapable of adequately formulating an understanding of, or programme for social change alone. In this way all other positions are transformed from difference to opposition: non-Marxists become anti-Marxists. They become examples of liberalism, reformism, leftism, irrationalism, functionalism, and pluralism: all degrees of bourgeois complicity. Marxism is able to represent all radical movements as variations, and inadequate ones at that, of a true (socialist) revolutionary theory and practice. In this way, these movements become objects of analysis for Marxism *within* Marxist theory and are subjected to a logic of reinterpretation and representation.

Given the institutional power of Marxism and its domination of the left political field, it becomes extremely difficult to combat this reduction and to insist on a multiplicity of aims, practices, and theories directed towards revolutionary social change. This may be illustrated in the Marxist search for Feminist Theory and a Unified Movement, where differences between women in feminism are seen as fragmented, subjective, or based on confused ideas about political organization. If Marxism speaks of the need for an autonomous women's movement it actually means a homogeneous entity capable of taking care of or rather keeping in check the struggles over women's issues, those which the theory of capital has not yet managed to allot a place within the ambit of its core principles. The fragmentary, non-unified theoretical perspectives and practices of feminist struggles are deplored as a weakness rather than applauded as a strength. Feminism is seen as being in need of unification, tighter organization, and a more comprehensive programme that will include all women, somehow, under a single banner. Marxism's claim to one movement with one (true) theory and a singular programme is simply transposed onto feminism as if fragmentation and regionality were a problem instead of a mode of self-determination. Feminism is judged by Marxist criteria which seem to have little appreciation of the issues and struggles faced by women *as women*.[16]

MARXISM AND THE THEORETICAL DOMAIN

The so-called 'crisis in Marxism' is not simply a political crisis, a crisis in effectivity, organization, or popular appeal. The crisis Marxism faces is also a theoretical crisis, a crisis at the level of its adherence to problematic concepts of Knowledge, Truth, Reason, and Power which it holds in common with the mainstream of western philosophical thought. This crisis affects not only its place as revolutionary vanguard, it also raises questions about the very politics of scientificity – the *political* function of knowledge, truth, and representation. Questions about the relation between power and knowledge have until recently been discussed with Marxism only in relation to the 'ruling class' or the state. The claim to truth, the will to knowledge, the primacy of reason, are rarely examined in their relation to power, and are taken as somehow pure and neutral values.[17]

Marxism's adherence to these philosophical assumptions is central to its functions of representing all other political groups and its operations as a system of thought. These adherences include: the claim for a universal totalizing theory, capable of explaining various conflicts and disturbances at all levels of the social formation with a concept of (dialectical) causality and a belief in *telos*, in an immanent singular meaning to social events in their diversity. It is these which lead to a desire for programmes and prescriptions to direct practice towards the realization of reason, to a need to construct a system of social order, and so on.

Marxism, contrary to its own assertions, has a great deal invested in traditional philosophical concepts of knowledge, truth, reason, and the universal rational intellect, which have precise political effects. In the face of a world that increasingly finds itself confronted with regional, marginal, and minority groups which revolt against the denial of their claims to a unique irreducible difference, a commitment to concepts of universality may prove historically inappropriate and politically oppressive. A few primary points of intersection between Marxist theory and traditional philosophy serve to indicate Marxism's ensnarement in phallocentric and logocentric assumptions.[18]

The primacy of reason

The concept of reason that Marxism shares in common with bourgeois thought has an illustrious genealogy in the history of philosophy which dates from Plato.[19] This concept presupposes a unified mind, unhampered by any internal contradictions which may result from its relations to a lived body. Reason is not simply based on a psychical unity, it is also the principle that organizes reality. Reason is the link, the mediating connection between the unitary mind and a singular reality. Reason provides a double guarantee: it ensures that the mind comes progressively to approximate reality (making knowledge, truth, and science the major embodiments of reason); and that reality is grasped in its fullness by the mind, as may be illustrated from effective intervention in practical reason. This double guarantee can be stressed in various ways: by stressing the mind's capacity to *make* the world understandable, the idealist position is developed; by privileging the world as *having* a determinate reason which the mind adequately grasps when it is rational, we are led to materialism. What is perhaps ironic about Marxism's epistemology is that, while claiming to overthrow idealism, it simply takes the opposite side, remaining locked into its underlying assumptions and values.

In common with its historical and philosophical heritage, Marxism does not characterize reason positively, in its own terms, but defines it dichotomously. Reason as a privileged value (or value of the privileged) must be contrasted with what it defines as *not* reason. In this way, reason establishes a positive value and content for itself by creating oppositions, 'others' that serve to locate and implicitly define reason. These 'others' of reason give up their independent content to define the ground on which something else can be called rational becoming the completely negative task of illustrating what reason is not. A whole 'anatomy of otherness' is established if the list of all the dichotomies that serve to anchor reason is added together. Taken together, these are constituted as an infinite, homogeneous other levelled to an amorphous category of 'the irrational'. Among the relevant oppositions that serve to define reason are: reason/madness, reason/passions, reason/emotions, reason/sense, reason/experience, reason (mind)/body, reason/spontaneism, reason/barbarism, and reason/anarchy.

Moreover, reason is not simply in opposition to various 'others'; its primacy depends on a transcendence, an overcoming or avoiding the dangers this otherness poses. In order to attain the status of reason, the knower must disengage from lived experience, the body, senses, emotions, and so on, putting them on one side, as it were. In separating these 'others' from reason, philosophical tradition must neglect their place, operation, and effects. Only procedures based on reason are

376

acceptable and valuable theoretical contributions – reflection, analysis, synthesis, logical arguments, the dialectic, clear and straightforward expression. Marxism, as heir to this tradition, is able thereby to claim a power and appeal as a rational theory and method of change, guiding and informing other political groups who are in some way 'less rational'.

Our point here is not that there are systems of thought which are so naive as to believe in reason; nor, on the other hand, do we wish to claim a positive value to 'the irrational' as a category, for this would amount to accepting the dichotomy while attempting to reverse its value. Our criticism has to do with the political investments in this process of separating the rational from the irrational. Our criticism is not that Marxism uses a concept of reason, but with the particular conception that it uses – a hierarchical, transcendent, and unitary one. Reason is not defined by its incidental properties or qualities, but by its capacity to stand over and above particularities and specificites. Reason, in shedding itself of all particularity, not only leaves behind its own history, it becomes the yardstick or measure for all the forms that it constitutes as irrational. The unified, singular, global form of reason, Reason, prevents a political and historical understanding of the dichotomous mode of characterizing reason. This model of rationality cannot accord a place to other forms of rationality derived from different concrete contexts. This position, however, must not be equated with relativism. There is nothing relative about politics or power unless for those who presume themselves to be outside of it in some universal position of knowledge. Marxism retains the belief that there can be no thought which remains specific, local, particular, and yet theoretically justified. Thinking and understanding can only attain the position of Knowledge or Truth if it attains the universal.

The subject/object relation

Marxism also inherits the subject/object dichotomy. This presents a non-reversible hierarchy in which the subject of knowledge has a privileged status in relation to the object of knowledge. The use of this dichotomy has two related consequences: a radical distinction between the subject of knowledge, on the one hand, and the object of knowledge, on the other; and a bifurcation between 'subjective' and 'objective' interests in knowledge. These have important implications for the Marxist concept of knowledge, of the knower or intellectual and of the relation between these and those who are ignorant.

While Marxism insists that material conditions of existence shape the subject's consciousness, when it comes to the *subject of knowledge* the concept of a disembodied, rational, or universal consciousness is posited instead. *This* subject, the subject that produces truthful knowledges, is

377

not implicated in such 'subjective' ensnarements as political, economic, or personal interests, for the subject is not a living, experiencing subject at all, but a rational, knowing subject. This rational subject is a neutral subject, a disinterested knower who may be committed or involved with political struggle, but whose commitment does not interfere with the objectivity of the theoretical work that is engaged in. This subject is unhinged from lived experience and the particularity of a position in the world. This is perhaps what explains the notable absence of self-critical awareness of the privileged social position of the Marxist intellectual or academic.

Marxist social science divides the politico-social field into objects or potential objects of knowledge – oppressed workers, women, blacks, and also capitalists. These 'objects' of knowledge do not, at least in crude versions, produce knowledge themselves, but ideology and self-interested rationalization. They can be known, but not themselves knowers. Their existence as potential objects of knowledge is given. What is significant about this opposition between subject and object of knowledge is that the knowing subject, the agent of the theory's truth never becomes the object of the other's gaze, never gets analysed in turn. Knowledge mediates between the subject and the object in one direction only.

Knowledge produced by a rational subject using the appropriate methods wilfully manipulated in the hands of propagandists or advertisers yields a knowledge that is objective, true in all circumstances, for all subjects. Objective knowledge is objective because it is not relative to space and time, because it is independent of all 'subjective' particularities, and because it is politically neutral. All knowledge that does not attain this position is thereby deemed subjective and demoted to the status of opinion or belief. The particular, the experiential, what is variable, the question or viewpoint or perspective are considered subjective, and thus not suitable for the kind of generalization that structures objectivity. The politics of knowledge-production and the position and function of those who produce knowledge remains untouched on this conception of knowledge. As a neutral object, the subject of knowledge is not considered to be implicated in the structure or content of knowledge. It is only when the relations of power between the knower and the known are openly discussed that the question of the power of the knowing subject over the object of knowledge can be challenged or overthrown altogether.

Reality and truth

Marxism's reliance on a traditional concept of rationality is, as we have already suggested, directly connected to a particular conception of reality. Reality and reason are somehow mirror-images of each other, for reality is in principle rational in its underlying structure. It is presumed that reality is governed by particular causal laws which are determinable and understandable, that it is a reality amenable to scientific understanding.

The idea that there is *no* meaning or reason *in* the world other than that which is contributed to it by human thought is unacceptable for Marxism. Indeterminacy, chance, discontinuity, event, or accident are only ever acknowledged as operating in reality when it is understood that these are only apparent occurrences without meaning, which can be given their real explanation by attributing specific causes to them by uncovering their real determination. Adequate or true knowledge is then a knowledge which grasps the underlying structure and totality of reality. Reality is in essence whole, a given object of thought, even if it can be admitted that reality is *perceived* differently from different perspectives. This is why, for Marxism, 'lived experience' is a second-order phenomenon which requires knowledge of what structures it so that it may be seen as first-order relation. It is precisely Marxism which can provide this knowledge of the real relations which structure phenomena, because it grasps reality properly in its underlying totality.[20]

The adherence to the concept of a unified and singular reality has led Marxism to conceptualize the relation between this given reality and the processes of signification that present us with knowledge of it as one of correspondence (see below). While two or more theories may signify this reality in quite different ways, underneath or beyond these representations is a reality to which they may or may not correspond, and which exists quite independently of their representations. Incommensurable positions are regarded as forms of interpretation of one and the same underlying reality. As interpretations they are mere embellishments, or acts of consciousness, reflecting a reality other than their own. Interpretations, it may be conceded, are the products of differences that are explicable in terms of interests or politics (ideological adherences), but their referent, the real, is outside this arena, free from ideology. It is this neutral reality that determines the true objectivity of competing statements.

We do not want to suggest that there is no reality or that the material world does not exist. Such a traditional form of opposition to realism is hardly a useful concept, politically speaking. But to admit that the world exists does not commit us to a singular truthful mode for accounting for it. Marxism seems to assume an implicit parallelism between the totality of the world (reality) and the totality of knowledges (truth) as well as the function of reason in grasping this totality. A singular reality requires a singular true theory and a singular form of reason to formulate or know it. No place can be accorded to other modes of conceptualization, other forms of experience, and other knowledges. The complexity and multiplicity of the world is reduced to the manifestation of a singular underlying reality which can be used to explain the apparent plurality of the perceived world.

The essential and material unity of reality is what is shared among all human beings. It is thus no surprise that Marxism insists on the need for unitary action. The struggles of women, blacks, gays, or youth can, as a result, be labelled directionless, unorganized, unrealistic, but most of all, particularized and thus incapable of grasping the real in its totality and thus of even their own *real* interests.

In accordance with its conception of a singular form of reality and a singular mode of rationality, Marxism relies on an absolutist and singular concept of truth. Truth is conceived, as in traditional philosophy, as a relation of correspondence between a proposition or discourse and that part of the world that it depicts. The image or representation of reality, and the reality it represents have a certain isomorphism such that one could say the image is a true representation of reality. Truth in other words is established by the process of *reference*. From its commitment to a singular and independent reality already, as it were loaded with meaning and from its adherence to a rather naive materialism,[21] language as a medium of truth is seen as a passive, reflective second-order phenomenon. Language is capable of being a neutral tool of description and analysis, clearly and simply referring to a reality outside and beyond discourse. Truth is a form of bridge between these two distinct systems, the form in which discourse grasps reality.

In so far as a proposition is true it is regarded as neutral, objective, universal, and ahistorical – true under all conditions at all times.[22] It is only in so far as a body of true propositions is organized by systematic rules or laws that it can aspire to the status of science. Marxism becomes a science from the moment its knowledge is no longer dependent on political or sectarian interests. It becomes scientific when *internal* interests to knowledge itself become primary. Such knowledge is not the partial or contingent discourses of workers, oppressed groups, or even intellectuals, but a knowledge directed at and based upon an understanding of the totality and underlying reality of society. The separation of truth from all investments in power relations is based on the belief that the truth condition is established merely by the correspondence of discourse and reality. As *re*presentation, is is a more or less transparent phenomenon that can be nevertheless capable of being used neutrally, disengaged from power.[23]

Since it is presumed that power lies with political interests or that true knowledges derive from a situation outside of power, Marxism relieves itself of the need for self-examination or questioning of its desire for truth as a desire for power. Marxism, it seems, cannot accept the relativity of scientific discourses – a relativity not only with respect to history, different cultures, or individuals, but a relativity with respect to *power*.

Marxism is able to justify itself as a truthful and objective theory in two quite different ways. First, as we have just outlined, Marxism presents itself as a true representation of reality. This marks its aspirations as a social science. Second, Marxism presents itself as a true representative of a universal proletariat, as the position that most ably or truly represents the interests of the working class. It is able to represent those who need the truth. Both these positions amount to a refusal to see that science, whether 'proletarian science' or 'universal science' and the formations of true knowledges are already deeply implicated in power relations. Marxists have spent considerable time and effort connecting the operations and functioning of false or ideological discourses to power (e.g. to the interests of particular groups); but they refuse to acknowledge the 'stakes' of knowledge and science production are just as high as those of ideology, the political investments just as great.

Marxism, as a result, does not need to scrutinize itself or allow other competing theories an existence as adequate or true accounts of particular historical realities. Since, as we have argued, reality is singular and unified for Marxism, it is a reality flattened of depth and diversity. Particular experiences, positions, and forms of oppression are relevant only in so far as they relate to this common, universal reality, the mode of production as the 'arche' of all societies, past, present, and future.[24] Direct experience and true knowledge seem, on the Marxist conception, to be mutually exclusive – experience mitigates the globality, objectivity, and universality of true knowledge, while presenting experience to the grid of truth somehow mitigates its subjective, experiential nature.

It must be noted here that our claim is not that Marxism includes some phenomena and not others in a highly selective manner. The inclusion of some and the exclusion of other objects of analysis, the existence of criteria which constitute them as appropriate objects, and the establishment of criteria and rules of adequacy all mark the operations of any discourse or theoretical systems. The point however is *what* it is that is included and excluded and the political effects of this selection process. In other words, the openness of objects, methods and the closure to other systems of thought marks an unacknowledged set of political investments that belie the claim to neutrality and objectivity made by scientific or true systems.[25]

Marxism can be seen to be waging a battle on two fronts on the battleground of truth. First, it struggles against so-called bourgeois knowledges, particularly those that claim some scientific status in social, political, and economic theory. Its claim here is that these social theories are developed and maintained in order to justify the social order – they are bourgeois in so far as they represent bourgeois interests and hence are false and ideological.[26] Second, it uses its claims to scientificity and truth to combat, suppress, or supersede other knowledges, knowledges based on concrete experiences of exploitation and oppression, analysing, explaining, and representing these knowledges in its true discourse. A strategy that evolves out of this double-barrelled investment in truth is an attempt to reduce the latter to versions of the former. Out of this results a dominance over the field of left politics that cannot be questioned – as a truth able to point out the 'ideological investments' both bourgeois and some radical theories share in common, Marxism stands outside and beyond them.

The significant question that needs to be posed here – one which Marxism cannot ask as soon as it presents itself as a science or true discourse – is at the level of the *desire* for totality, unity, synthesis, reductive singularity, and what power is invested in it, all of which effects theoretical closures.[27] Why is it necessary to unify/solidify what may be fluid, diverse, and changing, if not in order to block or control it? Diverse, changeable, strategic knowledges pose a potential threat that must be minimized – that of the incapacity of theory, of *any* theory to capture reality in its entirety or in its essence. To invoke truth in the way that Marxism does as a singular, universal, absolute, and exhaustive meta-principle is to prevent the question being asked: who poses truth, from where, to whom, and for what purpose?

The theory/practice relation

Marxism's investment in truth and rationality leads it to a rather paradoxical and circular conception of the relation between theory and practice. Admittedly, it is within Marxist discourse that the necessity of theory being tied to action, and of action being infused with theory is developed. But the establishment of a dichotomous concept of the relations between theory and practice almost in spite of itself privileges one of the terms of the dichotomy (theory) and reduces the other (practice) to more an object of rather than a complement to theory. This dichotomy is represented in the old distinction between mental and manual labour, which Marxism has never successfully been able to exorcise other than by attributing its existence to the evils of capitalism. A bifurcation between theory and practice is, in fact, a corollary of Marxism's adherence to a traditional concept of reason; for theory to be reliable and effective, it must be produced elsewhere than practice.

Within Marxism there is an implicit assumption about what constitutes theory and what counts as practice. They must be distinct for a dialectical relation between them to be possible. Theory is presumed to be what is written in books in the quiet reflection before and after action, remote from polemic or politics; while practice consists in the energies of bodies of individuals and groups in concrete struggles. While this radical separation is to some extent a caricature (it is a firm belief that theory is always at least implicit in *effective* struggle), nevertheless the two remain quite distinct and in need of mediation. Theory is supposed to provide a rational guide to practice, directing, controlling, interrogating, and analysing it; while practice informs, reforms, corrects, and is reflected in theory. Practice without theory (if such a thing were possible) would be without aims or objectives, blind in its direction, chaotic or haphazard in its effects. It would be irrational, without sense. Theory, on the other hand, cut off from practice becomes stale, idealist, irrelevant, and untested. A dialectical relationship between these two terms is necessary to provide an adequate context for each and to account for their interrelationships. Whichever side is privileged depends on the strategy necessary in a given conjuncture: theory can be invoked when the masses start to define their own practice (Althusser); practice can be invoked when the masses have to be wooed (Mao).

Under scrutiny, this dialectical relation between the terms is not an equal or reciprocal one, for theory always retains a primacy with respect to practice. While theoretical interventions, or more pertinently, interventions by theorists, academics, and party officials representing the truth have an enormous power in relation to struggles and political practice (witness the role of the PCF in Paris, 1968), practice changes or directs theory only in its outer protective shell, but does not touch its core. Indeed, it is only from the position of the core that practices, including Marxism's own, and all other theories are evaluated. No possible practice could ever undermine its fundamental axioms. The core is *a priori* confirmed by any possible struggles, successes, or even failures.[28]

This is not to say that internal debates about the explanatory power of the core principle do not take place. In fact, they do, quite regularly. However, these take place by forcing the reality of successes and failures into the straitjacket of the theory, which can endlessly expand its definitions of basic principles by reinterpreting the sacred texts but never questioning their relevance or adequacy. Marxism has an immutable centre beyond debate, analysis, experience, or practice and is thus not regarded as a tool whose usefulness must be tested on the job at hand. The appropriateness of the theory is never in question, only the effectivity of struggles, practices, and strategies can be doubted.

Theory and practice, presented as if they were dialectical partners in revolutionary struggle, are in fact judged and assessed *only* by theoretical criteria. It is *theory* that judges the effects of theory on practice and practice on theory. To speak of practice in Marxist terms can only be done in terms of what practice means to Marxist theory. So, even if it is seen as a complement or supplement to theory, practice remains secondary, undirected. Practice is judged by a *theory of practice* as good/bad, relevant/irrelevant, etc., but theory itself is generally not subjected to practical criticism.

This emphasis on the guiding role of theory in relation to practice is supposedly what distinguishes Marxist politics from other forms of political struggle. Because theory is considered either absent, problematic, or non-directive in other struggles, these struggles are considered irrational, confused, chaotic, unfounded. Marxism, in contrast, derives from a close relation between theory and practice, mediated by the theory in the figure of the theorist/intellectual who claims to master knowledge and thus be capable of representing the other. The subject/object relation in knowledge is reinforced by a mental/manual split that characterizes the relations between theory and practice. Those that act in concrete struggles are generally considered not to be those who produce theory; they can become so if they conduct their struggles according to the theoretical directives laid down by Marxism.

BEYOND MARXISM

Marxism, in uncritically adopting traditional concepts of subjectivity and the body, presents an inherently phallocentric or masculinist characterization of the subject. This phallocentrism establishes an implicitly normative account of the subject, equating it with characteristics associated with masculinity. This normative commitment, in our view, blocks any well-meaning attempts by socialist feminists to find a place for women in Marxist theory, or alternatively, drastically to change the theory's outer shell while adhering to its basic principles. In the last resort, this leads to adopting the tactics of representation that Marxism utilizes – globalizing and totalizing difference in the service of an assumed sameness.

The concept of subjectivity in Marxism

It has been generally assumed since Althusser's work on ideology and subjectivity that any form of humanism is anathema to Marxism. Whereas earlier versions of Marxism (and Marx's own 'pre-scientific' writings) may have adopted concepts of a basic human nature and an unalienated essence of human existence, the development of 'scientific' Marxism meant that the determination of any human essence must be rejected as a form of idealism. Reference to a definite human nature is criticized for being bourgeois or ideological, since it is claimed that needs, desires, beliefs, and meanings are ahistorically determined. To suggest that these might have a definite form or content is seen as contrary to the goals of socialism.

Yet, a form of essentialism remains undetected in even the most rabid anti-humanist version of Marxism, since this so-called empty category of human nature nevertheless does have some given characteristics.

Human existence is still ultimately defined by the basic activity of the production of material goods by labour. All social relations derive, in the final analysis, from economic relations (the only material relations that fill the category of subject). Apart from the fact that what is material is narrowly defined to include economic relations but to exclude linguistic, libidinal, and other forms of power relations, this simply assumes that the condition of being human – the condition of labour – is the prerogative of men. The domination over nature and the creation of consumable and exchangeable goods through labour, i.e. production as meaningful activity on a world in order to transform it, has in fact been a description of the place accorded to men in patriarchal culture. What counts as labour and as production is narrowly defined in such a way that generally only the activities of men (and those of women in so far as they are the same as men) count.

Although Marxism holds that there is no determinate human nature in terms of the beliefs, wishes, aims, and projects of individuals, there is nevertheless something which fills the category of subject, prior to any social determination being grafted onto it. Marxism assumes a subject as the raw material for a process of social stratification that permits no differences and is therefore a neutral subject. This subject operates in the same manner as the subject of reason.[29] The fact that there is such a collection of undifferentiated subjects is a presupposition of the idea of a socialist or communist revolution. Communism can become a future reality because, basically, if all the social conditions are equalized and evenly distributed, individuals must themselves be equalized, the same. This levelling is possible because of a suppressed assumption of sameness, which perhaps represents the desire of the theorist or intellectual: to reduce the amorphous mass to a manageable category of 'universal human being'. In this way, underneath it all, the theorist = the worker = everyman, and Marxism becomes the universally true representation of the *telos* of human existence and human potential.[30]

Our point here is not to enter the debate between humanist and anti-humanist versions of Marxism but to examine the truth effect of a discourse which functions on the basis of a universal singular, unified, and implicitly masculine entity, just as much as it is necessary to examine the truth effect of the anti-humanist position which speaks of structures and agencies rather than subjects. Both views pre-empt a scrutiny of the politics of representation which denies the sexual specificity of women in the interests of men. Both sets of discourses block a *claim to difference*, denying or regarding as insignificant the *sexed* nature of human beings and the sexed nature of modes of representation and knowledge in patriarchal societies. It is only on the assumption that the naturalness of patriarchal relations between the sexes is an incontrovertible fact that the effect of both humanist and anti-humanist Marxism as universal representations of human existence and a covering over of female specificity is possible.[31]

Marxism has been prepared to admit, given its views on subjectivity and agency as being determined by social and economic relations, that it has no adequate theory of the subject. It is at this point that the relevance and usefulness of psychoanalytic theory is acknowledged. The incorporation of the psychoanalytic account of the development of subjectivity has helped Marxism to explain the constitution of consciousness, by reference to the structure of the (bourgeois, patriarchal) family and the processes of socialization it develops for the (unconscious) production of subjects. The concept of the unconscious fits rather neatly (although in a form that distorts Freud's use of the term) with the Marxist epistemological requirement of a dichotomy between knowledge and ignorance. Today it is not so much the concept of 'false consciousness' but the unconscious that is used to explain why the masses are ignorant of their own real interests, why they suffer from bourgeois, individualist, or liberal tendencies. In other words, psychoanalysis has provided the basis of a theory of ideology, or of the production of a suitable bearer of capitalist relations. Moreover, the fact that the subject cannot know its own truth – the unconscious – other than through the mediation of the analyst reproduces the same truth effect as Marxism: namely that knowledge is not derived from experience or consciousness of its own conditions of existence, but comes from elsewhere, from outside. The truth of Capital and the truth of Oedipus together represent the truth of the primary determining term. Both theories take the male norm for granted, assume a universal determination, one in terms of masculine relations of production, the other in terms of a universal complex that takes the phallus as its primary determining term. Both theories take the male norm for granted. However, the fact that psychoanalysis bases its theory of the subject on the question of the differences between the sexes has provided Marxist feminists and others with the possibility of inserting a 'gender' specification onto the subject of capitalism. Probably the most striking example is Juliet Mitchell's *Psychoanalysis and Feminism* (Harmondsworth: Penguin, 1975) which attempts to bring Marxist and feminist theory together using psychoanalytic precepts. Unfortunately, Mitchell (and a number of others) affirmed, in concurrence with Freud, that the female is a lack in relation to masculine, phallic fullness. Hence there can be no question of overcoming the patriarchal unconscious for women other than by an initiation into the male, rational norm, which implies an uncritical adoption of the universal truths of Marxism and psychoanalysis.

The outcome of Marxist interest in and use of psychoanalytic concepts is to a large extent guided, not by the details of psychoanalytic theory itself (for that, Marxists acknowledge, would be to accept an individualism that is contrary to them) but by the spectre of the twin evils of biologism and essentialism.[32] Although psychoanalysis in its orthodox form embodies both of these assumptions, it is nevertheless claimed to be capable of being purified of its essentialist and biological traits and to provide the necessary elements for a Marxist theory of subjectivity. Anatomical differences between the sexes can be admitted, but they can play no role in either modes of representation or in characterizing the type and form of subject, for these anatomical givens are outside of social and psychological spheres. To conflate them together is a form of biologism and reductionism. This implies a highly selective use of Freud's work: either his work on the unconscious is used to enhance or develop the concept of ideology, ignoring altogether the relations between the unconscious and sexuality; or else Freud's account of the distinction between the sexes is wholeheartedly adopted without any indication of the eternally oppressed position of women that his account entails.

What remains problematic about any 'union' of Marxism and psychoanalysis is the presumption of masculinity as the norm of subjectivity. It is significant that what remains ignored by both Marxism and psychoanalysis is precisely the specificity of the *female* body, and the consequent differences in psychical functioning between the sexes.[33] A recent critical questioning of psychoanalytic theory by feminists[34] has been aimed at revealing the phallocentrism of psychoanalysis, seeing it as an expression of male subjectivity, male desire, and male projections, rather than, as Mitchell did, as an accurate description of both sexes under patriarchy. Such a reading regards the construction of femininity as a lack, not as a sociological fact, but as a programme established by male desires and based on the incapacity of men adequately to deal with the limits of their subjectivity. Women are represented in phallocentric discourse as the other, the lack that men cannot tolerate within themselves.

Power and the sexually differentiated body

If Marxism and psychoanalysis have, as we have argued, developed a concept of the subject that is universal and neutral, then this subject is implicitly a male subject. The assumption of a universal category of subject, to which one can add a class, a race, or a sex, belies the already assumed *structure* of a male subject. Psychoanalysis explains this universal structuring of subjects by assuming a norm of subjectivity as phallic and, by virtue of the fact, assigns women to the category of un-phallic, that is, castrated. This homogeneous category of the subject is an effect of the levelling of all differences to the category of the same, which

387

allows a comparative evaluation of the presence or absence of already valorized qualities, attributes, and capacities as they are distributed between men and women respectively. The most fundamental level of difference begins with the differences between sexed bodies.

One of the most striking elisions in Marxist theory is its neglect and ignorance of the role of the body in constituting consciousness and in characterizing exploitation and oppression. Admittedly, Marx does discuss the body of the worker as a locus of labour power, but his comments simply reflect a naive positivist assumption of unitary bodies as functional organisms which is inadequate to explain the complex place the body occupies in the social world. For Marxist theory, discussions of bodies and their specificities belongs to the realm of biology, and attempts to introduce them in social and political theory have to be regarded as biologism or essentialism. In this way Marxism has seriously arrested work done by feminists and others on specifying that particular forms of bodies and bodily processes mark out differences between subjectivities, that subjectivity is sexed. By simply dismissing all of this as biologism and essentialism, the necessary analysis of biological existence and its representation in psychical life is neatly pre-empted, and the role of men in women's oppression is conveniently ignored.

This threatens to annihilate the specificity of women's lived oppression, since that oppression is prevented from being represented in terms of the existence of sexually differentiated bodies, and more particularly in their significance in psychic and social life. And yet, no explanation can be offered for why it is *women's bodies and sexualities that operate as the site for this*. The same blind spot characterizes psychoanalytic theory, although this theory at least openly admits it is in fact *women's* bodies and sexualities that serve, by their characterization as a lack or deprivation, in the construction of the universal (male) subject. In other words, the body's specificity can be ignored by these Master-knowledges only because their concepts of subjectivity are already implicitly masculine. The female body has already given up its 'use-value' in the process of exchange; its value is established by a phallic economy.

The point is that we are not disembodied subjects, consciousnesses distinct from bodies. Our psychologies and subjectivities are bounded by our morphologies,[35] the psychical and libidinal relations we have to our bodies. The body as lived is what constitutes subjectivity, and structures and organizes consciousness. This implies that there cannot be one or even two kinds of subject, but many different kinds, bounded not simply by the biological body but by its necessary social and individual signification. The body is not simply the 'seat' of subjectivity; it is also the target of technologies of power and forms of social control in all cultures. Its relations are not limited to capitalism, for even after a so-called socialist revolution, the cultural necessity of harnessing and inscribing the body as a *social* body remains – a fact not often acknowledged in utopian conceptions of life 'after the revolution'. If, as we have suggested, there are irreducible differences between sexed bodies and if any culture imposes itself by marking these differences, then the two sexed bodies require different technologies of power to organize and supervise the development of each.[36]

Any theory that is based on the unquestioned assumption of a singular, non-differentiated concept of subjectivity denies these irreducible differences, blocking an understanding of the specific conditions which create the inscription and codification of bodies as sexually differentiated. Indicating sex differences cannot simply be a matter of a general model which differs only in its detail or by degrees, for the two sexes, but entails a radical rethinking of whether models, instruments, and discourses appropriate for describing male subjectivity are, in fact, appropriate for female subjectivity. That Marxism takes little or no interest in these considerations is grounded in the fact that it is only interested in the subject as a reflection or product of ultimately economic demands – a tool in the service of capital – instead of recognizing the 'mediation' of sexual difference that helps structure consciousness and behaviour.

By suppressing the specificity of the body's morphology, and thus denying sexual differences (only admitting it in so far as it can be explained by the mode of production in the last instance), capitalism and not patriarchy becomes the locus of all social power. Patriarchy can then either be reduced to an effect of capitalism, or alternatively to a functional prop for it, and the centrality of the Marxist paradigm is saved in the face of a threatening blow to its edifice. In other words, what can be parried in this way is the question how far the values and concepts of Marxism, and its 'natural' dominance over the left political field are, in fact, effects of the suppression of the problem of sexual difference. This evasion helps to relegate the debate about sex/class or capitalism/patriarchy continually to the 'private sphere' (where the relations between the sexes are admitted to be problematic) or to the catch-all phrase 'the sexual division of labour', which in itself hides *male* domination *over* this division into spheres. Moreover, since only capitalism represents power, Marxism prevents the possibility of questioning the relation between technologies of power on sexually differentiated bodies and power as the organizing principle of all social order. So, it is not just that Marxism is sex-blind, as so many recent socialist feminists recognize, but much more that it assumes (in union with the whole history of western cultural thought) the unproblematic primacy of one term of a dichotomy installed by patriarchy. In other words, it is phallocentric. The opposition between masculine and feminine constitutes a picture of subjectivity, the body, and social relations which, while it gives a place to women, does so only in terms of what they are not and never can become: independent categories of analysis. Femininity is seen as deficient, variant masculinity. Women can only exist dependently. There can never be any question of a theoretical perspective which takes women as subjects, nor takes its point of departure from women's specificity and femininity as an independent and autonomous category.

Different not equality

One of the major effects of the levelling of the specificity of the female existence to male models is the reduction of feminist struggles for autonomy and self-determination to struggles for equality. The strategical evasion of the problem of the body began with the introduction of gender, not the sex of the body, as the key term. Originally devised as a radical feminist response to reactionary theories about the natural inferiority of women, this sex/gender dichotomy has since been happily incorporated within Marxist feminist theories.[37] This is not so surprising, since underlying the Marxist assumption that feminist theory needs completion, is the assumption that what all women are and should be after is equality with men. The various arguments about women's economic relations and familial position imply that women need an equal share in production, reproduction, and consumption and an equal place in socialist struggles. If, however, the connection between sex and gender is an integral one, then the assumption that the aim of women's struggles should be equality with men needs to be seriously questioned.

This equality is based on a denial of the sexed body as the defining characteristic of subjectivity. It is only in so far as women are similar to men that they are part of the same struggles; and it is their reduction to a common denominator determined by masculinity that defines all struggles as ultimately one androgynous struggle. The levelling implied by the concept of equality works in conjunction with a number of familiar dichotomies in Marxist theory: subjective/objective and political/psychological. Lived experience is equated with subjectivity, while structured, formalized knowledges derived, not from experience but from an analysis or synthesis of it, are equated with objectivity. This dichotomy allows men to speak the truth of women's experience because they are 'unattached' in their lived experience, and thus capable of 'objectivity'. This position completely denies the possibility of autonomy, of speaking for and of oneself, and moreover involves a glaring disavowal of the male position within patriarchal grids of power and knowledge. This 'objective' discourse invalidates the truth of a different perspective, a different point of view, a different interest.

It is argued by Marxist feminists that autonomous forms of knowledge that are based on women's lived experience are already the effect of patriarchal domination. Assertions about femininity or female sexuality are always caught in the trap of unwittingly reproducing the 'eternal feminine', in so far as they are bound up with the body and its experiences. This argument presumes a pervasive and complete system of ideology and deception such that the oppressor's position is completely absorbed by the oppressed in a passive, non-resistant way.

What we are suggesting here is that the autonomy of self-determined theories and practices is implicit in the idea of *difference*. This autonomy is not simply taking up the right to determine one's own terrain and the extent of one's own oppression, but also the right to interpret and develop any theories, any politics, and any struggle from the position established by the lived oppression of women. So that, for example, the point is not simply to acknowledge the body's existence, as Marxist-feminists are prepared to do, if only to acknowledge women's limitations, but to *affirm* and *claim* it as independently representable. To argue that such a feminist claim amounts to subjecting women to patriarchal power once again is to miss the basic feature of the claim to autonomy: namely that one form of challenge to patriarchal power is to reject its definitions and characterizations of femininity, and to appropriate for itself the right to a self-determined and independent perspective on the world.

CONCLUSION

If, as we have claimed, the morphology of the sexed body establishes the limits of lived experience and the socio-political meaning of that experience, then it seems justified to maintain that all non-feminist theories – those which do not start from women as such – including Marxism, are founded on masculine norms. Any bringing together of Marxism and feminism implies feminism's acceptance of these terms – adopting a male norm as universally applicable. This amounts to an unquestioned acceptance of phallocentrism as the natural and inevitable paradigm for all possible forms of being, thinking, and acting. The domination of Marxism over feminism cannot fail to result because even any presumed complementarity is necessarily governed by this principle of equality in sameness. 'My wife and I are equals' is the ruse of phallocentrism, as Wilden remarked.[38]

The unwillingness of Marxists and Marxist-feminists to recognize the need for a genuine autonomy for women's theories and practices – one which claims a positive difference – has led to some peculiar evaluations of the status and potential of feminist theory. Feminist theory is conceived in one of two ways: either feminist theory is about 'women's issues' (abortion, rape, prostitution, pornography, domestic labour, sexuality, the family, health and welfare, and so on) – i.e. it is about

391

women's place in a man's world; or it is seen simply as a form of critique of already existing non-feminist theories (Marx, Freud, etc.). Neither of these alternatives sees the possibility of a completely different perspective on problems of truth, reason, reality, knowledge. Feminist theoretical work is assumed to attempt to overthrow, reverse, adapt, modify, deconstruct 'male' theory. Its methods must be adopted from elsewhere, not only from Marxism and psychoanalysis, but also existentialism, anarchism, aesthetics, semiotics, etc. Feminist theory is considered to be at most a critique of male theories, but never as capable of developing its own theories.

To see a feminist theory either as a critique or reworking of Master-knowledges or as an adoption of the other's theoretical tools is to underrate considerably what feminist theory has achieved and to consider it in limited terms. But what is perhaps more important is that it involves a reduction of the multiplicity and plurality of feminisms, equating differences here with oppositions once again. There is a wealth of feminist theory (some good, some bad) that falls entirely outside the scope of this either/or split. Differences between women as well as women's difference from men need to be affirmed without reducing either to a common denominator. Because the concept of difference does not permit assumptions about commonness or meta-principles of a universalizing nature, it is well suited for acknowledging the specificity of any struggles by oppressed and exploited groups on their own particular terms.

In concluding, we are led by these considerations to ask whether the recurrent emphasis on equality in Marxist politics does not, in the final analysis, have the effect, not only of bringing feminisms into line with Marxism, but of reducing them to a commonness with it. The political and institutional power of Marxism is such that any feminism can only be tolerated in so far as it accepts Marxism's fundamental premises and modes of thinking. This amounts to a form of subjugation that can never provide the space for developing theories and practices independently. If feminism is a movement or series of them directed not so much at equality as at autonomy, then the coupling of Marxism and feminism together is problematic, to say the least. Perhaps what is at stake is our capacity to adopt a conceptual separatism, i.e. the ability to take ourselves as the independent norm of our thinking and being. Such a conceptual separatism has nothing to do with tired old disputes about whether to work with or to relate to men. It simply means that any political or theoretical alliance with other radical movements, such as Marxism, cannot and never will involve an allegiance to concepts, categories, principles, and modes of procedure that are derived from a negation of women's experience *as women*.

NOTES

We would like to thank the following people for advice, comments, and suggestions: Judith Allen, Katherine Ingram, Margaret Grafton, Rebecca Albury, Paul Patton, and particularly Moira Gatens.

1 Phallocentrism, a term coined by Ernest Jones in his criticisms of Freud has been used by Irigaray and Kristeva to designate systems of representation that collapse the two sexes into a single (implicitly masculine) model, identifying male interests with human interests. See L. Irigaray, 'Women's exile', in *Ideology and Consciousness*, No. 1 (1977), and 'This sex which is not one', in P. Foss and M. Morris (eds), *Language, Sexuality and Subversion* (Sydney: Feral, 1978), and Part VI, this volume.

2 The phrase 'seeing women first' is from M. Frye's 'To be and be seen: metaphysical misogyny', in *Sinister Wisdom*, No. 17.

3 See P. Dews, 'The *nouvelle philosophie* and Foucault', in *Economy and Society*, Vol. 8, No. 2 (May 1979); and R. Jacoby, 'What is conformist Marxism?', in *Telos*, No. 45 (Autumn 1980).

4 The comparison with the official trade union movement is instructive. Just as discipline and surveillance over the rank and file is effected by union representation of workers' struggles at the conference table with management, so the intellectual recognition of academic Marxism has contributed to its deradicalization, and its attempts to restrain other subversive discourses, among them feminism.

5 It is tempting to compare Marxism's hegemony of the left intellectual field with that of various feminisms. Only in so far as feminism remains within the area of women's issues is it acknowledged, whether inside or outside academic circles, trade unions, parties, organizations, etc. Within the university its non-recognition is reflected in the virtual absence of senior *feminist* women academics, the low status of the few related courses, the inferior reputation of feminist publications, and the virtual exclusion of the feminist perspective in all core courses and areas which are assumed to be outside the specific scope of 'women's concerns'. In fact, the idea that there might be a feminist perspective on the very concept of knowledge production and the role and development of the social sciences is in itself something that meets with considerable disbelief. This subordinate position to which any autonomous mode of feminist thinking is relegated within intellectual circles is not eased in any way by Marxism, but is probably aggravated by it.

6 Phallocentric theory in general, of which Marxism is just one example, has the function of either making women disappear from history and thought, or appear but only in so far as women are comparable to men, and can be judged by the same criteria. Women's specificity *as women* cannot be acknowledged and has no place within a phallocentric economy.

7 A case in point here is the function of the phrase 'the sexual division of labour'. The presumed centrality of this notion to explanations of women's oppression simply reduces the relations between the sexes to a productivist definition of human existence, neatly obliterating the fact that exploitation and oppression in the division of labour is perpetrated by one side only – men. The concept cannot explain sexual domination other than by removing the agents of domination from the scene and explaining inequality by means of a faceless system, capitalism. This conception, which privileges labour as the essence of human value, must explain sexuality, language, subjectivity, etc., derivatively from the division of labour, a problem which has plagued Marxist feminists

attempting to analyse women's oppression *as a sex* as a function of capitalist relations of production and reproduction.

8 See D. Fernbach, 'Towards a Marxist theory of gay liberation', in P. Mitchell (ed.), *Pink Triangles: Radical Perspectives on Gay Liberation* (Boston, Mass.: Alyson, 1980).

9 M. Godelier, 'The origins of male domination', *New Left Review*, No. 127 (May/June 1981); and M. Daly's critique in *Gyn/Ecology: The Metaethics of Radical Feminism* (London: The Women's Press, 1979).

10 See, for instance, M. Hartwig, 'Capitalism and Aborigines', in E.L. Wheelwright and K. Buckley (eds), *Essays in the Political Economy of Australian Capitalism* (Sydney: ANZ, 1978, Vol. III), pp. 119–38; and V.G. Kiernan, *Marxism and Imperialism* (London: Edward Arnold, 1974). The recent switch from discussions of imperialism to a benign cultural relativism since the rise of Aboriginal land rights as a political issue should not blind us to the fact that the Aboriginal claim to difference is subject to a form of levelling and subsumed under the class struggle against capitalism. Aboriginals may well be doomed to keep playing the role of 'noble savage' with his or her dreamtime, where every rock is of eternal symbolic significance, preventing an autonomous development into modern blacks, whatever that means *for them*. At any rate, it is not clear why the wonders of socialism have an automatic relation to struggles by the black race. See C. Alexander, 'Power and the Australian Aborigines' in J. Allen and P. Patton (eds), *Beyond Marxism? Interventions after Marx* (NSW: Intervention Publications, 1983), pp. 73–90.

11 Marion Tapper, in 'Dichotomous thinking', unpublished PhD, has developed in considerable detail the strategies involved in the use of dichotomous modes of thought in the history of philosophy. See also Nancy Jay, 'Gender and dichotomy', in *Feminist Studies*, Vol. 7, No. 1 (Spring 1981).

12 The position of many feminisms is characterized by Marxists as 'non-political', 'psychological', 'individualist', and so on. These positions are regarded as less objective or historical partly because their relation to concepts like class, unions, workplace, and the economic sphere are not clear. Moreover, feminisms are continually accused of being white middle-class movements, which neglect or ignore working-class and black women. This can, on occasions, become extended into remarks like: 'It is imperative that feminism develop a position *vis-à-vis* working-class men' (Ann Curthoys on 'Razor's edge', 2SER radio: reporting the absence of a primary focus on the relation between class and sex at the recent *Women and Labour Conference* discussion).

13 It is at this level of a politics of representation that a 'Marxism of Marxism' makes sense. If it is true that consciousness is shaped by social relations (the *Critique of Political Economy*) and that the middle class imagines itself to be beyond or outside of class oppositions and thus truly representative of the universal (Eighteenth Brumaire) then it is not clear how the Marxist intelligentsia (self-confessed white, middle-class subjects) can simply declare by fiat that *it* is the exception to the Marxist rule. The way this is done is to declare itself representative of the exploited and oppressed. This trick can only work by invoking the truth of its knowledge and the initial ignorance of those it seeks to represent by forgetting the social relations of the theory and its speakers.

14 It is precisely this notion of an underlying unity/homogeneity of capitalism, expressed in the ever-widening concept of the mode of production which guarantees the 'truth' of a common enemy. Even if it is admitted that power relations in advanced western cultures are diverse, complex, and affect

different groups in different ways, the belief in an expressive totality of capitalism underlies the Marxist project.

15 More sophisticated versions of socialist feminism now present capitalism as the most advanced state (or the most oppressive version) of patriarchy, though this may seem perilously close to the radical feminist view, we would argue that it co-opts radical feminism for two reasons. First, it conveniently displaces the problem of patriarchy once more from the question of male domination to its apparent expression in social reality: capitalism. Second, it makes it virtually impossible not to combat capitalism as the *primary* target, if indeed it is the most oppressive version of patriarchy. There is no immediate reason for feminists to periodize patriarchy according to Marxist epochs, just as much as it is not necessary to accept a traditional concept of descent and progress. This does *not* amount to an ahistorical account of patriarchy nor to a denial of the need to have a particular mode of periodization, only not a Marxist one.

16 Hence the frequent allegation that non-Marxist feminisms ignore the centrality of the oppression of working-class women. The invariably middle-class Marxist intellectuals who make it evidently see no problem in *their* politics of representation. Moreover, they are unable to accept the many *self-defined* attempts to conceptualize themselves as women *first* made by working-class, immigrant, and black women, i.e. not just or primarily in relation to the men in their race, class, or ethnic group. Such attempts are judged inimical to their 'real interests'.

17 For relevant discussions of the relations between power and knowledge, see M. Foucault, *The History of Sexuality* (London: Allen Lane, 1978); 'Politics and the study of discourse', *Ideology and Consciousness*, No. 3 (1978); 'The discourse on language', in The *Archaeology of Knowledge* (NYU: Harper and Row, 1972); 'The intellectuals and power', in D. Bouchard (ed.), *Language, Counter-Memory, Practice* (Ithaca, NY: Cornell University Press, 1977); 'Power and norm', in M. Morris and P. Patton (eds), *Foucault: Power, Truth, Strategy* (Sydney: Feral, 1978); 'Truth and power', in C. Gordon (ed.), *Michel Foucault: Power/Knowledge* (Brighton: Harvester, 1980); and 'The west and the truth of sex', in *Substance*, 20 (1978).

18 Logocentrism is used here in Derrida's sense, meaning 'being as presence: the absolute proximity of self-identity, the being-in-front of the object available for repetition', *Speech and Phenomena* (Mass.: North-Western University Press, 1978). Logocentrism involves the assumption of the primacy of presence, self-identity, and unity.

19 G. Lloyd, 'The Man of Reason', in *Meta Philosophy*, Vol. 10, No. 1 (1979), argues that from the Enlightenment period, rationality has always been associated with masculinity.

20 For example, Althusser's model of ideology as a system of representation of lived relations as opposed to Marxist science as the correct and true knowledge of the real relations. Experiences or forms of knowledge that do not correspond with precepts of this true knowledge are explained away as misrepresentations of reality. Hence the theory provides self-validation by the initial assumption that only Marxism can explain reality.

21 A materialism based only on the materiality of material objects is crudely reductionistic. Language both as speech and structure poses great difficulties; dealt with in such a materialist account by reduction to mere tools of communication instead of a structured institutional system exerting considerable power of its own.

22 While on the one hand Marxists have attempted to ground truth in history,

there is only one acceptable truth in history – determination by modes of production.

23 Foucault's lecture, 'The discourse on language', op. cit., presents a general outline of this.

24 It is often objected that Marxism does not entail such an absolutist idea of truth/science/knowledge, since it is based on the historicity of knowledges – knowledges determined by social relations specific to modes of production. Yet this is an obfuscation since at the same time it purports to grasp the totality of causes or reasons for these historically specific forms of knowledge – the determining principle of all historical formations – namely, the inevitable relations between the productive forces and the relations of production.

25 In fact, the very claim to neutrality and objectivity made by any system of thought reveals the desire for power. It is the attempt to present what is particular and specific as universal and absolute.

26 Marxist justifications for its own scientificity have shifted from that of Lukács (and many others), namely that it represents the proletariat (the universal class/non-ideological) to that of Althusser, that Marxism is a scientific representation of reality in itself.

27 For example, there is a lot of talk in Althusserian epistemology of 'closure' as a characteristic of ideological systems of thought. Sciences are characterized as open continually subject to change and to questions that arise out of problems confronted by the theory in its relation to reality. Ideologies only ask questions to which the answers are already known and set. These 'closures' are ultimately derived from external interests, i.e. the interests of political and economic power. The question of what governs the principle of scientificity itself cannot be put intelligibly, since if it can be shown that no external interests interfere in the theoretical discourse, the condition of truth is satisfied. Hence, the equation of closure with non-scientificity prevents an enquiry into Marxism's existence as 'true discourse', affecting its own form of closure.

28 See Jacoby, op. cit., for discussion of the way Marxism constructs these. He, of course, concludes that *critical* Marxism should erase the pieces of a Marxism that has become a caricature of conformism.

29 Paul Q. Hirst, in his article 'Althusser's theory of ideology', in *Economy and Society*, November 1976, notes this fact too in claiming that even Althusser's anti-humanism is not anti-humanist enough, and is still bound to the Cartesian assumption of a given subject. But Hirst's position itself seems unable to accept the concept of difference – for him there can be *nothing* given about subjects. Human subjects, bodies, consciousnesses, and the unconscious are all for him only effects produced by structures.

30 Such a presupposition lies behind the Marxist (and existentialist) conceptions of the universal subject. This becomes clearest, not specifically in relation to discussions about the position of women, but in discussions on Judaism and anti-Semitism. Julia Kristeva, in 'L'anti-sémitisme, aujourd'hui', in *Libération* (August 1979), argues that Christianity and Marxism (and by implication existentialism) necessarily suppress the difference of Jew in favour of a sameness with universal humanity. Marx in *On the Jewish Question* and Sartre in *Anti-Semite and Jew* implicitly and explicitly suggest that it is only by shedding difference – a difference which is socially imposed in any case (by anti-Semitism?) that we all become equal. The use of the claim to difference as a *strategy* of defence against a levelling process is ignored and in its place is put a universal equality of subjects whose histories, specific

positions, and knowledge must be ignored.
31 The Marxist view is Hegelian in this sense. In *The Phenomenology of Spirit* (London: Allen and Unwin, 1966), Hegel's discussion of the movement from consciousness, self-consciousness, reason, spirit to Absolute Knowledge is implicitly a discussion about relations between men. This only becomes clear when Hegel specifically discusses women in the context of the family and the private sphere in terms of their limited capacity to attain Absolute Knowledge. Similarly, in Marxist theory social relations are quite clearly relations between men (exchange and production). It is only in the context of the family that once again women figure as a specific group. Marxism in this sense shares in common with all phallocentric theory the assumption that what really is essential to any social formation are patriarchal sexual relations. The oppression of women by men thus becomes thinkable only in terms of what it means for class exploitation or some other political concern. It is not regarded as an issue on its own.
32 While examples of these critiques are abundant in many Marxist-feminist journals, some particularly influential and instructive examples can be found in the journal *m/f*. See P. Adams and J. Minson, 'The subject of feminism', and M. Cousins, 'Materialist arguments and feminism', in No. 2 (1978); B. Brown and P. Adams, 'The feminine body and feminist politics', No. 3 (1979); M. Plaza, 'Phallomorphic power and the psychology of woman', in *Ideology and Consciousness*, No. 4.
33 While Freud himself rarely discusses anatomy and physiology in the context of psychoanalysis and is very careful to specify that his object is a psychical representation of anatomical and physiological processes, nevertheless he never considers the woman's body as a specifically *female* body – instead he regards it as a castrated male body. This may perhaps explain one of the most striking omissions in Freud's analysis and discussion of female sexuality – the absence of any discussion of menstruation and its effects on women's psychical lives.
34 Luce Irigaray is perhaps the most well known. See 'Women's exile' and 'This sex which is not one', op. cit.
35 The concept of morphology, a term Irigaray (op. cit.) uses frequently, mediates between a purely anatomical and a purely psychological account of the body and its pleasures. It denotes the determinancy of the body's form in the formation of the imaginary body or body image (cf. Lacan's mirror-phase for the construction of the libidinal and identificatory relation to the child's own body as constitutive of the boundaries and structures of its ego in 'The mirror phase . . . ' in *Ecrits* and 'Some reflections on the ego', in *International Journal of Psychoanalysis*, Vol. 34, 1953). The body's morphology is thus both constitutive of and constituted by how it is inscribed, marked, and made meaningful.
36 This seems to pin-point a problem not only with Marxist accounts but also with the positions of recent French theorists such as Foucault and Deleuze. Since their work, the importance of the body to political analysis has been recognized but no account has been given of the fact that there are at least two different kinds of bodies and two different technologies of power at work in patriarchal societies.
37 For analysis of this incorporation and its implications for feminist theories, see M. Gatens, 'A critique of the sex/gender distinction', Part IV, this volume.
38 A. Wilden, *Systems and Structure: Essays in Communication and Exchange* (London: Tavistock, 1974), p. 279.

NOTES ON CONTRIBUTORS

ELIZABETH GROSZ teaches in the General Philosophy Department at the University of Sydney. She is the author of *Sexual Subversions. Three French Feminists* and *Jacques Lacan. A Feminist Introduction*, and has co-edited a number of anthologies on feminist theory.

SNEJA GUNEW has studied in Australia, Canada, and England. She currently teaches in literary studies at Deakin University, Victoria. She has published widely in the area of feminist theory. Her most recent research has concentrated on questions of cultural, in relation to gender, differences through an examination of non-Anglo/Celtic writing in Australia. She has edited two anthologies of such writings (*Displacements: Migrant Storytellers* and *Displacements 2: Multicultural Storytellers*) and co-edited *Beyond the Echo: Multicultural Women's Writing*; *Telling Ways: Australian Women's Experimental Writing*; and *Striking Chords: Multicultural Literary Criticism* (forthcoming). She is completing a monograph (*Framing Marginality: Non-Anglo/Celtic Writing in Australia*) which redefines ways of theorizing Australian literature and culture.

LOUISE C. JOHNSON was trained primarily as a geographer but left Sydney and that discipline in 1979 as a Marxist geographer to teach Australian studies and then women's studies at Deakin University. She became involved in socialist feminist politics in Melbourne and this guided her research into sexual and spatial divisions of labour in the Australian textile industry. The problems of seriously using Marxist theory to answer feminist questions on women's work began a process of questioning, most recently informed by a critical reappraisal of radical and socialist feminist writing. This is still occurring in her current activities of trying to define feminist geography in her teaching and published work.

GISELA T. KAPLAN studied in Berlin, Munich, and Melbourne and gained her Ph.D. from Monash University (Melbourne). Major publications include: a jointly-edited book, *Hannah Arendt: Thinking, Judgement, Freedom* (Sydney: Allen & Unwin, 1989) and chapters in the following: *Feminine/Masculine and Representation,* edited by A. Cranny-Francis and T. Threadgold (Sydney: Allen & Unwin, 1989); *Women's Movement of the World,* 4 (Hamburg: Argument Redaktion, 1989); *Australian Welfare: Historical Sociology,* ed. R. Kennedy (Melbourne and London: Macmillan, 1988). She is joint editor of *The Australian and New Zealand Journal of Sociology* and is currently completing a book on contemporary Western European feminism. Her research interests include: political sociology; sociology of culture; gender and ethnic issues. She is currently based in the Department of Economic History, University of New England, Armidale, NSW.

RENATE D. KLEIN holds degrees from Zurich University in biology (M.Sc.), the University of California at Berkeley (BA), and London University (Ph.D.), both in women's studies. With Gloria Bowles she co-edited *Theories of Women's Studies* (1983) and since 1981 she has been the European editor of *Women's Studies International Forum.* She also co-edits (with Gloria Bowles and Janice Raymond) the ATHENE series, an international collection of feminist books.

Her current work is on reproductive and genetic engineering and its impact on women. She is co-editor with Rita Arditti and Shelley Minden of *Test-Tube Women: What Future for Motherhood?* (1984), co-author with Gena Corea *et al.* of *Man-Made Women* (1985), and editor of *Infertility: Women Speak Out About Their Experiences of Reproductive Medicine* (1989). In 1986 she was awarded the Georgina Sweet Fellowship to do research on the experiences of women who drop out of test-tube baby programmes in Australia which she continued as post-doctoral research fellow at Deakin University, Australia till 1989. In 1990 she will be a Distinguished Visiting Professor in Women's Studies at San Diego State University, USA. She is a founding member of the Feminist International Network of Resistance to Reproductive and Genetic Engineering (FINNRAGE) and acted as its international co-ordinator from 1985 to 1987.

LESLEY J. ROGERS obtained her first degree, B.Sc. with First Class Honours, from Adelaide University. She then lived in the USA for four years, some of which time was spent in post-graduate studies at Harvard University and the rest working in research at New England Center Hospital in Boston. She completed her Doctorate of Philosophy degree in ethology at Sussex University before returning to Australia in 1972. For the next thirteen years she taught medical and science students at Monash University, apart from one year at the Australian National University, and conducted research into brain development and behaviour. In 1987 she was honoured by being awarded the degree of Doctor of Science from Sussex University for this research. Throughout the 1970s until now she has been an active feminist, lecturing and writing widely in the area of gender and biology. She is now an Associate Professor of the Physiology Department at the University of New England.

PHILIPA ROTHFIELD has a Ph.D. in Philosophy, from Monash University, which was written on textual analysis in relation to phenomenology, structuralism, and Marxist theories of ideology. Since then, she has written on French feminism, semiotics, and cultural/media analysis. More recently, she has published on the body, in relation to both French feminism and dance. This latter work is influenced by her experience as a performer in contemporary dance and in women's theatre. Her current research project is on feminist theory, politics, and post-modernism. This project involves developing a decentred theory of knowledge, which allows for a politics of difference at a number of levels.

ROBYN ROWLAND's doctorate is in social psychology. She is senior lecturer in women's studies at Deakin University, Deputy Dean of the School of Humanities and has taught women's studies for over fifteen years. She is author of *Woman Herself: A Transdisciplinary Perspective on Women's Identity* (Oxford University Press, 1988) and editor of *Women Who Do, and Women Who Don't, Join the Women's Movement* (Routledge & Kegan Paul, 1984). Her most recent publications are a feminist analysis of the new reproductive technologies, in, for example, *Made to Order: The Myth of Reproductive and Genetic Progress* (Pergamon Press, 1987). She is Australian and Asian editor of *Women's Studies International Forum* and Australian editor of *Issues in Reproductive and Genetic Engineering: Journal of International Feminist Analysis*. She is author of *Living Laboratories. Women and the new Reproductive Technologies* (Macmillan, Australia: Indiana University Press, Indiana, forthcoming). She has two books of poetry published: *Filigree in Blood* (Melbourne: Longman Cheshire, 1982) and *Perverse Serenity* (Melbourne: Heinemann, 1990).

HAZEL ROWLEY studied French and German at Adelaide University and wrote her Doctorate on French women's autobiographical writing – in particular Simone de Beauvoir and Violette Leduc. Since 1984 she has been teaching literature and women's studies at Deakin University. She is currently writing a biography of Christina Stead. Her research interests are feminist theory, Australian literature, and contemporary European and Australian autobiographical writing.

SUSAN SHERIDAN lectures in women's studies at the Flinders University of South Australia and has been involved in women's studies since 1973. She is a graduate of the universities of Sydney and Adelaide and has taught literary studies at the South Australian College of Advanced

Education and Deakin University. An editor of *Australian Feminist Studies*, she has published widely in feminist and literary journals. Her book on the fiction of Christina Stead has appeared in the Harvester Key Women Writers series and she has edited *Grafts: Feminist Cultural Criticism* (1988).

MARIE TULIP graduated from the University of Queensland and spent four years in the United States, doing an MA in French and teaching French and Latin in Chicago. Since 1970 she has been active in the women's movement in Sydney, especially in the area of religion, working on the Commission on the Status of Women of the Australian Council of Churches and on the *Magdalene* collective. She teaches continuing education courses in feminism and religion and contemporary women's poetry. Recent publications include *Women in a Man's Church* (ACC, 1983), and chapters in *Force of the Feminine* (Allen & Unwin, 1986) and *Opening the Cage* (Allen & Unwin, 1987).

INDEX